ON SOCIOLOGY, SECOND EDITION: VOLUME TWO

ON SOCIOLOGY, SECOND EDITION

VOLUME TWO: ILLUSTRATION AND RETROSPECT

John H. Goldthorpe

STANFORD UNIVERSITY PRESS

STANFORD, CALIFORNIA

2007

Stanford University Press
Stanford, California

Printed in the United States of America on acid-free,
archival-quality paper

First edition: Oxford: Oxford University Press. © 2000
by John H. Goldthorpe.

Chapter 2 was originally published in the *British
Journal of Sociology*, vol. 47, 1996; and chapter 3
in *Rationality and Society,* vol. 9, 1997.

Library of Congress Cataloging-in-Publication Data

Goldthorpe, John H.
    On sociology / John H. Goldthorpe. — 2nd ed.
        v.   ; v.   ; cm.
    Originally published: Oxford : Oxford University
Press, 2000.
    Includes bibliographical references and index.
    Contents: v. 1. Critique and program
    ISBN-13: 978-0-8047-4997-3 (cloth : alk. paper)
    ISBN-13: 978-0-8047-4998-1 (pbk. : alk. paper)

v. 2. Illustration and Retrospect
    ISBN-13: 978-0-8047-4999-X (cloth : alk. paper)
    ISBN-13: 978-0-8047-5000-9 (pbk. : alk. paper)

    1. Sociology.   2. Sociology—Philosophy.
3. Sociology—Methodology.   4. Sociology—
Research.   5. Social action.   6. Social classes.
I. Title.
HM585.G65   2007
301—dc22
                                        2006020316

Typeset by G&S Book Services in 10/14 Sabon

CONTENTS

PART II

ON SOCIOLOGY, SECOND EDITION: VOLUME TWO

CHAPTER ONE

Introduction to Volume II

The essays brought together in Volume I of this book were concerned with the present state of sociology. This state I had to regard as one of general intellectual disarray—although with some more encouraging developments being very recently discernible. In line with such an assessment, the essays were of two kinds: critical and programmatic. Taken together, these essays form in effect an extended prolegomenon to those of Volume II; and, thus, a brief recapitulation of their main themes may here be helpful.

FROM VOLUME I TO VOLUME II

The critical essays of Volume I focus on basic methodological difficulties that, I believe, arise with certain current styles of sociological work. I single out what I label as 'grand' historical sociology (to which may be assimilated 'grand' treatments of globalisation as representing, say, 'epochal transformation'), case-oriented macrosociology, and sociological ethnography. These are all styles of sociology that involve processes of data collection and analysis that are primarily qualitative in character; and it might then be thought that my aim in these essays is to launch an all-out attack on such qualitative research. This is not in fact the case. Rather, I try to establish three specific points.

First, I seek to demonstrate that the qualitative styles of sociology in question do face methodological problems—and ones that their proponents have to a large extent neglected. These are problems ultimately of the reliability and validity of the kinds of data on which chief reliance is placed and of the ways in which such data are used in processes of theory construc-

S

N

1

tion and evaluation. In their essentials, such problems are also encountered in quantitative work. But while quantitative sociologists have, over time, evolved various techniques, grounded in statistical theory, through which these problems can at all events be assessed and managed, even if never entirely resolved, sociologists committed to qualitative work have been far more inclined simply to disregard or discount them or to beg off from the technical efforts for which their treatment calls.

Second, insofar as qualitative sociologists are in fact ready to recognise the methodological difficulties that confront them, they tend, I try to show, to look for ways of coping with them that would in some sense be distinctive to their own style of work, and that would in particular allow them to avoid any complicity in 'positivist' (read statistical) approaches. However, the special procedures that are suggested are not well elaborated or codified, they often lack transparency, and, insofar as they are made explicit, seem open to rather obvious objections. Furthermore, and quite ironically, they appear in various respects to lead their proponents into positions that are in fact of an *ur*-positivist kind. This occurs, for example, when grand historical sociologists seek to justify their empirical reliance on secondary sources by envisaging historical facts not as—often challengeable—inferences from incomplete and possibly biased primary sources but rather as discrete and stable 'items' that can be excerpted and reassembled at will as the building bricks of their wide-ranging inductivist constructions; or again when case-oriented macrosociologists or sociological ethnographers seek to overcome difficulties of generalising from insufficient or possibly quite unrepresentative data by resorting to entirely deterministic logical methods of analysis or by invoking theory that, supposedly, allows certain knowledge of lawlike relations.

Third, I underwrite the argument previously made by King, Keohane, and Verba (1994) that all styles of social research, whether qualitative or quantitative in character, have to respect a similar logic of inference: that is, a similar logic governing the way in which one may properly move from data about the world to claims that go beyond the data, whether in a descriptive or an explanatory mode, or, one might say, a logic that governs the interplay of evidence and argument. Such a logic can in fact be regarded as applying to all forms of science and scholarship. It does not dictate any particular set of research strategies or techniques but has rather to be expressed through methodologies elaborated in ways that are found appropriate to different subject-matter areas and substantive issues. Sociology in its more quantitative forms uses methods that are grounded in advances made in the statistical analysis of observational data from the later nineteenth century onwards—which can be understood as extensions of the logic of inference as expressed in the experimental methods of the natural sciences. And what, then, I wish chiefly to maintain is that it can be fairly required of practitioners of more qualitative forms of sociology that they too should attempt further extensions of this logic that they would regard as appropriate to their particular research fields and interests. As I recognise in the Introduction to Volume I and elsewhere, there are at the present time welcome indications that movements in this direction are indeed occurring—although ones still contested by those who would rather see qualitative sociology grounded in some form of relativist epistemology or who believe that it should be judged more by literary than by scientific standards.

In the programmatic essays of Volume I, I then aim to outline, and to give a rationale for, the kind of sociology that I would wish to see emerge as a new mainstream—to serve not as a basis of exclusion but rather as an exemplar of shared standards, in relation to which methodological discussion and debate can be carried on expressive of a genuine pluralism rather than of a merely convenient, 'anything goes' counterfeit. I am naturally influenced here by what I would judge to be, on the one hand, those respects in which sociology has thus far been most successful and, on the other hand, those in which potential for the future is most apparent.

On the side of research, I believe that the most notable achievements have been made in quantitative work: in particular, in the demonstration, through the analysis of large-scale, usually survey-based, data-sets, of a wide range of empirical regularities, often extensive in time and space, that were hitherto unrecognised or only inadequately described. I thus maintain that such work will, and should, remain central to sociology, and that continuing progress can be expected as survey research becomes more diverse in its designs, as quantitative techniques become more powerful and refined, and as data collection and analysis alike become more specifically adapted to sociological concerns.

On the side of theory, it is not possible to claim any similar record of achievement. However, encouraging developments can, I believe, be observed in the revival, following on the apparently final collapse of functionalist thinking, of what Boudon (1987) calls the 'individualistic tradition' in sociology; and also in a reassertion of the idea that theory does not exist, as it were, for its own sake but must serve the primary task of providing a basis for explanation. In particular, I see major potential in the expression of the individualistic tradition via rational action theory—used as a more general term than rational choice theory—and in the context of what I describe as mechanism-based theorising: that is, theorising that attempts to explain phenomena of interest not by subsuming them under general, covering laws but rather by identifying the causal processes, or mechanisms, through which they are generated and sustained and perhaps changed or disrupted.

The programmatic essays have therefore two main concerns. First, they aim to bring out the essential complementarity of the quantitative analysis of large-scale data-sets and rational action theory. The quantitative analysis of data (QAD) can provide increasingly sophisticated descriptions of empirical social regularities but is not in itself capable of also providing explanations of them. Causal accounts cannot be simply cranked out of statistical analyses; a theoretical input is also needed. And rational action theory (RAT) appears as an especially apt basis for the specification of the patterns of action and interaction out of which relatively large-scale social regularities are produced. Moreover, through the development of such generative models and their subsequent testing by means of further empirical research, the explanatory potential of the underlying theory can be evaluated, and especially insofar as it can be set in competition with that of other, rival theoretical approaches. In this way, then, as I seek to show, the possibility is created of overcoming what I refer to as 'the scandal of sociology', the manifest lack of integration of research and theory, and thus of achieving an intellectually more coherent discipline.

The second concern of the programmatic essays of Volume I is then with trying to clarify RAT, as I would wish to understand it, and to remove misconceptions that appear widespread and persistent about such theory and, more generally, about the individualistic tradition within sociology, of which RAT is one major expression. I aim to show that it is a mistake to equate RAT simply with those versions of it that are most commonly found in economics, and in turn to regard RAT, and the principle of methodological individualism that it embodies, as alien and threatening to the very nature of the sociological enterprise. Rather, RAT in different versions and the individualistic tradition itself have deep roots in the history of sociology. A form of RAT developed so as to meet the particular requirements of present-day sociology—around the idea of subjective and bounded, rather than objective and infinite rationality—offers, I suggest, a means of overcoming the long-standing opposition between the explanation and the interpretation of social action and also the best prospects for making headway in regard to various other basic problems of sociological theory.

Turning now to the present volume, the essays I include again fall into two kinds: six that I label as illustrative and the two final essays that I label as retrospective. In the remainder of this introductory chapter I discuss these two sets of essays in turn, beginning in each case with some general observations that aim to show their continuity with those of Volume I and then going on to comment on the essays separately so as to bring out their more specific contexts and motivations.

THE ILLUSTRATIVE ESSAYS

The six illustrative essays follow on directly from the programmatic essays of Volume I: that is to say, they are intended to show what the kind of sociology that I there envisage and advocate might look like in practice, and in particular to indicate how the closer integration of research and theory that I believe such a sociology makes possible can actually be realised. However, while the essays have this broad purpose, they do in fact relate to one particular research field in sociology: that of social stratification and mobility, in which my own expertise and experience chiefly lie. I naturally hope that they will be of interest to other specialists in this field, and that they will not prove too off-putting to sociologists with different interests. The latter will no doubt wish to ask themselves whether similar illustrative material could be derived from their own research fields—and to consider the implications, positive or negative as they may see them, of the answers they arrive at. The essays, as will be discovered, vary a good deal in their form and content, but they do, I hope, achieve a certain unity in the three following respects.

First, each essay aims to bring out, though with differing emphases, the potential for the interplay between research and theory that I would see as following from the three-phase schema discussed at various points in Volume I (see ch. 9 esp.). This comprises:

1. establishing social phenomena to be explained in terms of the empirical regularities through which they are manifest,

2. hypothesising processes or mechanisms at the level of individual action adequate to generate these regularities, and then

3. testing the validity of the explanations thus advanced by means of further empirical enquiry.

Second, and again following on arguments advanced in Volume I (see esp. chs. 6 and 7), those features of social stratification and mobility that are taken as phenomena to be explained are ones established primarily through the quantitative analysis of large-scale data-sets, and the generative processes that are suggested as adequate to their explanation are ones couched in terms of rational action theory.[1] At the same time, though, RAT is taken as only a special, if privileged, theory of action and is thus always seen as being in competition with other theories of action or of 'social behaviour'. And further the possibility is kept open of other kinds of empirical inquiry than QAD being used in the testing of theoretical explanations.

Third, the regularities empirically established in the field of social stratification and mobility on which theoretical attention primarily focuses are ones of a particular kind. They are regularities, of a macrosocial character, that take the form of relative constancies over time and commonalities across sociocultural contexts rather than regularities expressing variation in the form of secular trends or systematic cross-societal or cross-cultural differences.

I might add that while this last feature is to some extent a matter of accident—in the recent past the more notable regularities demonstrated in research in social stratification and mobility have been ones of relative constancy and commonality—the accident is rather fortunate. There is advantage to be gained from concentrating on regularities of the kind in question for reasons that have been well set out by Lieberson (1987: 99–107). To begin with, the reliance of much quantitative analysis on regression methods creates the danger that the study of variation, of one kind or another, is privileged simply because it is variation that this statistical technology is designed to handle. Variation in the phenomenon of interest is presupposed and is then accounted for in terms of independent or 'explanatory' variables. But in the case of phenomena that are characterised by little variation, their treatment via such methods is problematic, and they may therefore be neglected.[2] Moreover, it is entirely possible that the processes or mechanisms that underlie the very presence of some phenomenon are different from those that underlie such variation as it may display. And, as Lieberson argues, we may then be seriously misled if we try to deal with causes of variation without first having an adequate appreciation of 'fundamental' causes—that is, the causes of the phenomenon per se. Thus, to take examples from what is to follow, we need to have some theoretical understanding of why an association exists and persists between children's class origins and their educational attainment or between their class origins and the class positions that they themselves eventually attain *before* we attempt to explain why—should this appear to be the case—this association is strengthening or weakening over time or differs in its strength or pattern from one society or culture to another.[3]

The illustrative essays are then chiefly concerned with aspects of the interplay of research and theory in a particular context of enquiry. If they are found lacking in some desirable features of the essay form, such as elegance of composition and a sense of completeness, this may reflect, I would like to think, not just my own inadequacies in writing expository prose but also the inherent messiness of what one finds on, as it were, the edge of any attempt at bringing research and theory together. Uncertainties can and do arise over the precise nature of what is to be explained, over just what the explanatory theory advanced does and does not claim, over what exactly would count as corroborating or disconfirming evidence, and so on. I have not tried to cover up such uncertainties or the difficulties to which they give rise. Many issues are left open and problems unresolved, and the attentive reader will no doubt find more weak spots and loose ends in the arguments put forward than I have myself appreciated. I can only plead in mitigation that the essays are essentially concerned with giving an account of sociology in the making—a process that is in its nature open-ended and provisional.

At the same time, though, I do not wish here to take up a too defensive position. Even if the essays do reveal the more seamy underside of work in progress, they also, I submit, provide clear enough evidence that a sociology of the kind that they are intended to illustrate is in fact capable of actually *achieving progress,* and not just in extending our empirical knowledge of social phenomena but in developing theoretical understanding as well. In a thoughtful contribution, Cole (1994) has argued that while on the periphery or 'research frontier' there is little difference in the way in which the social and the natural sciences proceed, sociology, at least, falls behind the natural

sciences in its ability to convert new knowledge produced on the—often un-
tidy and disputed—frontier into 'core' knowledge that is generally accepted
as valid. It would be difficult to deny the descriptive force of this argument.
But, as I think Cole would agree, the problem is not entirely insurmount-
able: sociology is not, by the very nature of its subject matter, prevented from
producing cumulative knowledge, as the 'impossibilists' to whom I refer in
the introductory chapter to Volume I would suppose.[4] And, as I have sought
to show more fully elsewhere (Goldthorpe, 2005; and cf. Hout and DiPrete,
forthcoming), the study of social stratification, and of social mobility in
particular, can count as one area in which new knowledge has been steadily
gained *and* has, in some part, been formed into what is recognisable as core
knowledge.

One last general comment may be made, with American readers chiefly
in mind. Although I have not, I hope, neglected relevant American literature,
a good deal of the work that has influenced my own, and with which I engage, is European. The essays may then serve the further purpose of increasing transatlantic awareness of what have, I believe, been significant, even if
still minoritarian, developments in European sociology over recent decades.
On the one hand, the style of micro-to-macro, and primarily RAT-based,
explanation that is highlighted, while of course having important American
origins, especially in the work of Coleman (1990), would seem of late to
have been pursued with greater enthusiasm and effect in Europe than in the
United States. And, on the other hand, a substantial part of the quantitative
empirical work on which I draw is of a cross-national comparative kind,
the growth of which in Europe has in various ways been promoted by post-
1989 political events and is today underpinned by levels of funding for both
research and organisational support that American colleagues may well find
enviable.[5]

These developments are, moreover, being matched by an expanding
professional infrastructure. The European Consortium for Sociological Research, established since 1991, has a present membership of over 50 research institutes and university departments with active research centres,
holds regular conferences on comparative European sociology, and spon-
sors the *European Sociological Review*. In addition, the European Academy
of Sociology, founded in 2000, under the presidency of Raymond Boudon,
has a strong representation of scholars with a general commitment to the
individualistic tradition of sociological analysis and an interest in sociologi-

cal applications of RAT. Through these bodies in particular, an increasingly favourable context is being provided for the advancement of sociology as social science, in the interests of which the illustrative essays are written.[6]

Considering these essays in more detail, the first three could be said to form a closely related trio. They are all concerned with regularities that have been demonstrated in social class differentials in educational attainment in modern societies and with the explanation of these regularities.

The first essay, 'Class Analysis and the Reorientation of Class Theory: The Case of Persisting Differentials in Educational Attainment', begins with an attempt to locate the problem of educational differentials in a larger context. I argue that until recently class theory, whether Marxist or liberal in inspiration, has been preoccupied with the dynamics of class and in turn, and rather strangely, with developments that have not in fact taken place: in the Marxist case, with class formation, intensifying class conflict, and the emergence of working-class revolutionary politics; in the liberal case with class decomposition and the emergence of a 'classless' form of society. Somewhat more relevantly, I suggest, the central *explananda* of class theory could rather be seen as various well-established regularities that point to the *stability* of class in modern societies or, at all events, to the powerful resistance to change that class relations and associated inequalities in life chances and differences in patterns of social action would appear to display.

I then take continuing class differentials in educational attainment, despite a general expansion of educational provision and increases in overall levels of educational qualification, as providing a major example of such resistance to change—in contrast, for example, to the very rapid decline, if not reversal, of gender differentials previously favouring males. I go on to outline a RAT-based account adequate to explain the degree of persistence of class differentials: that is, an account that shows how this aggregate outcome results from central tendencies in educational decision-making by children and their families that can be understood as rational, given their differing class situations and the nature of the opportunities and constraints that characterise these situations. I further indicate how this account may be appropriately extended to one of the more obvious deviant cases, that of Sweden, where a decline in class differentials in educational attainment over a fairly lengthy period has in fact been demonstrated.

In the second essay, 'Explaining Educational Differentials: Towards a Formal Rational Action Theory', which is coauthored with Richard Breen, the theoretical argument of the first essay is developed and, as the title indicates, is given a more formal, mathematical expression. Such formalisation is still rather rare in sociology and is here undertaken in a largely experimental spirit. Formalisation can, however, undoubtedly serve to bring out the full implications of a theoretical argument and thus to increase both the coherence with which it is stated and the extent to which it becomes open to empirical test. In the present case, for example, we were helped to see, and to spell out, more clearly the crucial part played in our explanation of persisting class differentials by two ideas: (1) that some degree of perceived risk attaches to children continuing in education rather than leaving or, more generally, in making more rather than less educationally ambitious choices, and (2) that this risk tends to be greater in the case of children from less rather than more advantaged class backgrounds, although *equal relative* risk aversion can be supposed in regard to the common goal of avoiding downward social mobility.

The general explanation of how educational differentials are created, sustained, and in some cases reduced that is put forward in these two essays has attracted an encouraging amount of attention, both in the form of critical discussion of the type of theory involved—that is, RAT—and, more important, in the form of attempts to test the explanation through further empirical enquiry. In the third essay, 'The Theory Evaluated: Commentaries and Research', which is published here for the first time, I aim to review these differing responses and to assess their significance. As regards RAT, I remain convinced that, where based on the idea of subjective and bounded rationality, this is in fact the type of theory that can most appropriately be pursued. It allows educational choice to be seen as action guided by perceived costs and benefits in the context of given opportunities and constraints, rather than as merely socioculturally conditioned behaviour, while at the same time not supposing the infinitely rational expectations of the standard economics treatment of educational choice. As regards the specific claims of the theory that Breen and I have developed, I conclude, first, that a good deal of evidence has been produced that is consistent with the operation of the key mechanism of risk aversion that is invoked, but, second, that what is so far lacking is evidence of a more direct kind that it is indeed this mechanism that is crucially at work. In this connection, I note the problem of an adequate research methodology for reliably establishing individuals' goals and expectations—for example, about what level of employment they aim to achieve and about what level of education they see as being necessary for this. I suggest that further progress in evaluating the theory may depend on how far this problem, to which there would seem analogues in many other contexts, can be overcome.

The fourth illustrative essay, 'Social Class and the Differentiation of Employment Contracts', may seem to mark a rather abrupt change of focus. However, it relates to those preceding it in the following way. The 'class schema' from which the essay starts out has become widely used in research in the field of social stratification and mobility, including in studies of class differentials in educational attainment, and has, I believe, both empirical and theoretical advantages in these respects over classifications or scales of 'socioeconomic status'. The understanding of class that informs the schema is in fact directly reflected in the explanation of educational differentials that Breen and I advance: in particular, in our stress on the importance of class differences not just in current levels of income but also in security and stability of income and in long-term income prospects—which the class schema can be shown to reflect.

The conceptual basis of the schema is the definition of class positions in terms of employment relations, but on practical grounds, it is actually implemented in research through information on individuals' employment status and occupation. The question does then arise of how far, when thus implemented, the schema captures those differences in employment relations that, conceptually, it is supposed to capture—or, more technically, the question of its criterion validity. In fact, empirical analyses that have been made to test the schema in this regard, especially in connection with its adoption as the basis of a new official social classification for the UK, have given generally encouraging results (Rose and O'Reilly, eds., 1997; Rose and O'Reilly, 1998; Rose and Pevalin, eds., 2003; Rose, Pevalin, and O'Reilly, 2005). What this means, therefore, is that a fairly systematic association exists between individuals' employment status and occupation, on the one hand, and, on the other, the kind of employment relations in which they are involved as indicated by form of payment, perquisites, control of working time, employment security, promotion opportunities, and so on. And in turn, therefore, the further question of evident sociological interest can be raised of why this should be so. Why, especially in the case of employees (as distinct from self-employed persons), should those in different occupational groupings have their employment regulated in such differing ways?

I suggest an explanation of this empirical regularity—that is, in effect an explanation of why classes exist—in terms of employers' rationally motivated attempts to deal with problems of the employment contract as these arise in the case of employees engaged in different kinds of work and, specifically, with the problems of **work** monitoring and human asset specificity. Although, ideally, employers **might** wish to reduce all employment contracts to simple money-for-effort spot contracts—or in effect to 'commodify' labour—these problems mean, I argue, that approximations to spot contracts are likely to meet the needs of organisational effectiveness only with rather basic forms of labour, and that in the case of professional and managerial employees especially contracts with a quite different rationale are typically required. This leads therefore to the prediction that the differentiation of employment contracts will continue on its present pattern to a far greater extent than much fashionable discussion of 'the future of work' would suggest. In developing a RAT-based explanation in this case, I am more influenced than elsewhere by current theory in economics, but chiefly of a kind that shows notable divergences from orthodox utility theory and in ways that in fact bring it closer to RAT in the form that I would see as especially appropriate for sociology.

The next essay, 'Class Analysis: New Versions and Their Problems', does indeed represent something of a diversion but, I hope, a worthwhile one. It can be read as my response to other recent attempts to reformulate class analysis that have been made in addition to, and in part in critique of, my own, although out of very similar concerns for the closer integration of research and theory. In particular, I seek here to develop relatively brief comments that I have earlier offered on the work of Aage Sørensen and David Grusky (Goldthorpe, 2000, 2002a). While not Marxists themselves, both these authors regard class analysis as having more specifically Marxist origins and objectives, and, for this reason, as currently facing more severe challenges, than I would myself be ready to accept. Consequently, their proposals for the renewal of class analysis—advanced from sometimes apparently similar but in fact quite divergent 'neo-Ricardian' and 'neo-Durkheimian' positions, respectively—are, in my view, unnecessarily radical. Sørensen would wish to make the prime focus of class analysis the study of conflict among social collectivities over differing kinds of rent, while Grusky urges that the level at which analysis is undertaken should be 'ratcheted down' from that of 'aggregate classes', the mere constructs of sociologists, to that of specific occupational groupings, meaningful to their members and thus a far more likely basis for the formation of real sociocultural entities and for collective action of any kind.

The research programmes that follow from Sørensen's and Grusky's proposals have, I believe, significant potential. Rent-seeking activity on the part of different collectivities is indeed widespread in modern societies and has been neglected by sociologists—and, among rent-seeking collectivities, occupational groupings figure very prominently. Furthermore, some occupations no doubt do represent sociocultural entities exerting a powerful influence over their members' social identities and patterns of action, and we need to know more about which they are and whether, overall, such 'occupational communities' are becoming more or less important. However, while I would see these programmes as providing valuable complements to class analysis as more conventionally understood, I aim in my essay to show that they cannot serve as substitutes for it. I argue, on conceptual and empirical grounds, that under the new versions that Sørensen and Grusky envisage, class analysis would in effect be virtually displaced from the field of macrosociology. The very idea of a class structure becomes problematic; serious difficulties in turn arise in studying class effects as opposed to occupational and other more sectional effects—and including the effects of class origins on class destinations or, that is, intergenerational class mobility; and such class action as may occur at a societal level rather than in more localised contexts cannot be adequately accommodated.

In the final illustrative essay, 'Outline of a Theory of Social Mobility', I return to my central concern with wide-ranging social regularities, established through quantitative analysis, and their explanation. A substantial body of research by now exists to show that within modern societies relative rates of intergenerational class mobility have a surprising degree of constancy over time, and also that a large commonality at least in the pattern if not the level of these rates exists across societies. I extend theoretical arguments already introduced in the preceding essays to provide an account of these features of 'endogenous' mobility regimes and also of the part that education plays in mediating mobility. I argue that mobility regimes are conditioned by the nature of the class structures of modern societies and, in particular, by the systematic inequalities in resources that they create, but that regularities in relative mobility rates derive more immediately from the mobility strategies that are typically pursued by individuals of differing class origins. These strategies are understandable as rational adaptations to the opportunities and constraints that characterise different class situations. However, especially in their interaction with the selection policies of employers in regard to different kinds of work, they can, and quite typically do, have the overall effect of maintaining the state of intergenerational class competition for more or less desirable class positions largely unaltered over time.[7]

An implication of this account is, then, that inequality of *opportunity,* as reflected in relative mobility rates, is only likely to show substantial temporal change or cross-national variation in association with corresponding change or variation in inequalities of *condition* among the members of different classes. This implication, I argue, is borne out by the results of research in at least some national cases, such as that of Hungary during the Communist era or of Sweden under social democratic hegemony from the 1930s through to the 1970s, in which clear, if not continuing, shifts towards greater social fluidity followed on significant reductions in class inequalities of condition brought about by political means. In turn, I would expect that insofar as trends towards greater class inequalities in income, as recently evident in the UK, the United States, and elsewhere, persist, and at the same time social welfare provision becomes less redistributive, then instances of significantly *decreasing* social fluidity will become apparent—an expectation that currently emerging research findings would appear to bear out.[8]

THE RETROSPECTIVE ESSAYS

The two long retrospective essays with which Volume II ends are intended as a coda to the book as a whole. They are retrospective in the sense that they seek to answer a particular question that refers to the history of sociology but that is posed, quite explicitly, from the standpoint of the present. This question is one that may indeed have occurred to readers at some stage in this or the preceding volume. I argue, from several different standpoints, in favour of a sociology that attempts to combine the quantitative analysis of social data, and especially of data extensive in time and space, with explanation of the empirical regularities thus revealed through a theory of action, and especially one in which rational action is privileged. But if a sociology in this style has the potential that I would like to suppose for the advancement of sociology as social science, why then has it taken so long for it to emerge or even to be explicitly proposed?

In the history of sociology concerns with furthering the quantitative study of social phenomena and with elaborating and applying a theory of action have in fact been largely pursued in isolation from each other. Is it therefore the case that this historical experience reflects some inherent incompatibility between the two key components of the kind of sociology I would favour that I have simply overlooked? Or has their failure to come together been a matter largely of various unfavourable circumstances, intellectual or institutional, that have tended to recur?

The two essays in which I take up this general question are not then ones of pure historical scholarship but rather examples of 'history with a purpose'—which always carries the danger that present concerns are read back into the past in a quite anachronistic way. I have to suppose that I avoid this danger sufficiently for my question still to be meaningfully addressed.

At the same time, the two essays do, I believe, also serve to throw further light on transatlantic differences in the development of sociology—in this case, in development of a long-term kind—that, as will be seen, are of direct relevance to various issues previously discussed in this volume. These differences are in fact especially apparent if due attention is given to the history of research as well as of theory or 'social thought' more broadly, and in particular to the hitherto rather neglected relationship between sociology and one of the major scientific developments of the later nineteenth and earlier twentieth centuries—the probabilistic revolution and the creation of modern statistics. In concentrating on this relationship, and on associated questions of the integration of sociological research and theory, in comparative perspective, the essays may, I hope, lend some support to the efforts of those scholars on both sides of the Atlantic, such as Martin Bulmer, Charles Camic, Anthony Oberschall, and Jennifer Platt, who have produced pioneering historical studies in this area.

In the first of the two essays, 'Sociology and the Probabilistic Revolution, 1830–1930: Explaining an Absent Synthesis', I review selected features of the history of sociology in its formative years in France, England, and Germany. As its title indicates, the main focus of the essay is on the changing relation between emerging sociology and the more or less concurrent probabilistic revolution in scientific thinking. I show that in the initial stages of this revolution sociology represented a research field of major importance, chiefly on account of the work of Quetelet; but that by the time that the revolution culminated, around the turn of the century, in 'the new English statistics', sociology had lost this centrality, even as its own development created a growing need for the kind of theoretical and methodological support that the new statistics could have provided. I conclude, however, that the 'absent synthesis' has to be explained essentially in terms of barriers—of in fact an intellectual more than an institutional character—that were specific to the time and places in question rather than necessary, and of other yet more contingent, difficulties.

Rather ironically in view of the more recent identification of quantitative sociology with positivism, by far the most serious of the intellectual barriers turns out to be the positivistic conception of science, as upheld by Comte and his followers, which was inimical to probabilistic analysis and to the development of a theory of action in equal measure. In some instances, the barrier of positivism was reinforced by that of an undue empiricism—a 'cult of the facts' that recognised little need for theory of any kind; and in others, by persisting confusion over the principle of methodological individualism in sociology and 'psychologism'.

The second essay, 'Statistics and the Theory of Social Action: Failures in the Integration of American Sociology, 1900–1960', then addresses the same question as the first but in a new context. Over the first half of the twentieth century, there was in general a greater readiness in American than in European sociology to exploit the widening possibilities in the analysis of social phenomena that the advance of statistical methods afforded. However, problems clearly remained over the part that quantitative work was to play within the larger sociological enterprise and, in particular, over its relationship to theory. I treat these problems by examining three episodes in the history of American sociology in the period in question that, I believe, are especially illuminating: these relate to sociology at Columbia from 1900 to 1929, at Chicago from 1927 to around 1935, and at Columbia again from 1940 to 1960.

On this basis, I find in fact important similarities with the European situation that I previously considered. Again, I would argue, there was no inherent difficulty in the way of a closer integration of the statistically informed analysis of social data and the attempt to explain the regularities thus revealed from the standpoint of a theory of social action. Rather, movement in this direction was largely frustrated by much the same intellectual barriers as I identified in the European case and by ones that, at least in the case of positivism and empiricism, can be regarded as simply historical variants of the latter. However, it is with psychologism that I see the most serious difficulties as arising, and especially in regard to the development of theory. A concern to ground or indeed embed sociological theory in psychology, whether behavouristic in character or mentalistic in the more indigenous American style of 'the psychology of social life', was not conducive to the reception of a Weberian idea of social action that seeks only minimal psychological foundations. Thus, in America, insofar as a theory of social action—as distinct from one of social behaviour—came to be elaborated, the emphasis was placed on the origins and constitution of action in highly contextualised microsocial situations rather than on the development of accounts of 'central tendencies' in action operating across differing contexts, and thus adequate to explain empirical regularities quantitatively established and analysed at a macrosocial level. The essay ends with the suggestion that the problems of the integration of research and theory that are revealed in the historical episodes examined have by no means been resolved in American sociology today.

CHAPTER TWO

Class Analysis and the Reorientation of Class Theory

The Case of Persisting Differentials in Educational Attainment*

In an essay published some years ago, Gordon Marshall and I set out the case for class analysis as a research programme. The aim of this programme could be summarised as that of enquiring into the interrelations that prevail among class structures, class mobility, class inequalities, and class formation (or decomposition). Viewed in this way, we argued, class analysis 'does not entail a commitment to any particular theory of class' but, rather, provides a context in which 'different and indeed rival theories' may be formulated and assessed (Goldthorpe and Marshall, 1992: 382).[1]

It is specifically to such theoretical development and critique, within the research programme of class analysis, that I wish to turn in this chapter and those that follow. I take the development of theory to be a more ambitious and difficult enterprise than simply the elaboration of concepts. The key requirement of theory, as here understood, is that it should have *explanatory* force. A sociological theory is of value to the extent that it can provide an account of how established social regularities come to be as they are—and to the extent that, through the wider implications it carries, it remains open to further empirical test. Because, then, the prime purpose of theory is to explain, an exercise in theory development in any particular substantive area may appropriately start from a consideration of the relevant *explananda*: of just what it is that calls for explanation. In the present case, a historical perspective may perhaps best serve to clarify matters.

---

*This essay is a revised version of a paper presented at a conference held in honour of David Lockwood at the University of Essex in 1996. I am grateful to Tony Atkinson, André Béteille, Richard Breen, Robert Erikson, Jean Floud, Chelly Halsey, Anthony Heath, Janne Jonsson, Walter Müller, and Adam Swift for helpful comments on earlier drafts.

Looking back over the nineteenth and the twentieth centuries, two broad strands of theory can be distinguished, the Marxist and the liberal, which are addressed to obviously related yet significantly differing *explananda* regarding social class. Marxist theory, as Elster (1985: ch. 6 esp.) has well brought out, is primarily concerned with class formation and, in particular, with explaining the incidence and forms of collective class action. Such action was, of course, of key importance in Marx's overarching theory of history: all history was 'the history of class struggle' and was periodised by the revolutionary outcomes of such struggle. But all history was also the history of the development of the forces of production and of the contradictions thus created with established relations of production. For Marx, and for his followers, therefore, a crucial problem was that of how exactly these two lines of argument should be integrated and especially as they were applied to capitalist society (cf. Lockwood, 1981, 1992: parts 3 and 4). The abiding theoretical task was to explain just what were the processes through which intensifying internal contradictions would actually generate the degree of class consciousness and of class conflict necessary for the working class to act out its historically appointed role as the 'gravedigger' of capitalism.

Liberal theory emerged largely in reaction to its Marxist equivalent. Its starting point was the fading prospect of working-class revolution as the economic advance of capitalist societies proceeded without any sustained threat to their political stability. However, as elaborated in the context of a supposed 'logic' of industrialism, rather than of capitalism, it became in effect a theory of the general decline of class (see, e.g., for general statements Parsons, 1967, 1971; Kerr et al., 1973; Kerr, 1983; Bell, 1973, 1980; and for more specific application in the field of social stratification, Blau and Duncan, 1967; Treiman, 1970). What the liberal theory aims primarily to explain is how, in the course of development of industrial societies, class formation gives way to class decomposition as mobility between classes increases and as class-linked inequalities of opportunity are steadily reduced. These tendencies, it seeks to show, follow most importantly from the demand imposed by the logic of industrialism for an ever more efficient utilisation of human resources—as reflected in the expansion of educational provision, the egalitarian reform of educational institutions, and the progressive replacement of criteria of ascription by criteria of achievement in all processes of social selection.[2] Thus, it may be understood how, within an increasingly 'open' and 'meritocratic' form of society, conditions are created that at a political level first of all facilitate the 'democratic translation of the class struggle' (Lipset, 1960)—the abandonment by national working classes of revolutionary for civic, electoral politics—and then further undermine the connection between class membership and political action even in the individualised form of voting behaviour (cf. Goldthorpe, 2001).

However, while the *explananda* of Marxist and of liberal theory may in this way be contrasted, it is one feature they have in common that is here of main significance: namely, that of being essentially spurious. In both cases alike, major theoretical efforts have been made to elucidate the generative processes of something that has not in fact happened.

That this is so on the Marxist side is of course notorious. As Lockwood has bluntly put it (1992: 166): 'Nothing has been more disconcerting to Marxist theory than the massively awkward fact that no advanced capitalist society has produced anything resembling a revolutionary proletariat since the upsurges in working-class protest after the First World War.' Marxist sociologists have then had to resort to a variety of means of coming to terms with this fact, including, especially in recent years, that of ceasing to be Marxists. Indeed, if class analysis is conceived of in a Marxist or *marxisant* fashion, so that its ultimate purpose can only be the understanding of class formation and collective class action as key dynamic factors in long-term social change, then a sceptical view of its future might well be taken—or, at very least, its radical reconstruction be thought necessary (see further ch. 6, this volume). However, what chiefly serves to show that class analysis—in a quite different version to the Marxist—can still lay claim to a viable and important *problematik* is a further 'massively awkward fact': namely, that the general 'withering away' of class, to the explanation of which the liberal theory is addressed, is also a historical outcome that, while often scheduled, has yet to be observed.

In the decades following World War II, during which the liberal theory achieved its fullest expression, the economic development of industrial societies went ahead at a quite unprecedented rate. It would therefore seem reasonable to suppose that, over this period, any logic of industrialism with the potential to undermine the prevailing force of class within these societies should have initiated well-defined trends of change indicative of this potential. But such trends have proved remarkably hard to establish. Indeed, to have shown that, in a number of key respects, they have simply not occurred might be regarded as the main achievement to date of—non-Marxist—class analysis as a research programme.

Thus, as Marshall and I sought to document, the available evidence from investigations into both educational attainment and social mobility is scarcely supportive of the idea of a generalised and decisive movement towards greater equality of life chances for individuals of differing class origins. Rather, class inequalities in these respects appear typically to display a surprising degree of stability. Further, studies that have purported to show a comprehensive decline in class politics within the advanced democracies have of late been called into doubt by results from more sophisticated analyses that reveal that class-party linkages are of a more enduring kind than has been supposed and that, insofar as changes are apparent, they are cross-nationally quite variable and often driven as much by party political strategies as by inexorable social change (see, e.g., Evans, ed., 1999; Evans, 2000; Brooks, Nieuwbeerta, and Manza, 2006; and the discussion in vol. I, ch. 5, pp. 107–13).

Research findings of the kind in question do then pose grave difficulties for the liberal theory. But this is not their only significance. For present purposes at least, the more important point is that such findings should themselves now be regarded as constituting the serious *explananda* to which class theory needs to be directed. Macrosocial regularities, expressing salient features of the class stratification of modern societies, have been empirically demonstrated. But, thus far, these regularities have been left opaque. The theoretical challenge that arises is, therefore, to develop some explanation of just how they are created and sustained. A major reorientation of class theory is here implied. Rather than such theory being, as in both its Marxist and liberal forms, concerned ultimately with explaining the dynamics of class, in regard either to class formation or decomposition, what would now appear of central importance is to account for the stability of class or, at all events, for the very powerful resistance to change that class relations and associated life chances and patterns of social action would appear to display.

In what follows, I will, first, outline what kind of theory appears to me most appropriate and promising for the task in hand. I will then seek to make a start in applying such theory by attempting an explanation of just one of the regularities referred to above: that of the persistence of class differentials in educational attainment. As noted, the widening of educational opportunity and its supposed effects in weakening the influence of class on individual life chances plays a central role in the liberal theory, and an attempt to explain why liberal expectations in regard to class and education have not been met might in turn point the way to accounting for other failed expectations and, in particular, in regard to class mobility (see further ch. 7, this volume).

RATIONAL ACTION THEORY AND CLASS ANALYSIS

Both Marxist and liberal theories of class form part of larger theories of long-term societal change that are of a functionalist and also a teleological or historicist character. The inherent developmental logic of capitalism, on the one hand, and of industrialism, on the other, are seen as impelling societies on a particular course of change directed towards a particular end. However, the source of the failure of these theories may in large part be traced back to the fact that the functional exigencies that they envisage have not proved to be sufficiently powerful over the course of history to make social actors 'follow the script' that was written for them. Or, one could say, the supposition that macrosocial change could be understood in an essentially top-down fashion left both theories alike fatally lacking in micro-foundations.

Here, I seek to avoid any such difficulty by starting from an acceptance of methodological—though not ontological—individualism: that is, from the position that all social phenomena can and should be explained as resulting from the action and interaction of individuals.[3] Thus, the theory that I shall try to develop will be one that aims to show how the macrosocial regularities that I take as *explananda* are the outcome of such action and interaction, whether in simple or complex, intended or unintended, or desired or undesired ways. In the course of providing such an account, I shall indeed make reference, without further elaboration, to institutions or other social structural features that, for the purposes in hand, I simply take as given. Nonetheless, the assumption remains that these features too are no more than the products of past action and its consequences and could, in principle, be shown to be such.

I shall, furthermore, opt for rational action theory. That is to say, I shall aim to give an account of how the *explananda* I treat derive from individual action that can itself be understood as rational. I take this option because, on grounds already set out in Volume I, I would see such an appeal to rationality as representing the most satisfactory terminus of any sociological analysis. As Coleman has put it (1986b: 1), rational action has 'a unique attractiveness' as a basis for theory in that it is a conception of action 'that we need ask no more questions about'. Or, in Hollis's words (1977: 21), 'rational action is its own explanation'.

The version of RAT that I take up implies, however, a conception of rationality that is of only intermediate strength or that, in other words, implies rationality of a subjective and bounded kind. I assume that actors have goals, have usually alternative means of pursuing these goals and, in choosing their courses of action, tend in some degree to assess probable costs and benefits rather than, say, consistently following social norms or giving unreflecting expression to cultural values. I also assume that actors are to a degree knowledgeable about their society and their situations within it—in particular, about opportunities and constraints relative to their goals—rather than, say, being quite uninformed or ideologically deluded. In sum, I take it that actors have both some possibility and some capacity for acting autonomously and for seeking their goals in ways that are more or less appropriate to the situations in which they find themselves.

At the same time, though, I would recognise that departures from the standard of objective rationality are very frequent. I make no assumption that actors are always entirely clear about their goals, always have the information or calculating power necessary to determine the optimal means of pursuing them, or in the end always follow the course of action that they believe to be rational. For present purposes at least, these latter assumptions are not in fact required in order to create the possibility of a viable RAT approach. Because the concern here is with explaining macrosocial—and probabilistic—regularities that result from the actions of large numbers of individuals, all that need be supposed is that the propensity of actors to act rationally as best they can in the circumstances that prevail is the most important *common* factor influencing them, even if perhaps relatively weak, while propensities to depart from rationality operate randomly in many different ways. The 'law of large numbers' will then ensure that it is the central, rational tendency that dominates in the overall outcome (cf. vol. I, ch. 6, pp. 128–30).

The focus of RAT is on how actors come to choose particular courses of action in pursuit of their goals, using the resources that they command

and adapting to the opportunities and constraints that characterise their situation. If, then, RAT is to be applied in the context of class analysis in the way envisaged, it will be essential to show not only how actors' goals are intelligible in relation to the class positions they hold but, further, how their actions directed towards these goals are conditioned by the distribution of resources and in turn of opportunities and constraints that the class structure as a whole entails.

In the following, class positions will be taken as defined by employment relations in labour markets and production units and, more specifically, by two main principles: first, that of employment status, which distinguishes among employer, self-employed, and employee positions; and, second, that of the regulation of employment, which distinguishes employee positions according to whether this regulation occurs via a 'labour contract' or a 'service relationship' (see further Erikson and Goldthorpe 1992: ch. 2 and, for a fuller discussion, ch. 5 this volume). Classes themselves will then be understood, in a minimal sense, as collectivities of individuals and families holding particular class positions over time. In elaborating the theoretical arguments that will be advanced, I shall concentrate, simply to keep the discussion within bounds, on the two employee classes that most clearly exemplify the second principle noted above: on the one hand, the 'service class', or salariat, of largely professional and managerial employees (cf. Goldthorpe, 1982, 1995)[4] and, on the other hand, the working class of wage earners in routine, chiefly manual occupations. It should, however, be evident enough how the arguments in question might be appropriately extended.

As most class analysts have recognised, the differentiation of class positions in terms of the resources their incumbents command, the opportunities available to them and the constraints imposed on them does not imply that classes can be consistently ordered on any single dimension. This is so because the differences involved may be ones of kind as well as level, as, say, in the case of those that would set apart the class positions of self-employed workers and of employees (cf. Goldthorpe and McKnight, 2006). Nonetheless, broad contrasts can of course still be made between what might be described as 'more advantaged' and 'less advantaged' classes. Thus, by virtue of the employment relations in which they are involved, members of the salariat are typically advantaged over members of the working class, not just in the level of their current incomes, but further through their more favourable chances of maintaining continuity of employment, through the greater stability of their earnings, and through their generally more favourable economic prospects deriving from incremental salaries and career opportunities.

In trying to explain the persistence of class differentials in educational attainment, I shall invoke only such basic, or constitutive, features of class—that is, those that derive directly from employment relations—rather than ones of a more contingent kind. In particular, I shall avoid reference to distinctive class values, norms, 'forms of consciousness', and the like. For this would of course mean going beyond the minimal conception of classes earlier indicated: that is, it would be to imply that class formation was at a level at which a 'capacity for socialisation' (Featherman and Spenner, 1990) was present. And not only might such a claim, in some instances, prove difficult to justify empirically (cf. Erikson and Goldthorpe, 1992: 217–27) but, as will emerge, explanations that rely on the existence of such systematic subcultural differences between classes do not in any event appear apt to the *explananda* in question.

Since I regard this essay as only a first step in theory development, I shall set out my arguments in a quite informal way. An attempt at formalisation is presented in Chapter 3. I shall, however, seek to clarify my position by contrasting wherever possible the empirical claims and implications that follow from it with those deriving from apparent alternatives.

CLASS DIFFERENTIALS IN EDUCATIONAL ATTAINMENT AND THEIR EXPLANATION

I take the degree of temporal stability of class differentials in educational attainment to be a genuine rather than a spurious problem for class theory—or, to follow Merton (1987: 6), I take it to be a phenomenon that is 'established' in the sense that we have 'enough of a regularity to require and allow explanation'. Nonetheless, the nature of the regularity should still be spelled out rather more exactly.

With the expansion of educational provision in economically advanced societies, primary and then secondary education, in some form or other, became universal, compulsory, and free; further, especially from the mid-twentieth century, growing numbers of young people have remained in education beyond the compulsory period and have also gone on into higher education, being often supported in this latter case by grants, soft loans, or other forms of subsidy. Within national populations, the average level of educational attainment has thus risen substantially. However, across the western world, class differentials in educational attainment would seem to have changed surprisingly little, if considered net of the effects of expansion per se.[5] More specifically, if educational careers are envisaged as comprising a series of transitions, or 'branching points', then, at each successive transition, children of less advantaged class origins have remained, to much the same extent, more likely than children of more advantaged origins to leave the educational system rather than to continue in it or, if they do continue, to follow courses leading to lower levels of qualification that in turn reduce their chances of continuing further (cf. Shavit and Blossfeld, eds., 1993). Moreover, in those national cases where declining class differentials have to some extent been found, these would appear for the most part to be rather episodic and also to be limited to particular transitions within the educational system—usually in fact to early transitions—while in later transitions as, say, in those to higher secondary or tertiary education, differentials remain rather little changed. What, in other words, is *not* found is any clear and compelling evidence of a *generalised, sustained, and substantial* decrease in class differentials in educational attainment, concomitant with the economic development of modern societies, of the kind that the liberal theory would lead one to expect.[6]

Why, then, should these differentials show such a degree of resistance to change? The explanatory approach that has thus far been most favoured is one that starts from a supposed connection of some kind between class and culture. In its weaker forms, this approach simply takes over earlier theories of the *famille educogène* (see, e.g., Halsey, Floud and Anderson, eds., 1961: part IV; Banks, 1971: chs. 4 and 5). The prevailing culture of more advantaged classes, it is held, leads to parents within these classes setting a higher value on education than parents in other classes and being better equipped to encourage and promote educational success on the part of their children. Such theories, one may accept, contribute significantly to the explanation of why class differentials in educational attainment should exist in some degree or other. However, they do not take one very far with the problem of their temporal stability. That is to say, they do not give any indication of why the cultural effects that they invoke should have maintained their differentiating force, virtually undiminished, over generations, and especially in the context of the social transformations engendered by advancing industrialism, including major educational expansion and reform. All that is offered in this regard seems to be an essentially circular argument: the fact that differentials have not been reduced is itself the evidence that the influence of class cultures persists.[7]

In stronger versions of the approach, an attempt is made to meet the difficulty in question in that theories explicitly of 'cultural reproduction' are advanced (e.g., Bourdieu and Passeron, 1970; Bourdieu, 1973; Bowles and Gintis, 1976; Willis, 1977). The educational system, as it functions within the totality of class relations, is seen not as means of utilising talent more effectively or of widening opportunities but rather as an agency of social control. Cultural reproduction, it is maintained, is necessary to social structural reproduction, and 'dominant' classes therefore use their power in order to ensure that schools operate in an essentially conservative way. This they do by imposing a pedagogy that requires of children an initial socialisation into the dominant culture as a condition of educational success. Class differentials in attainment are thus created via the unequal endowments of appropriate—though in large part arbitrarily defined—'cultural capital' that children bring with them into the educational system; and they are maintained because schools do not seek to offset, but rather to exploit, such inequalities, albeit in the name of recognising merit. Moreover, being thus debarred from educational success, children of working-class origins in particular are led to collude in their own disadvantage, whether through a passive acceptance of their 'failure' or through involvement in counter-school subcultures that enable them to express resistance to the established order even though at the same time reinforcing their position of subordination within it.

However, while theories of cultural reproduction do in this way offer an account of why class differentials persist, this account again still founders on the very facts of educational expansion. It is simply not the case that children from less advantaged class backgrounds have been excluded from, or have themselves rejected, the educational system to anything like the extent that these theories would suggest. As Halsey, Heath, and Ridge (1980: ch. 5 esp.) have argued, specifically against Bourdieu, educational expansion—in many respects *demand led*—implies not the reproduction of cultural capital but rather its very substantial growth. In Britain, as these authors show, and indeed elsewhere, the *majority* of children entering more selective and academic forms of secondary education during the postwar decades were 'first generation', and, by now, the same thing could also be said of those entering higher education. In other words, proponents of theories of cultural reproduction would appear to be betrayed by their rather gross misunderstanding of the degree to which in modern societies' opportunities for upward educational—and also class—mobility between generations have indeed been enlarged *and* exploited.[8]

Although, then, theories of a culturalist inspiration, despite their currency, must be reckoned as for one reason or another unsatisfactory for the explanatory task in hand, the nature of the difficulties they encounter does at all events help clarify just what must be required of a theory of a more adequate kind. That is, it must be able to offer an explanation of why class differentials in educational attainment have persisted, but one that can at the same time accommodate the more or less continuous increase in the participation of young people in education and in their overall levels of attainment across all classes that has been the general experience of advanced societies.

To try to meet this requirement, I would suggest a theory that is in direct line of descent from that advanced by Boudon (1974). Although, as will be seen, I diverge from Boudon at a number of points—as well as in my definition of the problem to be addressed[9]—I follow him not only in his general RAT approach but further in two more specific respects: first, in starting from the 'structural' theory of aspirations of Keller and Zavalloni (1964) and, second, in regarding the processes that generate class differentials as operating in two different ways.

Keller and Zavalloni argue, in opposition chiefly to Hyman (1954), that rather than class differences in levels of aspiration, educational or occupational, being interpreted culturally—that is, as reflecting differing class values and related norms—they may be alternatively, and more parsimoniously, understood in structural terms. The aspirations individuals report, Keller and Zavalloni propose, should be assessed not by an absolute standard but *relatively*: that is, relative to the class positions in which the individuals are presently located. From this standpoint, for example, aspirations to attend university on the part of children of working-class and of salariat origins would not be treated as being on the same level; rather, the former would be regarded as having the *higher* aspirations. In turn, then, it need not be supposed that the tendency of children from working-class families to pursue in general less ambitious educational careers than children from salariat families derives from a poverty of aspiration: the patterns of choice made could be more or less equivalent ones. It is simpler to assume that there is no systematic variation in levels of aspiration, or related values, among classes, and that variation in the courses of action that are actually taken arises from the fact that, in pursuing any given goal from different class origins, different 'social distances' will have to be traversed—or, as Boudon (1974: 23) more usefully puts it, different opportunities and constraints, and thus the evaluation of different sets of probable costs and benefits, will be involved.[10]

Such an assumption has, moreover, not just the virtue of parsimony but further that of being consistent with the experience of educational expansion. As greater opportunities for secondary and higher education have been created, children from less advantaged class backgrounds *have* proved ready to take these up and indeed to *a similar degree to children from more advantaged backgrounds.* That is to say—and the point is an important one—although class differentials appear in general to have been only very modestly if at all reduced, there is no evidence from any modern society that these differentials have appreciably *widened*—which is the consequence of expansion that theories invoking the reproduction of class cultural divergence would lead one to expect, as children from more advantaged backgrounds accept to the full the growing opportunities that working-class children spurn.

Boudon's adoption of the structural theory of aspirations is then related to the distinction that he proposes between the 'primary' and the 'secondary' effects that serve to stratify educational attainment. Primary effects are those that create class differentials in initial achievement or 'demonstrated ability' in school. It is at this level that Boudon would acknowledge the importance of class cultural influences—that is, in regard to actual performance rather than to values and aspirations, and to this extent he thus underwrites the idea of the *famille éducogène.* However, it is on secondary effects that his attention is focussed: that is, on those effects that come into play as children reach the various transitions or branching points comprised by the educational system and that condition the choices they make. Some choices may of course be formally denied to some children simply on grounds of insufficient ability. Nonetheless, what is important to recognise is that most children do still have significant choices open to them: whether to leave school or to stay on, to take more vocational or more academic courses, to seek to enter higher education, and so on. And it is at this stage that considerations arising from the relationship between class origins and envisaged destinations— educational and in turn occupational—become crucial. That is to say, Boudon sees the choices in question as being determined via the evaluations that children and their parents make of the costs and benefits of, and the chances of success in, the different options that they might pursue. Further stratification of educational attainment, he then argues, will result through the evaluation of more ambitious options tending to be the less favourable, the less advantaged the class position from which they are viewed and the greater, therefore, the *relative* level of aspiration that they entail. Thus, even among children who, through the operation of primary effects, reach similar educational standards early in their school careers, secondary effects will still produce class differentials in attainment insofar as these children start from—and view their prospective careers from—differing class origins.

Following this approach, Boudon's main concern is to establish that, as children's educational careers extend, it is the influence of secondary rather than of primary effects on attainment that becomes increasingly dominant— a claim that has in fact met with a good deal of opposition (see, e.g., Halsey, Heath, and Ridge, 1980: 128–33; Erikson and Jonsson, 1993). However, for my own purposes, I would wish to develop Boudon's theoretical approach towards a different end: that is, to show that it is on secondary rather than primary effects that attention must centre if the question of change, or absence of change, in class differentials under conditions of educational expansion is to be effectively addressed.

Primary effects can in fact be understood more broadly than by Boudon (cf. Halsey, Heath, and Ridge, 1980: 127) as comprising all those influences, whether cultural or genetic, that shape what is taken (arbitrarily or not) to be the distribution of ability in the earlier stages of schooling. These effects can be seen as establishing, together with the structure of the educational system, a *potential* range of educational outcomes overall and, likewise, of class differentials in these outcomes. However, it is then secondary effects, operating through the decisions actually made by children, together perhaps with their parents, regarding particular educational options that will determine just how these potentialities are realised. With educational expansion and reform, the constraints on choice that primary effects impose will tend to weaken (and even if these effects do persist throughout educational careers) in that the degree of selectivity in successive transitions, in terms both of ability and resources, will be reduced. More children, in total, will stay on in education beyond the compulsory period, take more academic courses, enter higher education, and so on. And greater scope is thus created, at the level of secondary effects, for less advantaged children to bring their take-up rates of relatively ambitious educational options closer to those of more advantaged children. In other words, educational opportunity is increased in the sense that the objective structure of opportunities is made generally more favourable. But, for present purposes, the crucial question is of course that of the particular pattern on which these enlarged opportunities are in fact exploited.

It may at this point be instructive to refer to the case of gender differentials in educational attainment. What has emerged from research in this area (see esp. Shavit and Blossfeld, eds., 1993) is that in the course of the decades of educational expansion these differentials have shown a marked decline across virtually all advanced societies. Former disparities in favour of males have been largely eliminated—and in some cases reversed—as, one might suggest, parents and their daughters have come to reach more positive cost-benefit evaluations of education for women in the light of changing gender relations and labour market conditions. Thus, the problem of class differentials is thrown into sharp relief: why is it that a comparably comprehensive and rapid process of equalisation, such as would be predicted by the liberal theory, has not in this case also been apparent? [11]

From the theoretical position that I have taken, I would suggest an explanation that may be summed up in the following proposition. Class differentials in educational attainment have persisted because, even though with educational expansion and reform, the *general* balance of costs and benefits associated with more ambitious options has steadily changed so as to encourage their take-up, little concurrent change has occurred in the relativities between *class-specific* balances: that is, between such cost-benefit balances as they are on average assessed from the standpoints represented by different classes of origin. What needs then further to be shown, or at all events hypothesised, is why, in this latter respect, such stability should have prevailed.

THE RAT EXPLANATION DEVELOPED

In the liberal theory, one of the main bases of the expectation that class differentials in educational attainment will decline is the idea that costs will be a steadily waning influence on educational decision making by parents and children. The direct costs of education, in the form of fees, maintenance, and the purchase of books and equipment, will be much reduced through growing public provision of free or subsidised education at all levels; and indirect costs, usually estimated in terms of earnings foregone by children who remain in education beyond the minimum school-leaving age, will tend to be discounted in a context of economic growth and generally rising family incomes. Thus, there will be rather few children, of whatever class background, who do not continue in education simply because of a lack of the necessary economic resources. Here, as indeed in other respects, the liberal argument undoubtedly has force, but at the same time several important considerations are neglected.

To begin with, the obvious point is that even if family income no longer represents a constraint *stricto sensu* on children's educational careers, it may well still affect the *probability* of their taking one rather than another of the various options facing them. And it has then further to be recognised that while generally rising affluence has indeed characterised modern societies, it is far less clear that there has been any major and continuing reduction in class differentials in family economic resources. Over recent decades class inequalities in the distribution of personal and household incomes have in fact widened significantly in many societies, and, perhaps still more relevantly, there is little evidence of any decline in the effects of class position on the security or stability of earnings or on the course that earnings typically follow in lifetime perspective (see further vol. I, ch. 5, and chs. 5 and 6, this volume).

On the one hand, manual wage workers remain far more likely than professional or managerial employees to experience job loss or recurrent or long-term unemployment. And, even when in employment, the fact that they are more often paid on a piece- or time-rate basis rather than receiving a fixed salary means that their earnings are far more subject to fluctuation. Thus, the consequences for family living standards of incurring a certain level of costs on children's education will be less easily calculable within the working class and, in turn, a greater degree of caution in this regard can be expected. On the other hand, differences persist, and may even have been accentuated, in the tendency for earnings in professional and managerial positions to show rising curves with age over a longer period than in the case of manual or routine nonmanual employment. It is in fact towards the end of the period of children's compulsory education, when crucial educational choices have to be made and when the question of opportunity costs first arises, that the earnings curves of parents in different classes are likely to be at their most divergent. In the course of their forties, the earnings curves of parents within the salariat will still tend to be moving upwards, while those of parents in less advantaged class positions will already have flattened out (for British data, see Goldthorpe and McKnight, 2006). Thus, for families in such differing class situations, absorbing the costs, direct and indirect, of children remaining in education is likely to have quite contrasting implications for the *trend* in their living standards (cf. Lane, 1972).[12]

It should in this connection be further noted that public subsidies for education are not always targeted on those families with the greatest need for them. To the extent that the principle of universal, compulsory, and free education applies, means testing is precluded and, further, those eligible for subsidised higher education can only be those who have opted for it—and, previously, for the school courses that lead to the requisite qualifications. Thus, insofar as state support for education does not succeed in reducing class differentials at early branching points in the system, it will thereafter tend to help families in more advantaged classes to maintain their higher take-up of what is in fact the most expensive kind of educational provision (cf. Goodin and Le Grand, 1987).

In sum, the declining influence of costs is surely part of the explanation of the growth in all modern societies in the total number of children remaining in education beyond the compulsory period. But it is not at all apparent—and the liberal theory throws no light on the matter—just what, so far as costs are concerned, might result in children of less advantaged class origins choosing to stay on in school and to pursue more extended educational careers *at a more rapidly increasing rate* than others. Rather, it may in this regard be suggested that the more or less unchanging class differentials in educational attainment that are observed do no more than reflect similarly unchanging relativities as between the costs of education and typical levels and dynamics of family income from class to class.

A further basis of liberal optimism regarding the reduction of class differentials is the assumption that, while the costs of education to the individual diminish, its perceived benefits will increase. As criteria of ascription give way to criteria of achievement in social selection, education becomes the key to economic success, and is generally recognised as such. Thus, the tendency will be for children of all class backgrounds alike to continue in education for as far as their abilities will take them. However, it is once more the case that although the liberal argument is relevant to explaining the general rise in educational levels, it underestimates the self-maintaining character of class inequalities. It neglects the fact that educational decision making remains conditioned by the class situations in which it takes place, and that this is likely to lead to differing evaluations of benefits, as well as of costs, so that change is again inhibited in the ways in which, from class to class, primary effects are modified by secondary effects in producing the pattern of ultimate educational outcomes.

For example, one may suppose that, in viewing education as an investment good, the chief concern of families in more advantaged class positions is that their children should obtain qualifications sufficient to preserve an intergenerational stability of class position or, at very least, to guard against any decisive downward mobility. Thus, parents within the salariat will be more likely than others to encourage their children to go on from school into higher education of some kind. And, moreover, they may be expected to give such encouragement more frequently, and with an increasing commitment of resources, as a consequence of educational expansion itself. As Thurow has argued (1972), the development of a generally better educated population means that more advantaged families are under constant pressure to make greater investments in their children's education as a form of 'defensive expenditure': that is, as one necessary just to maintain their advantage. Considered as an investment good, education is, to an important degree, 'positional' (Hirsch, 1976): what counts, so far as returns in employment are concerned, is not the actual amount of education that individuals have but the amount relative to their competitors in the labour market. In the case of salariat families, it may then be expected that the importance that is attached to qualifications adequate to maintain class stability, together with parents' capacity to absorb the costs involved, will lead to children attempting to enter higher education even where their ability levels are such that, as regards the chances of a successful outcome, the investment is a rather high risk one.

Boudon (1974: 30) has suggested that this tendency is accentuated as a result of higher education becoming a social norm that children are induced to follow through family or peer-group pressures. But while this argument may hold good for certain status groups or milieux *within* more advantaged classes, it is not one that I would myself wish to invoke in the explanation of regularities as extensive, temporally and spatially, as those here in question. A more important consideration might be that, with rising living standards, more salariat families are able to regard higher education for their children as, in the first instance, simply a desirable *consumption* good—although, of course, with resources still being available to create further opportunities, whether through additional education or otherwise, in the event either of failure or the qualifications initially achieved not appearing to offer sufficiently attractive labour market prospects.[13]

Turning now to families in less advantaged class positions, the theoretical expectation must be that they will view the possibility of higher education for their children in an altogether more guarded way. In their case, other, less ambitious, and less costly, educational options would be adequate to the goal of maintaining class stability, while also providing quite good chances of some eventual degree of upward movement. For working-class families, for example, the 'best buys' for their children, despite places in higher education becoming more widely available, could still appear to be vocational courses, linked perhaps to subsequent on-the-job training, which would reduce the chances of relegation into the ranks of the unskilled or unemployed (cf. Arum and Shavit, 1995; Müller and Shavit, 1998) while increasing those of relatively quick entry into skilled manual or technical or supervisory positions. It is, moreover, important to recognise that, in the case of working-class children, a failed attempt at obtaining higher-level academic qualifications is likely to be more serious in its consequences than for children from families enjoying superior resources. For as well as representing a loss in itself, it would also imply further opportunity costs if an alternative, say, vocational option were then to be taken up, and in some cases might actually preclude such an option or impose direct costs as a result of age limits on entry or on the provision of financial support.[14] Thus, among children of less advantaged origins, a prevailing tendency just the opposite of that among the children of the salariat may be anticipated: that is, for academic courses of the kind leading to higher education to be turned down even by some of those with ability levels that would favour a successful outcome.[15]

Boudon would here too wish to bring social as well as purely economic considerations into the analysis. Working-class children, he suggests, may be reluctant to pursue academic routes that would imply their eventual mobility away from their communities, as well as their class, of origin (1974: 30). However, I would again not wish to follow him, if only because of scepticism about the social costs that mobility entails (cf. Goldthorpe, 1987: chs. 6 and 7); and his suggestion does, in any event, seem of doubtful relevance to explaining the persistence of class differentials in educational attainment, since working-class communities of the solidaristic kind that are presupposed have in most modern societies been in steady decline.

What thus emerges from the foregoing are two, related, arguments that develop my initial explanatory proposition regarding the lack of convergence in class-specific evaluations in educational decision making:

1. class differentials in the take-up of more ambitious educational options have been maintained because so too have conditions in which the perceived costs and benefits of these options lead to children in less advantaged families requiring, on average, a greater assurance of success than their more advantaged counterparts before such options are pursued; and

2. the persistence of these differing propensities over time can be seen to have a basis in action of a rational kind once the implications of the resources, opportunities, and constraints that continue to typify differing class situations are taken into account.

The first of these arguments is one that, I believe, can now be left to empirical assessment. The main implication is that a particular pattern of association prevails between class origins, children's demonstrated academic ability, and the kinds of educational decision that they make. A number of studies, from different periods and places, have in fact already revealed a pattern of just the kind in question: that is, they have shown that *even when demonstrated ability is held constant,* children are more likely to enter longer-term and more academic courses, the more advantaged the class origins from which they come (see, e.g., for Britain, Micklewright, 1989; Wadsworth, 1991; Jackson et al., 2005; for the United States, Sewell and Hauser, 1976; for France, Duru-Bellat and Mingat, 1989; Duru-Bellat, Jarousse, and Mingat, 1992; for Sweden, Erikson and Jonsson, 1993). Such findings have sometimes been taken to indicate that children of less advantaged backgrounds face discrimination in their academic careers in the form of an 'ability handicap' that is imposed, consciously or otherwise, by teachers or academic administrators. But an alternative, or at all events additional, interpretation is here proposed in terms of the higher level of ability that less advantaged children will need to show before they, and their parents, are likely to regard more ambitious educational options as, on balance, the best ones for them to follow. The question to be further investigated is then of course that of whether there is also evidence that within particular nations this tendency has indeed remained, as would be hypothesised, rather little altered over time, and despite educational expansion and institutional reform. This is a matter to which I return in Chapter 4, this volume.

As regards the second argument, further clarification of just what is at issue empirically could still be thought desirable. An attempt to provide this may be made by further reference to the work of Gambetta (1987; cf. vol. I, ch. 6, p. 136). From his study of decision making by parents and children within the Italian educational system, one of the leading conclusions Gambetta reaches is that working-class families are indeed far more sensitive to the chances of success than are middle-class families. He contrasts the way in which the latter 'lightheartedly' expose their children to failure in high school and beyond with the 'extreme caution' of the former (1987: 171–72). But Gambetta then raises the question of how far these differing orientations can be regarded as rationally grounded. Although he is in general sympathetic to the RAT approach to explaining class differentials, as pioneered by Boudon, it is here that he sees a possible need to qualify it. His empirical results show that class still exerts an influence on educational choices even when family income and parental education are controlled: that is, middle-class families are still more ambitious and working-class families less ambitious, in the choices they make relative to their children's ability. This finding he then takes as an indication that parents and children do not simply respond to the limits and possibilities that are typical of their class situations in a conscious manner but, subintentionally, *over*adapt. They 'short-circuit' themselves by attempting, on the one hand, too much and, on the other hand, too little, as compared with what a rational appreciation of the probabilities of success and failure would suggest. In other words, parents and children are subject to the influence of 'behind-the-back' processes that, in their very nature, must lie beyond the scope of RAT (1987: 86–100, 180–86 esp.).

Now I do not believe that Gambetta's analysis in this regard is all that secure, and it certainly calls for confirmation. He is engaged in the dangerous practice of providing an ex post interpretation of a residual effect, which could well be no more than the result of misspecification in the model he applies. Furthermore, as he recognises (1987: 93–99), the question of how the 'inertial forces' to which he appeals might actually operate has to be left with no very plausible answer. Nonetheless, Gambetta's work does have the merit of bringing out the way in which, in relation to educational decision making, the boundaries of the explanatory potential of RAT are in principle to be drawn and, in turn, the general form that would need to be taken by radically alternative accounts of how the differing propensities of more and less advantaged families are determined.

The key empirical issue that arises can be stated as follows. In accounting for persisting class differentials in educational attainment, do 'inertial forces' of some kind or other need to be invoked, implying the overadaptation of parents and children to the realities of their differing class situations, even if this would provide an essentially 'black-box' explanation? Or is it rather the case, as I have sought to argue, that persisting differentials are simply one expression of the way in which the unequal distributions of opportunities and constraints that characterise a class society contribute to their own perpetuation through the quite rational adaptive strategies that they induce on the part of those who must act under their influence? To produce evidence that would allow adjudication between these two possibilities will surely not be easy. It will mean entering into a closer examination of how educational decisions are actually made and in particular, I would believe, of what quantity and quality of *information* actors typically have available to them, or actively seek, and further of how they process this information (cf. Manski, 1993). The methodological resources of sociologists in this area are a good deal less developed than those that have enabled them to analyse the pattern of the eventual outcomes of educational decisions across populations and subpopulations and over time. But the challenges that arise must be accepted if empirical research is to go beyond its descriptive task of establishing the phenomena and become effectively allied with the development of theory that has real explanatory power.

EVIDENCE FROM A DEVIANT CASE

In the foregoing, the emphasis has been on the need to reorient class theory so that, instead of offering accounts of processes of class formation or class decomposition that have not in fact occurred, it addresses well-documented macrosocial regularities testifying to the resistance to change that prevailing class relations express. There is, however, no suggestion here that such regularities have the status of 'iron laws' that operate entirely without exception (or that must extend indefinitely into the future). Thus, in the case of educational attainment several instances can now be cited in which the effects of class have to some extent changed and indeed weakened. In conclusion of this essay, it is therefore pertinent to ask how promising the theoretical approach that I have outlined would appear to be when it is a matter not of explaining the long-term persistence of class differentials in educational attainment but rather their diminution. The value in theory development of deviant case analysis, or of the exception that 'proves' (*sc.* tests) the rule, has long been recognised.

Where research findings have indicated declining class differentials in educational attainment in a particular national society, the trend shown up has usually been of a limited kind and sometimes, too, its reality has been open to question in the light of the results of other enquiries. However, there is at all events one case in which the evidence of a fairly general decline in differentials has been demonstrated and consistently confirmed on the basis of different data-sets, namely, that of Sweden (see, e.g., Jonsson, 1988, 1993, 2004; Jonsson and Mills, 1993; Erikson and Jonsson, 1993, eds., 1994). In Sweden in the period from the 1930s through to the 1990s, educational expansion has been accompanied by a narrowing in the probabilities of children of different class backgrounds staying on in school rather than leaving after the compulsory period and, likewise, in the probabilities of their taking up more advanced secondary courses and entering higher education. In particular, children of working-class and farm families have improved their levels of educational attainment as compared with those of children of the salariat.

If then, as I have argued, class differentials in general persist because little change occurs in the relativities of cost-benefit evaluations of educational options as these are—rationally—made in different class situations, what should also be found in the Swedish case is evidence of change, that is, of *convergence*, both in these relativities and in the social realities they reflect. In other words, evidence should exist of the features of employment relations that differentiate class positions being modified or their effects in some way offset.

In fact, quite extensive research findings are already available to show that over the period in question economic inequality in Sweden has for the most part been in decline. Personal incomes have become more equally distributed (Spånt 1979), and to a rather extreme degree as viewed in comparative perspective (Smeeding, O'Higgins, and Rainwater, 1990; Fritzell, 1993), while income differences between broad occupational groupings also fell, to the disadvantage especially of higher-level professional and managerial employees (Åberg, Selén, and Tham, 1987). It would in addition seem likely that in Sweden highly developed social policies, 'active' labour market policies, and powerful trade unions have together reduced to a greater degree than in most other advanced societies the differences in economic security that exist as between wage workers and salaried staff (cf. Esping-Andersen, 1985, 1990; Vogel, 1987; Persson, ed., 1990; Hibbs, 1991).

Further, though, as well as such circumstantial evidence, results are available from a sophisticated time-series analysis undertaken by Erikson (1996), aimed at establishing more specific linkages between changing economic and social conditions in Sweden and the trend in educational differentials. Three points of main importance can be noted. First, there is little sign of economic growth, rising levels of consumption, or educational expansion per se having any connection with greater educational equality. Second, the trend in this direction is in certain respects associated with educational reform—notably, with the introduction of comprehensive schools that eliminated early branching points in the educational system. But, third, the trend is more generally and more strongly associated with what Erikson would interpret as increasing economic security, in particular for the working class, and as indexed primarily by declining rates of unemployment.[16]

It would surely be premature to claim that increased educational equality in Sweden has in fact come about in a way that confirms my account of why, in general, class differentials in education remain little altered: again, the need for further, more detailed, evidence is apparent. Nonetheless, what emerges from analyses of the Swedish experience is at all events consistent with this account, and, it may be added, by the same token must tell clearly against the contentions of the liberal theory. As Erikson (1996) concludes, not just the deviant character of the Swedish case but what is further known of its dynamics, points to the fact that increasing equality in educational attainment is by no means the more or less automatic outcome of inherent features of advancing industrialism. At very least, other conditions must be present, and the strong indication is that 'one of these is political action'. Indeed, it could be that the egalitarian tendencies apparent in Sweden in this, as in various other, respects will in the end have to be seen as being quite specific to, and thus limited by, the period of a distinctive political conjuncture—that of social democratic hegemony (cf. Castles, 1978; Esping-Andersen, 1985; Tilton, 1990)—and one that has, perhaps, by now reached its close.[17]

The general conclusion that I would draw is, then, that a duly reoriented class theory should aim to break with the functionalist and teleological character of both its Marxist and liberal forerunners in two different ways. In present circumstances, its major task, I have argued, must be seen as that of accounting for the long-term stability of class relations and associated inequalities—for, in effect, their inherent self-maintaining properties. And here the prime need is for secure micro-foundations in the analysis of individual action and of its intended and unintended consequences, where individuals are seen as acting as members of classes in the sense of being subject to the differing levels and forms of opportunities and constraints that their particular class situations imply. However, insofar as such theory is also called on to explain processes of change, suggestive of a significant weakening—or, should the case arise, a strengthening—of the influence of class, it would seem likely that it will then have to turn to the analysis of action at a different level: that is, to the action of political elites, and of the organisations they command, insofar as this is specifically directed to modifying relations in labour markets and production units that constitute the matrix of class. Strangely, or perhaps not so strangely, this last point is one that many years ago I argued, together with David Lockwood, in a very different context—in fact, in the last chapter of the last volume of the *Affluent Worker* series (Goldthorpe et al., 1969)—but there, too, against the claims of Marxist or liberal immanentism and by way of asserting the importance of the 'degrees of freedom' that always remain to political creativity.

CHAPTER THREE

Explaining Educational Differentials

Towards a Formal Rational Action Theory*

with Richard Breen

In the light of recent research in the sociology of education, which has involved extensive over-time and cross-national analyses (see esp. Shavit and Blossfeld, eds., 1993; Erikson and Jonsson, eds., 1996), it would seem that the following empirical generalisations can reliably be made and constitute *explananda* that pose an evident theoretical challenge.

1. Over the last half-century at least, all economically advanced societies have experienced a process of educational expansion. Increasing numbers of young people have stayed on in full-time education beyond the minimum school leaving age, have taken up more academic secondary courses, and have entered into some form of tertiary education.

2. Over this same period, class differentials in educational attainment, considered net of all effects of expansion per se, have tended to display a high degree of resistance to change: that is, while children of all class backgrounds have alike participated in the process of expansion, the association between class origins and the relative chances of children staying on in education, taking more academic courses or entering higher education has in most societies been reduced in only a rather modest and uncertain fashion, if at all. Children of less advantaged class origins have not brought their take-up rates of more ambitious educational options steadily and substantially closer to those of their more advantaged counterparts.

3. Some cross-national variation in this respect has, though, to be recognised. In one case at least, that of Sweden, there can be little doubt that class

*I am grateful to my coauthor, Richard Breen, for permission to include this essay. For the—very minor—changes made to the present version, I alone am responsible. Helpful comments on earlier drafts of the essay were provided by David Cox, Robert Erikson, Michelle Jackson, Ineke Maas, Cecelia Garcia-Peñalosa, Brendan Halpin, Aage Sørensen, and Tony Tam.

differentials in educational attainment have indeed declined over several decades (Erikson and Jonsson, 1993); and, while some conflict of evidence remains, a similar decline has been claimed for France (Thélot and Vallet, 2000; Vallet, 2004b), the Netherlands (De Graaf and Ganzeboom, 1993), and Germany (Müller and Haun, 1994; Jonsson, Mills, and Müller, 1996). Thus, any theory that is put forward in order to explain the persistence of class differentials should be one that can at the same time be applied mutatis mutandis to such 'deviant' cases.

In addition, it would be desirable that such a theory should be capable of yet further extension in order to account for one other regularity that has emerged from the research referred to.

4. Over a relatively short period—in effect, from the 1970s onwards—*gender* differentials in levels of educational attainment, favouring males over females, have in nearly all advanced societies declined sharply and, in many instances, have been eliminated or indeed reversed. In other words, while the process of educational expansion has not led to children from less advantaged family backgrounds catching up with those from more advantaged backgrounds in their average levels of attainment, in families across the class structures of contemporary societies daughters have rather rapidly caught up with sons.

In Chapter 2, an explanation of persisting differentials in educational attainment, sensitive to the further requirements indicated above, was developed from the standpoint of rational action theory. Here, our aim is to refine this theoretical account and to express it in a formal model. In this way we would hope to clarify its central arguments and in turn the wider implications that it carries. Since such attempts at the formalisation of theory are still not very common in sociology (as compared with economics, where they are standard), this essay may also serve to stimulate discussion of the merits or demerits of this kind of endeavour. In the remainder of this introductory section we set out certain background assumptions of our subsequent exposition that will not be further discussed. The more specific assumptions on which our model rests will be introduced and their significance considered, as the chapter proceeds.

We assume, to begin with, that class differentials in educational attainment come about through the operation of two different kinds of effect which, following Boudon (1974), we label as 'primary' and 'secondary' (see further Jackson et al., 2005). Primary effects are all those that are expressed in the association that exists between children's class origins and their average levels of demonstrated academic ability. Children of more advantaged backgrounds are in fact known to perform better, on average, than children of less advantaged backgrounds on standard tests and in examinations. Primary effects, as will be seen, enter into our model but, fortunately, in such a way that we need not take up the vexed and complex question of the extent to which they are genetic, psychological, or cultural in character. It is, rather, secondary effects that for us play the crucial role. These are effects that are expressed in the actual choices that children, together perhaps with their parents,[1] make in the course of their careers within the educational system—including the choice of exit. Some educational choices may of course be precluded to some children through the operation of primary effects: that is, because these children lack the required level of demonstrated ability. But, typically, a set of other choices remains, and it is known that the overall patterns of choice that are made are in themselves—over and above primary effects—an important source of class differentials in attainment.

We then further assume that, *in their central tendencies*, these patterns of educational choice reflect action on the part of children and their parents that can be understood as rational: that is, they reflect evaluations made of the costs and benefits of possible alternatives—for example, to leave school or to stay on, to take a more academic or a more vocational course—and of the probabilities of different outcomes such as educational success or failure. These evaluations, we suppose, will be in turn conditioned by differences in the typical constraints and opportunities that actors in different class positions face, including the levels of resources that they command. However, what we seek to dispense with is any assumption that these actors will also be subject to systematic influences of a (sub)cultural kind, whether operating through class differences in values, norms, or beliefs regarding education or through more obscure 'subintentional' processes. Not only do we thus gain in theoretical parsimony, but we would in any event regard the culturalist accounts of class differentials in educational attainment that have so far been advanced as in various ways unsatisfactory (cf. ch. 2).

Finally, two other assumptions, regarding the structural context of action, should also be spelled out. On the one hand, we suppose the existence of a class structure: that is, a structure of positions defined by relations in labour markets and production units. And, in addition, we need to assume that within this structure classes are in some degree hierarchically ordered in terms of the resources associated with, and the general desirability of, the positions they comprise.[2] On the other hand, we suppose an educational system—a set of educational institutions that serve to define the various options that are open to individuals at successive stages in their educational careers. And here, too, we have a more specific requirement. That is, that this system should possess a diversified structure that provides options not just for more or less education but also for education of differing kinds, and that in turn entails individuals making choices at certain branching points that they may not be able later to modify, or at least not in a costless way. It might be thought that this latter requirement will tend to limit the applicability of our model to educational systems of the more traditional European, rather than, say, the American variety: that is, to ones where the type of school attended is likely to be more consequential than the total number of years spent in education. However, we would argue that, on examination, educational systems such as that of the United States turn out to be more diversified than is often supposed, so that children do in fact face educational choices that involve considerations that go beyond simply 'more' or 'less': for example, in the American case, with the choice at secondary level between academic and vocational tracks.[3] It is further of interest to note how two American authors have specified in this regard the divergence between assumptions that we and they would share and those of most economists working within the human capital paradigm. Although for the latter, education appears as a 'fungible linear accumulation, like a financial investment', a more realistic view would be that educational systems, the American included, 'offer an array of choices and constraints that defy simple linear formulations' (Arum and Hout, 1998:1).

A MODEL OF EDUCATIONAL DECISIONS

The model we present is intended to be generic: that is, one applicable in principle to the entire range of decisions that young people may be required to make over the course of their educational careers as regards leaving or staying on or as regards which educational option to pursue. However, in the interests of simplicity, we will here set out the model as it would apply just to the choice of leaving or continuing in education. The salient elements of the exposition are shown in Figure 3.1 by means of a decision tree. Here

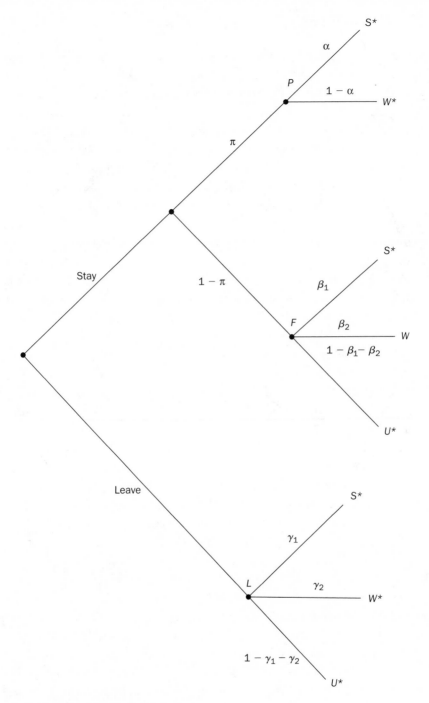

Figure 3.1 A single decision tree

we assume that pupils must choose whether to continue in education—that is, follow the 'stay' branch of the tree—to the completion of a further level (as, say, in the decision in the British case of whether or not to continue to A-level after GCSE) or to leave and enter the labour market, that is, follow the 'leave' branch. Continuing in education has two possible outcomes, which we take to be success or failure. Because remaining at school often leads to an examination, we equate success with passing such an examination. This is indicated by the node labelled P in Figure 3.1, while failing the examination is indicated by the node labelled F. Leaving is then the third educational outcome in our model, that is, in addition to those of staying in education and passing and staying and failing, and is indicated by node L.

In deciding whether to continue in education or leave, parents and their children, we suppose, take into account three factors. The first of these is the cost of remaining at school. Continuing in full-time education will impose costs on a family that they would not have to meet were their child to leave school: these include the direct costs of education and also forgone earnings. We can therefore express these costs relative to the costs of leaving by setting the latter to be 0 and the former as $c > 0$. The second factor is the likelihood of success if a pupil continues in education. Because we distinguish only between success and failure, subjective beliefs about the chances of success at the next stage of education can be captured in our model by a single parameter, which we label π. This parameter measures the subjective conditional probability of passing the relevant examination given continuation. The third factor is then the value or utility that children and their families attach to the three educational outcomes represented by P, F, and L in Figure 3.1. In our model this factor is expressed in terms of beliefs about the chances of access that each outcome affords to three possible destination classes.

For the purposes of our exposition, we take these classes as being the salariat of professionals and managers (S^* in Figure 3.1), the working class (W^*) and the underclass, (U^*)—the class, say, of those with only a precarious place in the labour market and in only the lowest grades of employment if not unemployed. However, it should be emphasized that nothing of significance attaches to this choice of classes, except that, as earlier noted, we need to have a hierarchical ordering. Thus, the salariat is regarded as comprising the most advantaged and most desirable positions and the underclass the least advantaged and least desirable, with the working class falling in between. This ranking of classes is, moreover, assumed to be universally recognized or, at all events, not to vary across the population in any socially structured way.[4]

As we have said, each of the three possible educational outcomes in our model has attached to it subjective probabilities of access to each of the three possible destination classes. So, as Figure 3.1 shows, for pupils who remain at school and pass their examination, node P, the probability of access to the salariat is given by α. There is no path linking this educational outcome to the underclass. This means that anyone who reaches this particular outcome is believed to be certain to avoid this class. It follows, therefore, that the probability of entering the working class, conditional on having been educationally successful, is given by $1 - \alpha$. At the other two outcome nodes, F and L, there is a positive probability of entering all three destination classes. So, for the outcome F (remaining at school and failing) the probability of access to the service class is given by β_1, the probability of access to the working class by β_2, and the probability of access to the underclass by $1 - \beta_1 - \beta_2$. For the L outcome the corresponding probabilities are then given by the γ parameters.

We repeat that these are all subjective probabilities. Just as with π, the values for our various α, β, and γ parameters reflect people's beliefs: in this case, about the returns to various educational outcomes conceptualised in terms of access to more or less desirable locations in the class structure. In principle, therefore, these parameters could vary widely across individuals and families. Again, though, we assume a societal consensus in regard to a set of beliefs that then serve as conditions on the parameters in question and that may be stated as follows.

> 1. $\alpha > \beta_1$ and $\alpha > \gamma_1$. It is generally believed that remaining at school and succeeding affords a better chance of access to the salariat than does remaining at school and failing or leaving school. Our model does not require that we make any assumptions about the relative magnitude of β_1, and γ_1. It could, for example, be the case that a young person's chances of access to the salariat are improved simply by acquiring more years of education, even if this does not lead to examination success. Alternatively, such time spent in education may be wasted in the sense that leaving school and embarking earlier on a career will yield a better chance of access to the salariat.

2. $\gamma_1 + \gamma_2 > \beta_1 + \beta_2$. Remaining at school and failing increases the chances of entering the underclass. This means that there is a risk involved in choosing to continue to the next level of education.

3. $\gamma_2 / \gamma_1 > 1$; $(\gamma_2 / \gamma_1) \geq (\beta_2 / \beta_1)$. Those who leave school immediately have a greater chance of entry to the working class than to the salariat. This may or may not be the case among those who remain at school and fail, although, if it is, their odds of entering the working class rather than the salariat are no greater than those who leave school immediately.

4. $\alpha > 0.5$. Staying on at school and passing the examination makes entry to the salariat more likely than entry to the working class.[5]

In the interests of realism, especially as regards conditions (2) and (3) above, it ought to be noted that 'leaving' and entering the labour market need not in most educational systems be equated with a definitive ending of the individual's educational career. Taking this option could lead to further vocational courses pursued in conjunction with employment.

THE GENERATION OF CLASS DIFFERENTIALS

Given the model previously outlined, we can now turn to the question of explaining why differences exist across classes in the proportions of young people who make one kind of educational decision rather than another. For ease of exposition here we consider only two classes of origin, the salariat, S, and the working class, W. In all of what follows we assume that these classes differ in only two ways. First—and it is here that we give recognition to primary effects—children of the two classes differ in their average ability. Ability is taken to be normally distributed within each class with means $a_S > a_W$ and variance given by σ_a^2. Second, the two classes have different levels of resources, r, which they can use to meet c, the costs of education. Resources are taken to have a logistic distribution with mean values $r_S > r_W$ for the two classes and a common dispersion parameter, σ_r^2. Throughout, we make no other assumptions about differences between the classes. In particular, and as earlier noted, we do not suppose any class-specific cultural values or social norms nor any class differences in the subjective α, β, and γ parameters of our model.

We then propose three mechanisms through which class differentials in educational attainment may arise at the level of secondary effects. Of these three, we would wish to stress the particular importance of the first, since this provides an account of how these differentials may be created and sustained through the apparently 'free' choices made by those in less advantaged classes. Our second and third mechanisms can be understood as accentuating the differing patterns of choice that derive from this initial source.

Relative Risk Aversion

We begin with an assumption regarding aspirations: that is, that families in both classes alike seek to ensure, so far as they can, that their children acquire a class position at least as advantageous as that from which they originate or, in other words, they seek to avoid downward social mobility.[6] This means that the educational strategy pursued by parents in the salariat is to maximise the chances of their children acquiring a position in this class. In terms of our model their strategy is to maximise the probability of access to S^*. For working-class parents the implication is that they should seek for their children a place in either the working class or the salariat, since either meets the criterion of being at least as good as the class from which they originate. In terms of our model their strategy is then to maximise the probability of access to S^* or W^*, which is the same as minimising the probability of access to U^*. This establishes families in both classes as having identical relative risk aversion: they want to avoid, for their children, any position in life that is worse than the one from which they start.

To see the consequence of these two strategies, maximise $pr(S^*)$ for those of salariat origins and minimise $pr(U^*)$ for those of working-class origins, let us assume, for the moment, that continuing in education is costless ($c = 0$). Then we find that whether a pupil believes it to be in his or her best interests to continue in education rather than leave depends on the value p_i (where i indicates the ith pupil) given by

$$p_{iS} = \frac{\pi_i \alpha + (1 - \pi_i)\beta_1}{\pi_i \alpha + (1 - \pi_i)\beta_1 + \gamma_1} \tag{1}$$

for the ith pupil of salariat origin, and by

$$p_{iW} = \frac{\pi_i + (1 - \pi_i)(\beta_1 + \beta_2)}{\pi_i + (1 - \pi_i)(\beta_1 + \beta_2) + (\gamma_1 + \gamma_2)} \tag{2}$$

for the ith pupil of working-class origin.

Here we have allowed π to vary among pupils but we have assumed the values of α, β, and γ to be common to all. If p takes a value greater than one-half, this indicates expected returns to remaining at school exceed those of leaving. Thus, without taking account, as yet, of the costs of pursuing the former strategy, pupils for whom $p_i > 0.5$, can be said to prefer to remain in education. Even if subjective expectations of future success, as captured by π, do not differ between the two classes, it will nevertheless be the case that, given conditions (1) to (4) above, $p_{is} > p_{iw}$ for any value of π less than 1.[7]

This is proved as follows: $p_{is} > p_{iw} \; \forall \; \pi \leq 1$ if and only if

$$\frac{\pi\alpha + (1 - \pi)\beta_1}{\gamma_1} > \frac{\pi + (1 - \pi)(\beta_1 + \beta_2)}{\gamma_1 + \gamma_2} \tag{3}$$

Taking the first term on the left-hand side of (3) we have

$$\frac{\pi\alpha}{\gamma_1} = \frac{\pi}{\frac{1}{\alpha}\gamma_1} > \frac{\pi}{\gamma_1 + \gamma_2} \tag{3a}$$

by conditions (3) and (4) in the text above. Taking the second term of the left-hand side of (3) we have

$$\frac{(1 - \pi)\beta_1}{\gamma_1} \geq \frac{(1 - \pi)(\beta_1 + \beta_2)}{(\gamma_1 + \gamma_2)} \tag{3b}$$

by conditions (2) and (3). Together (3a) and (3b) imply (3), which in turn implies $p_S > p_W$ as required.

This result establishes that if continuing in education is costless and there are no class differences in the subjective probability parameters α, β, and γ, children from more advantaged class backgrounds will more strongly 'prefer' (in the sense of perceiving it to be in their best interests) to remain in school to a further level of education rather than leave.

The proportions in each class who prefer to stay are derived as follows. Assume that p has an unspecified distribution with means in each class p_S and p_W and dispersion parameters σ_{pS} and σ_{pW}. Because $p_{is} > p_{iw}$ for any common value of π, and assuming, for the moment, no class difference in the distribution of π, it follows that $p_S > p_W$. Then, given that only those pupils for whom p exceeds one-half prefer to stay at school, the proportions in each class preferring this outcome are given by the area under the unspecified distribution function above the point

$$z_S = \frac{\frac{1}{2} - p_S}{\sigma_{pS}}$$

for the salariat, and analogously for the working class.

Differences in Ability and Expectations of Success

Thus far we have been assuming that the option of continuing in education is open to all pupils. But, of course, this is often not the case and successive levels of education may be open only to those who meet some criterion, such as a given level of performance in a previous examination. Let us assume, for the sake of simplicity, that this criterion can be expressed directly in terms of ability, so that, for example, a pupil may continue in education only if his or her ability level exceeds some threshold, k: that is, we impose the condition that a_i must be greater than k. Given our assumption regarding primary effects, that the mean level of ability is higher in the salariat than in the working class but that both have the same variance in ability, it then follows that the proportion of children of salariat origin who meet this condition exceeds the proportion of those of working-class origin.

However, we might also suppose that pupils' own knowledge of their ability helps shape the subjective probability they attach to being successful in the next stage of education, which we labelled π_i. So we can write $\pi_i = g$ (a_i), where g indicates that π is a function of a. If we then denote by π_S^* and π_W^* the required minimum subjective probabilities compatible with continuing in education (these are the smallest values of π_i for which $p_i > 0.5$) we can write the probability of continuing in education as

$$pr(a_i > k)\, pr(\pi_i > \pi^* | a_i > k)$$
$$= pr(a_i > k, \pi_i > \pi^*)$$
$$= pr(a_i > k, g(a_i) > \pi^*) \tag{4}$$

If

$$pr(g(a_i) > \pi^*) \leq pr(a_i > k)$$

then equation (4) reduces to

$$pr(\pi_i > \pi^*)$$

If pupils' expectations about how well they will perform at the next level of education are upwardly bounded by how well they have performed in their most recent examination—for example, if there are no pupils who, although they have failed to exceed the threshold k, are nevertheless sufficiently optimistic about their future examination performance to wish to continue in education—then ability differences will be wholly captured in differences in the subjective parameter π. This will cause the average value of π to be lower among pupils from the working class than among pupils from the salariat because of the class difference in average ability levels.

Differences in Resources

Thus far we have assumed education to be costless. If we relax this assumption, we need to take account of class differences in the resources that families in different locations in the class structure can devote to their children's education. Assume, therefore, that pupils can continue in education if and only if $r_i > c$ where r_i is the level of resources available for children's education in the ith family. Given that families in the salariat have, on average, greater resources than families in the working class ($r_s > r_w$) and that resources have the same dispersion within each class, it follows that the proportion of salariat pupils for whom this resource requirement is met will exceed the proportion of working-class pupils.

We have now suggested three mechanisms that, taken together, give rise to class differentials in the proportions of children who choose to stay on in education. Our first mechanism shows how, solely because of the relative risk aversion that is seen as being common across classes, there will be a stronger preference among salariat than among working-class pupils for remaining in education given that no costs attach to doing so. Our second mechanism then allows for class differences in average ability levels and in turn in expectations of success. The effect of this is to introduce class differences in the values of π (the subjective probability of future educational success), which further widen class differences in the value of p and thus in the strength of the preference for staying on in education. Finally, our third mechanism takes account of the costs of continuing in education and allows for a further source of class differentials, the average resource levels available to meet these costs. The effect of this is to promote class differences via the proportion of families in each class whose resources exceed the costs of their children continuing in education or, more simply, who can afford to allow their children to continue.

HOW IMPORTANT ARE OUR ASSUMPTIONS?

Throughout the foregoing exposition of our model we have made assumptions of two distinct kinds. First, there are assumptions that serve to restrict differences between classes, for which we have theoretical reasons. Second, there are assumptions that we have introduced just to make our model more tractable. As regards the latter, it might reasonably be asked: how far are our results dependent on these simplifying assumptions?

The assumption that the educational decision problem has three possible outcomes, each of which results in eventual entry to the labour market, is innocuous. In reality, the decision about whether to continue to educational level n may well be made with a view to gaining access to level $n + 1$: for example, a decision about whether to remain at school to sit certain examinations might be made in the light of possible entry to university. Such a situation could be represented through a decision tree such as that shown in Figure 3.2 in which there are two branching points, labelled 'Choice 1' and 'Choice 2', both referring to decisions on whether to continue in education. Note that the second choice is open only to those who reach the node labelled P_1, that is, who pass the examination at the end of the previous level of education. In this model there are five educational outcome nodes, labelled L_1 (immediate leaving), F_1 (staying at the lower level but failing the examination), and, correspondingly, L_2, F_2, and P_2. These five nodes have associated probabilities β, γ, δ, ε, and ϕ and there are two parameters measuring subjective beliefs about the chance of success at each level: π_1 relating to educational level 1 and π_2 relating to educational level 2. Recall that anyone who passes the examination at the end of level 1 is assumed to have a zero probability of entering the underclass. This implies that for any outcome consequent on passing this examination there will only be one identified probability: that is, there will only be one value of δ, of ε, and of ϕ.

In this setup the decision analysed in Figure 3.1 could now be seen as Choice 1 embedded in a more realistic sequence of educational decisions. However, the situation is readily analysed using backward induction. We first solve the final decision in Figure 3.2 (i.e., the decision at Choice 2) in the same way as we analysed the decision in Figure 3.1. This yields

$$p_{iS2} = \frac{\pi_{i2}\phi + (1 - \pi_{i2})\varepsilon}{\pi_{i2}\phi + (1 - \pi_{i2})\varepsilon + \delta} \tag{5}$$

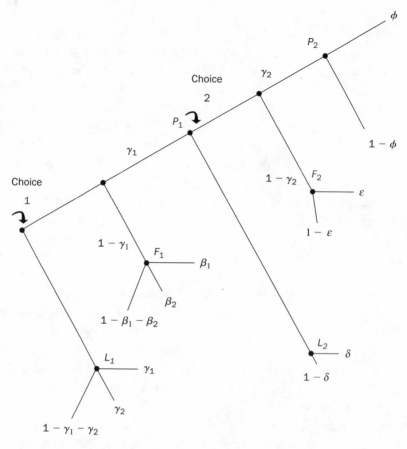

Figure 3.2   A multiple decision tree

which is the value of p for the ith pupil of salariat origin at Choice 2. If we assume that at the time at which Choice 1 is made pupils and their parents have formed the subjective expectation π_{i2}, then we can solve for p_{iS2} in equation (5), and similarly for p_{iW2}. Having done this, we solve for α in equations (1) and (2), which, for pupils of either salariat or working-class origins, is

$$\alpha_i = q_{i2}(\pi_{i2}\phi + (1 - \pi_{i2})\varepsilon) + (1 - q_{i2})\delta$$

Here q_{i2}, which is a function of p_{i2}, is the expected probability of remaining in education at Choice 2.

   Figure 3.2 shows that if we assume no class differences in the parameters

δ, ε, and ϕ, then, holding constant class differences in ability and resources, class differences in choices at a lower educational level will be influenced by expectations about choices that will be made at higher levels of the system. However, these higher-level choices will, again net of class differences in resources, show less variation according to social class than will earlier ones. Not only will successive choices have reduced class differences in ability among those making these later choices, but the riskiness of making more ambitious educational choices will have been reduced or even eliminated. So, for example, in looking at Choice 2 in Figure 3.2, we see that there is now no risk of demotion to the underclass: all the educational outcomes will serve to secure for children of working-class parents a position at least as good as that from which they originated. Under these circumstances, it seems reasonable to assume that, although pupils of salariat origin will still be more likely than their working-class counterparts to choose to continue in education, the class difference should be lessened because this more ambitious educational option now carries with it no risk of downward mobility for working-class pupils. Indeed, were we to make finer distinctions in the labour-market outcomes in our model, we might find that, as we move to higher educational levels, the riskiness in choice comes to affect successively more advantaged classes.

The fact that our model allows only for a pass or fail outcome at the end of each educational level is similarly trivial. It would be easy to allow for three outcomes (e.g., do well, do modestly, or fail) or for a continuum of outcomes, without doing any violence to the model. Again, we have presented the choice to be made as staying in education versus leaving, but the basic approach represented by our model would apply equally well to other educational decisions that might be no less important, as, for example, the choice between following an academic or a vocational educational track. We could then consider four possible outcomes, defined as pass or fail in each track; in turn, there would be no difficulty in embedding this choice in a more complex set of sequential decisions such as that shown in Figure 3.2.

One might also consider the possibility that the α, β, and γ parameters in the model of Figure 3.1 should differ according to class origins, so reflecting class differences in beliefs about the returns to education. Although we have sought to minimise the extent of class differences in subjective parameters, there would be no difficulty in incorporating this modification into our model. In this case, the results would depend on the exact nature of such differences, since what is important here is the pattern of relativities in the values of these parameters both within and between different class origins. For example, if we suppose that $\alpha_S > \alpha_W$ (the returns to staying in education and succeeding are **believed** greater in salariat than in working-class families) or that $\beta_{1S} > \beta_{1W}$ (the chances of access to the salariat among those who fail are believed to be better for salariat than for working-class children) then, referring to equation (3), it is clear that class differences in the proportions of pupils who prefer to stay on in education will be greater. On the other hand, if $\gamma_{1S} > \gamma_{1W}$ the effect will be indeterminate, depending on the size of this difference relative to the extent of class differences in the α and β parameters. For example, if $\gamma_{1S} > \gamma_{2W}$ (among those who leave school, salariat children have a better chance of access to the salariat than have working-class children to the working class), then class differences in preferences will be less marked. However, perhaps the most plausible class difference in assumptions about returns to education is that concerning access to the salariat among young people whose chances would otherwise be diminished by educational failure. Here, salariat families may be in a better position to compensate for such failure than working-class families by providing other channels through which their children could gain access to a service-class destination (see further ch. 7, pp. 000–00). If this were the case, it would be reflected in our model in a class difference in β_1, which, as we have seen, will tend to exaggerate the extent of class differences in choice.

Finally, our assumptions that salariat families seek to maximise $pr(S^*)$ while working-class families seek to minimise $pr(U^*)$ imply that the former do not differentiate between downward mobility to the working class and to the underclass, while the latter attach no more positive weight to upward mobility (into the salariat) than to immobility. If, however, we do suppose that such distinctions are drawn, does the basic result—namely, that the preference for remaining in education rather than leaving is stronger among pupils of salariat than of working-class origins—still hold? As an example, assume that salariat pupils attach weights of $-x$, 0, and 1 to destinations in the underclass, working class, and salariat, respectively, and that working-class pupils attach weights 0, 1, and x^* to these three destination classes, with $x > 0$ and $x^* > 1$. In this case, the salariat considers U^* to be less preferable than W^*, while the working class considers S^* to be preferable to W^*. In this case $p_{iS} > p_{iW}$ holds only if

$$\frac{\pi\alpha + (\alpha - \pi)\beta_1 - x(1 - \pi)(1 - \beta_1 - \beta_2)}{\gamma_1 - x(1 - \gamma_1 - \gamma_2)} >$$

$$\frac{\pi + (1 - \pi)(\beta_1 + \beta_2) + (x^* - 1)(\pi(\alpha - \beta_1) + \beta_1)}{\gamma_1 + \gamma_2 + (x^* - 1)\gamma_1} \tag{6}$$

Compared with expression (3), there is an extra term in both the numerator and denominator for both classes in expression (6). In the case of the salariat (the left-hand side of (6)), the greater penalty attached to U^* makes both the numerator (the payoffs to choosing to stay) and denominator (the payoff to choosing to leave) smaller, because both alternatives carry some possibility of ending up in U^*. However, providing that π is not small, the overall effect will be to increase the probability of staying in education because this option provides a more advantageous trade-off between S^* and U^* than does leaving. For the working class the extra terms in the equation will increase the payoffs to both staying and leaving, because in all cases there is at least one path that leads to S^*, which now carries a greater reward. But, assuming $\beta_1 > \gamma_1$, the net effect will be to make staying more attractive than hitherto. For both classes, the larger the value of π, the greater the increase in the attractiveness of staying rather than leaving. Whether the effect will be a narrowing of class differences in p then depends on the actual configurations of the expected payoffs to S^*, W^*, and U^*. The important considerations are the extent to which the chances of the extra return x^* counterbalance the risk associated with choosing to stay among the working class; and the extent to which the penalty of $-x$ attached to U^* makes the salariat susceptible to the same kinds of risk associated with choosing to stay.

One situation in which class differences in p will narrow (though not necessarily be eliminated) is when $\pi < 1 - \gamma_3 / \beta_3$ (where $y_3 = 1 - \gamma_1 - \gamma_2$ and similarly for β_3). In this case the risk of entering U^* and receiving the very low payoff of $-x$ will come to reduce p_{is} compared with its value under our earlier assumptions that the payoffs to U^* and W^* were the same. But the extent to which this will reduce class differences in p is limited. This is because, under this new setup, the increase in the probability of working-class pupils remaining at school depends on the extent to which they benefit more from the extra return to S^* through remaining at school rather than leaving (so offsetting the riskiness of choice). Yet precisely when π is small the degree to which this is so is limited, so that, as π gets very small, their advantage arises solely because of our assumption that $\beta_1 > \gamma_1$.

The upshot is that, under these alternative assumptions about the weights attached to the various destination classes, a threshold value of π, say π^* exists, such that among young people for whom $\pi_i < \pi^*$, $p_{iS} < p_{iW}$. For values of $\pi > \pi^*$, we find $p_{iS} > p_{iW}$ as before, with the difference widening as we move to larger values of π. At the low values of π there is a very high expectation of failure if young people continue in education. But now, failure is more costly for salariat than for working-class pupils because of the extra penalty associated with the greater downward mobility they risk experiencing. However, for parameter values that meet conditions (1) to (4) given at the start, together with the assumption that $\beta_1 > \gamma_1$, it transpires that for any reasonable values of x^* and x, p^* will be less than 0. By reasonable we mean values of x^* that are less than 2 (so that, for members of the working class, the cost of downward mobility into U^* is greater than the benefits of upward mobility) and of x, that are marginally greater than $x^* - 1$ (meaning that the cost of extra downward mobility into U^* for the service class is greater than the perceived desirability of the extra upward mobility into S^* on the part the working class). These conditions on x and x^* are, in fact, further risk-aversion assumptions, albeit weaker than the ones with which we began this chapter. Young people and their families value upward mobility less than they fear downward.

Our original choice of payoffs reflects our belief that educational decisions are driven by the desire of families to ensure that their children do not experience downward mobility. However, the central result of our risk-aversion assumption, namely, that children from more advantaged backgrounds will more strongly prefer to continue in education, is robust to other choices of pay-off, which seek to capture distinctions in the attractiveness of upward mobility rather than immobility and in the aversion to the amount of downward mobility.

Given this list of what is not essential to the model, it may then be asked what are those features of it that need to be preserved. We have in fact already indicated the answer to this question in noting that it is the first of the three mechanisms we have proposed—that of equal relative risk aversion—that basically drives the model and leads to its most novel and, perhaps, counterintuitive results. More specifically, we may say that what the model crucially depends on is the general structure of the educational decision problem that we have set up, as this is constituted by our initial conditions (1) to (4).

What is essential is that there should be some measure of risk, in terms of eventual class of destination, that is attached to continuing in education or, more generally, to making certain more ambitious educational choices, relative to leaving education or taking less ambitious options. And then further, in order for the model to provide an explanation of class differences in the probabilities of the choices made, risk has in this respect to be unequally distributed across origin classes. Thus, in our model, riskiness is a cost imposed on the working class, but not the salariat, through the possibility of their dropping into the underclass. This is why, with only two origin classes, we still have three destination classes, although it should be stressed that the notion of an underclass is not here of any particular importance in itself. All that is required is that there should be some outcome that can be considered as implying an inferior position to that from which children begin and that, for children of some class origins, this outcome should be less likely if they opt for less ambitious but 'safer' educational careers.[8]

EXPLAINING EMPIRICAL REGULARITIES

We may now seek to apply our model to the explanation of the empirical regularities that were set out in the introductory section, beginning with that of the widely observed persistence of class differentials in educational attainment in the context of an overall increase in educational participation rates. To account for the latter trend is fairly easy: the relative costs of education have declined over time in all economically advanced countries. As the period of compulsory schooling has been extended, the costs of successively higher levels of education have been reduced through the abolition of fees, the introduction of maintenance grants, soft loans, and so on. In our model this change is treated via the third mechanism suggested—the effect of class differences in resources—and is captured in a decline in the size of the parameter c. This will lead to an increase in the proportions of children of both salariat and working-class origins continuing in education, providing, of course, that the preference for continuing (given by our p parameter) does not decline. However, far from p_i declining over time, it is more plausible to suppose that there is a widespread increase in the desire to remain in full-time education as educational credentials are believed to have increasing importance in the labour market and in securing a relatively advantaged class position. Indeed, insofar as education is regarded as a 'positional' good (Hirsch, 1976), p_i could be expected to rise steadily simply as a consequence of educational expansion itself.

At the same time, our model can provide an explanation of how, within a context of educational expansion, class differentials may nonetheless persist. To see this, recall that class differences in educational attainment are usually measured by odds ratios that compare the odds of continuing in education versus leaving for pairs of origin classes. Under our model, the odds ratio between the service and the working class is equal to

$$\frac{\phi_S / (1 - \phi_S)}{\phi_W / (1 - \phi_W)}$$

where we use ϕ_S to mean the proportion of salariat pupils who remain in education and similarly for ϕ_W. It is then possible to show (see the appendix) that, given a decline over time in c, together with an increase in the proportion of both salariat and working-class pupils who consider it in their best interests to remain in education, the odds of continuing in education increase by a roughly constant amount for each class, and so preserve a similar constancy in the odds ratio. This tells us that, under these circumstances, a uniform decline in the costs of education—that is, uniform across classes—will result in the odds for children of all classes choosing to continue being multiplied by something like a common factor. So if, for example, some level of education is made free of charge (in the sense that fees are no longer levied), class differences in participation (as measured by odds ratios) at this level will remain more or less unchanged even though the overall participation rate will increase.

Our model also sheds some new light on the concept of 'maximally maintained inequality' in education (Raftery and Hout, 1990; Hout, Raftery, and Bell, 1993). These authors argue that class differences in educational attainment will only begin to decline when participation in a given level of education of children of more advantaged backgrounds reaches saturation. In our model, such a reduction will occur once c declines to the value at which all members of the salariat have resources that exceed it. At this point, all salariat families will possess resources that exceed the costs of remaining in education and thus the proportion in this class who choose to continue in education will be equal to the proportion who perceive it to be in their interests (i.e., for whom $p_i > 0.5$). Further reductions in c will then have no influence on the numbers of salariat children who choose to continue but will still increase the proportion of working-class children who do so. Under these conditions, the relevant odds ratio could be expected to move towards unity.[9] However, it should be recognised that, as understood in terms of our model, maximally maintained inequality does not imply that a decline in class differentials can commence only at the point at which all children of more advantaged class origins continue in education. Rather, this effect occurs once all such children whose p_i is greater than one-half continue; in other words, once all those who perceive it to be in their best interests to continue are able to act accordingly. It is true that in some instances the achievement of this latter condition will, in fact, give rise to 100 percent continuation among children of more advantaged classes.[10] But further declines in c, even if they lead to $r_{iW} > c$ for all members of the working class, will not lead to equality in the proportions continuing in education in each class so long as there still remains a class difference in the proportion who prefer to continue.

It further follows from our model that class differentials in educational attainment will also respond to changes in the costs of education, which, rather than being uniform, have a variable impact across classes. Such changes could be brought about directly through the selective subsidisation of young people according to their class of origin but essentially the same effect could follow from a general reduction in inequality of condition between classes. Specifically, if class differences in resources, r, become smaller, our model would predict that differentials in educational attainment, as measured by odds ratios, would in turn decline.

It is then in this way that the model may be seen as applying to the national case that most obviously deviates from the pattern of largely persisting class differentials in educational attainment, that is, that of Sweden, in which, as earlier noted, a narrowing of such differentials over the postwar decades is well attested. There is indeed further extensive evidence (cf. ch. 2) that in this same period the average income levels of different classes in Sweden became more equal, while the degree of economic insecurity experienced by the working class was steadily reduced. And through time-series analysis, correlations can in fact be established between these latter tendencies and the growing equality in educational outcomes that are at all events consistent with the hypothesis of a causal influence (Erikson, 1996).

Compared with the degree of stability of class differentials in educational attainment, the decline in gender differentials that has occurred in virtually all advanced societies since the 1970s must appear as rather dramatic. Because gender differentials arise within rather than between families, neither changes in the costs of education nor in inequalities in resources among families are appropriate to explaining their reduction. In the light of our model, this may rather be seen as resulting from shifts in the perception of educational returns that have been prompted by changes in women's labour market participation. It would be fair comment to say that the pattern of returns to different educational decisions that we have thus far envisaged would, for most of the twentieth century, be more applicable to young men than to young women. Until quite recently, it is likely that educational decisions in the case of girls were shaped in the main by the expectation that their primary social roles would be those of wife and mother, and that their class positions would therefore be determined more by whom they married than by how they themselves fared in the labour market. Insofar as this were the case, then the relative returns to education for women would be somewhat different to those we have supposed in the exposition of our model: at all events, the returns associated with any particular educational decision would be less highly differentiated than for men. So, for example, young women of salariat origins could be thought best able to retain their position in this class through marriage. But to meet young men holding positions in the salariat did not necessitate that women should themselves acquire the educational qualifications that led to these positions. Rather, their qualifications had to be such as to provide them with employment that would bring them into contact with potential salariat husbands, and this requirement might be met through only relatively modest levels of educational attainment, leading to a job as, say, a secretary or nurse. And within both the home and the educational system alike, as much emphasis was indeed placed on the acquisition of social and domestic skills as on skills that would have value in the labour market.

Such a flatter gradient in the returns to different educational pathways would, if incorporated into our model, have two consequences. First, the proportion of women choosing to remain in education at each decision point would be smaller than the proportion of men. Second, class differentials would tend to be less among women than among men. The former result follows from the lesser incentive to continue in successively higher levels of education that would be held out to women of all class origins alike; the latter comes about because the magnitude of the class differences among those choosing to remain in education (for given values of ability and resources) is directly proportional to the differences in returns associated with the various possible educational outcomes. If we consider equations (1) and (2) as earlier shown, then as the difference between, say, α_1, β_1, and γ_1 diminishes, so the difference between p_{iS} and p_{iW} will also diminish.

Over the past 20 years, we would suggest, the pattern of returns to education for women has drawn closer to that for men, as rates of women's labour market participation and, especially, rates for married women, have increased and as a woman's own employment has taken on greater significance in determining the standard of living enjoyed by her family and further, perhaps, her own class position. In other words, our model as expressed in Figure 3.1 has come increasingly to apply to women: the gradient in their returns to education has steepened. According to our model, then, such a change should have two effects: gender differentials in educational attainment should decline, as indeed they have,[11] and at the same time the magnitude of class differentials among women should increase.

EMPIRICAL AND THEORETICAL IMPLICATIONS OF THE MODEL

It was in order to account for the empirical regularities that we have just addressed, in particular, that of persisting class inequalities in education, that our model was developed. However, we earlier remarked that an advantage of the formal approach that we have adopted is that, as well as serving to clarify theoretical arguments that are advanced with explanatory intent, it also helps to bring out the wider implications that these arguments carry. In this concluding section, we draw attention to a number of implications, both empirical and theoretical, that stem from our model.

The chief importance of empirical implications is that they provide opportunity for further testing of the model. Insofar as the explanation that we have advanced of certain established empirical regularities would in turn lead to the expectation of other regularities, the possibility arises of further enquiry that could corroborate or undermine the model. For example, in the course of the foregoing, at least three such implications of our model have emerged that would seem worthy of restatement on account both of their apparent openness to test and of their own substantive interest.

1. Before they go on to a further level of education, children of less advantaged class backgrounds will require a higher expectation of success at that level—as indicated, say, by previous academic performance—than will children of more advantaged backgrounds.

2. As children proceed from lower to higher levels of the educational system, the pattern of choices that they make will (in addition to any continuing primary effects) lead to class differentials in participation becoming smaller.

3. As gender differentials in educational participation and attainment diminish over time, class differentials among women will increase from a level initially lower than that among men so as to approximate the male level or, in cases where class differentials are in general decline, will decline less than among men.

A good deal of evidence is in fact already available to lend support to the first two of these propositions that we have had occasion to refer to earlier.[12] As regards the third, the decline in gender differentials would by now seem sufficiently well established in many societies for data relevant to its assessment also to be brought together, and an obvious research opportunity arises.

In addition, in Chapter 4, I consider a number of further empirical implications of the model that others working in the field have noted, in the context of a general evaluation of the model in the light of recent research.

The theoretical implications of the model we would see as being of main significance in their bearing on explanatory strategy. The model represents children and their families as acting in a (subjectively and boundedly) rational way: that is, as choosing among the different educational options available to them on the basis of evaluations of their costs and benefits and of the perceived probabilities of more or less successful outcomes. It then accounts for stability, or change, in the educational differentials that ensue by reference to a quite limited range of situational features. For example, in the case of persisting class differentials, the explanatory emphasis falls on similarly persisting inequalities in the resources that members of different classes can command in the face of the constraints and opportunities that their class positions typically entail. Class differences in demonstrated academic ability are also recognised as relevant, but not—as we have emphasised—class differences in values or norms bearing on educational choice.

To the extent, then, that our model holds good—that is, that it can provide an adequate account of the regularities we have considered and that its further empirical implications are not rejected—the relatively parsimonious strategy of the rational action approach is supported, and, we might add, in an area in which culturalist theories of one kind or another have hitherto enjoyed great popularity, even if not great explanatory success. In turn, the case for attempting to pursue this strategy in other areas of sociological enquiry is strengthened.

Finally, though, we would wish to allude to certain theoretical implications that might be regarded as following from our model but that do not in fact do so (cf. vol. I, chs. 7 and 8). To begin with, we are not required to suppose that, in making educational choices, children and their parents in fact go through all the processes of ratiocination that the model might appear to attribute to them. We do take it to be the case that the actors in question have some knowledge of how their society works, have some concern for their own or for family interests, and seek to use the former to promote the latter. But we can at the same time accept that the decisions they make may only rarely result from any entirely explicit procedures rather than, say, 'emerging' over a period of time and, in all probability, reflecting also various nonrational influences. What underlies our approach is the idea that it is rational considerations that are, not the only, but the *main common* factor at work across individual instances, and that will therefore shape patterns of educational choices in aggregate and, in turn, the regularities that constitute our *explananda*. Our model then aims to represent these considerations in an idealised way, so as to capture the key generative processes involved, rather than to represent decision making as it actually occurs at the level of particular families.

Further, while we do not in explaining class differentials in education invoke systematic variation in values or derived norms, this does not mean that we have to deny their very existence. Thus, insofar as class-specific norms may be identified—which is an empirical issue—we could recognise them as serving as *guides* to rational action that have evolved over time out of distinctive class experience and that may substitute for detailed calculation when educational choices arise. Understood in this way, such norms could conceivably be of some independent explanatory significance as inertial forces in cases where the structure of constraints and opportunities is changing. But what we would in fact expect—and the decline in gender differentials would, at least by analogy, lend support to the idea—is that norms, in being essentially epiphenomenal, would rather quickly come into line with patterns of action that display a rational adaptation to the new circumstances that have come into being.

In sum, our model implies an explanatory strategy that is undoubtedly 'reductionist' so far as the relation of norms to rational action is concerned (cf. Elster, 1991). However, we do not in this regard seek what Popper (1972: ch. 8) has criticised as reduction by *fiat*, but reduction only insofar as it is warranted by the empirical support that our theoretical arguments can obtain in the particular area in which they have been applied.[13]

APPENDIX

The Constancy of Class Differentials over Time

In this appendix we show in detail how our model can account for the widely observed approximate constancy of class differentials in educational participation rates in the context of increasing overall levels of participation.

Let ϕ_{St} be the proportion of salariat pupils continuing in education at time t, given costs c_i, and ϕ_{St+1} the proportion at time $t + 1$ (given costs c_{t+1}) and similarly for the working class. Then we require that

$$\phi_{St+1} > \phi_{St} \tag{A1a}$$
$$\phi_{Wt+1} > \phi_{Wt} \tag{A1b}$$

and

$$\frac{\phi_{St+1} / (1 - \phi_{St+1})}{\phi_{Wt+1} / (1 - \phi_{Wt+1})} \approx \frac{\phi_{St} / (1 - \phi_{St})}{\phi_{Wt} / (1 - \phi_{Wt})} \tag{A2}$$

Equations (A1a) and (A1b) say that overall participation rates increase in both classes over time; equation (A2) says that inequalities between them (measured as odds ratios) remain unchanged.

Our model posits two conditions that must be met if a pupil is to continue in education: family resources must exceed the costs ($r_i > c$), and it must be perceived as in the pupil's best interests to continue in education ($p_i > 0.5$). If the costs of education decline over time from c_t to c_{t+1} ($c_t > c_{t+1} > 0$), this leads to an increase in the probability of resources exceeding costs. Given the reasonable assumption that the values of p_i do not decline over time, equations (A1a) and (A1b) follow immediately. Under the assumption that r has a logistic distribution, the probability of resources exceeding costs is given by

$$L(S, c_t) = \frac{\exp[-(c_t - r_S)/\sigma_r]}{1 + \exp[-(c_t - r_S)/\sigma_r]} \tag{A3}$$

It is easy to demonstrate that the odds ratio as between the salariat and the working class

$$\frac{L(S, c_t) / (1 - L(S, c_t))}{L(W, c_t) / (1 - L(W, c_t))} \tag{A4}$$

is equal to

$$\exp[-(r_S - r_W)]$$

and thus does not depend on the value of c_t (under the assumption that the dispersion parameter, σ, is common to both classes). It follows that if the distribution of resources does not change over time, neither will the odds ratio, equation (A4). However, the overall odds ratio between the two classes is equal to

$$\frac{\dfrac{p_{St} x_{St}}{1 - p_{St} x_{St}}}{\dfrac{p_{Wt} x_{Wt}}{1 - p_{Wt} x_{Wt}}} \tag{A5}$$

and similarly at time $t + 1$. Here, for convenience we use the abbreviations

$$p_{St} = pr\left(p_{St} > \frac{1}{2}\right)$$
$$x_{St} = pr(r_S > c_t)$$

and similarly for the working class. To show that equation (A5) will be approximately constant over time despite change in c, we first rewrite it as

$$\frac{\dfrac{x_{St}}{(e_{St} - x_{St})}}{\dfrac{x_{Wt}}{(e_{Wt} - x_{Wt})}} \tag{A6}$$

where

$$e_{St} = \frac{1}{p_{St}}$$

and likewise for e_{Wt}. Note that if $e_{St} = e_{Wt} = 1$, then equation (A6) reduces to equation (A4). But given $e_{Wt} \geq e_{St}$, a decline in c over time will cause the odds ratio in equation (A6) to decline rather than remain constant. However, recall our earlier argument that educational qualifications increase in importance over time and that this is reflected in an increase in the values of p in both classes. Then if e_S grows proportionately smaller than e_W over the interval t to $t + 1$, the tendency for equation (A6) to decline will be offset. In turn this will occur if

$$\frac{p_{St} / (1 - p_{St})}{p_{Wt} / (1 - p_{Wt})} > \frac{p_{St+1} / (1 - p_{St+1})}{p_{Wt+1} / (1 - p_{Wt+1})}$$

In words, the odds ratio in preferences for remaining in education increases as educational qualifications take on more importance in the labour market.

To summarise: our argument is that, given a decline in the costs of education, the proportions continuing in education in each class will increase, provided that there is no decline in the strength of preferences for so continuing. Thus, equations (A1a) and (A1b) will hold. We then argued that equation (A2) (approximate constancy in the between-class odds ratios of continuing in education) has held as the result of two processes that have had offsetting effects. The decline in the costs of education has a tendency to cause odds ratios to diminish but the increasing importance of education (leading to a widespread increase in the strength of preference for continuing in education) has a tendency to cause odds ratios to widen. In the Swedish case, where odds ratios have declined, this can be explained as being due to the reinforcing of those factors pushing in this direction through the diminishing of class inequalities in resources.

CHAPTER FOUR

The Theory Evaluated
Commentaries and Research*

In the two previous essays a theory aimed at explaining persistent class differentials in educational attainment is set out, first in a rather discursive fashion and then through a formal model. The theory has in fact attracted a surprising, though of course gratifying, degree of attention. In the present essay my aim is to review the critical reception of the theory and a body of empirical research that has, in part at least, been prompted by it and, ultimately, to arrive at an assessment of its present standing. Some of the critical commentary and research has taken the initial version of theory that I outlined as its starting point but research, especially, has tended to relate to the formal model, developed with Richard Breen—which found a place in David Grusky's classic reader, *Social Stratification: Class, Race, and Gender* (2001). In what follows I shall therefore in general refer to the Breen-Goldthorpe (BG) theory or model.[1]

As a preliminary, it may, I believe, be useful if I say something more—and now of course with benefit of hindsight—about the wider intellectual context within which the formulation of the theory could be situated.

APPROACHES TO EDUCATIONAL DIFFERENTIALS FROM ECONOMICS AND SOCIOLOGY

From Chapter 2 it will be clear how the theory relates to debates in the field of class analysis. I there start from the argument that a major reorientation

*For helpful information, advice, and observations, I am indebted to Rolf Becker, Richard Breen, Anders Holm, Stephen Morgan, Alice Sullivan, and Herman Van de Werfhorst.

of sociological theory in regard to class is required. Rather than such theory being, as in both its Marxist and liberal versions, focused ultimately on the explanation of the dynamics of class, whether in regard to class formation or decomposition, more attention needs now to be given to the *stability* of class, in the sense of the powerful resistance to change that class relations and associated differences in life chances and patterns of social action display. The general persistence of class differentials in educational attainment, despite the major expansion of educational opportunities that characterises all modern societies, represents one notable manifestation of the enduring power of class that I then seek to address. However, what needs to be added here is that the nature of educational differentials and the way in which they are to be explained are in themselves issues that give rise to differences and disagreements of rather large significance within the social sciences, in particular as between sociologists and economists. And—as I might have anticipated at the outset—these are issues that will sooner or later require consideration, since they are ones that in any discussion of the BG theory will sooner or later surface.

For economists, following standard human capital theory, decisions on the length of time to be spent in education are made by individuals comparing the costs of the various options open to them with the (discounted) returns that they would expect from pursuing these options. Costs are taken to be the earnings foregone by remaining in education plus any direct costs of education itself, and returns are usually understood in terms of expected lifetime earnings. As regards the formation of such expectations, it is in effect assumed that individuals have knowledge of the processes through which, conditional on certain personal attributes such as sex and ability, lifetime earnings are actually generated, and that they apply this knowledge correctly in order to forecast the outcomes of the different courses of action they might themselves take. In other words, their expectations are assumed to be rational expectations, and on the basis of a conception of rationality that makes extremely strong demands regarding both the information available to individuals and their information-processing capacities (cf. the discussion in vol. I, chs. 7 and 8). From this standpoint, then, class differentials in educational attainment are simply the result of class differences, on the one hand, in average ability and, on the other, in the availability of the funds that are needed to invest in education.

Sociologists do not have a similarly standard theory on which to draw.

However, it would be widely held that systematic differentials in educational attainment of all kinds have to be seen as resulting from processes of socialisation and thus, ultimately, from differences in the cultures or subcultures into which individuals become socialised. From this standpoint, therefore, class differentials are seen as reflecting not so much processes of choice under constraint as the psychological responses of young people to the distinctive value orientations and normative expectations of 'significant others'—parents, peers, and so on—in the class subcultures in which they grow up.[2]

As I did previously note (pp. 29–31), such culturalist positions are in fact expressed in weaker or stronger versions. In weaker versions, all that is claimed is that within different class subcultures education is more or less highly valued and normatively supported and that parents have greater or less cultural resources that they can use to help their children to gain educational success. But in stronger versions, usually deriving from the work of Bourdieu and his followers, the idea of socialisation into subcultures with differing potential for educational attainment is radically extended to that of 'cultural reproduction'. 'Dominant' classes, it is argued, impose a quite *arbitrary* form of pedagogy throughout the educational system that favours their own children and disfavours those socialised into the subcultures of 'subordinate' classes. Thus, class differentials in educational attainment exist, and persist, because schools, rather than seeking to offset the subcultural attributes of children that may inhibit their academic performance, function as essentially conservative institutions that in fact reinforce inequalities in 'cultural capital' across generations. Children who are thus excluded from any serious possibility of educational success can only react by a passive acceptance of their failure or through a rejection of the values of the school and 'acts of resistance'.

The rather stark opposition that is apparent between the approach of the economists and that of at least some sociologists thus disturbingly recalls the old joke that while economics is all about how people make choices, sociology is all about why they have no choices to make. For anyone who finds little satisfaction in interdisciplinary *apartheid* and is, moreover, committed to the idea of an increasingly unified social science, such a situation can only appear as unfortunate and, indeed, as directly challenging. Consequently, while I was initially led to take up the question of educational differentials through an involvement in debates on class analysis, a further concern that I found unavoidable was with the radical disjunction between the ways in which economists and sociologists typically treat this question and with the problems that are thus highlighted.

In this connection, the BG theory can then be seen as one that attempts, following on the earlier work of Boudon (1974), to bring together certain features of the approaches of both economists and sociologists, while of course at the same time necessarily jettisoning others. This attempt is chiefly apparent in the following three respects.

1. The idea is accepted that in general children do make educational choices—in conjunction, perhaps, with their parents and teachers—on the basis of some kind of cost-benefit evaluation. These choices are subject to differing constraints and in particular, to constraints deriving from class background. But, despite this emphasis on differing constraints, it is not accepted, even for children of the most disadvantaged backgrounds, that choice is illusory in that they are effectively prevented from achieving academic success. Class differentials in educational attainment are known to result not only from differences in academic performance but also from the fact that, over their academic careers, children of less advantaged backgrounds tend to take up less ambitious educational options than do children from more advantaged backgrounds even when their academic performance is of a comparable standard (Boudon's 'secondary' effects—see pp. 32–3). At the same time, though, the idea that the cost-benefit evaluations that are involved in educational choices extend to the calculation of expected lifetime earnings, as economists would assume, is rejected as being just too unrealistic. There are no serious grounds for believing that the actors concerned will have either the range of information or the information-processing capacity that would be required.[3]

2. The further assumption, at least implicit in standard economic theory, that educational decisions are no different from other economic decisions— such as, say, which vegetables to buy in the market—is also rejected. Rather, it is recognised that educational choices are made in specific social contexts and will be influenced by them. In particular, it is supposed that class background will be an important factor in such choices in that children will be concerned to obtain a level of education sufficient to enable them *at least to maintain* their parents' position. In other words, instead of aiming to maximise their expected lifetime earnings, they will seek, as first priority, to minimise their risk of downward social mobility—which would appear a rather easier 'criterion function' with which to operate and thus one more compatible with the idea of bounded as opposed to infinite rationality. However, while in *this* sense educational decisions are seen as being 'social' decisions, no appeal is made to class subcultures, and to the distinctive values and norms that they are believed to embody, as conditioning children's educational aspirations and objectives. Children of less advantaged class background may appear more risk

averse in their educational decision making than children of more advantaged background. But, rather than this expressing some subcultural difference, it is seen as reflecting the fact that both are pursuing the same priority—to at least maintain their parents' class position—with, however, differing average levels of ability (Boudon's 'primary effects'), and thus expectations of success, and also differing resources. In other words, *equal relative* risk aversion is supposed.

3. Although educational choices are taken to involve some kind of cost-benefit evaluation, it is not envisaged, in the way of economists working within the human capital paradigm, that obtaining education can be understood as a investment of a straightforward, more-or-less kind that can, for example, be measured simply in terms of years of education. As was in fact earlier noted (p. 48), it would appear more realistic to see modern educational systems as requiring a sequence of choices concerning not only how much but also what type of education—for example, academic or vocational—should be acquired. And it is further recognised that the choices that are made at certain crucial branching points may be ones that are not later modifiable, at least in any easy or costless way.

Finally, in the present connection, it is of interest to compare the position outlined above with that which emerges from another attempt to find some accommodation between the standard approaches of economics and sociology—in this case one made by an economist. Akerlof (1997) addresses questions of educational choice and of class or ethnic differentials in educational attainment in the context of a more general discussion of social decisions and of the externalities that may result from them.

At first sight, Akerlof's approach may in fact appear to go clearly beyond that of the BG theory in a 'sociological' direction. While the latter treats educational decisions as being social decisions only in the relatively weak sense indicated above, for Akerlof these decisions are social in that they involve action that is crucially guided by the individual actor's sensitivity to the responses of 'significant others': that is to say, his or her utility is dependent on theirs. More specifically, Akerlof argues that educational choices are strongly influenced by norms that prevail within the subcultures and social networks to which individuals belong, and it is then through individuals' compliance with these norms that secondary effects in educational differentials (though Akerlof does not actually use this terminology) are generated. On the one hand, children from advantaged backgrounds who have been socialised into norms favouring educational achievement are inclined to stay on in school too long, given their ability. But, on the other hand, children from less advantaged backgrounds tend to leave education, even if they have the ability and actual opportunity to go further, because in their case other norms carry greater weight: in particular, norms of loyalty to their friends, their neighbourhood, or, ultimately, their class or ethnic group. In this way, then, what Akerlof calls a 'low equilibrium trap' is created and educational differentials persist despite educational expansion and reform: 'loyalty to the social network in each generation trumps the evolution towards the social optimum that would otherwise occur' (1997: 1010, 1017).

However, while Akerlof's position might thus seem an essentially culturalist one, taken over from the typical sociological approach, two further features need also to be noted. First, Akerlof, unlike many sociologists, does not simply take it for granted that educational choices are formed within sociocultural milieux capable of exerting strong normative pressures on their members. He accepts that the 'contextual effects'—of peer groups, neighbourhoods, and so on—to which he appeals have to be demonstrated, and further that in quantitative, survey-based research apparent demonstrations tend, for various reasons, to be somewhat suspect.[4] On this account, therefore, he sees it as necessary (1997: 1007) to turn to ethnographies (and biographies) that can provide 'a level of thick description' at which it may be possible to discern 'unambiguously' the presence of subculturally conditioned social interaction and its effects on individual motivation. I believe that Akerlof's confidence in ethnographies may in this respect be excessive, on grounds that I have earlier set out (see vol. I, ch. 4),[5] and, to repeat, the BG theory avoids the assumption that in modern societies class subcultures (as distinct, perhaps from the 'ghetto' subcultures to which Akerlof often refers) do in general have the coherence and normative force that his position would require. Nonetheless, it is a virtue of Akerlof's contribution that this key issue is so clearly recognised.

Second, Akerlof, unlike sociological adherents of strong culturalist positions, does not seek to deny the reality of choice. To the contrary, he emphasises that his concern is to develop the analysis of choice, and indeed of *rational* choice, within the economics tradition (1997: 1023). What is new, from an economics point of view, in the models that he proposes in regard to educational choice is the broadening of individuals' utility functions so as to include 'social' considerations—presumably along with the standard 'individual' considerations such as expected lifetime earnings. But it is still assumed, and apparently with little question, that individuals will then seek, and will be able, to optimise the rather complex functions that result in a highly rational way. In this respect, the BG model may be regarded as a good deal less demanding.

The full relevance of these introductory remarks will, I hope, progressively emerge as in the next two sections I consider, first, several general critiques of the BG theory that have been made and then a number of more specific attempts at empirical tests in one form or another.

GENERAL CRITIQUES

For reasons that will become apparent, I cannot in fact regard the reactions to the BG theory that I review in this section as having any great force, negative or positive: that is, as either doing any serious damage to the theory or helping significantly with its development. However, these reactions do serve to raise in a particular context, and thus to allow more detailed treatment of, a number of larger issues that were central to the later chapters of Volume I. I there argue, from several different angles (with the last section of Chapter 9 providing in effect a summary statement) for a paradigm for sociological work that can be represented schematically in three stages:

> 1. establishing the phenomena: that is, demonstrating and clarifying the nature of social regularities of one kind or another, which then form the *explananda* of sociological analysis, and especially where they are regularities of an opaque kind—where it is unclear how they are created and sustained;
> 2. hypothesising generative processes: that is, proposing how established social regularities might result, ultimately, from the actions and interaction of individuals and their intended and unintended consequences, and with privilege here being given to action that can in some sense be understood as rational, since it is such action that provides the most satisfactory end point for sociological explanation; and
> 3. testing the hypotheses advanced: that is, carrying out further empirical research aimed at determining whether the generative processes that are seen as producing particular social regularities are in principle adequate to do so and, further, whether or how far it is these processes that are actually at work.

These three stages can then be usefully taken as a basis for the discussion of the present section, although the third stage, the stage of empirical testing, is that with which the following section will be more specifically concerned.

To begin with, much confusion has arisen because commentators on the BG theory have failed to understand just what are the social regularities for which it seeks to provide an explanation, although these have, I believe, been always clearly specified. To repeat: the main *explanandum* is the degree of stability in class differentials in educational attainment that, contrary to the liberal theory of industrialism, has persisted in most advanced societies—throughout periods of major expansion in educational provision, of educational reform aimed at increasing equality of opportunity, and indeed of steady growth in levels of educational attainment *overall*.[6] This stability in differentials is puzzling chiefly because it is unclear just why, as the objective opportunity structure has become generally more favourable, children from less advantaged class backgrounds have not regularly and decisively exploited this change so as to 'close the gap' in attainment with children from more advantaged backgrounds—even though they *have* taken up the new opportunities to more or less the same extent as the latter. That is to say, while the degree to which class differentials have narrowed may be thought surprisingly small, these differentials have in no case substantially *widened*.

It is then in order to address *this* issue that the BG theory focuses on secondary effects on class differentials: that is, effects deriving from class differences in the patterns of choice made by students on whether to continue in education, what courses to take, and so on, rather than on the primary effects of class differences in levels of academic performance. It was seen as a crucial weakness of the liberal theory that it disregarded such secondary effects and implicitly assumed that, given formal equality of educational opportunity, all children would alike seek to translate demonstrated ability into actual educational attainment as fully as possible.

Unfortunately, this basic motivation of the BG theory has in several instances been overlooked, and it has, for example, been supposed that what the theory is concerned with, or at least turns on, is the relative importance of primary and secondary effects in the creation of class differentials. Both Devine (1998) and Nash (2003) labour under such a misapprehension in their efforts to demonstrate—contrary, they believe, to the BG theory—that primary effects carry by far the greater weight.[7] However, as reference back to Chapters 2 and 3 will show, the part played by primary effects, whatever their relative importance might be, is fully recognised in the theory. The emphasis on secondary effects stems from recognition of the need to bring choice into the explanation of persisting class differentials, and choice that, while conditioned by a structure of opportunities and constraints, is still more than merely the expression of unchanging and compelling subcultural values and norms. Neither Devine nor Nash appears to grasp this point or, at all events, both alike fail to respond to it.[8]

Next, as regards the BG theory as an attempt to identify a generative process—that underlying the stability of class differentials in educational attainment—what has first to be noted is that its starting point, as a theory of action, in methodological individualism and its privileging of rational action have aroused much critical comment of an a priori and, it must be said, rather predictable kind (cf. vol. I, ch. 8). Thus, Hatcher (1998: 16; cf. also Savage, 2000: 86) objects that the theory marks the importation of a 'reductionist economic model of the individual'; Devine (1998: 34) complains that it is 'based on an overly economistic view of social action' and subsequently (2004: 7) that cost-benefit analysis has an 'often brutal sounding nature'; while Nash (2003: 442) contends that the theory derives from a 'strangely anti-sociological' position.

Insofar as such remarks display merely misconceptions and underlying fears concerning rational action theory and at the same time a disregard for what Boudon (1987) has called the individualistic paradigm within the sociological tradition, I need not add to what I have previously said on these matters (see esp. vol. I, chs. 6 and 8). For present purposes, it is more relevant to consider how the authors cited seek to develop their criticisms. Essentially, and again quite predictably, what they claim is that RAT is too narrowly conceived. In Hatcher's words (1998: 16) it neglects 'the richness and complexity of social action'. What is taken to be the truly sociological position is reiterated: that the actions of individuals are influenced not only, or even primarily, by cost-benefit assessments of their likely consequences but by individuals' socialisation into distinctive (sub)cultures and their internalisation of culturally specific values and norms. In particular, the fact that the BG theory invokes no more than basic or 'constitutive' features of class—that is, those deriving directly from differing employment relations—and does not appeal to differences in class subcultures as shaping educational choice produces particularly strong reactions in which shock, annoyance, and disbelief appear to commingle.[9]

However, in this connection two points need to be made. The first is that a priori objections to a theory of the kind that are illustrated above are in fact largely irrelevant. Even if it were the case (though, as earlier shown, it is not) that the BG theory does represent some kind of betrayal of sociological thinking and a capitulation to economics imperialism, this would still have little bearing on its value. Theories, like all other ideas, have to be judged not by their provenance but by their consequences, and, with theories, the important questions about consequences are those of whether or how far they lead to adequate explanations and stand up to empirical test. As regards the BG theory, these are issues to be dealt with subsequently.

The second point, on which I concentrate here, is that in developing a theory and related model of microsocial processes capable of accounting for given macrosocial regularities, one is necessarily engaged in an exercise in simplification. The aim is indeed to 'narrow down' the factors included and the assumptions made to the minimum that appears required, not in order to deal with *all* the various forms of action and interaction that may actually be involved at the micro-level, but simply with those 'central tendencies' through which the macro-regularities that constitute the *explanandum*—and which are after all only probabilistic regularities—are generated. Parsimony and consistency are in this respect virtues: a good theory allows one 'to do a lot with a little'.[10]

Thus, in the case of the BG theory, differing class subcultures were left out of consideration because, as was earlier indicated, serious doubts arose over their normative force in relation to educational choice and in turn over the explanatory payoff that might be expected from including them. In this connection, it may again be emphasised that an explanation is being sought of persisting class differentials *in the context of rapidly rising levels of educational attainment overall*—that is, among children of all class backgrounds alike. For example, in Britain in the mid-1970s only around one in ten children of working-class background did well enough academically to be able stay on in school after the compulsory period of education in order to take 'A-level' examinations *and* took up this option. But by 2000 this proportion had risen to over three in ten (Jackson et al., 2005).[11]

Given, then, a change of this magnitude, it is difficult to see the relevance, and indeed to avoid questioning the validity, of any idea of a working-class subculture that, through the normative constraints it imposes, systematically inhibits those who are socialised into it from realising their demonstrated academic potential. A subculture of such a kind may perhaps exist in particular locales: for example, in the 'sink estate' or decayed industrial neighbourhood, where anti-school values and norms inimical to social mobility—of the kind envisaged by Akerlof—can be sustained though high levels of class homogeneity and relatively dense social networks. But insofar as any more pervasive working-class subculture is invoked as an influence on educational decision making, it would surely have to be seen, in the light of the evidence cited, as one that is rather rapidly losing its normative force or at all events its distinctiveness.

In contrast, the BG theory readily accommodates rising levels of educational attainment 'across the board'. These rising levels are seen as the outcome of the upgrading of the objective opportunity structure and of the reduction of the direct costs to students of taking up the opportunities provided, and also of the pressures stemming from 'credentials inflation' and the fact that education is in important respects a positional good. The persistence of class differentials is then accounted for by reference not to continuing subcultural variation among classes but, primarily, to the stability of patterns of relative risk aversion that can be understood as rational, given prevailing differences in class situations and given that actors' first priority in educational decision making is to avoid downward mobility. To repeat, the argument is that children from less advantaged backgrounds will, all else equal and on average, need to have a higher subjective probability of succeeding than will children from more advantaged backgrounds before they are ready to take up more rather than less ambitious educational options at the point at which safer options appear to give them good chances of at least maintaining their parents' class position.[12]

Furthermore, focusing thus on one form of action—that is, action that is at least boundedly rational—helps avoid the inconsistency or ad hoccery in explanation that can all too easily follow when efforts are made to comprehend social action in all its 'richness and complexity'. The critics referred to above themselves demonstrate this problem. Thus, although at one point Devine flatly asserts that individuals 'do not calculate the costs and benefits of various courses of action', she is elsewhere quite ready to argue that middle-class parents 'pay for and buy educational success' for their children through opting for independent schools or through ensuring that they 'attend the best schools in the state system' (1998: pp. 35, 38; cf. also 2004)—which are surely not courses of action that parents take in innocence of costs and benefits. And the problem is revealed yet more clearly when Hatcher (1998: 13–15), in a discussion of educational decision making 'in real life', accepts that within the middle classes this *is* mainly carried out on the basis of 'rational choice', that is, of some kind of cost-benefit evaluation, and with the aim of maintaining children's class positions, but then goes on to argue that within the working class such decision making tends not to be conducted rationally, except perhaps where young people and their parents have aspirations for upward mobility into the middle-class positions.

A resort to such dualist, 'elite and aborigine' models[13] is not only empirically suspect, as will later emerge, but does in any event at once raise the question of why one set of actors should act rationally and another not. Or, more specifically, the question of why working-class children and their parents should be supposed to be disadvantaged not only in the resources available to them, as indeed they are, but further in their capacity to apply what resources they have to the effective pursuit of their goals. And until answers to these questions are provided—and the authors cited make little attempt in this regard—it is explanatory regress rather than progress that has been achieved.[14] A similar objection may, moreover, be raised against arguments that claim that within different classes different kinds of 'culturally constructed' rationality operate (e.g., Savage, 2000: 87). Such arguments do in fact give the impression of being little more than verbal flourishes, but if they are to be taken seriously, one would want to know just how such class-specific rationalities are believed to differ from each other and, again, how they originate and are sustained.

Against this background, it would then seem in all respects a preferable strategy in theory construction to suppose, and with now growing empirical support (see vol. I, ch. 8), that a human capacity and propensity for—bounded—rationality in action, that is, for evaluating trade-offs between the expected costs and benefits of different possible courses of action, exists as in fact a cross-cultural universal.

Finally, then, as regards the empirical testing of the BG theory, it has to be said that this is not a major concern of the general critiques considered in this section. As indicated, their main objective is to call the theory into doubt on account of its very form—as being reductionist, economistic, anti-sociological, and so on. It is, nonetheless, of interest to note that insofar as any more empirically grounded criticism is advanced, this derives largely from enquiries of a particular kind that have of late become increasingly common in educational sociology, and in Britain especially. That is, what are described as 'qualitative' studies of the processes and contexts of educational choice, but ones less often based on sustained ethnographic work in specific locales than on the interviewing, usually characterised as 'intensive' or 'in-depth', of rather small numbers of individuals who may, but often do not, constitute a sample of some defined population.[15]

What, however, seems to be overlooked is the general unsuitability of such qualitative studies for testing theories that are concerned with explaining regularities at the macrosocial level. There is, to begin with, the rather obvious danger, pointed to in a recent review of British research, 'of assuming that findings that are based on a few arbitrarily chosen young people, observed in very particular circumstances, are generally true and firmly established, when the evidence base is in reality very slender' (Payne, 2003: 60). Further, though, even if qualitative studies are taken, as it were, at their face value, it has still to be noted that, despite the small numbers of individuals covered, they typically lead to the conclusion that a rather wide range of variation exists in the ways in which educational choices are arrived at (some, perhaps, exhibiting rationality, others not) but with no assessment then being possible of which variant patterns are of major, and which of only minor, quantitative importance. Consequently, while in such studies *some* amount of support can be found for just about any and every theory of educational choice, the BG theory included,[16] one cannot gain from them any reliable idea of what might be the central tendencies in action capable of producing the macrosocial regularities that are of interest.

For more appropriate attempts at the empirical evaluation of the BG theory it is then necessary to turn to research that has a more secure methodological rationale and that is also more specifically focused on the theory. This turns out in fact to be survey-based research, undertaken on samples of generally well-defined populations and large enough to allow the multivariate analyses for which the sometimes rather complex issues involved would appear to call.[17]

EMPIRICAL TESTS

Theories can be subjected to empirical test in a variety of ways. A distinction is often made between testing theories according to whether or not their underlying assumptions appear valid, that is, empirically justifiable, or according to whether or not the implications or predictions that would appear to follow from them are empirically borne out. However, this distinction can scarcely be treated as a hard and fast one and, further, other approaches can also be taken. For example, a theory may be applied in an attempt to resolve an explanatory problem and then be judged by how well it succeeds in this respect. I do not believe it is helpful to try to order these different methods in any principled way according to their strength or any other criterion. I would rather regard the empirical testing of a theory as being essentially a catch-as-catch-can matter in which opportunities of all kinds should be seen as open to exploitation and their results as all contributing to the evaluation of the theory.

In what follows I consider six different attempts at testing the BG theory, which divide, conveniently, into three pairs: the first pair are concerned mainly with underlying assumptions, the second are attempts at applying the theory in the case of particular problems, while the third aim at more comprehensive testing, in which both assumptions and implications of the theory are to some extent considered.[18]

Tests of the Assumptions of the BG Theory

The first of the two studies reviewed here is that reported by Need and de Jong (2000). Drawing on a national longitudinal survey of students in the Netherlands, these authors address the question of whether there is evidence that the mechanism of relative risk aversion, central and distinctive to the BG theory, is of importance in producing the differentials in educational choice that the survey reveals.[19] They focus their attention on a subsample of over 900 students who were at the end of their general secondary education and who were faced with a three-way choice of leaving school, enrolling in vocational courses, or seeking university entry. The main limitation of their data-set is that it contains no information on students' class backgrounds, only on parental income and education. Consequently, the equal relative risk-aversion argument is recast in terms of students giving priority to attaining an *educational level,* rather than a class position, that is not inferior to that of their parents.

From the several multivariate analyses that Need and de Jong undertake, the main finding to emerge is that parental education has a strong effect on students' own educational aspirations—that is, the higher the level of parental education, the higher the level of education that students want for themselves—and even when their previous academic performance and their own assessments of their ability are controlled. It is also found that the effect of parental education on the educational choices that students eventually make is largely mediated through students' aspirations. On this basis, then, Need and de Jong conclude (2000: 94) that the results of their analyses are at all events highly consistent with the idea that relative risk aversion is at work and is indeed a 'crucial factor' generating differentials in educational choice in the case they consider.

One further result that Need and de Jong report does, however, lead them to suggest that another mechanism that does not figure in the BG theory may also be operating in a supplementary fashion. Students' beliefs about their own ability, as well as their aspirations, are associated with parental education: that is, the higher the level of parental education, the further students believe that they can themselves go in their educational careers, whatever the actual standard of their past academic performance. And in turn, then, the more favourable their assessments of their ability, the higher are their aspirations and the more ambitious the educational options that they in fact take up.

The second study considered here is one by Sullivan (2006). Sullivan's main concern is with the issue earlier referred to of the 'minimalist' conception of class used in the BG theory and the supposition that subcultural differences are not such as to exert a systematic influence on class differentials in educational attainment via secondary (as opposed to primary) effects. Through a questionnaire enquiry involving 465 sixteen-year-old students in four British comprehensive secondary schools, Sullivan investigates whether among students of differing class background differences in 'attitudes to education' do exist of a kind that would indicate that subcultural effects should not be disregarded in the way they are in the BG theory. To this end, she develops an 'educational attitudes scale' that can be used to measure students' positive or negative attitudes towards education in general and also their views on both its 'instrumental' and 'intrinsic' value.

The leading results from Sullivan's analyses of her data are that students' attitudes to education are only very weakly associated with their class backgrounds, that they are far more strongly associated with their examination performance at age 16, and that the association with class background disappears altogether once examination performance is controlled. Further, no significant association emerges between level of parental qualifications and students' attitudes to education overall, even before controlling for performance.[20] These results do then provide powerful support for the discounting of class subcultural effects in the BG theory and, in particular, as Sullivan observes, they call into serious doubt the idea that anti-school values or other negative orientations towards education are, at the present day at least, a prevalent feature of working-class subculture.

There is, though, one respect in which Sullivan does discover robust class differences: that is, in students' own assessments of their ability. Students from more advantaged class backgrounds have higher estimations of their ability than do students from less advantaged backgrounds and can, moreover, be regarded as being overoptimistic while the latter are overpessimistic. This finding is then in line with that of Need and de Jong that students' assessments of their ability are positively associated with parental educational level.[21] But, unlike Need and de Jong, Sullivan does not see here simply an indication of a further mechanism, supplementary to and tending to intensify, that of relative risk aversion. A problem, she believes, is created for the BG theory in that students' beliefs are shown to be not rationally formed but rather distorted by social class in a way similar to that suggested by Gambetta (1987) and discussed in Chapter 2.

The possibility that such distortion occurs cannot be ruled out. And Sullivan's claim raises questions of the formation of beliefs and related expectations that, as will subsequently emerge, are of quite general and major importance. However, it has at the same time to be said that her claim is not securely established. Her ratings of students' self-assessments of their ability as being too optimistic or too pessimistic are based on comparing predictions they made of their results in their examinations at age 16 with the results they actually achieved. What it would be crucial to know—but Sullivan's research does not extend this far—is whether students then tended to adjust their estimations of their ability in the light of their results. If so, this would be entirely consistent with the assumption of the BG theory (see above ch. 3, pp. 55–6 esp.) that students' expectations about how well they will do in their future academic careers are rational, in the bounded sense of having some appropriate grounding in information that is readily to hand—such as recent examination performance.[22]

Applications of the BG Theory

The first study to be considered in this section is that of Becker (2003). Becker presents his research as constituting an empirical test of the BG theory as embodied in a more general formal model developed by Esser (1999).[23] Rather than focusing directly on the assumptions or the implications of the

BG theory, Becker first draws on the theory to provide an explanation for a particular, empirically demonstrated problem and then considers how consistent this explanation is with further empirical analyses that he undertakes in which he attempts to operationalise the Esser model.

The problem that Becker identifies in the context of postwar West German society is, in general terms, the same as that which initially motivated the BG theory: how to explain the coexistence of educational expansion and rising standards of educational attainment overall with persisting class inequalities. In Germany, however, secondary education is more institutionally differentiated and selective than in many other modern societies, and Becker's analysis is thus more specifically concerned with the question of why the steadily growing number of parents in all classes who seek places for their children in the highest level and most academic type of secondary school—the *Gymnasium*—is accompanied by only very modest change in class differentials among the children who eventually gain entry.

Following the BG theory, Becker argues that, in consequence of educational expansion and credentials inflation, education is of increasing instrumental importance for parents as a means of maintaining their children's class positions, but that while the expected benefits of education have thus risen and the costs have fallen across all classes alike, *class-specific* balances of costs and benefits have altered rather little. In particular, the more advantaged the class position of a family, the more it stands to lose if its children do not do well educationally, and the less risk averse—in absolute terms—will parents then be in regard to the educational options that their children take.

Becker's operationalisation of the Esser model uses data from three surveys conducted in different West German federal states in the 1960s, 1970s, and 1980s, and, on this basis, he produces results that are for the most part in line with his explanation of persisting educational differentials. In particular, the hypothesis of unchanging class-specific costs and benefits is supported. In addition, Becker suggests that although children's performance in primary school and teachers' recommendations appear to carry increasing weight in determining entry to the *Gymnasium*, parents in more advantaged class positions remain not only more motivated but also better able than others to 'push through' their preference for the *Gymnasium*, and even if their children have only modest academic records.

The second application of the BG theory to be noted is that reported by Schizzerotto (1997), which concerns the case of Italy. In Italy, Schizzerotto observes, class differentials in educational attainment are marked and as in many other societies appear to have changed little if at all. However, the larger context is rather distinctive. While some amount of educational expansion has occurred, still only quite low proportions of young people, by comparative standards, successfully complete higher secondary education and then graduate from university, and this despite the fact that the direct costs of education are relatively low and the returns to education are relatively high in terms both of level of entry into the labour market and subsequent protection against unemployment. The problem then is that of why these apparent incentives to continue in education do not appear to be effective, and least of all in encouraging changes in patterns of educational choice that would lead to a reduction in class differentials.

The answer that Schizzerotto advances, with supporting empirical evidence from official statistics and survey research, is on the following lines. In Italy particular conditions obtain that in effect give special force to the main mechanism invoked by the BG theory, that of relative risk aversion. On the one hand, the Italian systems of secondary and tertiary education impose unusually high failure rates, which mean that students have often to repeat years or, perhaps, are forced to drop out. Moreover, the risks of dropping out are clearly greater for students from less advantaged class backgrounds, whether because of their lower ability or of their more limited resources and thus lower capacity to absorb the direct and opportunity costs of protracted periods of study. On the other hand, primarily *because* Italian labour market institutions afford a high degree of employment protection to individuals in positions that typically call for higher secondary or tertiary academic qualifications, appropriately qualified young people are exposed to high rates of unemployment before they manage to gain access to these positions. In fact, such individuals tend to wait significantly longer before entering their first job than do those with lower-level academic or vocational qualifications.

Together, then, these conditions mean that pursuing high-level qualifications is in general less attractive than it might at first sight appear. Further, wide differences in educational choice are likely to be maintained as between children of more advantaged class origins who see such qualifications as essential to maintaining the class position of their parents, and who are relatively well placed to meet the costs involved, and children of less advantaged origins who are able to move towards the equivalent goal through less costly and less risky routes.

The two studies reviewed do then show that the BG theory has proved useful to other sociologists engaged with issues of educational inequality and that it can lead to explanations that appear adequate to accounting for class differences in patterns of educational choice under varying institutional conditions. Such applications can be regarded as constituting tests of the theory in that the theory could in fact have turned out to be quite unhelpful. Nonetheless, the possibility cannot of course be excluded that some other theory might have served as well, or better, or indeed that, despite the seeming adequacy of the explanation derived from it, the theory is still in some respects flawed.

More Comprehensive Tests

There is one study in which the BG theory is tested not only in itself but also, to an extent, against rival theories of educational choice: that is, the standard human capital theory and Akerlof's theory, both of which were previously outlined. The authors of this study, Davies, Heinesen, and Holm (2002), draw on data from a large-scale and nationally representative survey of young people in Denmark that they are able to supplement with data from administrative registers. They then carry out sophisticated analyses of patterns of student choice at the unusually large number of transitions that are possible within the highly flexible Danish educational system. A shortcoming of their data-set is, however, that it does not contain adequate information on students' class origins and thus, in the same way as was noted in the study of Need and de Jong, the relative risk aversion argument has to be treated in terms of students aiming to minimise the risk of not attaining their parents' educational level rather than their parents' class.

The analyses reported by Davies and his colleagues derive their force from the fact that they are able pick out an implication of the BG theory that would not usually arise with the two other theories that they consider. They observe that, if the BG theory is correct, then, in the form in which they treat it, level of parental education should have an effect on students' educational decisions and, moreover—controlling for other relevant variables, in particular, for students' ability—an effect that is 'kinked' rather than smoothly continuous. Specifically, this effect should peak for the transition in which students reach their parental educational level, and thus achieve the goal of avoiding downward educational mobility. In other words, the kink will occur at different educational transitions for students whose parents have different levels of educational attainment.[24] In contrast, neither human capital theory nor Akerlof's theory would lead one to expect any finding of this kind. Under human capital theory, other than in some rather special versions, parental education should have no effect on students' educational choice (apart, perhaps, from spurious effects resulting from omitted variables), while Akerlof's theory, it is argued, would lead to the expectation of an effect that shows a steady increase across successive transitions.[25]

For the choices that are possible at each transition within the Danish educational system, Davies and colleagues then run a series of binary logistic regressions and seek to evaluate the BG theory, as against the two rival theories, by examining the structure of parameter estimates for the effects of parental educational level, and in particular with an eye for kinks of the kind referred to above. In total, they undertake 17 analyses. The BG theory is clearly or partially supported in 10 of these, while Akerlof's theory is clearly or partially supported in nine—with its predicted effects sometimes occurring additionally, rather than alternatively, to those favouring the BG theory. Human capital theory is supported in five analyses in that no systematic effects of parental educational level show up. However, it also emerges that the BG theory generally does worse in those analyses where the number of observations is relatively small, which, as Davies and colleagues acknowledge, may prevent the detection of significant kinks in the effects of parental education. If attention is limited to the five analyses where the largest numbers of observations are available, three provide strong support for the BG theory and two for the Akerlof theory, with there being also some support for the Akerlof theory in two of the former cases and some support for the BG theory in one of the latter. Human capital theory finds little or no support. Overall, then, while it could not be claimed that the BG theory is conclusively endorsed, it could be said to emerge quite creditably from the competition that is set up.

The second more comprehensive test of the BG theory is that reported by Breen and Yaish (2006). This is notable in that it focuses on the mechanism of relative risk aversion that is central to the theory and, further, treats this in the form originally specified: that is, as deriving from a concern by students to minimise the risk of downward *class* mobility, relative to their parents, rather than of downward educational mobility (the latter being the interpretation forced on other investigators simply on account of data limitations). For Breen and Yaish, the key empirical issue in testing the theory is then the following. What evidence is there that students do make educational choices consistently with the idea that they recognise a threshold level of education that is the minimum necessary for securing a class position at least as desirable as that of their parents—that is, a threshold that can be expected to vary with their class origins?

To address this issue, Breen and Yaish draw on the British National Child Development Study, a birth-cohort study covering all children born in Britain in one week in 1958, and examine the educational choices made by boys in the cohort on completing compulsory education at around age 16. In effect, three choices were open to them: staying on in full-time education, entering the labour market and at the same time taking up an apprenticeship or other form of vocational training, or entering the labour market without vocational training. Breen and Yaish then seek to derive from the BG theory, and specifically from the idea of children of different class backgrounds having differing threshold levels of education, a set of hypotheses about the pattern of choices that would in this case be expected. However, they point out that, to implement this strategy, some way is required of representing the beliefs that students hold about the 'class returns' that can be expected from different levels of education—on which matter the BG theory is itself silent. In order to fill this gap, they therefore turn to data on the *actual* relationship between educational level and class position, as was found for men in the Oxford national mobility study of 1972, and they assume that students' expectations are—rationally—grounded in the probabilities that these data demonstrate.

On this basis, Breen and Yaish proceed to test their hypotheses through multinomial logistic regression analyses in which they include controls for students' basic ability, their examination performance and their families' economic resources as well as their class position. In the outcome, the hypotheses receive broad, if not total, support. That is to say, there is in general evidence that educational choices are influenced by threshold levels of education that students could be taken to define in relation to minimising their risk of downward class mobility, as the BG theory would propose.

However, Breen and Yaish go on to stress the crucial role that is played in their analyses by the particular way in which students' beliefs about the class returns to education are proxied. They show that if, for example, these beliefs were to be derived not from the experience of men of earlier generations, as represented in the 1972 enquiry, but rather from the students' *own later* experience, that is, in the labour markets of the 1970s and 1980s, then results far less favourable to the BG theory would be produced. These results need not in fact be taken all that seriously in themselves since they largely reflect the advantage that members of the 1958 cohort gained from the high, structurally induced, levels of upward mobility in the decades in question. And as Breen and Yaish point out, it would be difficult for this development to have been anticipated at age 16.[26] But the general point that Breen and Yaish make here remains important, and also important is the way in which their concern with questions of students' beliefs about linkages between education and class position echoes that earlier noted, arising from the work of Sullivan, with questions of students' beliefs about their own abilities and their chances of educational success.

THE PRESENT STANDING OF THE THEORY

How, then, in the light of the foregoing, can the present standing of the BG theory be best assessed? In trying to answer this question, it will, I believe, be helpful to operate at two levels: first, to consider the case for a theory of persisting class differentials in educational attainment of the *general kind* that is represented by the BG theory, and then, second, to consider the case for this theory itself.

As noted at the outset, the BG theory aims to bring together certain features of more standard approaches in economics and sociology while rejecting others. It takes over from economics the idea that educational choices are real choices—although subject to varying degrees and forms of constraint—and choices that are, moreover, best understood as being rational in the sense of tending to follow from cost-benefit evaluations of some kind. However, the BG theory seeks to avoid the requirement for such evaluations to depend on rational expectations of a quite unrealistic order. Thus, the criterion function of minimising the risk of downward social mobility is taken as one that is more readily applied than that of maximising (discounted) lifetime earnings, and in turn more consistent with rationality in action that is inevitably bounded by the extent of actors' information and of their information-processing capacities.

In this way also educational decisions are treated as being, in a particular sense, social decisions: that is, as being conditioned by the reference point of individuals' class origins as well as influenced by ability, academic performance, and economic resources. At the same time, though, the BG theory rejects the assumption made in standard sociological accounts of class differentials that educational decisions are social in a much stronger sense—and one that indeed threatens to reduce them to the status simply of social behaviour: that is, the assumption that they derive from the socialisation of children into distinctive class subcultures and thus more or less automatically reflect the values and related normative expectations that are specific to such subcultures. While the BG theory does not seek to deny that children's academic performance is importantly influenced by class inequalities in cultural resources, it does not appeal to subculture in seeking to explain the further class differences that arise in children's propensities to translate such performance as fully as possible into educational attainment over the course of their academic careers.

At this level, then, the two claims that I would wish to make most strongly, on the basis both of empirical studies directly prompted by the BG theory and of the body of research concerned with educational choice more generally, are the following. First, in constructing explanations of persisting class differentials in educational attainment, the future does indeed lie with theories that aim to bridge the gap between more standard approaches from economics and sociology. And, second, greater success is likely to result from attempts to do this in the manner illustrated by the BG theory rather than in that illustrated, for example, by Akerlof's theory: that is to say, from attempts to move away from the usual emphasis of sociological analyses on the normative conditioning of educational choice to an emphasis on boundedly rational action within class structural constraints rather than by attempts to incorporate positive or negative normative sanctions into the utility functions of conventional economic analyses.

As already argued in this and previous chapters, theories of class differentials in educational attainment that rely in effect on the idea that the values and related norms of working-class subculture in some way inhibit working-class children from taking up widening educational opportunities—whether or not through the contrivance of a 'dominant class'—are rendered highly problematic by one major and quite general empirical finding: namely, that over recent decades in all modern societies working-class children *have* taken up the new opportunities that have been created at a more or less similar rate to children of more advantaged class backgrounds, and with the result that, by the present time, the numbers staying on into higher secondary and tertiary education cannot possibly be regarded as constituting only a small and normatively deviant minority. Any adequate theory must be capable of explaining *this* finding *as well as* the finding that an increasingly favourable opportunity structure has not in general led to class differentials being consistently and substantially reduced.

Furthermore, there seems to be little direct evidence, for recent times at least, to suggest that class subcultures are anything like as distinctive, coherent, and compelling as the theories that invoke them would suppose. To the contrary, the findings of relevant research would seem largely in line with the results of Sullivan's study concerned specifically with the question of whether the 'minimalist' conception of class adopted in the BG theory is justifiable. That is to say, these findings point to only rather slight cross-class differences in orientations towards education. For example, Payne, in her review of British research on educational choice at around age 16, concludes (2003: 17–19, 33–34) that most young people of all class backgrounds alike view education in a primarily 'instrumental' way—that is, as a means of obtaining qualifications that will improve their chances in the labour market, and that most parents hope for their children to perform well educationally and give them whatever help and encouragement they can. Thus, Payne rejects the idea that secondary effects in the creation of class differentials, or what she refers to as the 'gap' in class staying-on rates even when educational performance is controlled, can be attributed to class subcultural differences, as opposed, say, to inequalities in economic or social resources.[27]

In turn, suggestions made on the basis of some qualitative studies that while middle-class families may engage in rational educational decision making, working-class families do not are also called into question by more systematic research. Thus, fairly pervasive instrumental views of education would seem readily linked to a similarly pervasive 'pragmatic rationality' in educational choice, for which in fact Payne (2003: 13–14) records widespread evidence from both qualitative and quantitative studies. And it may be added that in one of the largest-scale and most sophisticated studies bearing on this issue, Beattie (2002) finds that among young American males, those of lower socioeconomic status are seemingly *more* rational in their educational decision making than those of higher status, at least in the sense of being more responsive to prevailing levels of earnings returns to education in their local labour markets.[28]

Finally, it is here also a matter of interest—and encouragement—to note that the BG theory does not represent the only current attempt to move towards a better understanding of processes of educational attainment through seeking some middle ground between economics and sociology. For example, Morgan (1998, 2002, 2005) in a constructive engagement with the Wisconsin 'status socialisation' model, for so long dominant in American educational sociology, has developed a theory of educational attainment that, while differing from the BG theory in its main focus (see further below), is of very similar intellectual inspiration. Morgan too seeks to go beyond a reliance on explanations grounded purely in appeals to socialisation and the conformity of young people with the examples and expectations of their 'models and mentors' and to give greater weight to their 'deliberative powers' and capacity to act rationally in the light of their beliefs, while at the same time still recognising the importance not only of structural constraints but further of the social contexts of belief formation.[29]

Coming now to the BG theory itself, the claims that I would make at this level have to be somewhat more qualified. For reasons that have been earlier stated—and restated—the BG theory, in seeking to provide an explanation for the persistence of class differentials in educational attainment, concentrates on secondary effects. And insofar as secondary effects appear to be themselves generally present and persistent,[30] the relevance of the theory, at least, is underlined. However, the crucial issue is of course that of whether the main mechanism postulated by the BG theory, that of (equal relative) risk aversion in regard to the possibility of downward social mobility, is that which chiefly underlies secondary effects. Is it in fact the case that secondary effects come about primarily because, in making their educational decisions, children of less advantaged class origins will on average need to have a higher subjective probability of success than children of more advantaged origins before taking up more ambitious educational options?

In certain respects, the research reviewed above could be said to give a large measure of support to the idea that students' social origins are consequential for their educational choices, and via a mechanism of the kind that the BG theory proposes. It is essentially through the application of this idea that Becker and Schizzerotto draw on the BG theory to make some explanatory sense of the pattern and development of class differentials in attainment that they describe within the German and Italian educational systems respectively. And further, more direct support is provided by the work of Need and de Jong and, especially, by that of Davies and his associates. But the point has then to be reiterated that in these two latter inquiries the BG theory is not in fact tested in its full form: risk aversion is considered only in terms of the avoidance of downward mobility relative to parental education, not parental class. And as the work of Breen and Yaish brings out, when the attempt is made to test the theory in full, the difficulty arises of how to treat the threshold levels of education that students of differing class origins are supposed to take as the minimum necessary to counter the risk of failing to maintain their class positions. In empirical research the issue is that of the appropriate way to proxy students' beliefs as regards class returns to education, and especially insofar as different proxies may lead to different results. But the deeper problem is of course that of establishing how such beliefs are in fact formed and, in turn, whether the expectations to which they lead can be viewed as rational expectations, if not in the 'infinite' sense of conventional economic analysis, at least in the bounded sense that the BG theory assumes.

Moreover, as was also earlier noted, similar difficulties arise in the case of students' beliefs about their own abilities and chances of academic success. Are these beliefs formed, and if need be adjusted, in some rational fashion in the light of students' actual academic performance or are they, as Sullivan would suggest, irrationally distorted by class—which could then imply an alternative, or at least an additional explanation of secondary effects in the creation of class differentials that significantly diverges from that proposed by the BG theory.

In these respects, the position is not that the BG theory is clearly undermined—as, say, by Breen and Yaish's experiments with alternative proxies for students' expectations of the class returns to education or Sullivan's results on their own assessments of their ability. It is, rather, that, as regards the ways in which students are supposed to determine the goals that orient their educational decision making and to develop the beliefs that inform it, the theory so far lacks any quite direct corroboration. In other words, as Morgan (2005: 111) fairly observes, the main problem with the BG theory is that too little is known about whether or how far the microsocial processes that it implies do actually operate. In effect, the theory relies essentially on a 'revealed preferences' approach in which it is assumed that what individuals are observed to do is just what they aimed to do and believed that they should do, given their aims. Thus, within his own theory of educational attainment, previously referred to, Morgan seeks to embody an explicit model of the evolution of beliefs that generate the 'prefigurative' and 'preparatory' commitments to 'educational plans'—or, that is, to envisaged future educational choices—by which the theory is chiefly driven.

What is then required in the case of the BG theory, I would suggest, is for it to be elaborated in an analogous fashion. The results of empirical tests thus far do encourage one to believe that the mechanism of (equal relative) risk aversion in regard to downward social mobility does quite regularly influence educational decision making and in turn plays a significant part in the maintenance of class differentials in educational attainment. Students, one might say, do often appear to act, or at least can be plausibly represented as acting, *as if* the theory were correct. However, the matter of how their goals, beliefs, and related expectations are actually formed now obviously requires more explicit theoretical and empirical examination. For it is of course a basic difficulty with the revealed preferences approach that any observed pattern of choice may well be consistent with several alternative specifications of the goals, beliefs, and expectations of the actors who produce this pattern.

Finally, though, while the need to extend the BG theory in the way indicated may readily be recognised, the hard and long-standing question remains of just how efforts in this direction are to be empirically underpinned. That is, the question of on what basis—through what methodology—social scientists may most effectively seek to establish what individuals aim to achieve and the understandings that they have about how best to move towards their goals.

The revealed preferences approach was developed, chiefly by economists, as a result of an acute awareness of the problem of access to 'other minds' and of a consequent tendency to attach far greater importance to 'objective' data relating to what people did than to 'subjective' data relating merely to what they said. In contrast, sociologists have been far more ready to believe that techniques do exist through which such subjective data can be obtained with an acceptable degree of reliability and validity. For some time this appeared to be yet another issue on which economists and sociologists simply agreed to differ without any serious engagement. More recently, however, it has been reopened, largely as a result of a number of economists, led most conspicuously by Manski and his associates, becoming dissatisfied with the limitations of the revealed preferences approach (technically, in the form of the identification problems to which it gives rise) and urging their colleagues to overcome their hostility to subjective data (see, e.g., Manski, 1993; Dominitz and Manski, 1999). At the same time, though, these economists remain unimpressed by what sociologists have achieved in the way of producing such data. The looseness of the conceptualisation and the coarseness of the measurement involved mean that data on preferences and, especially, expectations, deriving either from surveys or from the 'intensive' interviews of qualitative studies, tend to be of limited use in the context of more formal theoretical models.

These criticisms are, I believe, ones that sociologists need to take seriously, and still more worthy of note are the attempts that Manski and others are now making, in more positive vein, to develop new techniques for the collection of subjective data, in particular, through the use in both surveys and laboratory experiments of questions that elicit respondents' expectations in *probabilistic* form. Promising results have in fact already been achieved in regard to expected earnings returns from education and also in regard to questions of job security and household income prospects (for a review, see Manksi, 2004). At the same time, some advances are also being made within sociology, as was earlier noted (vol. I, ch. 4: p. 82), in treating issues of the reliability and validity of subjective survey data on far more sophisticated lines than hitherto, which economists following Manski's lead might well adapt to their own purposes.

There is then at least the possibility, given a continuing interdisciplinary 'permeability' (cf. Steuer, 2002), that the middle ground between economics and sociology, within which the BG and several other theories of educational choice and inequality have of late been developed, could become an area for progress not only in theory construction but further in work aimed at overcoming a rather fundamental methodological problem in the social sciences at large.

CHAPTER FIVE

Social Class and the Differentiation of Employment Contracts*

My concern in this chapter is with the theory of social class: I aim to contribute to the ultimate goal of explaining why social classes exist. However, I start out from a way of conceptualising class, and in turn of making 'class' operational in empirical research, that I have developed, along with a number of colleagues, over the last 30 years. The fundamental idea that has been pursued is that class positions can be understood—in a way to be explained more fully below—as positions defined by *employment relations*. A class schema has been progressively elaborated that differentiates class categories by reference to such relations, and that can be implemented in research through information on employment status and occupation.

This programme of work was undertaken as the basis for studies of social mobility envisaged within a class structural context (Goldthorpe and Llewellyn, 1977; Goldthorpe, 1987; Erikson, Goldthorpe, and Portocarero, 1979; Erikson and Goldthorpe, 1992). However, the class schema, in one or other of its several versions,[1] has subsequently become used in many other areas of research and, more recently, has been adopted in Britain as the basis of the National Statistics Socio-Economic Classification (NS-SEC), which from the time of the Census of 2001 replaced the Registrar General's Social Classes in all official statistics (see further Rose and O'Reilly eds.,1997, Rose and O'Reilly, 1998; Rose and Pevalin eds., 2003; Rose, Pevalin, and O'Reilly, 2005).[2]

*I am indebted to Sam Bowles, Richard Breen, Jerker Denrell, John Ermisch, Duncan Gallie, Dan Krymkowski, and Aage Sørensen for comments on an earlier draft, and to Tony Atkinson, Geoff Evans, Abigail McKnight, Colin Mills, Meg Meyer, Karen O'Reilly, and David Rose for useful advice and information.

In consequence of its widespread use, evidence of the *construct* validity of the schema has steadily accumulated: that is, evidence of its capacity to display variation in other, dependent variables on theoretically expected lines: for example, in patterns of voting (Heath et al., 1991; Evans, Heath, and Payne, 1991, 1996; Evans, 1999), in differentials in educational attainment (Jonsson, 1993; Müller and Haun, 1994; Jonsson, Mills, and Müller, 1996; Jackson et al., 2005), or in health (Bartley et al., 1996; Kunst, 1996; Sacker et al., 2000). One line of further research that is then prompted—but that is not here my concern—is that aimed at elucidating exactly how class, as conceptualised in terms of employment relations, exerts its influence on such variables. What are the actual causal processes involved? For example, just how does the incumbency of different class positions operate so as to produce the empirical regularities that are apparent in the association between class and party support (cf. Evans, 1993; Weakliem and Heath, 1994; Andersen and Heath, 2002) or in that between class and educational choice (cf. chs. 2–4, this volume) or class and morbidity and mortality?[3]

At the same time, though, the wider use of the schema and especially its adoption in official statistics has encouraged interest in its *criterion* validity: that is, in the extent to which, as operationalised through occupation and employment status, it does in fact capture those differences in employment relations that it is, conceptually, supposed to capture.[4] The findings so far reported on this issue, based largely on British data, indicate that the schema does in fact perform quite well (see Evans, 1992, 1996; Evans and Mills, 1998, 2000; Rose and O'Reilly, eds., 1997; Rose and O'Reilly, 1998; and also specifically on NS-SEC, Rose and Pevalin, eds., 2003).[5] In particular, for individuals of employee status, occupation can, it appears, for the most part serve as an adequate proxy for those features of their employment relations that the schema takes as distinguishing class positions.

In this way, then, another line of further investigation is suggested and one that I shall here seek to pursue: namely, that directed to the question of why it should be that different occupations do tend to be associated with differences in the employment relations of those engaged in them of the kind that I would in turn see as implying different class positions. Insofar as this question can be answered—insofar as the empirical regularity that is here involved can be given a satisfactory explanation—the class schema will be provided with a fuller and more explicit theoretical rationale.

In the conceptualisation of class that underlies the schema (see further Erikson and Goldthorpe, 1992: 35–47), basic distinctions are made among employers, the self-employed, and employees: that is, among those who buy the labour of others, those do not buy the labour of others but neither sell their own, and those who do sell their labour to an employer or employing organisation. Why these three categories should exist is not itself especially problematic, or at least not in the context of any form of society that sustains the institutions of private property and a labour market. However, in such societies in the modern world the third category, that of employees, is numerically quite preponderant, usually accounting for some 85–90 percent of the active population. [6] Thus, what is crucial to the class schema is the further level of distinction that is introduced, applying specifically to the employment relations *of employees*. This focuses on the form of regulation of their employment or, one might alternatively say, on the nature of their employment contracts, explicit and implicit.

In this regard, the main contrast that is set up is that between, on the one hand, the 'labour contract', supposed typically to operate in the case of manual and lower-grade nonmanual workers, and, on the other hand, the 'service relationship' as expressed in the kind of contract taken as typical for the professional and managerial staffs of organisational bureaucracies, public and private.

> Employment relationships regulated by a labour contract entail a relatively short-term and specific exchange of money for effort. Employees supply more or less discrete amounts of labour, under the supervision of the employer or of the employer's agents, in return for wages that are calculated on a 'piece' or 'time' basis. In contrast, employment relationships within a bureaucratic context involve a longer-term and generally more diffuse exchange. Employees render service to their employing organization in return for 'compensation', which takes the form not only of reward for work done, through a salary and various perquisites, but also comprises important prospective elements—for example, salary increments on an established scale, assurances of security both in employment and, through pensions rights, after retirement, and, above all, well-defined career opportunities. (Erikson and Goldthorpe, 1992: 41)

It is recognised that these two basic forms of the regulation of employment may exist with degrees of modification and, further, that 'mixed' forms also occur, typically associated with positions intermediate between bureau-

TABLE 5.1

Categories of the Class Schema and Supposed Form of Regulation of Employment

Class[a]		Form of regulation of employment
I	Professionals and managers, higher grade	Service relationship
II	Professionals and managers, lower grade; technicians, higher grade	Service relationship (modified)
IIIa	Routine nonmanual employees, higher grade	Mixed
IIIb	Routine nonmanual employees, lower grade	Labour contract (modified)
IVabc[b]	Small proprietors and employers and self-employed workers	
V	Technicians, lower-grade supervisors of manual workers	Mixed
VI	Skilled manual workers	Labour contract (modified)
VIIa	Nonskilled manual workers (other than in agriculture)	Labour contract
VIIb	Agricultural workers	Labour contract

[a]The class descriptions given should be understood as labels only. In any implementation of the schema, the detailed occupational groupings to be allocated to each class are to be fully specified. For example, for Britain, see Goldthorpe and Heath (1992).
[b]IVabc is included only for completeness here, and no regulation of employment is involved.

cratic structures and rank-and-file workforces: for example, those of clerical or sales personnel or of lower-grade technicians and first-line supervisors. Table 5.1 summarises the argument in relation to the categories of the class schema.

The main significance, for present purposes, of the enquiries into the criterion validity of the class schema, referred to above, is then the following. They reveal that the regulation of employment of different occupational groupings of employees does in fact tend to follow the pattern indicated in Table 5.1. More specifically, when indicators of various relevant features of employment relations are considered for samples of the economically active population—concerning form of payment, perquisites, control of working time, job security, opportunities for promotion, and so on—then occupations as differentiated in terms of these indicators are found to map onto the class categories distinguished by the schema in ways broadly consistent with its conceptual basis.[7] The central issue that arises is therefore that of how this empirical regularity actually comes about. Why should there be such a tendency for individuals engaged in different kinds of work to have their employment regulated via different contractual arrangements and understandings?

In previous work (Goldthorpe, 1982, cf. also 1995), I have made some attempt at an answer to this question, with particular reference to the idea of the formation of a service class or salariat, but only in a brief and rather ad hoc fashion. Here, I aim at a more systematic and theoretically informed treatment. I draw, as in previous chapters, on rational action theory and in particular on such theory as deployed in recent organisational and personnel economics (see, e.g., Milgrom and Roberts, 1992; Lazear, 1995), and in the new institutional, especially transaction-cost, economics (see, e.g., Williamson, 1985, 1996). I would not regard this cross-disciplinary borrowing as in any way implying the abandonment of a sociological perspective, as is suggested, for example, by Pfeffer (1997: ch. 9). What is in fact striking about the economics literature referred to is how much of it can be read as a more rigorous development—from the standpoint of a particular theory of action—of observations and insights already to be found in the industrial sociology of the later 1940s and 1950s.[8] Moreover, the version of RAT that is chiefly in use, at least in transaction-cost economics, is not the utility theory of neoclassical orthodoxy but a version in which the idea of rationality as objective and infinite gives way to that of rationality as subjective and bounded: or, in the words of Simon (1961; cf. Williamson, 1985: ch. 2), actors are seen as being 'intendedly rational but only limitedly so'. As earlier argued (vol. I, chs. 6–8), this modification produces an obvious convergence with approaches to the theory of action that are central to the classic sociological tradition; and all the more so to the extent that rationality is seen as being restricted not only by psychological, cognitive constraints on information processing but further by social constraints on the availability of information, or knowledge, itself.

Such efforts as sociologists have previously made to account for variation in the form of employment contracts (see, e.g., Edwards, 1979; Wright, 1985, 1989, 1997: ch. 1) derive largely from Marxist political economy (cf. Marglin, 1974; Stone, 1974; Bowles and Gintis, 1976) and are in turn characterised by an almost exclusive emphasis on considerations of power and control. The basic assumption is that, under capitalism, the prime concern of employers will be to maximise the 'exploitation' of their workers: that is, to maximise the extraction of actual labour from employees' working time. Employers will thus in general aim to establish forms of contract that are to their greatest advantage in this regard in that they effectively 'commodify' labour. To the extent that variation in contracts does occur, it is then to be explained in terms of employers seeking to privilege their managerial and supervisory staffs as a means of buying their loyalty in the process of exploitation or to create conflicts of interest among employees as part of a larger strategy of 'divide and rule'. Organisational and transaction-cost economists have, however, been critical of such Marxist interpretations on both theoretical and empirical grounds. The main counter-claim that they have advanced is that, rather than being seen as expressions of power and means of exploitation, most features of employment contracts are better understood in terms of efficiency: that is, as serving not only to ensure the viability of the enterprise within a competitive market context but further to increase the *total value* of the contract, to the benefit of all parties involved (see, e.g., Milgrom and Roberts, 1992: ch. 10; Williamson, 1985: 206–11, 1994).

In what follows I aim to take up an intermediate position that avoids what I would see as ideologically induced weaknesses in the more extreme versions of both the 'exploitation' and the 'efficiency' arguments.[9] I treat employment contracts primarily from the standpoint of employers, with whom the *initiative* in their design and implementation does at all events lie. I first set out what would appear to be certain general problems of the employment contract as such, and I then try to show how the different forms that this contract may take can be understood primarily as employers' responses to the more particular ways in which these problems arise in the case of employees involved in different kinds of work. I make the assumption that in this regard the central tendency is for employers to act as rationally as they are able towards the goal of maintaining the viability and success of their organisations within the context of whatever constraints they may face. This may then lead them, depending on the specific circumstances that obtain, to view their contractual relations with employees in *either* zero-sum *or* positive-sum terms—just as employees may take a similarly varying view of their contractual relations with employers. In other words, I see no reason to treat the interests of employers and employees as being 'fundamentally' either in harmony or in conflict.[10]

GENERAL PROBLEMS OF THE EMPLOYMENT CONTRACT

It is has for long been recognised by economists and sociologists alike that the employment contract has distinctive features (see, e.g., Commons, 1924; Simon, 1951; Baldamus, 1961). These stem basically from the fact that the labour that is bought by employers on the labour market cannot be physically separated from the individual persons who sell it. What is in effect bought and sold through the employment contract is not a commodity, or at least not in the sense of some definite, objective thing, but rather a social relationship. Employment contracts are contracts through which employees agree, in return for remuneration, to place themselves under the authority of the employer or of the employer's agents.[11] Further, though, employment contracts are in varying, but often substantial, degree implicit or in fact incomplete, and especially in regard to what employers may demand of employees and what in turn the obligations of employees are. Employers buy the right to tell employees what to do while at work, and minimum requirements may be formally laid down concerning, say, hours of work, working methods and procedures, and so on. But contracts rarely if ever seek to specify just how hard employees should work—what intensity of effort they should make— let alone what degree of responsibility, adaptability, or initiative they should be ready to show in their employer's interest. Such matters would indeed seem largely to defy formulation in explicit contractual terms.

From the employer's point of view, therefore, a major objective must be that not merely of *enforcing* the compliance of employees with the authority that they have in principle accepted but, further, that of *inducing* their maximum effort and cooperation in the performance of the work allocated to them. Another way of putting the matter would be to say that within the employment contract employees will always have some non-negligible amount of discretion; and that it will then be of obvious importance to employers and their agents to ensure that this discretion is as far as possible used in ways that support rather then subvert the purposes of the employing organisation.

In the industrial sociology of the immediate postwar years (see, e.g., Miller and Form, 1951), which had a strongly managerialist orientation, the problems arising in this regard were treated in terms of the degree of congruence prevailing between 'formal' and 'informal' organisation—especially, that is, between employers' work rules and work-group values and norms. The greater the congruence that could be achieved, the higher, it was supposed, would be levels of employee motivation and morale. This goal was then to be pursued through 'human relations' policies, implemented by first-line managers and supervisors at the level of the work group—or, as critics would have it, through social-psychological manipulation.

In the economics literature previously referred to, essentially the same issues are addressed, also in fact largely from the employer's standpoint, but in a different idiom. The key issue is taken to be that of how the employment contract may be most efficiently elaborated, not only in its explicit *ex ante* design, to which limitations clearly apply, but, more important perhaps, in its *ex post,* and possibly quite implicit, interpretation and actual day-to-day execution: that is, in the way in which it serves as the basis for the continuing regulation of employment relations over time.[12] At a minimum, the employer must be given protection against employee shirking or opportunism, but it is a further requirement that employee interests should as far as possible be aligned with those of the employer or, in other words, that appropriate incentive structures should be set in place. And at the same time transaction costs have to be taken into account: that is, the arrangements and procedures involved in actually implementing the contract must be cost effective as compared with available alternatives.

The rational action theory that informs this latter approach does, I believe, endow it with greater intellectual coherence than that achieved by early industrial sociology (cf. ch. 4, this volume, pp. 83–4 and n. 14). However, for my present purposes its most immediate attraction is that it leads naturally to recognition of the fact that employment contracts will need to take on different forms in relation to the different kinds of work-task and work-role that employees are engaged to perform.

DIFFERENTIATION OF THE EMPLOYMENT CONTRACT AND TYPES OF WORK

What is to be explained here is, to repeat, the association between different occupational groupings of employees and the form of regulation of their employment that can, it appears, be empirically demonstrated on the lines indicated in Table 5.1. To this end, it is necessary to consider types of work analytically, and in a more abstract yet focused way than could be achieved by reliance on occupational designations themselves. The organisational and transaction-cost economics on which I draw would suggest two main dimensions in terms of which potential problems—or sources of 'contractual hazard'—from the employer's point of view can be identified (cf. Weakliem, 1989).

> 1. The degree of difficulty involved in monitoring the work performed by employees: that is, the degree of difficulty involved both in measuring its quantity and also in observing and controlling its quality; and
> 2. the degree of specificity of the human assets or human capital—skills, expertise, knowledge—used by employees in performing their work: that is,

the degree to which productive value would be lost if these assets were to be transferred to some other employment.

In pursuing the explanatory task in hand, I shall therefore find it helpful to refer to the two-dimensional space described in Figure 5.1.

Work that falls into the lower-left quadrant of Figure 5.1 is that which may be expected to give rise to fewest hazards for employers as regards the employment contract. The absence of serious work monitoring problems means that some kind of 'variable pay' system can operate or, in other words, employees can be remunerated in direct relation to their productivity. And the absence of serious asset specificity problems means that no understandings need be entered into about the long-term continuation of the contract. No such understandings are required in order to provide employees with an incentive to acquire skills of specific value in their present employment and then to remain in this employment. Under these conditions, the employment contract can simply provide for discrete, short-term exchanges of money for effort, in the way characteristic of the labour contract as earlier described,

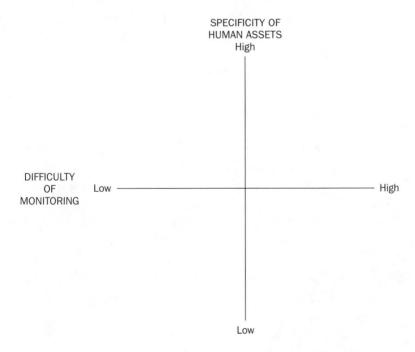

Figure 5.1.   Dimensions of work as sources of contractual hazard

and thus come in fact as close as is possible to a simple spot contract—albeit perhaps of a recurrent kind—for the purchase of a quantity of a commodity (cf. Kay, 1993: ch. 4).

However, the question does then at once arise of why it is that, despite the evident advantages of the labour contract to employers, the occupational range of its application would appear, as is indicated in Table 5.1, to be rather restricted: that is, in its pure form to nonskilled manual occupations and, somewhat modified, to skilled manual and lower-grade nonmanual occupations. What will here be argued is that this limitation is to be explained in terms of various *concomitant* features of the kind of work in regard to which a labour contract proves viable.

The Occupational Restriction of the Labour Contract

Difficulties in measuring the quantity of work done by employees will be least, and a variable pay system will thus be most easily implemented, where measurement can be based on actual *output*. In this case, a direct link between work and pay can be established through piece rates of some kind. However, work that can be thus measured and remunerated is likely to have various other characteristics. To begin with, the measurement of work by output implies output that is of a specific, well-defined kind, and efficient payment by output implies a production process that is relatively simple: first, so that output can be clearly attributed to particular individuals or at most to small work groups and, second, so that the employer—as well as employees—can have reliable knowledge of how quickly the work can be done and can therefore set an appropriate rate of pay.[13] Moreover, because piece rates give an inducement to workers to concentrate on quantity of work at the expense of quality, it is important, from the employer's point of view, that the quality of the product as well as its quantity is easy to monitor—that is, to observe and assess—and likewise such other aspects of work quality as the use of tools, equipment, and raw materials (cf. Milgrom and Roberts, 1992: 394–35). It could then be said that the kind of work with which piece rates are most likely to be associated is work in which workers, acting individually or in small groups, undertake physical (rather than mental) operations that lead in a fairly transparent way to discrete material (rather than symbolic) results. Typical piece-rate workers are in fact fruit and vegetable pickers, various kinds of loaders, fillers, and packers, and machinists in batch-production manufacturing industry.

It may also be possible for work to be more or less adequately measured by *input* in the sense of time spent at work, and thus for a variable pay system to operate through time rates, calculated, say, on an hourly or daily basis. Once more, though, for this to be the case—in effect, for time worked to be informative about output—restrictions would seem to apply to the nature of the work involved. If under piece rates the employer's main monitoring problem is that of quality, under time rates it becomes that of assessing and maintaining the level of worker effort. This problem will be least severe, and time rates thus most attractive to employers, where workers have in fact only limited autonomy in regard to their pace of work: where, for example, this is largely determined by technology, as in assembly line or continuous process production, or by the flow of customers or clients, as in the case, say, of checkout operators, ticket sellers, or counter staff. Otherwise, it will be important that worker effort should be easily observable, and thus open to control through supervision, and this would then again tend to imply work activity with a clear physical component, even if not necessarily of a kind conventionally classified as 'manual' (cf. Fama, 1991).

The payment of employees in return for discrete amounts of work done, whether by piece or time, is one defining element of the labour contract. The other is that the exchange is of a short-term nature in the sense that, while it may in fact be many times repeated, there is nothing in the contract itself, explicit or implicit, that is aimed at securing the relationship between employer and employee on a long-term basis. As earlier suggested, an employer is able to operate with such a contract where there is little to be gained in encouraging workers to invest in the acquisition of human assets specific to their present employment, and in turn little to be lost if employees should leave this employment—that is, the costs of labour turnover are slight. Here too, though, the argument may be made that where such a situation prevails, there are likely to be further implications for the type of work that is involved.

Thus, while in principle a workforce with which no problems of human asset specificity arose could still be a skilled workforce—that is, one reliant simply on general purpose skills—it would seem empirically to be the case that where general purpose skills are brought to particular employments, it tends to be both possible and advantageous for further, more specific skills, expertise, and knowledge to be developed around them.[14] Consequently, a situation in which employers need take no account of asset specificity in regard to their employees can be reckoned as most probably one in which employers are able to recruit the workers they require from a fairly homogeneous pool of labour, the individual members of which are substitutable for each other without serious loss of productive value on the basis simply of their physical capacities plus, perhaps, minimal literacy and numeracy.

In the light of the foregoing, then, what underlies the restriction of the occupational range of the labour contract should be more apparent. It is work with features that locate it in the lower-left quadrant of Figure 5.1 that allows employers to resort to this form of regulation of employment. But work that is easily measured and otherwise monitored *and* that in itself offers little potential for the development of specific human capital will have other characteristics too. Its archetype can in fact be regarded as manual work of a nonskilled kind, or what might be thought of as labour in its most basic sense. It is, then, with such work that the labour contract can operate in its purest form or, in other words, that employers can take the commodification of labour to its furthest possible point. Correspondingly, any extension of the labour contract beyond such work is likely to entail some departure from the pure form in one direction or another. For example, where the monitoring of work is not entirely straightforward, as regards either quantity or quality, the strict principle of pay in return for discrete amounts of work done will need to be modified in some degree. Thus, a *weekly* wage with, perhaps, provision for overtime pay or time off 'in lieu' for work in excess of a given number of hours is a fairly common arrangement among more skilled manual and lower-grade nonmanual employees. And likewise such workers may be given certain privileges of seniority—such as pay guarantees or a 'first-in, last-out' understanding in the case of redundancies—in circumstances where employers are compelled to recognise some need for the development and retention of human assets of an organisation-specific kind (cf. Doeringer and Piore, 1971; Weakliem, 1989).

The full significance of these latter points can, however, only be fully brought out by changing perspective somewhat. Having begun by asking what accounts for the empirically observed restriction of the labour contract to manual and lower-grade nonmanual occupations, I shall next ask why it should be that in the case of professional and managerial occupations, this form of regulation of employment would appear to be effectively precluded and is typically replaced by what has been called the service relationship. Again, I shall seek to give an answer in terms of employers' responses to the potential contractual hazards that are mapped out in Figure 5.1 and, more specifically, as these intensify as one moves from the lower-left quadrant towards the upper right.

The Rationale of the Service Relationship

The general problems of the employment contract, as outlined in the previous section, are sometimes represented (e.g., Pratt and Zeckhauser, 1984; Eggertsson, 1990) as ones of a 'principal-agent' relationship: that is, of a relationship in which a principal (the employer) engages an agent (the employee) to act in the principal's interest in circumstances in which the principal cannot observe the agent's actions, nor share in all of the information guiding those actions. This representation may seem somewhat strained where it is possible for labour to be more or less commodified and some approximation to a spot contract is thus viable. However, it takes on special force where employees act in a professional or managerial capacity.[15] Professionals are engaged to exercise specialised knowledge and expertise that they have obtained from a lengthy training; while managers are engaged to exercise the delegated authority of the employer. In both cases alike, therefore, the nature of the work-tasks and work-roles that are performed imply some asymmetry of information as between employer and employee and thus, for the latter, a significant area of autonomy and discretion into which monitoring by the employer cannot feasibly extend. Indeed, effective monitoring would here entail some kind of infinite regress. It would itself require precisely the kind of use of specialised knowledge and expertise and of delegated authority that creates the agency problem in the first place (cf. Simon, 1991).

Where such difficulty in monitoring work arises, it then becomes especially important for the employer to gain the commitment of employees, which in turn implies designing and implementing a form of contract that can as far as possible ensure that their interests are, and remain, aligned with the goals of the organisation as the employer would define them. In the case of profit-making organisations, one evident recourse is to link employee compensation to the economic success of the enterprise as, for example, through stock awards or stock options or profit-related bonuses or other profit-sharing schemes. However, while these kinds of remuneration may often play a major part in the compensation of chief executive officers and other very senior personnel, they are difficult to extend at a similar level of importance throughout the staff hierarchy, and they would appear to have no very effective analogues in the case of employees in public sector or non-profit-making bodies.[16]

Moreover, further circumstances may well obtain in which serious difficulties for any kind of performance-related pay system are created: that is, where employees are required—as professionals and managers typically are—to carry out tasks, or roles, of a very diverse character. In such a situation, payment can scarcely be related equally to every aspect of the work that is undertaken. It will, rather, have to be linked to just one, or at most one or two, aspects—those for which performance indicators can most easily be devised being most likely to be chosen. But such arrangements hold dangers for employers. For the incentives offered will in this case serve not simply to induce greater effort on the part of employees but further to influence their *distribution* of effort, and of time and attention, *among* their different responsibilities. That is to say, those aspects of their work to which pay is in fact related will tend to be favoured at the expense of others, and to a degree that need not be optimal from the employer's point of view (cf. Holström and Milgrom, 1991). Employers may 'get what they pay for' in an all too literal sense (cf. Gibbons, 1997). Moreover, given that work-tasks *are* diverse, monitoring that is then specifically aimed at preventing such unintended consequences, or 'perverse effects', may well not be cost effective, even if practical at all.

Since, therefore, in the employment of professionals and managers general principal-agent problems may often be compounded by the further ones posed by multitask agents, forms of employment contract in which either direct work monitoring or specific performance indicators provide the basis for pay would seem unlikely, in the main, to answer to employers' requirements. The alternative and generally more appropriate strategy will be for employers to seek to gain the commitment of their professional and managerial personnel, or in Simon's apt phrase (1991: 32) to shape their 'decision premises', through a form of contract with a quite different rationale. That is, one which relies on performance appraisal of only a broad and long-term, though perhaps comparative, kind and that then sets up, conditional on such appraisal, the possibility of a steadily rising level of compensation throughout the course of the employee's working life. In this regard, the contract provides for compensation primarily through an annual salary that may be expected to increase both in accordance with an established scale and further, and more substantially, as the result of the employee's advancement through a career structure. Given the prospect of such an 'upward-sloping experience-earnings profile', as Lazear (1995: 39) has termed it, both effective incentives for employees *and* effective sanctions for the employer are created—and especially so if, as Lazear would argue (cf. also 1981), what is typically entailed is paying employees *less* than they are worth, in terms of their productivity, when they are young or at all events in the lower levels of the hierarchy and *more* than they are worth when they are older or in higher-level positions.

On the one hand, the better employees perform (or at least are perceived to perform) in the pursuit of organisational goals, the further, and more rapidly, they will be promoted out of the levels at which they are underpaid and into those at which they are overpaid. On the other hand, because for most employees higher rewards will still lie ahead, and ones that they have already in part earned through their previous underpayment, 'hasty quits' are discouraged and the threat of dismissal, as, say, in the case of manifest shirking or incompetence or of malfeasance, becomes a more potent one. Furthermore, appropriately constructed pensions schemes can also be seen as an integral part of such 'deferred payment' contracts, encouraging employees to stay with their organisations up to the peak of the expected present value of benefits but then discouraging them from staying on too long (in the absence of a mandatory retiring age) in the phase when, relative to their productivity, they are being overpaid (Lazear, 1995: 42–45).[17]

In other words, the solution to the problem of agency, as it arises with professional and managerial employees, is sought essentially in the service relationship as this was earlier described. In place of any attempt at the immediate linking of performance and pay, the employment contract envisages, even if implicitly as much as explicitly, a quite diffuse exchange of service to the organisation in return for compensation in which the prospective element is crucial; and, by the same token, the contract is understood as having a long-term rather than a short-term basis. The key connection that the contract aims to establish is that between employees' commitment to, and effective pursuit of, organisational goals and their career success and lifetime material well-being.[18]

So far in this subsection, I have concentrated on employers' contractual problems associated with work located towards the right of the horizontal dimension of Figure 5.1: that is, those of monitoring. However, problems associated with work located towards the top of the vertical dimension are also relevant: that is, those of human asset specificity. I earlier suggested that these problems would be least demanding where employers could operate satisfactorily with workers who possessed no more than commonly available physical or cognitive capacities. Insofar as a higher quality workforce is called for, the probability increases that there will be advantage to the employer in ensuring that any general purpose skills that employees bring with them are, as Williamson has put it (1985: 242), 'deepened and specialized' in the particular organisational contexts in which they are to be applied. And, where this is so, a form of contract that does nothing to help secure the employment relationship on a long-term basis will obviously be deficient: it will fail to provide incentives for employers to engage in the training, or for employees in the learning, from which both parties could alike benefit.

Problems of human asset specificity are not confined to professional and managerial employees—as was earlier indicated and as will be seen further below. However, such problems may be thought to take on an importance in the case of these employees that is proportional to that of the organisational roles that they perform. That is to say, failure to provide for either the development or the retention of organisation-specific skills, expertise, and knowledge on the part of professionals and managers is likely to be especially damaging. Here again, then, the rationale of the service relationship, with its implication of continuing employment, is apparent. Through such a relationship, in contrast to one in which renewal is entirely contingent, employers can more securely embark on costly training and planned-experience programmes aimed at increasing employees' organisation-specific abilities, and employees can in turn more securely devote the time and effort necessary to acquire such abilities. In other words, it becomes possible for both the costs of and the returns to investments of this kind to be shared between employers and employees (Milgrom and Roberts, 1992: 363; Lazear, 1995: 74). The advantage of the long-term character of the service relationship as the basis of a solution to agency problems—that is, via the rising worklife compensation curve—is therefore reinforced in that at the same time the basis for a solution to asset specificity problems is also provided.[19]

Mixed Forms

Finally in this section some explanation should be attempted of the prevalence within certain occupational groupings—as indicated in Table 5.1—of mixed forms of the employment contract: that is, of forms that, in various ways, combine elements of both the labour contract and the service relationship.

Referring back once more to Figure 5.1, a tendency may be supposed, in the light of the discussion so far, for empirical instances to be concentrated on the lower-left to upper-right diagonal: or, in other words, for there to be some correlation between the severity of the monitoring problems and of the human asset specificity problems to which different kinds of work give rise. Nonetheless, instances lying off this diagonal can certainly be envisaged, and the suggestion I would advance is that it is in terms of work thus located that the occupational distribution of mixed forms of the employment contract is to be explained. Work falling in the lower-right quadrant of Figure 5.1, that is, work that confronts employers with real difficulties of monitoring but not of asset specificity, could be expected to lead to a form of contract in which features entailing some departure from the exchange of discrete amounts of money and effort characteristic of the labour contract would be more apparent than ones directed towards furthering a long-term relationship. And, conversely, work falling in the upper-left quadrant, where asset specificity problems are serious but not monitoring problems, could be expected to lead to a form of contract in which a fairly specific money-for-effort exchange is preserved but some understanding of the long-term nature of the contract is at least implied.

Some empirical support for this argument can in fact be provided, and indeed for a rather more precise version of it: namely, one which would associate the first of the two situations outlined above primarily with routine nonmanual occupations in administration and commerce that exist, so to speak, on the fringes of bureaucratic structures, and the second situation with manual supervisory and lower-grade technical occupations.[20] Thus, routine nonmanual employees—clerical workers, secretaries, and so on— would appear to enjoy fixed salaries and also relatively relaxed or flexible time-keeping arrangements almost to the same extent as the professionals and managers with whom they typically work in ancillary roles, although for the most part deploying only rather standardised skills (cf. Fama, 1991). However, they are not to the same extent involved in career structures within their employing organisations that would hold out the prospect of steadily increasing rewards over the entire course of their working lives.[21] Conversely, supervisors of manual workers and lower-grade technicians tend to have a larger variable element in their pay, especially as a result of overtime pay, or shift premia, in much the same way as many of the rank-and-file employees over whom they exercise direction and control. But their distinctive value to their organisations is more often recognised through agreements or understandings on employment and income security and also perhaps through opportunities to progress up job ladders that are based primarily on seniority—that is, in the manner provided for by the institutions of the classic firm-internal labour market (Doeringer and Piore, 1971; Osterman, 1987).[22]

Taking this argument together with those previously advanced in this section of the chapter, it is then possible to give an overall representation of how the analytical dimensions of Figure 5.1 are seen to relate to the empirical regularities implied in Table 5.1: that is, regularities in the association between different occupational groupings of employees and the form of regulation of their employment. This is done in Figure 5.2. On the understanding that the regularities in question are to be regarded as only probabilistic, and that exceptions to them will thus certainly be found, this latter figure can

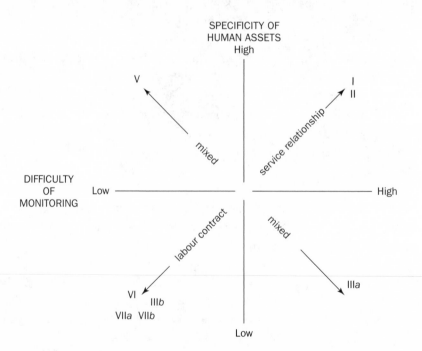

Figure 5.2. Dimensions of work as sources of contractual hazard, forms of employment contract, and location of employee classes of the schema

stand as a summary of the explanation that is here offered of how they are in fact generated and sustained through employers' responses to the problems of contractual regulation that arise from the engagement of workers to undertake differing kinds of work.

NEW EMPLOYER STRATEGIES AND THE FUTURE OF THE SERVICE RELATIONSHIP

One objection that might be raised against the foregoing analysis is that it seeks to explain in very general theoretical terms a pattern of differentiation in employment contracts that could well prove specific to a particular historical era. Several authors have indeed already broached the question of the continuing viability of the service relationship under conditions of rapid change in technological and market conditions and of intensifying global competition that impose ever greater requirements of organisational flexibility (see, e.g., Halford and Savage, 1995); and others have gone further in maintaining that, under these conditions, the service relationship is actually being eroded, and in the public as well as the private sector, as competitive tendering and other forms of market discipline are increasingly imposed (see, e.g., Brown, 1995 and also the globalisation theorists discussed in vol. I, ch. 5). There is constant pressure, it is argued, to 'downsize' or 'de-layer' management structures, to buy in professional services rather than to provide them in-house, to engage staff on fixed-term contracts, and to introduce performance-related pay systems at all levels of employment. From this point of view, then, the service relationship appears not as a form of contract with a rather sophisticated underlying rationale but as an expression merely of a conventional status distinction that could be sustained as an aspect of 'organisational slack' during the long boom of the postwar years but that is now being swept aside in a far more demanding economic environment.

Insofar as attempts *are* under way radically to reshape the form of regulation of employment of professional and managerial personnel, a valuable opportunity is then afforded for the empirical testing of the account I have offered of the logic of the differentiation of employment contracts. Some of the relevant evidence, pertaining, for example, to risks of job loss and unemployment and to the persistence of career structures, I have already reviewed in my critique of globalisation theorists in Volume I; and in the following chapter I return to the main empirical questions that arise in the larger context of current debates in class analysis. Here, though, it may serve as a useful preliminary and at the same time help further to clarify the theoretical arguments I have advanced if I attempt to spell out just what, from the point of view of their evaluation, has to be regarded as centrally at issue.

To begin with, it is entirely consistent with the general position that I have taken that employers *should try* to exploit any changes in labour market or other economic conditions that might enable them to modify contracts of employment, explicitly or implicitly, in ways that would be to their advantage or, more specifically, that would reduce their contractual hazard. And it is further consistent that such modifications should then, all else equal, be ones leading away from the service relationship and towards the discrete and short-term exchange of the labour contract; or, in other words, away from forms of the regulation of employment that presuppose a diffuse and continuing exchange and towards ones in which labour is to a greater degree commodified. As Breen (1997a) has observed, one can in this respect think of employers as seeking to transfer risk from themselves to their employees: that is, to free themselves from the inflexibility entailed by the 'quasi-generalised reciprocity' of the service relationship and to secure instead an 'asymmetric commitment' or in effect an *option* on the supply of labour, which they can then decline, if necessary, in order to avoid 'downside' risk while preserving the possibility of profiting from 'upside' risk. Evidence simply of employers being alert to the possibility of revising forms of contract in ways they would see as being in their interests is not therefore, in itself, of any great consequence. What matters is how far employers are thus led actually to abandon the service relationship in cases where it had previously applied.

In this connection, it has also to be recognised that some of the strategies that employers may pursue in search of greater flexibility need have little or no impact on the service relationship per se, and indeed may even help to make this relationship *more* viable. Thus, by downsizing and delayering management structures and also by buying in professional expertise, employers may reduce the proportion of their total workforce to whom the service relationship is extended, and in turn the degree to which they are involved in quasi-generalised reciprocity, but without abandoning this relationship for the professional and managerial staff that they retain.[23] Likewise, by creating greater flexibility in the employment of *other* grades of worker—as, say, by modifying features of internal labour markets for skilled manual workers (cf. Capelli, 1995)—employers may be better able to sustain the service relationship in the case of those employees for whom they would see it as specifically appropriate. In some influential models of the 'flexible firm' (e.g., Atkinson, 1985), the emphasis is in fact on the *divergence* between the employment relations that apply with the 'core' and with the 'peripheral' workforce.

What, therefore, emerges as the key question is that of how far in prevailing economic circumstances, and on what basis, employers do come to regard the service relationship itself as expressing a form of contract that they should aim in general to terminate rather than to preserve. And insofar as this relationship is in fact undermined in the case of professional and managerial staff, as, say, through the introduction of short-term contracts or performance-related pay, it will in turn be important to know just how employers then seek to handle those problems of work monitoring and of human asset specificity out of which, I have maintained, the rationale of the service relationship and of its occupational range initially arise.

Breen, for example, has pointed out (1997a) that, despite employers' concern to off-load risk within the employment contract onto their employees, there are still good grounds for supposing that the service relationship will prove durable since there is no other obvious solution to the agency problem deriving primarily from asymmetric information. Professionals and managers are employees in regard to whom it is generally less important that the employment contract should provide for flexibility (from the employer's point of view) than that it should ensure that the employee has strong incentives to show commitment to organisational goals (see also Gallie et al. 1998: 312–13). And to this I would add that even if improved techniques of monitoring may in some instances be capable of reducing agency problems (Halford and Savage, 1995: 129), attempts at basing pay on performance will still threaten to give rise to perverse effects in the way earlier noted where employees are engaged in work-tasks of a multifaceted kind.[24] In this respect, the requirements of contractual flexibility would seem to come into direct conflict with those of 'functional' flexibility (Atkinson, 1985), which in fact lead to demands on employees to be ready to take on an ever-wider range of tasks and responsibilities.

What is perhaps more plausible than the idea of the general abandonment of the service relationship is the suggestion that, at least with some employee groupings, the 'deal' that it comprises may be reformulated: in particular, so that what the employee is offered, in return for commitment and a readiness to develop organisation-specific assets, is an understanding not on continuity of employment but rather on continuity of *employability*. In this case, it falls to the employer to provide employees with training and experience that, as well as enhancing their organisation-specific skills, expertise, and knowledge, will also equip them for future career progression in the external labour market. However, it is still far from clear that even this modification of the service relationship would necessarily be to the employer's advantage. The evident risk that the employer incurs is that if investment is made in the development of human assets that are *not* organisation specific and if the employees who benefit from this investment are not then retained, the returns on the investment will largely be lost: they will be divided between the employees and their *subsequent* employers. Again, then, the force of the original rationale of the service relationship is brought out.

In sum, for a compelling argument to be advanced that the service relationship is in general decline, two things would seem to be required: first, direct evidence that employment contracts expressing this relationship are indeed being discontinued across the range of employee groupings for which they were previously typical; and, second, evidence that such a change is to be regarded as permanent—rather than being, say, a response merely to short-term economic exigencies or to the current vogue among management consultants—*because* the rationale that previously underlay the service relationship has now ceased to apply or has in some way been transcended.[25] The analysis that I have earlier presented obviously leads me to the view that evidence of the latter kind at least will not be readily forthcoming.

In this chapter I have started from an empirical regularity that has emerged from attempts to assess the criterion validity of the class schema that colleagues and I have developed as a research instrument. At least for the British case, a pattern of association has been established, among employees, between their broad occupational grouping and the form of regulation of their employment. I have then suggested, drawing chiefly on theoretical ideas developed in both more and less orthodox branches of modern economics, how this regularity might be explained at the level of social action: that is, in terms of employers' rationally intelligible responses to the problems that they face in devising and implementing employment contracts for workers engaged in different types of work—in particular, problems of work monitoring and of human asset specificity. I have also indicated how I believe that attempts at testing the explanation offered, within the contemporary economic context, might best be focused. To end with, I make two observations concerning what is and what is not implied by the central argument of the chapter for the more general understanding of the stratification of modern societies—on the assumption, of course, that the argument is basically sound. Since this assumption is, for the present at least, obviously open to challenge, the remarks will be brief, although they relate to large questions.

First, if the analysis I have presented is valid, it must follow that modern societies, at least insofar as they retain capitalist market economies of some kind, will have a relatively complex class structure as one of their concomitant and abiding features. In addition to the differentiation of employers, the self-employed, and employees, the latter will themselves be differentiated in terms of the employment relations in which they are involved as the result of a highly generalised 'situational logic' that applies, and that will have its effects, across a wide range of societal contexts. The further implication then is that although national societies may well show much variation in the historical evolution of their class structures—that is, in the rates of growth or decline of different classes and thus in their proportionate sizes—they will at the same time be characterised by class-related inequalities that run on far more comparable lines. The form of these inequalities is likely to be no less complex than the structure of class relations from which they derive, and therefore not open to adequate representation in a one-dimensional fashion. Nonetheless, it may still be said that insofar as employees are involved in a service relationship rather than a labour contract, they will be significantly advantaged not only in that they will tend to receive a higher level of income from their employment but, further, in that their incomes will be less subject to interruption through job loss and unemployment or to short-term fluctuation and will tend to follow a rising curve over the larger part of their working lives. It is in the case of intermediate classes that the problems of any one-dimensional ordering become most apparent.[26]

Second, though, it is important to recognise that the analysis advanced carries no particular implications for the overall *degree* of economic inequality, including inequality in incomes from employment, that will be found among members of different classes. Indeed, what should be noted in this regard is that substantial change in the extent of such inequality can occur over time while essentially the same *pattern* of class differentiation is maintained. For example, in Britain over the last quarter of the twentieth century class inequalities in income from employment widened sharply but with little effect on class differences in security and stability of income and in lifetime income prospects (Goldthorpe and McKnight, 2006). Moreover, a cross-national perspective might be expected to reveal an analogous situation: that is, that variation in the degree more than in the pattern of class inequality may be produced as the same situational logic of class relations works itself out in national societies with differing political economies, industrial relations systems and social welfare regimes.[27]

Esping-Andersen (1993: 2, 8) has complained that class theory, from Marx and Weber down to the present day, tends to assume that 'classes emerge out of unfettered exchange relations, be it in the market or at the "point of production"', and is thus 'nested in an institutionally "naked" world'. Regardless of how far such a characterisation is in fact correct, it is, I believe, still a mistake to see it as pointing to a deficiency. Rather, it would seem important that any theory of social class *should* aim to be as general as possible—to require only minimal assumptions about the institutional forms of labour markets and production units—precisely so that the impact of wider institutional variation, and likewise of underlying political and cultural factors, can then be assessed.[28] And the further question can of course in turn be raised of how far this variation, and also that in the differing shapes of national class structures previously referred to, are in fact themselves open to general theoretical explanation or have rather to be accounted for in more specific historical terms.

CHAPTER SIX

Class Analysis
New Versions and Their Problems*

Of late, sociologists have engaged in animated debate over the question of the continuing relevance of class analysis in contemporary, postindustrial, or postmodern societies (see, e.g., Lee and Turner, eds., 1996; Marshall, 1997; Evans, ed., 1999; Clark and Lipset, eds., 2001). For those who believe that in such societies class, as a social phenomenon, is in steady and inevitable decline, class analysis is merely a relic of the sociology of the nineteenth and twentieth centuries that must now give way to 'new paradigms'. But for those who would reject the idea of the decline of class, class analysis remains central to the sociology of contemporary societies, even though needing—as ever previously—to adapt its focus to changes in the forms of class structures and in the modalities of class relations.

In the present essay my concern is not with this debate, which has, I suspect, by now been pursued to the point of diminishing returns. I have, I hope, made my own position clear enough elsewhere: in short, that class and class analysis are of abiding importance (Goldthorpe and Marshall, 1992; Goldthorpe, 2001; and cf. also vol. I, ch. 5). Here, I seek to move on to a range of issues that have arisen among sociologists who would broadly share my view that class analysis retains its relevance but who would differ from me, and from each other, in the ways in which they would understand the nature and objectives of class analysis and wish to see it develop. I concentrate on

*This essay draws at various points on papers that appeared in the *American Journal of Sociology*, 105 (2000) and in *Acta Sociologica*, 45 (2002a). I am indebted to Tony Atkinson, Richard Breen, Robert Erikson, David Grusky, Stephen Morgan, Aage Sørensen, Kim Weeden, and Herman Van de Werfhorst for helpful conversations, information, criticism, and advice.

the strong, but contrasting, programmatic statements that have been made in this regard, and with the backing of at least illustrative empirical work, by two leading American sociologists, Aage Sørensen and David Grusky.[1]

However, the debate on the decline of class cannot be entirely ignored. This is so because the arguments of those who have sought to defend class analysis are rather systematically influenced by their evaluation of this debate. More specifically, insofar as class analysis is regarded as a project of inescapably Marxist inspiration, the more seriously has the charge to be taken that it is now outmoded, and, in turn, the more radical are the changes that seem necessary if it is still to remain viable and valuable. Crucial in this case is the idea that an essential concern of class analysis is with tracing the main lines of economic division that define classes and with the consequent 'formation' of these classes: that is, with their emergence as groupings of individuals with a sufficient sense of shared identity and interests to be capable of engaging in collective action in which class is set against class and a potential for societal change thus created. This idea is clearly threatened insofar as classes, as understood in Marxist terms, have tended to show only rather low levels of formation and the working class in particular has failed to realise the historic significance that was scheduled for it. Thus, it would appear that class analysis in a *marxisant* vein can only be saved through some quite basic reformulation of the concept of class. And, as will be seen, both Sørensen and Grusky, who would alike wish to see a theory of class-based action remain at the core of class analysis, are led to propose new versions that would mark clear, and in fact rather startling, breaks with what has hitherto been attempted under this heading.

In contrast, if class analysis in contemporary sociology is recognised as having other sources than Marxist theory, and indeed as having in certain important respects developed *in opposition to* such theory, then the debate over class can be viewed with far less disquiet. In particular, it would appear that claims of the decline, or even 'death', of class can only be made by those who are blinkered by the supposition that the debate must remain one essentially with the ghost of Marx over issues of class action.[2] What might be described as the non-Marxist, or even anti-Marxist, tradition of class analysis—and within which I would situate my own work as represented here and elsewhere—comprises in fact a relatively wide span of interests. These extend from the differentiation of class positions by social relations in labour markets and production units (class structure), to the distribution and redistribution of individuals and families among these positions over time (class mobility), and in turn to the consequences that then follow for a range of individual life chances and life choices.[3] In this last regard, issues of the degree of class formation and of the extent of class-based collective action do of course arise. But these are seen as issues to be treated empirically: that is to say, it is to be determined under what conditions class formation and action are likely to occur. And should it prove to be the case that these conditions are quite special, so that high levels of class formation and action are historically exceptional rather than recurrent, this in no way constitutes a threat to the project of class analysis as a whole. From the standpoint of this tradition, therefore, no pressing need arises for the radical reconstruction of class analysis; it can, rather, be left to develop, as it has in the past, according to its own dynamic.[4]

The foregoing remarks should then be taken as important background to what is to follow. In the next section, I outline the proposals that have been made for radically new versions of class analysis by Sørensen and Grusky, and aim to bring out the main ways in which departures from existing versions of class analysis are involved. In succeeding sections I then present, from the standpoint of the non-Marxist tradition and, more specifically, of my own position within it, a critical response in which both empirical and conceptual issues are raised.

NEW VERSIONS OF CLASS ANALYSIS

Sørensen and Grusky are not of course alone in having argued the need for a renewal of class analysis. However, I choose to focus on these two authors on the following grounds.

First, a number of earlier contributions, notably Wright's various efforts (e.g., 1985, 1997) at revitalising the Marxist tradition and Bourdieu's attempt (1984) at transcending Weber's 'opposition' of class and status, while having already attracted a great deal of commentary, have led more to the modification or extension of existing research interests and practices than to their radical transformation in the way that would follow from the positions taken up by Sørensen and Grusky. At the same time, other more recent proposals, influenced, like those of Sørensen and Grusky, by the debate on the decline of class, lack the theoretical sharpness that characterises the work of these latter authors, and are thus less clear in their implications so far as the transition from programme to performance is concerned (see, e.g., Cromp-ton, 1998; Devine and Savage, 2000; Savage, 2000).

Second, Sørensen's and Grusky's proposals provide a marked and reveal-ing contrast in their theoretical orientations. Sørensen is clearly an exponent of what I have earlier referred to, following Boudon, as the individualistic paradigm within sociology. He adopts in fact a rational action approach, draws freely on classical as well as Marxist economics, and comes in the end (2005) to label his approach as 'neo-Ricardian'. Central to Sørensen's under-standing of class relations is the idea that actors in different class positions, which he defines in terms of property rights and assets, will seek to use what-ever rights and assets they posses to their best advantage, and often, thus, to the disadvantage of others. It is then the structure of the 'antagonistic' rela-tions that arise between classes and their representative organisations that Sørensen believes must be the main focus of class analysis. Inequalities in the 'life conditions' and life chances of the members of different classes and any associated subcultural variation are matters of only derivative interest. For Grusky, on the other hand, it is precisely the social processes that pro-duce subcultural variation—processes of social selection, socialisation, and institutionalisation—that are essential to class analysis. In his view, it is only insofar as classes are formed as recognisable sociocultural entities that they can shape the life chances and the attitudes and behaviour of their members, and that the latter can pursue their shared interests through collective action. A major source of inspiration for Grusky is in fact Durkheim, the historic enemy of the individualistic paradigm. And in his most recent publications (see 2005a, 2005b) Grusky explicitly describes his position on class analysis as being 'neo-Durkheimian'.[5]

I turn now to a rather more detailed statement of the positions taken up by Sørensen and Grusky, with some comments on how these relate to those of various other authors.

Sørensen

Sørensen (2000b) distinguishes three types of class concepts, associated with ascending levels of theoretical ambition:

> 1. concepts that provide for a purely nominal categorisation of populations on some dimension or dimensions (e.g., occupational prestige or socioeco-nomic status) and that can then be used to display class inequalities in life con-ditions and life chances or class differences in attitudes and behaviour;

2. concepts that aim to delineate sets of positions (as, e.g., in the class schema discussed in the previous chapter), among which individuals or families within a population are distributed and can thus be recognised as empirical collectivities with a greater or lesser degree of sociocultural formation; and

3. concepts that aim to specify classes as collectivities within populations whose members are led to engage in conflict with each other in consequence of their interests being structurally opposed: that is, opposed by virtue of the positions that they hold and the social relations in which they are thus involved.

For Sørensen, the great virtue of Marxist class theory is that it treats classes in this last, theoretically most ambitious, sense. Classes are seen as collectivities engaged in structurally induced conflict as a result of their ownership or nonownership of the means of production and of the relations of exploitation that thus arise between them. In turn, a theory of societal change—indeed a theory of history—can be based on the logic according to which such class conflict is seen as evolving. At the same time, though, Sørensen recognises that the Marxist theory can no longer be sustained, not just because its historical predictions have evidently failed but, further, because exploitation as understood by Marx depends on a subsidiary theory, the labour theory of value, that is now quite discredited. Nonetheless, Sørensen believes that it is still essential, if class analysis is to survive, that it should maintain the Marxist emphasis on classes as collectivities in 'antagonistic' relations and on the idea of exploitation as the root cause of the conflict between class and class.

It follows, therefore, that a new understanding of exploitation is required, and it is this that is then basic to Sørensen's programme for the reconstruction of class analysis. What he is proposes (2000b: 1532) is that while exploitation should still be seen, following Marx, as deriving from property rights, it should be recognised that not *all* such rights create exploitation but only those that provide for the ownership (or de facto use) of assets that produce *rents*. Sørensen defines rents in a rather catholic way but usually as returns on assets, the supply of which is limited or controlled so that it is not responsive to increases in price in the way that it would be in a perfectly competitive market economy. Those who hold rent-producing assets can thus be said to exploit those who do not hold these assets in that the former obtain economic advantage at the expense of the latter—in effect, by preventing them from realising the full return they would otherwise get from their own assets.[6]

Sørensen identifies many different kinds of rent in both modern and earlier forms of economy but concentrates on those that are chiefly to be found in labour markets (2000a, 2000b), namely, 'monopoly rents' and 'composite rents'.[7] Monopoly rents arise where employees are able to restrict the supply of their labour, as, say, through controls exercised by trade unions or professional associations over levels of recruitment, training, and qualification, and in this way increase their pay above what would be the truly competitive rate. Composite rents arise where two different assets are more productive in joint use than separately, as where employees develop human assets specific to the work carried out in particular organisations and advantage thus accrues, via internal labour markets or bureaucratic hierarchies, both to employees in the form of pay or job security higher than they could obtain in the external market and to the employer in the form of increased profit.

For Sørensen, then, the primary concern of class analysis should be with conflict among classes over rents and the exploitation they imply: that is, conflict over the creation, protection, or destruction of rents. Sørensen acknowledges that differences and inequalities in the 'life conditions' and life chances, including the mobility chances, of members of different classes will be influenced by the outcome of such conflict, and that in turn class subcultural differences may be created through processes of socialisation under different life conditions. These phenomena can also be of interest to class analysts, but only, in Sørensen's view, in a secondary and in fact limited way. In this regard, he stresses that inequalities in life conditions reflect the 'total wealth' of class members—the total return from the use of *all* their assets—but that it is only certain assets that produce rents. In other words, insofar as inequalities in total wealth and thus life conditions derive from the use of assets that does not involve rent, and that therefore does not lead to exploitation, these inequalities cannot be regarded as a source of class conflict (cf. 2000b: 1525). While they may be relevant to the description of what Sørensen calls (2000b: 1526) 'the geography of social structure', through the use of type (i) or type (ii) concepts of class, as distinguished above, they have little relevance for the analysis of the actual dynamics of class—of structurally induced class conflict and of societal change following from it—which requires the use of type (iii) concepts.

Moreover, Sørensen believes that the value of type (i) and (ii) concepts even for descriptive purposes is likely to diminish on account of the course that is actually being followed by class conflict in contemporary societies.

For Marx, the internal logic of such conflict would lead to working-class revolution and the eventual establishment of a communist form of society. But, for Sørensen (2000b), the course of history is destined to go in a quite different, indeed contrary, direction: that is, towards the ultimate triumph of capital over labour so far at least as conflict in the labour market is concerned. Employers will progressively succeed in destroying employment rents previously secured by workers and in thus creating freer, more efficient labour markets that operate in ever closer conformity with the assumptions of neoclassical economics.

Sørensen would indeed regard this process as already well under way. On the one hand, workers' monopoly rents are being undermined through attacks on the power of unions and especially through restrictions placed on their ability to organise and mobilise workers. Sørensen points here to a general decline in union membership across advanced societies, to the greater difficulties experienced by unions in obtaining bargaining rights with employers, to widening pay differentials *within* occupations, and to falling strike rates. On the other hand, composite rents are being reduced by the redesign of jobs that previously created a basis for such rents and in turn by the breakup of internal labour markets and the downsizing and delayering of administrative and managerial hierarchies. These developments are reflected in the disappearance of well-defined career structures and in more frequent layoffs, decreasing job security, and more 'payment-by-results' in all grades of employment. As, then, labour markets are reduced to what Sørensen once memorably described as 'neoclassical soup',[8] the economic fortunes of employees at all levels become overwhelmingly individualised—that is, determined by their own endowments and productive capacities. And, in turn, therefore, the very point of conceiving and representing classes by reference to occupations or differing employment relations is undermined. Economic inequalities are likely to grow but at the same time to take on an increasingly 'classless' character.

Finally, this scenario envisaged by Sørensen serves to bring out the point that the concept of exploitation that is basic to his proposed new version of class analysis has always to be understood in a strictly technical sense. It does not, as in Marxist class theory or the neo-Marxist version of class analysis pursued by Wright, serve to bridge analytical and normative concerns.[9] In other words, it does not follow for Sørensen that the elimination of rents, and in turn of exploitation and class antagonism, is a goal to be pursued—one integral, say, to the replacement of present-day capitalism by a more equal or in some sense a more just or more humane form of society. Exploitation is simply the outcome of assets being used in such a way as to create rents. And thus, insofar as it is the agents of capitalism who are destroying employment rents, it is they, rather than the revolutionary working class, who are removing exploitation and related conflict from labour markets and acting as the midwives of the classless society—a view that causes Wright (2000) some evident consternation. However, as Sørensen fully, and quite consistently, recognises, the new society may well prove to be more unequal and, by most criteria, more unjust and inhumane than that which it supersedes. Once employment rents are removed, the economic inequalities generated by the operation of the free market will be modified only through state welfare provision. And it is this, Sørensen suggests, that will in the future take over from the labour market as the main area in which class conflict as conflict over rents—rents deriving in this case from rights to welfare—is fought out.

Grusky

For Sørensen, one might say, class-based collective action must be the ultimate concern of class analysis, and his typology of class concepts is intended to underline this point. For Grusky, to retain a focus on collective action—or, as he puts it, to retain class analysis in its 'strong idiom' (Holton, 1996)—is crucial in defending it against its critics. And, if this is to be done, Grusky argues, it is essential to recognise a twofold conceptual distinction on somewhat different lines to Sørensen's threefold one: that is, the distinction between *nominalist* and *realist* concepts of class (Grusky and Sørensen, 1998; Grusky, Weeden, and Sørensen, 2000).[10] Nominalist concepts treat classes as being no more than simply aggregates of individuals who share a ranking on a scale or an allocation to a particular category of a schema of class positions (such as that discussed in the previous chapter). Realist concepts, in contrast, aim to identify classes that exist as actual sociocultural entities and, in particular, that are social groupings recognised by and meaningful to the individuals who make them up.

In Grusky's view, the most powerful argument for the 'decline of class' thesis is that class, as understood in current analysis, whether Marxist or non-Marxist, is not now an idea that seems of any great importance in individuals' everyday lives: that is, in shaping their own social identities or the 'cognitive maps' by means of which they perceive and define others. Consequently, it is unclear through just what causal processes class could be expected to provide a basis for class-linked action of any kind. If, therefore, class analysis is to be protected against this argument, what is required is that concepts of class that are, today at least, no more than nominalist should be abandoned and a new, realist approach pursued. The way in which this can be done, Grusky then proposes, is by 'ratcheting down' the level at which class analysis operates: that is, from the level of classes understood as large-scale, societal aggregates, defined, say, in terms of property rights or employment relations, to that of classes understood as more disaggregated and primarily *occupational* groupings that 'form around functional niches in the division of labor' (Grusky and Weeden, 2001: 203).

Like Sørensen, Grusky recognises that the reconstitution of class analysis that he envisages does involve a major break with conventional thinking—and is likely to meet with resistance for this reason alone (cf. Grusky and Weeden, 2002). But, he maintains, if a realist approach is to be followed, then the ratcheting down that he advocates is an entirely appropriate move to make. For it is in fact at the level of particular occupations, rather than at the level of the 'big classes' of conventional analysis, that processes conducive to the formation of real social groupings, of significance to their members, are most evident. For example, recruitment to occupations goes on through specific processes of selection, including self-selection; occupational entry is typically associated with processes of socialisation, whether formal (i.e., via training and induction programmes) or informal; and it is occupations rather than 'big classes' that gain legal and other official recognition and are most often represented by organisations such as trade unions or professional bodies (Grusky and Sørensen, 1998; Grusky, Weeden, and Sørensen, 2000; Weeden and Grusky, 2005; and cf. also Weeden, 2002).[11]

In turn, then, Grusky would argue, it is at the occupational level that one most readily observes collective action, in pursuit of interests created at 'the site of production', that is the ultimate concern of class analysis in the Marxist or at least *marxisant* tradition. Occupational groupings may not be vehicles of revolution; but it is they, rather than classes understood as societal aggregates, that typically act in order to protect and improve the economic conditions of their members. Their organisations may engage in collective bargaining with employers but also operate more generally through various 'strategies of closure' aimed at the regulation of labour supply: for example, through customary restrictions on recruitment, through credentialism and formal licensing, or by otherwise establishing 'jurisdictional' control over the kinds of work that they cover (see esp. Grusky and Sørensen, 1998; Grusky and Weeden, 2001).

In other words, Grusky would here emphasise what, for Sørensen, would be classic rent-seeking action.[12] But, unlike Sørensen, Grusky sees no reason to suppose that such action will become increasingly difficult to sustain. He notes the claims made by several authors of the emergence of a 'post-occupational' workforce as a result of the extensive deskilling of work or of its reorganisation into new polyvalent jobs. But, as strong countertendencies, he points to the specialised yet decentralised forms of work organisation of 'post-Fordism' (Piore and Sabel, 1984), which revitalise artisanal production methods and set a premium on worker solidarity and communitarianism, and again to the drive among managers and administrators and also many workers in technical and personal services to achieve 'professional' status and organisation. Indeed, once class analysis is relocated at the level of occupational groupings, Grusky believes, it will be found that collective action 'flows quite unproblematically' from such groupings. Thus, it will be possible to dispense with the argument, characteristic of the weaker idiom of the non-Marxist tradition, that class formation and collective action are to be treated not as theoretical expectations but rather as developments likely only under rather special conditions: 'The [occupational] division of labour is rife with collective action that occurs so predictably as to eliminate any need to deploy the rhetoric of contingency' (Grusky and Sørensen, 1998: 1206).[13]

Further, though, Grusky would also be ready to argue that even if class analysis is understood in a version that does not privilege issues of collective action, the disaggregated but realist approach that he favours still offers major advantages. For example, as regards class mobility, he observes that standard mobility tables, based on 'big classes', will often hide the fact that certain occupational groupings have particularly strong 'holding power'— far greater than that of any class definable at an aggregate level. And this is so because the processes of closure and thus of 'reproduction' to which conventional class analysts refer in explaining immobility operate primarily in particular occupational contexts rather than at a societal level. Mobility is in general 'governed by the deeply institutionalised boundaries between occupations rather than by the aggregate interclass boundaries fashioned by academics' (Grusky and Weeden, 2001: 208).

Likewise, insofar as interest centres on class as a determinant of life chances and, especially, of attitudes and behaviour, Grusky would claim that its effects will emerge most clearly and strongly if class is equated with occupational grouping. And again this is so because the causal processes that have to be invoked are ones most likely to be found at the occupational level. Thus, while aggregate classes are no more than collectivities defined in terms of 'nonorganic', *gesellschaftlich* relations, occupational groupings are of a generally more *gemeinschaftlich* character, and indeed genuine occupational communities can often be identified. Consequently, occupational groupings far more readily provide social contexts that can serve as the source of shared values and normative codes and in turn of distinctive lifestyles. In other words, occupational groupings, in contrast to 'big classes', tend to be both economic *and* sociocultural entities. Analysts who wish to follow the 'cultural turn' in sociology or the lead given by Bourdieu (1984) in seeking to overcome Weber's distinction between classes, which are 'not communities', and status groups, which typically are (Weber, 1922/1968: 927, 932), will therefore be best served by taking up the disaggregated approach (see esp. Grusky and Sørensen, 1998: 1192; Weeden and Grusky, 2005: 149–54).

This last point is of particular interest and merits a final comment. The view that it is desirable to conceptualise classes as sociocultural as well as economic entities is of course by no means specific to Grusky. Of late, a number of other authors have argued on similar lines, usually under the influence of Bourdieu and in reaction to the view that the sociocultural formation of classes should be treated as merely contingent (see, e.g., Devine and Savage, 2000; Savage, 2000). However, what is then important to note is that these authors have not been as ready as Grusky to consider the implications of this position. That is to say, they have tended to rely on the largely unquestioned assumption that distinctive cultures or subcultures can still be associated with classes as understood in some more or less conventional fashion (cf. ch. 4, this volume, pp. 81–4) and to neglect the possibility that, at least in the context of modern societies, what Grusky labels as a neo-Durkheimian approach to class analysis cannot in fact be pursued *without* the quite radical revisionism that is involved in his regrounding of the enterprise at the occupational level.

Having outlined the proposals that Sørensen and Grusky advance for the reconstruction of class analysis, I now turn to a critical evaluation from the standpoint of my own position. From what has already been said, it will be apparent that some differences must from the first arise over the socio-logical purposes that class analysis is intended to serve. However, I wish as far as possible to avoid questions of what class analysis ought 'really' to be about. Rather, I organise my critique under the three substantive heads of class structure, class effects, and class action. In regard to the first of these topics I am chiefly concerned with various empirical issues that arise from the respective cases that Sørensen and Grusky make out for their new ver-sions of class analysis. In regard to the second and third topics, I take up conceptual as well as empirical issues relating to the implications for class analysis that would appear to follow from their proposals and that I would regard as in various respects problematic. The upshot of my critique is that while research programmes associated with these proposals may well pro-duce results of considerable sociological interest in, as it were, their own right, they cannot provide an adequate substitute for class analysis in the more conventional sense that I would myself favour.

CLASS STRUCTURE

Both Sørensen and Grusky are sceptical of, and seek to move away from, the idea of a class structure as this is understood in more conventional forms of class analysis: that is, as a structure of positions defined by social relations within labour markets and production units. For Sørensen, such an idea could be of value only in a descriptive sense—it would not in itself throw light on the sources and dynamics of class conflict—but it is now, in any event, being outmoded by the course of change in employment relations as contemporary capitalism creates its own version of the classless society. For Grusky, the conventional idea of a class structure is primarily a construct of sociologists, and one that, by the present time at least, does not map at all closely onto the ways in which social relations at 'the site of production' are actually experienced and understood by individuals in their everyday lives. Occupation, not (aggregate) class, is the dominant subjective reality, and sociologists need to acknowledge this if they are to be more successful in analysing how employment and its consequences impact on individuals and how they respond.

The arguments that Sørensen and Grusky here put forward, and that play a large part in justifying their claims that class analysis requires radical revision, have clearly differing motivation and direction but they are, I believe, alike open to question on various empirical grounds.

The claims that Sørensen makes regarding the dissolution of class structure, despite their different—and more rigorous—theoretical derivation, show evident affinities with those of globalisation theorists (as examined in vol. I, ch. 5) and also with those of authors (referred in the previous chapter, such as Halford and Savage), who believe that what I have called the service relationship is now being eroded as the typical form of regulation of the employment of professional and managerial staff. In my discussion of the supposed impact of globalisation on class structure (vol. I, ch. 5, pp. 1–107), I have already cited some of the evidence that, I believe, undermines such claims. Here, I refer back to this material and also note further relevant research findings.

The central issue to be considered may be set up as follows. In the previous chapter, I suggested that differences in employment relations should be taken as the basis for distinguishing class positions and thus for delineating the class structure. Sørensen's argument is in effect that these differences are fast disappearing as a result of the growing power of capital in labour markets. While the elimination of monopoly rents tends to widen inequalities in earnings within occupational groupings, the elimination of composite rents has a homogenising effect across different categories of employee as all employment contracts move closer in form to spot contracts and labour is in effect commodified. Thus, professional and managerial staff lose the well-defined career prospects that they previously enjoyed and become exposed to a similar degree of economic insecurity and instability as are rank-and-file workers. However, I would maintain that Sørensen's position here lacks adequate empirical support and indeed that the relevant research results that are available tell quite strongly against it.

First, as regards the risks of job loss and unemployment, there is, so far as I am aware, no consistent evidence to show that these are converging across classes in the way that Sørensen would suppose. In the case of Britain, where high quality longitudinal data exist, the most notable research finding is in fact, as I previously noted (vol. I: ch. 5, p. 103), the degree of stability over time that class differentials in these risks display, although large fluctuations may of course occur in the overall level of unemployment (cf. Gallie et al., 1998; Elias and McKnight, 2003). Moreover, the differentials are marked. Thus, being in unskilled wage work increases the odds of experiencing recurrent or long-term unemployment almost fourfold relative to the odds for members of the higher salariat, and even when a range of individual attributes is controlled (Goldthorpe and McKnight, 2006).

Second, as regards career prospects, there would likewise seem no compelling evidence for Sørensen's position. Again as earlier noted (vol. I, ch. 5: pp. 103–105), claims of a decline in the stock of 'career-type' positions in the American economy have been strongly challenged. And, further, the results of a major survey of working conditions in Britain in 2000 have been summed up as follows (Taylor, 2002: 7): 'The evidence simply does not sustain the view that we are witnessing the emergence of a "new" kind of employment relations, seen in the "end of the career" and "the death of the permanent job for life"'. In fact, the research in question finds the average length of job tenure to be *rising,* and *especially among* professional and managerial employees. Moreover, the large majority of these employees reported that they were in jobs with promotion ladders and recognised career structures.

Third, while in many, but not all, advanced societies inequalities in earnings have of late tended to widen, and within as well as between occupations and classes, there is little indication that this is associated with any major change in payment systems. Thus, in Britain, despite some tendency for 'payment by results', in one version or another, to be extended to professional and managerial employees, it emerges (Goldthorpe and McKnight, 2006: Table 2) that this and other potentially variable forms of pay still average out, in the case of men, at only around 7 percent of the total earnings of these employees, in contrast to a variable component in the earnings of male manual workers averaging out at over 20 percent. Furthermore, it is also apparent that little change has occurred over recent decades in class differences in the relation between earnings and age. For manual workers, and also for women in routine nonmanual work, age-earnings curves tend to flatten out by around age 30, while for members of the salariat they continue to rise up to around age 50—consistently, that is, with the 'upward-sloping experience-earnings profile' characteristic of the service relationship (Goldthorpe and McKnight, 2006: Figures 3–6; and see further McKnight, 2004: ch. 4).

That Sørensen's position finds so little evidence in its favour reflects, I would suggest, the error of his assumption that employment rents, like all other rents, always and necessarily imply inefficiency. The service relationship may indeed create composite rents, but it does not then follow that it involves an inefficient form of employment contract. Although employers have good reason, all else equal, to prefer approximations to spot contracts, with types of work that give rise to problems of human asset specificity and also of monitoring (which Sørensen tends to neglect), the rationale of the service relationship—relative security in working life and a steadily rising level of compensation in return for 'appraised' service in the interests of the employing organisation—is likely to provide a more efficient mode of regulation of employment: that is, one better suited to maximising the total value of the contract, even though employers and employees may well be in conflict over how this total value should be divided. And employers as rational actors will tend, overall, to recognise that employment relations embody positive-sum as well as negative-sum games.[14]

The same body of evidence that can be marshalled against Sørensen also provides a basis for questioning Grusky's rejection of the idea of a class structure. Although this evidence does not stand in direct contradiction to the position that Grusky takes up, it does serve to raise the issue of whether, in urging that class analysis be ratcheted down to the occupational level, Grusky is not missing something important: that is, features of their economic lives that individuals *across a wide range of occupations have in common.* Is it in fact the case that the differences in economic security, stability, and prospects that exist among members of 'big classes', as defined in terms of employment relations (cf. Goldthorpe and McKnight, 2006), are in fact present to no less a degree among their constituent occupational groupings, so that thinking in terms of classes adds little or nothing of value? Grusky has not in fact demonstrated that that this is so, and I would think it generally implausible.[15]

There is of course no reason why differences in occupational subcultures and social networks of the kind that Grusky emphasises should not coexist with similarities in economic circumstances deriving from similar employment relations. Thus, for example, factory machinists, bus drivers, and security guards could differ markedly in the former respects while still being quite comparable in the latter, as also could, say, plant managers, accountants, and librarians. And even if particular occupations may appear to have distinctive economic features—a high or low level of layoffs, especially favourable or unfavourable promotion opportunities, unusually variable pay, and so on—it would still seem dangerous simply to discount the possibility that these may be no more than occupational variations on strong class themes.

Grusky could of course reply that, however this may be, it scarcely bears on his claim that sociologists' aggregate classes are insufficiently realist—that is, find insufficient correspondence in individuals' everyday social awareness. This may actually be a claim that Grusky pushes rather too hard;[16] but, aside from this, a further, more serious issue arises. If it is the case that classes defined in terms of employment relations form collectivities of individuals and families whose economic lives do have much in common, underlying any occupational variation, then one may ask why conceptual schemes that represent such classes should not, on these grounds, be regarded as just as 'realist' as those representing occupational groupings. Or, as Grusky would seem to imply, is only what is generally recognised by 'lay actors' to count as social reality—thus excluding the possibility of sociologists identifying aspects of this reality that are not readily apparent to lay actors? In certain lines of investigation, in regard to class or more generally, it will clearly be essential for sociologists to take actors' concepts into account, and in turn how these concepts relate to their own. But for other purposes, I would maintain, it is entirely permissible and indeed desirable that sociologists should be free to develop concepts, and render them operational, without their degree of correspondence to those of lay actors being of primary concern. Class structure in a conventional sense I would see as being a concept of this kind. And it has then to be judged not by its degree of 'realism', in Grusky's rather special usage of this word, but by what it contributes to sociological understanding. This is a point that will recur with some importance in the section that follows.

CLASS EFFECTS

Both Sørensen and Grusky start out from the view that the central focus of class analysis should remain, as it was for Marx, on class-based collective action. The question of how class impacts on individuals, influencing their life chances and their attitudes and behaviour is, for them, of only secondary interest. Still, in advancing their proposals for new versions of class analysis, both do give attention to this question and, as will be seen, it is one that Grusky has taken up in systematic empirical research. In this section, however, I seek to show that Sørensen's and Grusky's proposals alike carry troublesome consequences so far as the study of class effects is concerned.

To begin with Sørensen, the main difficulty to which I wish to point stems from his equation of class conflicts and conflicts over rents. What has to be recognised in this regard is that conflicts over rents are both highly heterogeneous and differentiated. Thus, conflicts over employment rents are conflicts that arise not only between employers and workers but also among different groups of workers. That is to say, those employees who gain monopoly rents or composite rents in labour markets do so not only at the expense of employers but also at the expense of—or, as Sørensen would say, through the exploitation of—other employees or potential employees, often ones in similar grades of work or with similar qualifications.[17] At the same time, employers (or their agents) may of course be in conflict with each other over rents associated with the securing or terminating of business monopolies or of licenses, franchises, patents. and so on. And, further, the social welfare rents that Sørensen would see as destined to become increasingly important, and indeed to replace labour market rents as the main area of class conflict, are ones likely to set against each other any number of different categories of welfare claimants and taxpayers.

Now such conflicts over rents obviously do occur and sociologists should certainly pay more attention to them. Moreover, if Sørensen wishes to treat these conflicts as class conflicts, involving exploitation, there is little point in objecting in principle, despite the conceptual turbulence thus created. However, what can be pertinently observed is the following. If one were to take up Sørensen's innovation at the level of what he would distinguish as type (iii) class concepts—those aimed at identifying collectivities that are brought into conflict by structurally opposed interests—then the actual lines of class conflict that would be traced within a modern society would be of an extremely complex, cross-cutting, and probably quite unstable kind. Consequently, it is difficult to see how these lines of conflict could in any intelligible way map onto the inequalities in life chances—including chances of class mobility—or again onto the differences in attitudes and behaviour that would be established using any existing class concepts of Sørensen's types (i) or (ii). And it is likewise difficult to see how new type (i) or (ii) concepts could be derived from Sørensen's rent-based approach that would be serviceable and revealing in empirical research, and especially when one recalls that, for Sørensen, differences in individuals' total wealth, and thus in their life conditions, stem only *in part* from their success in securing rents. The use of assets that does not involve rents may well lead to inequalities in 'total wealth' but, in Sørensen's view, without thereby resulting in exploitation or thus creating any objective grounds for conflict.

In sum, one could say, Sørensen's concern to provide a new basis for class analysis, understood primarily as the analysis of conflicts between collectivities arising out of structurally opposed interests, does not allow for this to be undertaken in an integrated way with the study of class effects at the individual level. The latter, under Sørensen's proposals, would not simply be relegated to a secondary place in class analysis; it would in effect have to be split off as a more or less separate area of enquiry.

Turning now to Grusky, his proposal for ratcheting down class analysis to the occupational level is also aimed at enabling classes to be seen as an 'unproblematic' source of collective action. But Grusky does at the same time maintain that class analysis in this new version will be better suited than more conventional versions to investigating class effects and, in particular, will allow sociologists to move more readily from establishing associations or correlations between class and 'outcome' variables to tracing the actual causal processes involved. Indeed, little progress in this latter respect is likely to be made 'without abandoning aggregate formulations' (Grusky and Weeden, 2001: 209; cf. Weeden and Grusky, 2005).

Behind this claim lies, of course, Grusky's conviction that it is only when classes can be treated as in some significant degree sociocultural as well as economic entities that it is possible to see how they might exert an influence over their individual members: that is, through shared values and social norms and institutionalised practices. However, as against this, I would wish to return to the general argument that I have already elaborated and applied in regard to class differentials in educational attainment (chs. 2–4, this volume, and also vol. I, ch. 8, pp. 172–3): namely, that adequate microfoundations for class analysis can often be provided without appeal to causal processes that depend on classes possessing a high degree of sociocultural formation. Many kinds of social regularity can in fact be understood simply as the result of individuals acting in a (subjectively and boundedly) rational way in response to the differing patterns of constraint and opportunity by which their class situations are characterised (cf. Korpi and Palme, 2003).[18] And what then, from this point of view, is chiefly important about concepts of class is that they should capture these differing patterns of constraint and opportunity as effectively as possible, and not that they should relate to groupings that are 'real' in Grusky's sense. Indeed, it may sometimes be that the attempt to achieve such realism by ratcheting down class analysis to the occupational level rather than concentrating on what individuals across a range of occupations have in common, such as the form of their employment relations and its typical consequences, leads to a loss rather than a gain in explanatory potential.

This point is well brought out in regard to class mobility: that is, in regard to the effects of individuals' origin positions on their subsequent chances of remaining in these positions or moving from them. As earlier noted, Grusky contends that mobility is governed primarily by 'institutionalised boundaries between occupations' and that the effects of these boundaries in creating social closure and class reproduction are likely to be lost in work based on aggregate classes. However, the case he makes here rests largely on analyses of *intra*generational, or worklife, mobility (Sørensen and Grusky, 1996) and is far more questionable when considered in relation to *inter*generational mobility. It is true that some occupations tend, for various reasons, to have relatively high 'holding power' in inter- as well as intragenerational perspective: for instance, those of doctor or coal miner. But research into intergenerational mobility is concerned not only or even primarily with why doctors' children have a high propensity to become doctors or coal miners' sons a high propensity to become coal miners. More important are such questions as why those doctors' children (the majority) who do not become doctors are far more likely to move into other professional or managerial occupations than to become manual wage workers, or why those coal miners' sons who do not become miners (again the majority) are far more likely to move into some other kind of wage work than to become professionals or managers. And to treat these questions adequately, attention has then to focus on features of the *shared* class situations of members of the professional and managerial salariat and of the body of wage workers, and on central tendencies in the responses that they make to these situations (as I seek to show in the chapter that follows). The institutional boundaries of particular occupations or the closure practices of their members can be of little relevance.

Grusky does in fact recognise this difficulty but argues (Grusky and Sørensen, 1998: 1205; cf. Grusky and Weeden, 2001: 208–209) that the tendency to represent 'supply-side' effects in processes of intergenerational class mobility and immobility as being 'so diffuse in character that they necessarily generate reproduction at the level of [aggregate] classes rather than occupations' may do no more than reflect the limitations of research to date; through further research, following a disaggregated approach, more 'occupation-specific' processes may be revealed. This must of course remain to be seen. But scepticism is, I believe, warranted, and primarily on the grounds that 'closure' and 'reproduction' do not in any event seem apt concepts to apply in the case of intergenerational mobility, whatever value they may have in analysing worklife mobility. In intergenerational perspective, classes are not in any meaningful sense closed nor is class membership reproduced—if only because of the absolute amount of mobility that is typically generated by class structural change (Goldthorpe, 1987: ch. 2; cf. Erikson and Goldthorpe, 1992b: ch. 6; Breen and Luijkx, 2004a).[19] Where some notable degree of reproduction, over both time and place, could be claimed is in the underlying mobility regimes of advanced societies, as defined in terms of relative rather than absolute mobility rates (again see Chapter 7, this volume). But it is then in accounting for this 'deep' reproduction that a reliance on occupationally specific factors, which are likely themselves to be quite variable over time and space, would seem especially inadequate and that more generalised class effects will be of primary importance.[20]

It could perhaps be argued that mobility is a rather special case and that Grusky's approach, emphasising effects that could derive only from collectivities that have some degree of sociocultural formation, will prove more appropriate in other respects. Here in fact Grusky's own empirical work is relevant. Grusky has sought to investigate the explanatory power of 'big classes' as compared with that of a highly disaggregated, 126-category occupational classification in relation to a range of some 50 'outcome' variables, both attitudinal and behavioural, extending across four different 'topical domains'—with explanation being understood, for the time being, simply in terms of degree of association.[21]

Results so far available (Weeden and Grusky, 2005) indicate that, from domain to domain, a version of the class schema described in the previous chapter leaves unexplained from around half to three-quarters of the association that can be established between the occupational classification and the outcome variables. Grusky regards such results as strongly supporting his position: that is, as demonstrating that the explanatory power of any such 'nominalist' schema is necessarily limited. However, I too would regard the results reported as being encouraging, and especially when three further points are noted. First, the version of the class schema here used excludes one class, the petty bourgeoisie, that has often proved to be highly distinctive. Second, many of the outcome variables considered are simply not ones in regard to which more conventional class analysts would expect any marked class effects to be present: for example, variables relating to marital history and status, satisfaction from family life, religious beliefs and participation, or attitudes to abortion, pornography, homosexuality, or the treatment of criminals. And third, it is in the one domain where such class effects *would* be expected, the domain of life chances, that they do in fact show up most strongly—the six-class schema in this case accounting for more than half of the association found with the 126 occupational categories—and even though the particular outcomes included here are still not those that, theoretically, should be most closely linked to class in the sense represented by the schema.[22]

How, then, is it that I as well as Grusky can view his findings with some satisfaction? What has to be understood here is that Grusky seeks, ideally, to capture *all kinds of effects* deriving from 'the site of production'. This is, in his view, the task of class analysis, and his disaggregated occupational classification is designed to meet this task: that is, to pick up effects that are quite specific to particular occupations as well as effects that operate far more generally. The classification should therefore—and does—have more explanatory power, in the sense here in question, than the class schema. But the schema derives from a tradition of class analysis in which class positions are defined by reference only to *certain features* of social relations at the site of production—in my case, the kind of employment relations in which individuals are involved—that many occupations will have in common. And, in turn, class effects will be expected to show up only insofar as some plausible *causal* connection can be suggested between an outcome variable and these defining features.[23] Thus, while the schema does, unsurprisingly, explain less, in terms of degree of association with many outcome variables, than the disaggregated classification, it still should—and does—explain enough to show that 'aggregate' class effects are of real importance, and that conceptual clarity is seriously impaired if these effects are simply lost sight of in a plethora of more specific occupational effects of a highly heterogeneous character.[24]

It could perhaps be held that the issue between Grusky and me comes down in the end largely to one of labelling and is not therefore of any great consequence. What he would present as a new version of class analysis, I would rather see as a way of revitalising the sociology of occupations: in effect, by moving it on from a preoccupation with more or less ad hoc case studies. This does, though, still mean that I would have to view Grusky's proposed programme as being complementary to class analysis in some more conventional form and not as providing a substitute for it. And one other rather basic issue has in this connection to be raised.

This is that Grusky has, so far at least, given only very preliminary indication of how he would treat the question of *hierarchy* within the detailed occupational classification that he has developed (Grusky and Weeden, 2006).[25] Now from the standpoint of the sociology of occupations, there is in fact no requirement to take this matter further: occupations can and do differ from each other in many consequential ways that are not hierarchical, in the sense that they do not involve systematic social inequalities. However, while many conventional class analysts, myself included, would not envisage classes as always falling into a single hierarchical ordering (see chs. 2 and 5, this volume; and cf. Dahrendorf, 1959: 74–77; Giddens, 1973: 106), all would of course view class structures as being, preeminently, structures of social inequality. Thus, from my own position, members of different classes are advantaged and disadvantaged in differing, if not always entirely commensurable, respects as a result of the employment relations in which they are involved. And it is the inequalities that thus arise that are seen in turn as driving class differences in 'outcomes' across a range of life chances and life choices. But it remains to be seen just how, on the basis of Grusky's decomposition of class structure into occupational structure systematic social inequalities are to be recognised and, if so, in what terms they are to be understood.[26]

CLASS ACTION

Sørensen would believe that the ultimate concern of class analysis has still to be with class-based collective action. Marxist class theory has manifestly failed but the spirit of Marx must in this respect be preserved, even if this means that class analysis has otherwise to be radically transformed. Thus, it is essential to identify as classes groups that are in conflict with each other on account of their structurally opposed interests—hence, the crucial role given to rent as the source of exploitation. Grusky would likewise believe that for class analysis to be securely defended against its critics, it should seek to retain its 'strong idiom'. To make this possible, classes must be understood as groupings that show a significant degree of sociocultural formation and are thus meaningful to their members as well as to sociologists—hence, the need to ratchet down class analysis to the occupational level.

Taken on their own terms, both these strategies can claim some evident potential. Sørensen can point to numerous and varied examples of collectivities that are engaged in conflict over rents of one kind or another, and Grusky can point to the frequency with which occupational groupings pursue their interests through representative organisations and through formal or informal efforts at closure (cf. also Weeden, 2002).

However, what has here again to be noted is that the attempts that Sørensen and Grusky make to reconstitute class analysis carry their own limitations, and that, so far as class action is concerned, the limitation that they have in common is of a rather ironic nature. In attempting to overcome the problems of Marxist class theory by moving class analysis in a neo-Ricardian and a neo-Durkheimian direction respectively, Sørensen and Grusky alike make it difficult to give due recognition to class action of the kind that primarily concerned Marx: that is, class action occurring not at a sectional or local but rather at a *societal* level.

Sørensen wishes to treat all conflict over rent as being class conflict and, further, all class conflict as being conflict over rent. But since, as already noted, conflicts over rent are highly heterogeneous and differentiated, they are in turn essentially sectional and often, too, cross-cutting—so that some groups may be exploiters in one context but exploited in another.[27] It is then difficult to see how, in modern societies at least, conflict over rents could ever become class conflict on a totalising, societal scale. Sørensen does indeed appear to acknowledge this when he remarks that class conflict, in his conception of it, will be more severe under feudalism than capitalism precisely because, under feudalism, one axis of conflict, that arising over rents from *land,* is dominant. In advanced capitalist societies, where the distribution of advantage and disadvantage from rents is complex and changing, 'no revolution has occurred' (2000b: 1541).

The occupationally based action on which Grusky would focus, though perhaps on a less complex pattern in being largely restricted to labour markets, is likewise essentially sectional or, as Grusky himself often puts it, 'localised'. Occupational groupings pursue their particular interests not only against employers over pay and conditions but also, through their attempts at controlling labour supply, against others who are seeking to sell their labour. And Grusky, in a somewhat similar way to Sørensen, would appear to believe that the counterpart to this occupational restriction of collective action—or that is, to labour markets becoming 'Durkheimianised'—is the containment and reduction of class conflict at the macro-level, which, Grusky remarks, emerged in threatening form 'for only a brief historical moment'. In general, micro-level organization 'can crowd out and substitute for class formation of a more aggregate sort' (Grusky: 2005b: 56).

What Sørensen and Grusky would both appear to assume here is that class conflict on a societal scale must involve, at least so far as the subordinate, working class is concerned, action that is revolutionary in character. In other words, they envisage no alternative to the full, and by now generally discarded, Marxist model. However, one of the main concerns of the non-Marxist tradition of class analysis has from its inception been with the possibility, and in some instances the actuality, of class action on a societal scale that is not revolutionary, at least in a Marxist sense: that is, action aimed at the radical modification of capitalism rather than its overthrow and pursued primarily through the institutions of liberal democracy.

In those cases where such action is most readily documented, labour movements have typically pressed for wide-ranging and redistributive developments in social welfare policy that in effect set up an opposition between 'citizenship' and 'social class' and that are aimed at 'class abatement' in regard to inequalities of both opportunity and condition alike (Marshall, 1947). And greatest success in this regard would appear to have been achieved where organised labour has been able to engage in a 'political exchange' (Pizzorno, 1978) with governments, especially social-democratic governments, in which it offers cooperation in macroeconomic policy—for example, over the regulation of pay increases and labour market flexibility—in return for advances in social welfare policy. The most notable examples of such a 'democratic translation of the class struggle', to use Korpi's (1983) phrase, are provided by Scandinavian nations, most notably Sweden and Norway. But variants of essentially the same process have been widely discussed, most commonly under the labels of 'social partnership' or 'neo-corporatism', with reference to a wider range of European societies.[28]

Moreover, what emerges from the relevant body of research is that the effectiveness of such class-based action crucially results from trade union confederations having sufficient organisational and strategic capacity to be able to overcome occupational or other sectional and localised interests in labour markets. This enables them to become credible and reliable actors in what Korpi refers to as 'societal bargaining' and in this way to pursue class interests of, precisely, an aggregated kind (see, e.g., Lehmbruch and Schmitter, eds., 1982; Goldthorpe, ed., 1984; Garrett, 1998; and cf. vol. I, ch. 5, pp. 98–100).[29] Grusky is therefore supported in his view of micro- and macrolevel organisation as being in some degree of tension, but not in supposing that, under some kind of Durkheimian law, the former must always and everywhere prevail over the latter. As Birkelund (2002: 219) has observed, in a critique of Grusky from a Scandinavian standpoint, national confederations representing organised class interests do there exist and clearly exert power at a societal level. Thus, even if classes, in the conventional sense, are only doubtfully formed as *gemeinschaftliche* entities, an awareness of class interests can still exist and find significant expression (see also Korpi and Palme, 2003).

As against such criticism, Grusky's main line of defence (Grusky and Weeden, 2001: 214; 2002: 230–31) is that the continuing sociopolitical relevance of class organisation and action at a societal level may amount to no more than Scandinavian exceptionalism—itself of questionable durability. And Sørensen, as already noted, would point to the growing ascendancy of capital over labour in the advanced societies of the present day as manifested in falling union membership and declining power, both industrial and political. These responses can certainly claim some degree of empirical support. Over recent decades a clear tendency has emerged for social partnership or neocorporatist arrangements, where they existed, to be weakened or less frequently used, and chiefly as a result of employers and governments being less ready to participate. At the same time, collective bargaining has become generally more decentralised on sectoral, industrial, or occupational lines. Nonetheless, on the other side of the argument, the two following points have to be stressed.

First, as was remarked at the outset, class analysis in the non-Marxist tradition does not carry the theoretical expectation that class action on a societal scale will in fact come about, whether in a revolutionary *or* a reformist mode. It is rather concerned with the conditions that make such action more or less probable. This may be seen as a resort to 'the rhetoric of contingency', to use Grusky's phrase, when, by moving down to the occupational level, collective action could be treated as quite predictable. However, what is required by the more conventional position is that classes should be so conceptualised that action that transcends sectional and localised concerns, insofar as it does occur, *can in fact be recognised* rather than being precluded from consideration *ab initio*—which would, it seems, be the case with the new versions of class analysis that Sørensen and Grusky propose.

Second, and by way of underlining the importance of this first point, it should be noted that not all current changes in the political economies of advanced societies do in fact run in the same direction. For example, *contra* Sørensen, it can be observed that the decline in the density of trade union membership is not universal. In a number of societies, mostly in fact ones with neocorporatist traditions, density has been maintained over recent years or has actually been increasing, chiefly through the wider recruitment of nonmanual employees (for statistics, see Ebbinghaus and Visser, 2000; Iversen and Pontusson, 2000). And *contra* Grusky it can be pointed out that two tendencies that *are* virtually universal are, on the one hand, that towards union amalgamation, which has seen the growth of general or 'conglomerate' unions at the expense chiefly of craft and other single-occupation unions, and, on the other hand, that towards a reduction in the number of affiliates that national confederations comprise (Ebbinghaus and Visser, 2000). These, then, are tendencies that should obviously facilitate rather than impede action at a supra-occupational level. And indeed, as several authors have recently argued, the extent to which processes of institutionalised class conflict—and compromise—have declined should not be exaggerated. Even if employers and governments have sought to withdraw from older forms of societal bargaining, there is little indication that in 'coordinated' as opposed to 'liberal' market economies—those, say, of northern Europe as opposed to those of the United States or Britain—either of these parties would wish to lose the 'institutional comparative advantage' of being able to engage in negotiations with organisations capable of representing labour at the level of classes and, increasingly, those of nonmanual as well as manual workers (see, e.g., Iversen and Pontusson, 2000; Hall and Soskice, 2001; Thelen, 2001). Moreover, from this point of view, the increased competitive pressures resulting from globalisation appear more as a conservative than as a destructive force.[30]

In short, it would, as of now, still seem premature to suppose that if sociologists wish to retain an interest in class action on a societal scale, then it is one that they will have to pursue in historical rather than contemporary contexts, and that class analysis for the future should be accordingly reconstituted.

The main lines of argument of this chapter might then be summed up in the following way. Both Sørensen and Grusky, in seeking to preserve a *marxisant* style of class analysis, with its primary emphasis on collective action, propose new versions that would, in effect, largely displace class analysis from the field of macrosociology. In particular, the idea of a class structure, identifiable at a societal level, would lose its significance.

In the case of Sørensen, this is the consequence of his concern that central to class analysis should be the 'antagonistic' relations that arise out of exploitation, which must then, in his view, mean relations that are expressed in conflicts over rent. But such conflicts are ones that, in modern societies at least, occur in several different domains, that at the macro-level are as likely to cross-cut as to aggregate, and that cannot therefore be easily related to the overall pattern of class-linked inequalities of condition and opportunity. And in any event such inequalities are, for Sørensen, only partially the outcome of success in securing rents. In the case of Grusky, the retreat from the macro-level is more deliberate. It follows from his concern to ground class analysis in real—that is, occupational—groupings, from which effects at the individual level and related collective action can be expected to flow in a far more regular way than from 'big classes'. The latter, as primarily sociologists' constructs, carry little subjective significance for the individuals who are corralled into them.

This downward shift in focus entailed by Sørensen's and Grusky's proposals may well in itself prove sociologically rewarding. The kind of action that Sørensen would regard as rent seeking is pervasive, and no doubt does occur as much or more *within* than between classes as conventionally understood. It would certainly merit more systematic study from those concerned with the sociology of economic life. And Grusky is surely correct in supposing that if one wishes to identify collectivities within labour markets and production units that have some significant degree of sociocultural formation, then occupational groupings offer more promising possibilities than do aggregate classes. To map out the extent of such formation across the occupational structures of modern economies could well provide a new starting point for the sociology of occupations.[31] However, this does not mean that either Sørensen's or Grusky's proposals amount to an adequate alternative to class analysis as more usually practised. Several implications follow from them that are problematic, especially in regard to the study of class effects, including on chances of mobility, and class action.

In Sørensen's case, the evident difficulty is that the analysis of class effects can no longer be integrated with that of class action. The patterns of inequality in individuals' life chances and of differences in their attitudes and behaviour that can be associated with different locations within the class structure need not have, and are indeed unlikely to have, any close correspondence with the structure of conflicts over rents. The latter will in only a quite limited way relate to the former as either cause or effect.

In Grusky's case, difficulties arise chiefly from the fact that his concentration on the occupational level leads to a neglect of what, at the level of class structure—as delineated, say, in terms of employment relations—members of different occupational groupings may have in common. In regard to class mobility chances, at least as viewed in intergenerational perspective, this neglect threatens a serious explanatory deficit, since 'aggregate' class effects would appear of far greater relevance than occupationally specific ones. And in regard to differences in attitudes and behaviour, the distinction between these two kinds of effects becomes obscured, and thus in turn the distinction between, on the one hand, effects that can be traced back to class-linked inequalities at the macro-level and, on the other, those stemming from distinctive features of particular occupations, including ones that may not imply social inequalities of any kind. Significant regularities in individuals' orientations and actions can in fact be produced simply in consequence of their rationally intelligible responses to the differing constraints and opportunities to which their class situations give rise. And while bringing in occupationally specific factors may well increase variance explained, and allow greater causal importance to be given to shared values and social norms, it is unclear what, from the standpoint of class analysis, is gained if links to an economically grounded structure of inequality cannot then be made.

Finally, in Grusky's approach as in Sørensen's, class action has to be seen as being of an essentially sectional or localised kind. Both would believe, if for differing reasons, that class-based action on a societal scale, organised and pursued in such a way as to overcome intraclass differences is, or is on the way to becoming, a thing of the past, and need not therefore figure on the agenda of a class analysis for the future. This view would seem to be too much influenced by the historic failure of Marxist predictions of revolutionary working class action while giving too little weight to the far from negligible number of national cases in which still today societal bargaining, involving organisations capable of representing class interests at a macro-level, remains an important process within their political economies—and one therefore that class analysts will still wish to keep within their conceptual field.

CHAPTER SEVEN

Outline of a Theory of Social Mobility*

It would be widely recognised among sociologists that the field of social mobility research is that in which quantitative techniques of data collection and, especially, of data analysis have reached their highest levels of sophistication. However, such recognition could not be taken to imply approval. A series of articles by sociologists both within and outside the field could be cited (but see esp. Miller, 1998) in which it is charged that the concern with technique has become excessive and has had seriously detrimental consequences in at least two respects. On the one hand, it is held, the problems that are pursued by mobility researchers are to an undue degree chosen in the light of technique—that is, because they appear readily treatable via some favoured procedure; while, on the other hand, the preoccupation with quantitative analysis and the results that it produces has led to a crude empiricism and to an avoidance, or at least a disregard, of central theoretical issues.

As will be apparent from what I have written elsewhere (see, e.g., vol. I, ch. 6), I can have some sympathy with this latter claim. Sociologists engaging in the quantitative analysis of social mobility, or indeed of other macrosocial phenomena, have, I believe, often shown an insufficient appreciation of the importance of theory and, in particular, in failing to see that such analysis, no matter how sophisticated it may be, cannot itself substitute for theory in providing explanations of the empirical findings that it produces. At the same time, though, I would regard the former claim—that the range

*This is an extended, reorganised, and largely rewritten version of the chapter of the same title that appeared in the first edition of *On Sociology*. For help, advice, and constructive criticism, I am indebted to Richard Breen, Robert Erikson, David Firth, Michelle Jackson, Janne Jonsson, Ruud Luijkx, and Colin Mills.

of problems treated in mobility research is unduly restricted by technical considerations—as being mistaken and indeed as betraying a lack of understanding of what has happened in the field. It is not difficult to show how successive technical advances have permitted the more successful treatment of problems, *which for long antedated them* (Goldthorpe, 2005). And, further, even if the researchers who have made and exploited these advances have often neglected the need for their work to be complemented by appropriate theory, this does not mean that the results of their analyses have been without theoretical significance. To the contrary, the new findings that have been produced have made it far clearer than before just what the focus of a theory of social mobility should be—that is, just what such a theory should, and should not, seek to explain—and at the same time have revealed major problems with both the content and the form of the theory that has for long been of main influence in the field.

In this chapter I aim, first of all, to develop the above argument and then to move on to outline a new theory of social mobility. In its general conception this theory is inspired by the findings that advances in quantitative analyses have made possible, and it has, I believe, the potential to provide a fairly coherent explanation of these findings.

NEW FINDINGS AND THEIR GENERAL THEORETICAL IMPLICATIONS

The major illustration of my claim that technical advances in mobility research have proved to be of major theoretical significance is provided by the application, from the mid-1970s onwards, of loglinear (and logmultiplicative) modelling and then of logistic regression techniques to the analysis of mobility data.[1]

Mobility researchers realised at an early stage that where, as is virtually always the case, the marginal distributions of standard mobility tables—that is, the distributions defining the 'origins' and 'destinations' of possible mobility trajectories—were not identical, some amount of mobility would for this reason alone necessarily be displayed: it would not be arithmetically possible for all cases in the table to fall on the main diagonal. An issue which then came to attract much attention was that of how this 'structural' (or 'forced') mobility might be differentiated from that which could be thought of as occurring, independently of any marginal discrepancies, in the form of mutually offsetting instances of 'exchange' (or 'circulation') mobility. The efforts made to resolve this matter were in one way or another based on an accounting identity of the form:

Total mobility − Structural mobility ≡ Exchange mobility

However, this approach **did not** lead to any very satisfactory outcome. It entailed an attempt at partitioning total mobility into two notional components that could be identified only at the supra-individual, or macrosocial, level, whereas the mobility table itself was a record of individual cases. Not until the introduction of loglinear modelling was the difficulty overcome, although not, it should be said, directly by the application of this technique but rather by a new conceptualisation that the application prompted (cf. Hauser et al., 1975; Goldthorpe, Payne, and Llewellyn, 1978). Instead of distinguishing between structural and exchange mobility as two supposedly different components of total mobility, analysts using loglinear models were led to distinguish between *absolute* and *relative* mobility rates. The former were the total rates and inflow and outflow rates that could be derived from the standard table by straightforward percentaging, while the latter were expressed by the odds ratios that defined the pattern of net association of origins and destinations within the table. (Odds ratios do of course constitute the basic elements of loglinear models.) Thus, in place of the identity given above, it became possible to think of a set of relative rates in the form of odds ratios, when embodied within given marginal distributions, as then implying a set of absolute rates:

Marginal distributions, Relative rates ⇒ Absolute rates

By means of loglinear modelling, therefore, mobility tables could be analysed in a far more coherent way than hitherto. It became possible to separate out the impact on absolute rates, or on changes or differences in absolute rates, of marginal distributions or 'structural effects', on the one hand, and of relative rates or 'fluidity effects', on the other.

Subsequently, logmultiplicative models were proposed (Erikson and Goldthorpe, 1992; Xie, 1992) that allowed questions of the *levels* of fluidity implicit in mobility tables also to be addressed. More specifically, these models could provide tests of hypotheses to the effect that over a time series of mobility tables for a particular society relative rates were becoming more equal and fluidity was thus increasing (i.e., the odds ratios defining such rates were moving generally closer to a value of 1, implying a complete independence of social origins and destinations) or were moving in the opposite direction; or, analogously, tests of hypotheses to the effect that mobility tables for different societies embodied relative rates that implied higher or lower fluidity from one society to another.[2]

Finally, in a further significant development, it has been shown how loglinear models for the grouped data of mobility tables can be rewritten as logistic regression models for individual-level data (Logan, 1983; Breen, 1994). In this way, it has become possible to move beyond the bivariate analysis of the association between social origins and destinations and to bring additional variables of interest—such as, say, individuals' educational attainment—into the analysis of relative mobility rates and patterns (e.g., Hendrickx and Ganzeboom, 1998; Breen and Goldthorpe, 1999, 2001).[3]

The general theoretical implications of the results produced by these new techniques has become most apparent in the case of *inter*generational rather than *intra*generational, or worklife, mobility, and also, it might be added, where intergenerational mobility is studied within a class structural context rather than in the context of a hierarchy of, say, occupational prestige or socioeconomic status.[4]

The two central findings to emerge could be stated as follows. First, absolute rates of intergenerational class mobility display considerable variation, both over time within national societies and across these societies. But, second, this variation *is to an overwhelming extent produced by structural rather than by fluidity effects*—in other words, by differences in the ways in which class structures have evolved rather than by differences in underlying relative rates. Relative rates appear to be characterised by a rather surprising degree of *in*variance: that is, by a large measure of temporal stability and also by a substantial cross-national commonality at least in the general pattern of fluidity that they imply.

What follows, then, is that if variation in *absolute* mobility rates and patterns is to be explained, this will have to be primarily by reference to factors exogenous rather than endogenous to processes of class mobility themselves. In other words, the key factors will be those determining the 'shapes' of class structures, in the sense of the proportionate sizes and the rates of growth or decline of different classes, rather than those determining the propensities of individuals to retain or to change their positions within these structures. Moreover, it has also emerged from recent research that

such exogenous factors are extremely diverse—demographic, economic, political, and so on—and that they have interacted in the histories of particular
national societies in many different ways (see, e.g., Erikson and Goldthorpe,
1992: ch. 6 esp.; Miles and Vincent, eds., 1993). It thus becomes apparent
why attempts that were previously made to develop theory in this regard,
as, say, by seeking to link variation in absolute rates to levels of economic
development or modernisation or to types of political regime (e.g., Lipset
and Zetterberg, 1956; Fox and Miller, 1965, 1966), were not very successful.
And in turn a fairly clear indication is given that insofar as variation in absolute rates cannot be usefully regarded as systematic, explanations of such
variation, whether over time or place, will need to be provided far more in
specific historical than in general theoretical terms.[5]

In contrast, however, in the case of *relative* rates, the extent of the temporal constancy and cross-national commonality that have been displayed can
only be seen as posing an evident theoretical opportunity—and indeed challenge. While class structures themselves may often evolve in highly specific
ways, the patterns of relative mobility chances that prevail within them—or
what have become known as 'endogenous mobility regimes'—would seem
to be determined through processes that to a significant extent *are* systematic and also context independent: that is, that operate in much the same
way over a wide range of societies.

In this regard, then, the importance of the new analytical techniques
is that they have served to reveal extensive social regularities of a largely
unexpected and in fact quite opaque kind and, moreover, ones for which an
explanation grounded in theory with some claims to generality is evidently
required.

NEW FINDINGS AND THE FUNCTIONALIST
THEORY OF SOCIAL MOBILITY

At the same time as they indicate that theoretical efforts should focus on the
explanation of relative rather than absolute mobility rates, the new empirical findings also strongly underline the need for a renewal of such efforts:
that is, by creating a series of difficulties for existing theory. This theory
could be said to derive from a larger endeavour, in effect a general theory of
industrialism, developed in the 1960s and 1970s chiefly by American sociologists of a liberal, anti-Marxist persuasion (cf. ch. 2, this volume). It was

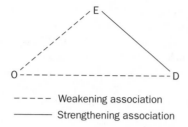

– – – – –   Weakening association
————   Strengthening association

Figure 7.1.   Changing relations over time among class origins, educational attainment, and class destinations as expected under the functionalist theory

then elaborated in its application to social mobility by American specialists in the field, notably Blau and Duncan (1967: ch. 12) and Treiman (1970).

The theory is, implicitly if not explicitly, functionalist in character, and thus the explanation of mobility rates and patterns that it provides is one couched in terms of societal responses to functional 'exigencies' or 'imperatives'.[6] In particular, emphasis falls on the way in which the dynamic technologies and economies of modern industrial, or postindustrial, societies impose requirements on their educational and employment systems that in turn carry direct implications for their mobility regimes. As regards relative mobility rates specifically, the three principal claims that are made by the theory can be set out, with reference to Figure 7.1, as follows.[7]

1. Technological and economic advance creates an inexorably rising demand for highly educated and qualified personnel and thus requires that human abilities or 'resources' should be as efficiently utilised as possible wherever within the social structure they may happen be located. To meet this requirement, educational provision is expanded and educational institutions are reformed so as to further equality of educational opportunity and selection on the basis of merit. Thus, the association between individuals' class origins and the level of their educational attainment—the OE association in Figure 7.1—tends to weaken over time.

2. Considerations of productive efficiency require that selection within labour markets and work organisations should also become 'meritocratic', that is, should reflect achievement rather than ascription; and in this regard educational attainment becomes the leading criterion of merit. Thus, the association between individuals' level of educational attainment and the class positions, or destinations, that they eventually reach—the ED association in Figure 7.1—tends to strengthen over time.

3. In consequence of (1) and (2) together, education becomes increasingly dominant in mediating intergenerational class mobility and in turn relative

rates become more equal or, in other words, social fluidity increases. Controlling for education, the association between class origins and destinations moves towards zero and, as mediated through education, moves towards the limit that is set by such genetic or cultural effects exerted by class origins on ability and motivation that education is unable to modify.

Up to the 1970s, this theory could be taken as providing a fairly coherent way of understanding the evidence that had so far emerged from mobility research. Or, at all events, the foregoing propositions, deriving from the theory, could not be regarded as being obviously inconsistent with this evidence. However, the far more refined, and also far more extensive, research findings that have subsequently been produced are such as to call the theory into serious doubt in several different respects.[8]

The most immediate difficulty is created by the finding that across modern societies, as earlier noted, relative rates of intergenerational class mobility show a high degree of temporal stability. Further, much of the change that can be detected is not of a directional kind—that is, towards greater or less fluidity overall. The most that might be said in favour of the theory in this regard is that so far as such directional change does show up, then this is more often towards greater fluidity rather than less. In other words, the association between class origins and destinations weakens rather than strengthens. However, such shifts are observed in some societies but not in others and are, moreover, usually related to particular birth cohorts or are otherwise episodic rather than sustained. In other words, they could scarcely count as compelling evidence of a tendency towards greater social fluidity of the 'worldwide' and 'secular' kind that the functionalist theory would predict.[9]

The functionalist theory also appears highly questionable in cross-national perspective. Again as earlier noted, the endogenous mobility regimes of modern societies reveal a notable degree of commonality in the general pattern of relative rates that they comprise. Sociologically as well as statistically significant differences can certainly be demonstrated, including in general levels of fluidity, but these would appear better regarded as 'variations on a theme' rather than as supporting any exceptionalist claims.[10] And still more damagingly for the functionalist theory is the fact that more technologically or economically advanced societies do not tend to show higher levels of social fluidity than those less advanced. Cross-sectional analyses have found no evidence of an association between fluidity and various indicators of development or modernisation, and a number of instances can be cited, notably those of Japan (Ishida, 1995; Ishida and Miwa, 2005) and Israel (Yaish, 2000, 2004a, 2004b), where relative mobility rates would appear to have remained essentially stable over periods of especially rapid and far-reaching economic and social transformation.

Finally, more recent analyses have examined the role of education in mobility processes, in terms of the OED triangle of Figure 7.1, and have also produced results that, overall, are scarcely compatible with the functionalist theory. Such analyses have considered, to begin with, the possibility of a 'global' decline (cf. ch. 2, n. 6) in class differentials in educational attainment, and in fact such a decline, even if often slight, has been detected in a number of societies, or, that is, the OE association weakens, as expected under the theory. However, when attention then turns to the relation between educational attainment and eventual class position—that is, to the ED association—the strengthening association that the theory would here predict is in fact rarely observed. Rather, the most common finding is that this association, too, is tending to weaken. And this is the case, it may be added, not only for countries characterised by a very high stability in relative mobility rates, such as Great Britain (Jackson, Goldthorpe, and Mills, 2005; Goldthorpe and Jackson, 2006) but also for countries in which some increase in fluidity has occurred, at least for a time, such as France (Vallet, 2004a) and Sweden (Jonsson, 1991, 1996, 2004). The indication then is of course that the mechanism producing this greater fluidity must be something other than the development of an education-based meritocracy in the way that the functionalist theory would envisage.[11]

One further finding of interest in this regard should also be noted: namely, that the OED triangle often comprises an interaction effect. Hout (1988) first showed this finding for the United States, but it has since been found to occur far more widely (see, e.g., Guzzo, 2002). One possible interpretation of this effect is that the strength of the association between social origins and destinations varies, inversely, with individuals' level of educational attainment. Thus, Hout (1988) observes that among American university graduates this association entirely disappears—while clearly still present among nongraduates. However, an alternative and, I would believe, preferable interpretation can be advanced: namely, that the association between education and class destination varies with class of origin, being weaker the more advantaged the origin.[12] From this standpoint, as will later become apparent, the idea can then further be questioned that in modern societies it is increasingly through an education-based meritocracy that class mobility is mediated.

Underlying the functionalist theory, two key assumptions can be noted. The first is that, prior to the exigencies of modern technologies and economies exerting their effects, human abilities were systematically underexploited: that is, were often not allowed to develop into merit, and especially in the case of individuals of less advantaged social origins. The second assumption is that, under the pressure of these exigencies, both public policy in the field of education and the personnel policies of employing organisations significantly change—indeed are forced to change—so as to enable merit to be more fully expressed and thus to play a steadily growing part in determining individuals' chances of mobility, whatever their social origins might be.

To the extent, then, that the theory does now appear increasingly inadequate in the light of empirical findings, these assumptions must be treated as suspect. What is most obviously suggested is that the exigencies to which the theory appeals, even supposing that they do exist, lack the transformative power that is attributed to them. It is true that educational expansion and reform have everywhere been the concomitants of technological and economic advance. But what has not come about is the envisaged restructuring of the chances of upward, and the risks of downward, mobility, as a result of educational systems creating greater variation rather than continuity in the class positions of families over generations. Moreover, it is in this connection further important to note that, because of its very form, the functionalist theory does not at any point provide specific accounts of just how the exigencies that it postulates are expected to work out actually at the level of individual action and interaction. As in all functionalist theories, the explanatory strategy is simply, as Coleman (1990: ch. 1) would put it, 'macro-to-macro', and individual action, insofar as it is considered at all, is reduced to little more than epiphenomenal status.[13]

In attempting to develop a more successful theory of social mobility, I therefore abandon all functionalist assumptions and also take it as a prime requirement that the theory should have as explicit micro-foundations as can be provided. That is to say, it should aim to spell out how the regularities that are empirically demonstrable in relative mobility rates and in the nature and extent of their mediation via education result from central tendencies in courses of action that are followed by the different categories of actor involved. I opt furthermore, as in previous chapters, to proceed on the basis

of rational action theory on the grounds that significant explanatory and interpretive advantage is gained insofar as action can be treated as rational, at
all events in a subjective and bounded sense, rather than as being understood
only in terms of actors' internalisation of the values of particular cultures
or subcultures or their commitment to social norms (cf. Boudon, 2003a,
2003b). This consideration would seem especially important in the present
case in view of the evident need to construct a theory of a rather high level
of generality.

I now to go on to outline a theory of the kind indicated that starts from
the idea of 'mobility strategies': that is, courses of action that are pursued by
individuals of differing class backgrounds, typically, though not necessarily,
in conjunction with their families of origin, in moving towards their own
eventual class destinations.[14] However, before I attempt to characterise such
strategies in detail and analyse their implications for relative mobility rates,
I need first to take up the questions of the resources that are available for
their pursuit and of the actual goals towards which they are directed.

MOBILITY STRATEGIES: RESOURCES AND GOALS

Resources

When social mobility is examined within the context of a class structure, this
structure has to be seen as conditioning rates and patterns of intergenerational mobility in two different ways. First, and as earlier implied, the shape,
and changes in the shape, of the structure in the sense simply of the proportionate sizes of different classes will determine the extent and nature of what
might be called 'objective' mobility opportunities. For example, a structure
in which higher-level class positions are expanding relative to lower-level
ones could be said to offer increasing opportunities for entry into the former positions, regardless of the class origins of the individuals who actually
take up these opportunities. In fact, as I have emphasised, empirical results
clearly show that both temporal and cross-national shifts in absolute rates
of intergenerational class mobility do overwhelmingly reflect the evolution
of class structures, with changes or variation in relative rates making only a
very minor contribution.

Second, though, and more relevant for the present concern with relative
rates, class structures can also be seen as conditioning mobility via the typi-

cal attributes of the positions they comprise. In this case, what is affected is not the overall situation as regards mobility opportunities but, precisely, the relative chances of mobility that individuals of differing origins have within the class structure, *whatever* shape or pattern of change it may display. Different classes, considered as classes of origin, provide varying degrees and forms of advantage to those individuals who are born and grow up within them. Or, one might say, from class to class, the resources that parents have available to help support their children's mobility strategies, or strategies that they themselves conceive on behalf of their children, will vary in both amount and kind, and such strategies will in this way be to a greater or lesser extent facilitated or constrained. In short, the class structure not only creates more or less favourable ground for the mobility stakes, it also plays a major part in determining the runners' handicaps.[15]

The nature and significance of this second way in which class structure influences mobility can, I would argue, be best appreciated if class positions are understood as being differentiated in terms of employment relations (see further chs. 5 and 6, this volume). An initial distinction has thus to be made among employers, self-employed workers, and employees. But more consequential, at least in the context of modern societies, are the further distinctions that can then be introduced within the numerically preponderant category of employees in regard to the form of regulation of their employment.

To recapitulate briefly the argument of Chapter 5, the major division to be recognised is that between, on the one hand, a working class, comprising employees in broadly manual and lower-grade nonmanual occupations and, on the other hand, a salariat, comprising professional and managerial employees. The former are typically engaged by their employer or employing organisation through a contract that implies a short-term and specific exchange of discrete amounts of labour in return for wages calculated on a piece or time basis. The latter are typically engaged through a contract that implies a longer-term and more diffuse exchange in which the employee renders service to the employing organisation in return for compensation that as well as a salary and various perquisites also includes important prospective elements—regular salary increments, some expectation of continuity of employment, and, above all, career opportunities. Further employee classes may in turn be distinguished that are intermediate between the working class and the salariat in that the regulation of employment in their constituent positions tends to be of a mixed form, in which elements of both the labour contract and the service relationship occur. These classes typically comprise routine nonmanual employees on the fringes, as it were, of professional and managerial bureaucracies and employees in lower-grade technical or manual supervisory positions.

From this standpoint, it is then, the salariat that appears capable of conferring the greatest degree of advantage as a class of origin, and the working class the least, specifically in respect of the resources that their members can command by virtue of the class positions that they hold. What is important here is not simply that salaried professionals and managers will have higher average earnings than rank-and-file wage workers. The former have also to be regarded as being advantaged over the latter, through the form of regulation of their employment, in at least three other highly consequential ways. First, they have greater economic security through their better protection against the risk of job loss and subsequent unemployment; second, they enjoy greater economic stability in that their incomes from employment will show less short-term fluctuation in relation to amount of work performed and will be less subject to interruption as a result of sickness or accident; and third, they have more favourable economic prospects in that their incomes will tend to follow a rising curve until a much later stage in the course of their working lives, peaking in their fifties rather than in their late twenties or thirties (see further Goldthorpe and McKnight, 2006). On all of these grounds, therefore, mobility strategies pursued from origins in the salariat are to be regarded as those least likely to be constrained by the availability of resources, while strategies pursued from working-class origins will be those most likely to be so constrained.

Matters become rather more complex when intermediate classes are considered, and especially when these classes are taken to include not just further employee classes, as referred to above, but also small employers and self-employed workers.[16] The advantages that such intermediate classes offer as classes of origin are not in fact readily ordered but can be better understood as differing qualitatively. For example, small employers and self-employed workers will typically be exposed to greater economic uncertainty and insecurity than members of intermediate employee classes but at the same time will have greater possibilities for the accumulation—and thus intergenerational transmission—of capital in some form. Or again, while employees in manual supervisory and technical positions may have higher average earnings than employees in routine nonmanual work, their earnings will tend to be more variable and perhaps to show less long-term progression. Although, then, the mobility strategies of individuals of intermediate-class origins may be taken as somewhat less constrained than those of individuals of working-class origins, the degree of constraint is likely to vary greatly with the appropriateness of the kinds of resources available to the particular strategies that are conceived.

Viewing relative mobility rates in a class structural context defined in terms of employment relations is by now of proven value in empirical research. Such an approach would be widely accepted as in various respects more revealing than that in which mobility is treated simply within a one-dimensional hierarchy of, say, prestige or socioeconomic status. What, though, for present purposes is of added significance is the possibility that the approach may be given a more developed theoretical basis. That is, by arguing, as I sought to do in Chapter 5, that, among the body of employees, the association that exists between the kind of work they carry out and the typical form of regulation of their employment is the outcome of decisions made by employers that have a clear rationale in considerations of organisational effectiveness. For, if this argument holds good—if the differentiation of class positions among employees can indeed be understood as deriving from employers' attempts to deal with such highly generalised organisational problems as work monitoring and human asset specificity—then this in itself gives grounds for expecting that endogenous mobility regimes will tend towards uniformity. The shapes of class structures, determining the overall distribution of mobility opportunities and in turn conditioning absolute mobility rates, may vary widely over time and place. But what might be called the principle of differentiation of these structures that constrains individuals' mobility strategies and in turn conditions relative mobility rates, could be thought to have a far more enduring character.

Goals

Mobility strategies pursued from different class origins will be backed by varying levels and kinds of resources. It has, though, further to be recognised that such strategies may differ in the goals towards which they are directed. Insofar as the question of individuals' goals has been previously taken up by analysts of mobility processes, two contrasting views can be identified.

The first view—and it is this that would seem to be taken over in the functionalist theory—is that the goals that individuals pursue can be treated as always and everywhere the same. On account of universal psychological impulses, defined as 'ego needs' or whatever, individuals aim to move, so far as they can, from positions that are less desirable to positions that are more desirable in terms of the various rewards that they offer (see, e.g., Lipset and Zetterberg, 1956; Kelley, Robinson, and Klein, 1981). The second view is that individuals' orientations towards social mobility, even within more advanced societies, show wide, subculturally determined, variation. In particular, it has been suggested, working-class subcultures may be inimical to the 'success ethic' that more generally prevails in such societies, either because these subcultures embody alternative values to that of individual achievement—for example, values of family or community solidarity—or simply because they engender fatalism and a 'poverty of aspirations' (see, e.g., Hyman, 1954; Richardson, 1977; Willis, 1977).

However, it is possible to suggest an alternative approach to this question that is at least as compatible with the empirical evidence as is either of the foregoing views,[17] and that would appear to offer greater explanatory potential. This approach requires that mobility orientations should be thought of as being basically similar across different social classes but at the same time as involving *priorities,* so that, given the differing degrees of constraint that are imposed by class origins, some systematic variation may indeed be observed in the actual goals that are pursued. More specifically, the suggestion is that what should be treated as common to individuals of all class backgrounds alike is a concern, in the first place, to maintain a class position that is no less desirable than that of their parents or, in other words, *to avoid downward mobility.* A concern to secure a more desirable class position, or, that is, to achieve upward mobility, is then to be regarded as a secondary objective, even if, perhaps, a still important one.[18]

If mobility is envisaged as occurring within a single, well-defined hierarchy of positions and if, further, educational attainment, understood in a linear, more-or-less, fashion is taken to be the crucial determinant of mobility chances, then the issue of priorities in mobility orientations may well appear of little importance. For in this case the *same* mobility strategy, that of maximising educational attainment, could be regarded as equally appropriate to improving the individual's chances both of avoiding downward and of achieving upward mobility: more education is always better. However, if mobility is envisaged as occurring within the more complex context of a class structure, if other factors than education are accepted as significantly influencing mobility chances, and if educational systems are in any event seen as diversified—that is, as providing options not just for more or less education but also for education of differing kinds—then a quite different perspective is gained. It is now at least conceivable that the strategies that would best serve to ensure that individuals of a given class origin maintain their class positions intergenerationally need not be the same as those that would best serve to promote their chances of upward mobility. Or, in other words, in this perspective the possibility can be recognised that significant choices of strategy may have to be made, implicitly if not explicitly, and ones that will entail differing degrees of risk. In pursuing one goal, the chances of realising another may be jeopardised.

Insofar as such situations do in fact arise, then, to repeat, the basic assumption that I would propose, and that will underlie the analysis that follows, is that the avoidance of mobility downwards will tend to be given priority over the achievement of mobility upwards. Thus, while it will not be supposed that individuals of working-class or other less advantaged backgrounds reject the goal of social advancement or are effectively precluded from pursuing it as a result of their subcultural conditioning, neither will it be supposed, as in the functionalist theory, that an equal commitment to this goal characterises all individuals.

MOBILITY STRATEGIES, EDUCATIONAL ATTAINMENT, AND ASCRIPTION

If it is taken that individuals engage in mobility strategies, subject to constraints and directed towards goals as outlined above, the general problem to be addressed is the following. How does it come about that this action actually generates, in aggregate outcome, the degree of constancy and commonality in relative mobility rates and also the empirical regularities in the mediation of mobility through education that must, for any theory of mobility, constitute the major *explananda*? Or, more specifically, one could ask: if it is indeed the case that much unexploited ability does exist among the members of less advantaged classes, why have educational expansion and reform and increased pressure for meritocratic selection not produced a more clear and consistent movement towards greater social fluidity, concomitantly with technological and economic advance? Or, again, why, given the educational systems of modern societies, have able children from less advantaged origins not come to compete more successfully for more desirable class positions, at the same time as less able children from more advantaged origins more often end up in less desirable positions?

In pursuing the agenda thus set, it will be a useful and, I believe, a not too misleading simplification to regard mobility strategies as being of two main kinds: that is, strategies 'from below' and strategies 'from above'. The former are strategies pursued from less advantaged class origins, which, following the discussion of the preceding section, will be taken as origins in the working class or in the various classes, which, in terms of the typical employment relations of their members, were considered as intermediate. The latter are those strategies pursued from more advantaged class origins or, that is, from origins within the salariat of professional and managerial employees.

I will now consider how these two kinds of strategies operate, first, via educational attainment—or what is usually regarded as achievement—and, second, via processes of ascription. In so doing, my aim will be to provide theoretical accounts or narratives that can show the courses of action involved to be ones capable of generating the empirical regularities in relative mobility rates that require explanation, and at the same time to be rational, and thus intelligible, responses by individuals to the situations in which they find themselves. As these narratives are developed, I will consider evidence that is, or that, if produced, could be, relevant to assessing their validity.

Mobility Strategies and Educational Attainment

I earlier suggested that within the conceptual approach to mobility that I here adopt, the choice of mobility strategy may be problematic. In particular, the strategy that would best guarantee the avoidance of downward mobility need not be that which would give the best possibility of achieving upward mobility. What I would now further argue, essentially on lines already developed in Chapters 2–4, is that it is in the case of educational choice within strategies pursued from below that this difficulty is most marked.

There can be little question that a strategy for upward mobility from relatively disadvantaged class origins into the ranks of the salariat will be most effectively pursued—that is, with the greatest chances of success—via the route of relatively high educational attainment (see, e.g., Ishida, Müller, and Ridge, 1995; Müller and Shavit, 1998; Goldthorpe and Jackson, 2006), and it would, moreover, seem reasonable to assume that there is wide public awareness of this fact. However, it does not follow that for children of disadvantaged origins, attempting to maximise their educational attainment will always be the most effective route towards what I would take to be their first priority, that of ensuring that they at least maintain the class position of their parents. Thus, for children of working-class origins, the safest option in this regard—to ensure, say, that they remain within the skilled as opposed to the nonskilled working class or in relatively continuous employment of some kind as against the possibility of becoming long-term or recurrently unemployed—may well be that of leaving mainstream education relatively early and of taking up vocational training, whether full-time or in conjunction with some appropriate kind of employment.[19] In addition, such a strategy could also give chances of short-range upward mobility into intermediate-class, especially manual supervisory or lower technical, positions. In contrast, continuing in general education could involve some significant degree of risk. In particular, if this option could not, for whatever reasons, be pursued through to the point at which relatively high level qualifications were actually achieved, it could well prove costly in terms of earnings foregone and of other—less ambitious but more realisable—opportunities missed.

Moreover, it has in this connection also to be recognised that those pursuing strategies from below are likely to be inclined towards educational choices of a more conservative kind—that is, ones more relevant to the achievement of class stability than of decisive upward mobility—simply on account of the economic constraints that their class backgrounds impose. Although reform programmes have in most modern societies removed or substantially reduced the direct costs of education, at least up to secondary level, the opportunity costs of remaining outside the labour market are still present. And, further, the successful passage of students through tertiary education is still much facilitated by, even if it does not actually demand, parental economic support in some form or other—the alternative to which is usually debt. One must then expect that the costs in question will be of greater consequence for individuals, the less advantaged are the class backgrounds from which they come. Especially in the case of children from working-class families, where income is relatively insecure, often subject to significant fluctuation and tends to peak early in parents' working lives, educational options that offer relatively short-term payoffs can be expected to have attractions over ones from which the economic rewards, though potentially larger, are longer delayed and carry a greater risk of not being successfully carried through.

The problematic nature of educational choice in mobility strategies from below is in fact highlighted if the comparison is made with strategies pursued from above: that is, by individuals of salariat background. These individuals, and their families of origin, face a situation, the logic of which is fairly straightforward. Given that intergenerational maintenance of class position is the prime goal to which their strategies should be directed, it is far clearer than in the case of strategies from below that attainment within the educational mainstream will be the safest and potentially most effective route to follow.[20] Thus, families within the salariat can be in general expected to give their offspring every encouragement and support to continue in full-time education beyond the minimum leaving age, to take up more academic options in secondary education, and to continue through to the tertiary stage. In other words, their strategy will be that of translating their children's ability as far as ever is possible into actual educational attainment as represented by formal qualifications.

Moreover, within these families a strategy of this kind can usually be backed by more or less adequate resources. What is important in this regard is not only the relatively high level and stability of their incomes but also the fact that at the same time as children are passing through the crucial secondary and tertiary stages of their educational careers, parental earning power will typically be moving up towards its highest point. Thus, investment in children's education is encouraged since the costs involved, direct and indirect, may well be absorbed without any seriously detrimental effect on established family living standards. However, even if some degree of sacrifice is involved, parents can still be expected to commit resources in various ways so as to improve their children's educational chances: for example, by buying homes in high status residential areas that provide good quality state schools, by supplementing state education with private tuition, or by opting out of the state system altogether and placing their children in private educational institutions.

It is, then, in these ways that children of more advantaged class backgrounds are given a clear competitive edge in seemingly meritocratic selection processes—or, as Halsey puts it (1977: 184) that 'ascriptive forces find ways of expressing themselves as "achievement"'. Moreover, the differential availability of resources can be seen as underlying the tendency (as already noted in ch. 2) for children of salariat background to be pushed to the very limits of their academic ability, or even beyond, while working-class children may decline educational options in which they would have good chances of success. For if strategies from above are threatened by academic failure, further resources can then often be deployed: for example, second or third attempts at relevant qualifications can be underwritten or alternative courses or institutions explored. In other words, a range of possibilities exist for what in French discussion has been aptly referred to as *récupération*. In contrast, for children pursuing strategies from below, and thus backed by fewer resources, a greater degree of caution is to be expected. For failure in a relatively ambitious educational option could well leave them and their families less well placed, in terms of opportunity costs and perhaps debt, than if they had never attempted it.

To the extent, then, that mobility strategies as outlined in the foregoing can be regarded as central tendencies in action within modern societies, the resistance to change that is shown by class differentials in educational attainment—or, to revert to Figure 7.1, the lack of any decisive weakening in the OE association—is made comprehensible. And while further research into the actual processes of educational choice within differing class contexts is certainly needed, it can at all events be claimed (see further ch. 4 above) that a model of choice that seeks to capture the key arguments I have deployed appears more consistent with existing empirical findings than others that have so far been proposed or implied.

In addition, evidence reviewed by Müller and Shavit (1998) is of particular relevance as regards the tendency for those pursuing strategies from below to leave mainstream education relatively early, even when, perhaps, they have good chances of successful continuation. In the light of research findings on the transition from education to employment in 13 advanced societies, these authors are led directly to question the idea that more—general—education is *always* better. They note that the completion of vocational courses does usually give individuals the best chance of entering skilled rather than nonskilled manual work, and, further, that it is quite often the case that the probability of being found in unemployment is lower for those with vocational qualifications than for those with more academic education of a comparable or even a somewhat higher level. In other words, insofar as class stability is prioritised, then for many children of less advantaged origins the choice of vocational over academic educational options may well reflect a large degree of realism and rationality—far more in fact than is allowed for in culturalist explanations that invoke a poverty of aspirations or unduly short time horizons and an inability to 'defer gratification' (e.g., Schneider and Lysgaard, 1953; Rosen, 1956).[21]

As was earlier remarked, the functionalist theory turns crucially on the idea that the 'release' of previously unexploited ability, through increasingly meritocratic social selection in education, and thence in employment, will serve as the main driving force behind steadily increasing social fluidity. However, the main implication of the present analysis is that such a release cannot be expected to occur in the quite unrestrained way that the functionalist theory would envisage. Even supposing that educational systems do operate on strictly meritocratic principles, the very nature of the class structure—the basis on which class positions are differentiated—is still capable of inhibiting the full exploitation of ability. That is, by creating circumstances in which individuals pursuing mobility strategies from below can have good reasons, in the light of perceived costs and benefits, for not in fact attempting to use educational channels to the fullest extent that would be open to them and that their ability would warrant.

Mobility Strategies and Ascription

In modern societies, educational attainment may be regarded as the single most important factor in determining class mobility chances—although, as indicated above, it would be naive to equate such attainment with purely individual achievement, uninfluenced by the ascribed advantages or disadvantages of differing class origins. Furthermore, it needs to be recognised that ascription may play a still more direct part in mobility strategies, whether pursued from below or from above. As well as contributing to children's educational success, various resources associated with family background may serve to help children in gaining access to particular class positions *independently of* their educational attainment. Where ascription is in this way involved, its importance is of course likely to be greater in strategies that are aimed at class stability rather than at major social advancement (cf. Goux and Maurin, 1997). And, in turn, for those engaging in strategies from below, the possibility of thus using ascriptive resources may itself be reckoned as a further factor favouring the adoption of goals of a relatively conservative kind.

This point is perhaps most readily brought out in the case of the children of small employers and proprietors, and self-employed workers. For these individuals, the maintenance of their class positions may well appear to be best guaranteed not through educational attainment, at all events beyond some threshold level, but rather through their direct inheritance of family businesses as going concerns or through the intergenerational transmission of capital sufficient to enable them to start up enterprises of their own. There is in fact clear cross-national evidence to show, first, that the propensity for intergenerational stability within the 'petty bourgeoisie' is relatively high, at least for men (Robinson, 1984; Erikson and Goldthorpe, 1992), and, second, that educational qualifications play very little, if any, part in sustaining this stability (Ishida, Müller, and Ridge, 1995).[22]

In addition, not only economic resources but also cultural and social resources can be transferred from generation to generation, and this may in various other cases of those starting out from relatively disadvantaged origins encourage strategies that have class stability as their prime objective. For example, traditions of family employment in particular skilled trades or specialised branches of commerce may endow individuals brought up within these traditions with knowledge and capacities and with contacts and social networks that are of greater value in maintaining class stability than qualifications obtained through the educational system.

For those pursuing strategies from above, however, the significance of ascription has to be seen in a somewhat different light. As earlier noted, the surest means of maintaining class stability within the salariat is through a high level of educational attainment, and family resources of every kind are likely to be exploited in order to help children towards such attainment. A more direct reliance on ascription is then to be expected chiefly where children's educational performance does not in fact reach the requisite standard: that is, as an *alternative* means of trying to secure their class stability or at very least to save them from any decisive downward movement.

Thus, children of salariat background may be able to benefit from 'connections' within the occupational and wider social milieux of their parents in order to find openings for employment that would not be available to those from other backgrounds and that their own educational qualifications would scarcely justify. There seems no reason to suppose that the requirements of modern societies for meritocratic selection in employment have entirely eliminated such possibilities or indeed the straightforward practice of nepotism. However, what is probably of more general importance is the fact, quite overlooked in the functionalist theory, that various ascriptive attributes of children of more advantaged class origins—that is, attributes that derive directly from their upbringing in particular family and community contexts—may themselves represent 'merit', at all events in the eyes of employers.

In the functionalist theory, employers have only a shadowy role. It is in effect assumed that what constitutes merit within the educational system—that is, the achievement of formal qualifications—will likewise constitute merit for employers. But it is now becoming apparent that this assumption is far too simplistic. For example, analyses of job advertisements (Jackson, 2001; Jackson, Goldthorpe, and Mills, 2005) indicate that while employers (or their agents) do indeed attach high importance to formal qualifications in the case of professional and ancillary positions, for many other types of employment qualifications appear less important than a range of other *desiderata*. In particular, for positions in the rapidly growing personal services and sales sectors, and including positions at managerial level, employers would seem less concerned with the certification of primarily cognitive abilities than with broadly defined social skills and with various personal or lifestyle characteristics: for example, appearance, self-presentation, savoir faire, manners and accent, and in general 'looking good and sounding right' (Warhurst and Nickson, 2001). And indeed it can scarcely be found surprising that it is attributes such as these that should be regarded as chiefly relevant to successful careers in, say, the leisure, entertainment, or hospitality industries, or in high-value sales, customer services, or public relations.

The implication then is that certain positions remain available within the salariat, and are even increasing in number, that, while not requiring a very high level of formal qualification, do call for attributes with which children from more advantaged class backgrounds will tend to be endowed simply as a consequence of their upbringing. And research findings are now in fact emerging to show, on the one hand, that individuals holding managerial positions in services and sales do on average have lower levels of formal qualification than managers in other sectors as well as professionals (Jackson, Goldthorpe, and Mills, 2005) and, on the other hand, that children of salariat origins with only modest educational attainment do gravitate towards such positions (Jackson, 2004).

The account earlier given of mobility strategies pursued through education led to an explanation for the resistance to change that class differentials in educational attainment display or, in other words, for the failure of the OE association of Figure 7.1 to weaken as clearly and consistently as the functionalist theory would require. The account now provided of the part that ascriptive factors may play in mobility strategies points to an explanation of two other empirical regularities earlier noted that likewise create difficulties for the theory: the tendency, at least over recent decades, for the ED association to weaken rather than to strengthen and the presence in the overall OED association of an interaction effect.

As regards the ED association, the suggestion is that employers will not automatically serve as the agents of an education-based meritocracy, as is supposed in the functionalist theory. Rather, employers must be seen as having their own ideas of what represents merit—or at least productive value—in employees, which, not unreasonably, will vary from one type of employment to another.[23] Thus, if employers believe that attributes that are more ascribed than achieved are nonetheless those most relevant to certain kinds of work, it is these attributes that they will select for in hiring, retaining, and promoting employees. There is, then, no overriding reason why the ED association *should* steadily strengthen. This is likely to happen only insofar as those positions for which employers regard educational qualifications as crucial are in expansion—as they probably were in many societies over, say, the middle decades of the twentieth century. Today, however, the most rapid growth in employment is often found in the services sector of the economy where employers' requirements for high-level qualifications and, even in regard to managerial positions, would appear to be least stringent.[24] And thus, the actual weakening of the ED association that has recently been observed in a number of societies could be the outcome of a simple compositional effect.[25]

As regards the interaction effect typically found in the OED relationship, it would seem best to interpret this, I earlier argued, as indicating that the strength of the association between educational attainment and class destination varies with class of origin. Viewed in this way, the interaction can then be seen as resulting from the differing part played in mobility strategies from below and from above by ascriptive factors, relative to educational attainment, on the lines I have set out. Thus, in the case of the children, or at least the sons, of the petty bourgeoisie, where the direct intergenerational transmission of economic resources is an obvious possibility, it has already been observed that education is of little importance in maintaining class stability and, in turn, that the ED association is especially weak (Ishida, Müller, and Ridge, 1995). Similarly, one would expect this association to be weaker among individuals with origins in the salariat than among those originating in the working class or in other intermediate classes apart from the petty bourgeoisie. For while, as suggested, the former can draw on various family resources to compensate for poor educational performance in their efforts to preserve their class position, the latter have few means of securing upward mobility other than through educational attainment. And again, empirical results would appear to confirm this expectation. Education is found to be of generally greater importance in mediating upward mobility into the salariat from relatively disadvantaged origins than it is in maintaining intergenerational stability within this class (Guzzo, 2002; Goldthorpe and Jackson, 2006).[26]

GENERAL IMPLICATIONS FOR RELATIVE MOBILITY RATES

Exploiting the idea of typical mobility strategies from below and from above, I have suggested explanations for an OE association more persistent than the functionalist theory would allow; for the failure of the ED association to strengthen as the functionalist theory would expect; and further for the tendency for the latter association to vary in its strength with class origins. Insofar as these explanations hold good, then an explanation is in effect also provided for the widespread failure of the overall OD association to weaken in any substantial way—for the absence across modern societies of any general and sustained movement towards more equal relative mobility rates or greater social fluidity. Or, to be more precise, an explanation is provided for the absence of any such movement *as the result of* the development of an education-based meritocracy on the lines indicated in Figure 7.1.

Class structures generate unequal resources among families differently located within them in ways that reflect the adaptation of employment relations to highly generalised problems of work organisation. Thus, the class structural constraints that bear on the mobility strategies in which individuals engage can be seen as in themselves making for temporal constancy and cross-national commonality in endogenous mobility regimes—and despite new opportunities that may be created by educational expansion and reform.

On the one hand, individuals of less advantaged class origins may have good reason not to seek to exploit these opportunities to the full—not to engage in supposedly meritocratic competition for more desirable class positions to the extent that the functionalist theory would envisage. Given the class-linked constraints to which they and their families are subject, they may, rather, favour strategies aimed primarily at achieving class stability or only modest social advancement, and even when their ability would be consistent with more ambitious educational and occupational aspirations. On the other hand, and likewise with good reason, individuals of more advantaged origins largely do engage in such competition via the educational system, while, however, being able to draw on family economic resources in order to raise their chances of educational success to some extent independently of their ability or, in the event of failure, being able to exploit other aspects of their family backgrounds so as still to avert any radical *déclassement*. Moreover, in the case of strategies from below a reliance on ascription rather than achievement typically implies making a choice in favour of stability rather than mobility, but in the case of strategies from above no such choice is required. Stability is the one goal to be pursued by means of achievement *or* ascription, so that the latter can in fact complement the former or, if need be, serve as substitute for it.

The constraints imposed by the class structure, one might then say, induce rationally adaptive responses from the individuals subject to them—their mobility orientations and the related courses of action that they follow— which serve to reinforce and to perpetuate the effects of these constraints on the mobility regime. To argue thus is *not* to underwrite the idea that among individuals of less advantaged class origins culturally grounded resistance exists to the idea of upward mobility. It does not rule out the possibility that many such individuals, and especially ones of relatively high ability, *will* engage in competition for more desirable class positions; nor yet the possibility that, at least where these positions are in expansion, they may do so with increasing relative success.[27] But what *is* implied is that any potential impact on the mobility regime that might in this way arise will tend always to be offset by individuals of more advantaged origins likewise exploiting the favourable conditions that prevail so as to improve *their* chances of preserving their class positions rather than experiencing downward mobility. And the degree of success that they thus achieve will of course itself operate as a further constraint on the extent to which those pursuing mobility strategies from below aimed at long-range upward mobility can in fact achieve their goals.[28] In other words, the point that is underlined is that greater social fluidity entails individuals of less advantaged class origins making gains vis-à-vis individuals of more advantaged origins in the 'positive' competition for more desirable class positions without losing out to a more or less similar extent in the 'negative' competition to avoid less desirable positions. However, insofar as mobility strategies from below and from above do tend to be pursued under the constraints and according to the rationales that I have suggested, there would seem little basis for expecting greater social fluidity to be produced simply in response, as it were, to economic and technological advance.[29]

CHANGE AND VARIATION IN RELATIVE RATES

It is the degree of temporal constancy and cross-national commonality in relative rates of intergenerational class mobility that poses the main theoretical challenge arising from mobility research and that in the foregoing has chiefly concerned me. In the field of social stratification, and indeed more generally, there is a danger that a preoccupation with change and variation, sometimes quite slight or indeed uncertain, diverts attention away from the more fundamental question of the source of the regularity by reference to which change and variation are identified (Lieberson, 1987: 99–107). However, as I have recognised, instances of shifts in relative mobility rates over time as well as cross-national differences can be demonstrated, and it is therefore pertinent to ask here to what extent the theory that I have outlined can apply in this regard also. I conclude by considering this question.

Two preliminary points need to be made. First, change or variation in relative rates need not imply greater or less social fluidity overall but only perhaps differences in the pattern as opposed to the level of fluidity. Differences of this kind, I would see as falling outside the scope of the theory, and, most probably, outside that of any other theory that has aspirations to generality, simply because of the extent to which they appear to be shaped by highly specific institutional or cultural influences (cf. Erikson and Goldthorpe, 1992: chs. 3 and 5 esp.).[30] Second, it is important to recognise that change or variation in relative rates that does pertain to the general level of fluidity can come about in diverse ways, some of which the theory will again not cover. For example, largely contingent factors, such as may be associated with wars, frontier changes, mass population movements, and the like, can impact on fluidity (cf. Breen and Luijkx, 2004b); or again what has been called 'perverse fluidity' (Goldthorpe and Mills, 2004; and cf. Duncan, 1968) can be created intergenerationally within class structures, in the case, say, of women or of ethnic minorities, as a result of unequal opportunities experienced in the course of working life.

However, since the theory that I have outlined sees the degree of invariance of relative rates of class mobility as being grounded in generic features of the class structures of modern societies, one expectation regarding change or variation clearly follows: namely, that fluidity will be greater, the more that class-linked inequalities in resources, or the immediate outcomes of such inequalities, are in some way modified. In other words, equality of *opportunity*, in the sense of more equal relative rates of mobility, should be more manifest within the class structure, the less the inequality of *condition* that derives from this structure.

In empirical research that is relevant to testing the theory in this respect one approach taken is that of cross-national comparisons. Analyses have been made of the extent to which levels of fluidity across different societies are associated with the degree of inequality in their (personal or household) income distributions—this being the only generally available indicator of class-linked differences in resources. An early study of 24 nations (Tyree, Semyonov, and Hodge, 1979) produced results to suggest that such an association was in fact present: nations with more equal income distributions tended to show (for men) more equal relative rates of intergenerational class mobility. Some later and more sophisticated analyses have confirmed this finding (e.g., Erikson and Goldthorpe, 1992: ch. 12) but others have not (e.g., Breen and Luijkx, 2004b). However, there is general agreement that the approach in question is fraught with methodological problems and that the significance of results derived from it, in whichever way they may point, is difficult to evaluate.[31]

The main alternative and more promising approach is that which focuses on changes over time in particular nations where high-quality data and evident theoretical interest happen to coincide. Two such cases are those of Hungary and Sweden, in both of which a good basis exists for analysing relative rates of class mobility over periods in which significant changes in class-linked inequalities occurred—and indeed, were largely brought about through political action.

In the Hungarian case a series of large-scale and well-designed mobility surveys have been carried out from 1973 through to 2000 and have been subject to much analysis (see esp. Andorka, 1990; Simkus et al., 1990; Erikson and Goldthorpe, 1992; Wong and Hauser, 1992; Szelényi, 1998; Róbert and Bukodi, 2004). What emerges of interest in the present connection is the following.

To begin with, in the period after the communist takeover in Hungary in 1947 there are clear indications of some increase in social fluidity. In particular among men and women who were born in the interwar years and who entered employment during the 1940s and 1950s relative mobility chances became more equal. This shift can, moreover, be plausibly seen as being, at least in part, the outcome of various forms of state intervention that were directly aimed at 'destratification'. The old land-owning and capitalist classes were eliminated, and, in the context of a command economy, inequalities in family incomes and wealth were significantly reduced. Further, a policy of creating a 'people's intelligentsia' led to formal discrimination in educational selection in favour of the children of peasants and workers and against children from 'bourgeois' or other supposedly privileged backgrounds. At the same time, relatively strict relationships were established between educational credentials and type of employment. An increase in social fluidity thus appears to have been brought about through an improvement in the relative chances of upward mobility of the children of peasants and workers that went *together with* a decline in the capacity of the professional and managerial salariat to maintain its intergenerational stability.[32]

However, in the later years of communist rule, and especially from the time of the so-called normalisation, following on the uprising of 1956, the trend towards greater fluidity appears steadily to weaken. In this period, a new understanding between the regime and the intelligentsia led to the progressive abandonment of educational discrimination, and then under the 'goulash communism' of the 1980s income differentials were allowed to widen substantially. Finally, in the years after the ending of communist rule in 1989, which saw the full transition to a market economy, the trend towards greater equality in relative mobility rates disappears, and the latest evidence for the 1990s points to an actual reversal of this trend, at least for men, or, that is, to declining fluidity within the Hungarian class structure (Róbert and Bukodi, 2004).

For Sweden also it is possible to track changes in class mobility over several decades, in the course of which a concerted political effort was made to create a more egalitarian form of society, although in this case through electoral rather than authoritarian politics. From the mid-1930s through to the 1970s, the Swedish Social Democratic Party was more or less continuously in power, and promoted the development of a distinctive political economy and of a comprehensive welfare state that together created a greater degree of equality in incomes, economic security, and living standards across classes than was found in most other modern societies. Evidence from repeated national surveys does then indicate that over the period in question social fluidity showed a steady increase (Erikson, 1983; Jonsson, 1991). By the 1970s, Sweden could in fact claim not only a rather distinctive position in regard to the reduction of class-linked inequalities of condition but likewise in regard to the degree of 'openness' of its class structure—which more detailed analysis showed to result chiefly from an unusually low propensity for *im*mobility within all classes alike (Erikson and Goldthorpe, 1992).

However, further survey evidence then reveals that from the 1970s onwards, as the Swedish model of economic and social policy lost its coherence, and its egalitarian impact was reduced, the trend towards greater fluidity clearly weakened (Jonsson and Mills, 1993; Jonsson, 1996). And although Sweden has still to be counted as one of the most fluid of modern societies, findings for the 1990s (Jonsson, 2004) would suggest that, at least among men, relative mobility rates have now tended to restabilise.

Both the Hungarian and Swedish cases do thus provide evidence that is at all events consistent with the theory I have advanced. Changes in fluidity are associated with changes in inequalities of condition across classes in the way that would be expected. At the same time, though, these cases must also be seen as underlining the degree of resistance to change that endogenous mobility regimes are likely to offer. The increases in fluidity that occurred were not large but still required political intervention of a determined and systematic kind, and, moreover, they appear not to have been sustained once egalitarian policies were relaxed or lost their force. Further, the effectiveness of educational reform alone is again called into question, unless, perhaps, as in early communist Hungary, it entails a degree of class-related discrimination and of state intervention in training and recruitment policies that would scarcely be acceptable in a liberal democratic context. For while in Sweden educational reform did indeed achieve its aim of reducing class differentials in educational attainment (cf. ch. 2, this volume), the effect of this in then raising fluidity remains uncertain, and especially in view of the weakening association between educational attainment and class destinations that was earlier noted (cf. Jonsson, 1991, 1996).

A final question that may be raised is that of whether endogenous mobility regimes would show a similarly strong resistance to change in the *op-posite* direction to that so far chiefly considered: that is, to change towards more *un*equal relative rates or reduced fluidity. The theory I have suggested implies that this would *not* be the case, or at least not if this trend were prompted by a widening of class-linked inequalities of condition. For individuals pursuing mobility strategies from below would thus face yet greater constraints and greater risks in engaging in competition for more desirable class positions, while those pursuing strategies from above would be still more advantaged in the resources that they could use so as, by one route or another, to ensure their class stability.

One striking, if perhaps somewhat special, case that illustrates the argument here advanced is that of post-communist Russia. In the years of transition to a market economy, class inequalities in both incomes and degree of economic security and stability widened sharply (Gerber, 2002), and, over the same period, a marked decline in fluidity within the class structure can be demonstrated (Gerber and Hout, 2004). A key factor in this change would appear to be that class origins have come to exert an increasing influence on the worklife mobility chances of men and women already in the active population as well as on those of children moving through the educational system and into employment for the first time. Consequently, a strong 'period' effect shows up in contrast to the more usual tendency where fluidity increases for this to occur predominantly through gradual 'cohort replacement' effects.[33]

Turning to the western world, one may here too note instances of a reversal in trend in economic inequality. Over the long boom of the postwar decades most societies experienced decreasing inequality in incomes, unemployment was at historically low levels, and at the same time governments extended citizens' rights to social welfare—a process aptly referred to by Marshall (1947) as one of 'class abatement'. It is, perhaps, against this background that one can best understand why insofar as directional changes can be detected in relative mobility rates, they are for the most part ones towards increasing fluidity, and also why such changes have shown up rather more frequently towards the end of the twentieth century than earlier—that is, as those birth cohorts that entered into employment during the long boom have progressively replaced older cohorts. However, since the mid-1970s trends in income distributions have become much more variable than before. In many societies the movement towards greater equality has been checked and in some, notably the United States and the UK, inequality has strongly increased (Gottschalk and Smeeding, 1997; Atkinson, 1999). Over the same period, double-digit unemployment rates have at times returned and there has been a general tendency for social welfare policy to become less class redistributive in its aims.

Under the theory that I have outlined the expectation must then be that at least in those societies in which economic inequality has widened most sharply, some decline in fluidity will eventually show up, and especially as birth cohorts entering the labour market since the 1980s replace those who lived through the long boom. Research over the course of the next few decades will determine whether or not this expectation is met, but there are in fact already some suggestive findings to hand. Thus, for the United States, Beller and Hout (2005) report preliminary results indicating that among men born between 1970 and 1979 a turndown in fluidity has indeed occurred, and one that can be at least in part associated with widening economic inequality. For the UK clear evidence has been produced of reduced intergenerational *income* mobility among men and women entering the labour market in the 1980s (Blanden et al., 2004), and this would seem likely to be paralleled in work on intergenerational class mobility, using the same data-sets, at least as regards the relative chances of long-range mobility.[34]

In this chapter I have argued that recent technical advances in social mobility research have not had the intellectually narrowing effect that various critics have claimed. I have sought to show how they have in fact led to empirical findings that have greatly clarified what the focus of theoretical effort in the field should now be. That is, to explain the degree of temporal constancy and cross-national commonality that are revealed in relative rates of intergenerational mobility, especially as viewed in a class structural context, and also the regularities observed in the mediation of such mobility by educational attainment. The extent of change and variation in absolute rates can be shown overwhelmingly to reflect the differing ways in which the class structures of particular societies have evolved, and will therefore require explanation of a primarily historical kind in which the invocation of contingencies and singularities is likely to play a major role. In contrast, the degree of invariance over time and place displayed by relative rates, or endogenous mobility regimes, clearly calls for theoretical explanation—and at a level of generality that can transcend the specificities of particular temporal or societal contexts and that can also provide a basis for some understanding of the more systematic aspects of such change and variation in relative rates as can be demonstrated.

I have sought to make a start on the development of such an explanation and have opted for one that is grounded in a theory of action, in contrast to the functionalist grounding of the most important attempt previously made to account for what were believed to be—often mistakenly, as it now appears—the main trends and patterns of relative mobility rates observable in modern societies. I do not intend at this point to recapitulate my outline theory but simply to make two final remarks for the benefit of potential critics and of those who might try to take the theory further (these categories being, I would hope, largely overlapping).

First, I have attempted to preserve coherence by relying throughout on rational action theory. It might at various points have been possible to give my argument at least a more immediate plausibility by shifting ground and treating action as, say, being ultimately shaped by individuals' adherence to cultural values or social norms. But this would in fact have been of little value if no more than ad hoc modifications were involved. I would therefore invite anyone inclined to improve the theory through such eclecticism to see their theoretical task as then extending to justification for so doing.

Second, while I would regard the existing empirical evidence as being generally supportive of both the direction that the theory takes and of expectations that in turn follow from it, I recognise that others might, in certain respects, wish to disagree. And it would, moreover, be only reasonable to suppose that either the reevaluation of old findings or the production of new ones will, sooner or later, create problems for the theory, of one kind or another, that cannot be denied. But I would then urge that theoretical efforts should nonetheless continue, whether on similar lines or different ones, in order to provide explanations of the highly significant results that social mobility research has produced and will, I believe, continue to produce, rather than the field being allowed to lapse into a condition of more or less unleavened, even if increasingly sophisticated, empiricism—for which it could indeed be rightly criticised.

CHAPTER EIGHT

Sociology and the Probabilistic Revolution, 1830–1930
Explaining an Absent Synthesis*

The essays that made up the first volume of this collection were of two kinds, critical and programmatic. They were intended to give, in their differing ways, a general idea of the kind of sociology that I would see as offering the best prospects for the future of the discipline. That is, a sociology concerned with establishing and explaining phenomena that can be described by reference to social regularities of a probabilistic kind—to their formation, continuity, interrelation, change, and disruption. As regards establishing such phenomena, and also determining their precise form, I would attach main importance to statistically based methods of data collection and analysis, as being, if not the only, then certainly the most reliable and versatile of those available to sociologists. As regards explaining such phenomena, I would, from the standpoint of methodological individualism, seek a basis in the theory of action, and give rational action theory a privileged, if not necessarily exclusive, role. And finally, as regards the testing of such explanations, I would see statistical analysis as again having a major role to play, and, most fundamentally, as providing a well-developed logic of inference for empirical, but nonexperimental, science, that can, however, be appropriately extended for use with qualitative as well as quantitative data.

In the essays so far presented in this second volume I have sought to provide some illustration of sociology of the kind in question as applied in a particular area—that, broadly, of social stratification. I hope thus to have

---

*For helpful comments on earlier versions of this essay, I am indebted to David Cox, Lorraine Daston, Alain Desrosières, Daniel Krymkowski, Gordon Marshall, Karl Ulrich Mayer, Stephen Stigler, and Wout Ultee.

brought out how, insofar as such a sociology might be further extended, several significant advantages could be expected to follow. First, the lack of integration of research and theory—the long-standing scandal of sociology—could at last be overcome. It would no longer be supposed that statistical technique alone is capable of providing sociological explanations or, in other words, that 'variable sociology' can be complete in itself; while at the same time theory would no longer be able to claim autonomy from the findings of empirical research but would be called on to demonstrate its explanatory power in relation to these findings. Second, vexatious differences between 'scientific' and 'humanistic' conceptions of sociology could be transcended. It would be apparent that sociology can, and ultimately needs to, combine the collection and analysis of data in ways informed by statistical science with efforts to make the results that emerge both explicable and at the same time intelligible: statistics and hermeneutics are complementary. And, finally, a major contribution could thus be made to a new sociological mainstream, capable of replacing the current, largely spurious pluralism that does sociology little credit in the context of the social sciences or the humanities and indeed bodes ill for its future as an academic discipline of any sort.

I recognise, however, that to argue in this vein does raise at least one rather obvious question. If a sociology on the lines that I would advocate does hold out such promise, why is it that it has been so very slow to make its appearance?[1] More specifically, why is it that through most of the history of sociology the statistical treatment of social data, on the one hand, and the theory of social action, on the other, have been concerns pursued for the most part separately from each other and by individuals or schools with, apparently, rather little in common. One answer that might be given is that this divergence is not at all accidental: that inherent problems have faced, and will continue to face, any sociology that seeks to achieve a synthesis of these concerns since they reflect what are ultimately incompatible understandings of the nature of sociology or even, perhaps, of society itself. Alternatively, though, it might be held that the difficulties that stood in the way of such a synthesis in the past were contingent rather than necessary—the result, say, of specific institutional or intellectual circumstances, or even perhaps in some cases of the courses of personal histories and their intersection, that could, in principle, have been otherwise and that at all events need not be taken as indicative of problems of any fundamental and abiding kind.

In the two concluding, retrospective chapters in this volume, my aim is to consider which of these views comes nearer to the truth. In the present chapter, I pursue this aim through an essay on the history of sociology in its key formative period from, roughly, the 1830s to the 1930s, and with special reference to the cases of France, England, and Germany. In the next chapter, I turn to the United States in the first two-thirds of the twentieth century, when American sociology came to achieve, at least in numerical and organisational terms, a position of international dominance, and focus on what, for my purposes, would appear to be three crucial historical episodes.

Two other preliminary remarks are in order. First, the history that follows is, quite openly, history written from the standpoint of the present and specifically in order to address a current issue. The reader should therefore be warned that there are more than the usual dangers of bias and distortion—of 'Whig history' or, more likely perhaps, of what Bulmer (1981) has referred to as 'inverse Whig history', which represents the past not as leading inexorably to a glorious future but rather as a catalogue of errors that can only now be recognised as such.

Second, in view of my earlier critical remarks (vol. I, ch. 2) on sociologists' uses of historical materials, I should make it clear that, for my present purposes, my primary sources are texts from the periods with which I am concerned. I have sought to document my arguments fairly extensively by reference to such texts, so that those who do not find my interpretations acceptable should at all events be able to pin down just where differences arise. Where I refer to secondary sources—that is, to commentaries on these texts—I do so largely as a convenience, and it can be taken that, unless otherwise indicated, I share their authors' interpretations of the primary sources.

SOCIOLOGY AND THE PROBABILISTIC REVOLUTION

In order to provide an essential context for the discussion of my three national cases, I need first of all to take up a topic that is in fact almost entirely neglected in standard histories of sociology: the initially important, but later faltering, involvement of sociology in what has become known as the 'probabilistic revolution' in scientific thinking (cf. Krüger, Daston, and Heidelberger, eds., 1987; Krüger, Gigerenzer, and Morgan, eds., 1987; Gigerenzer et al., 1989).[2] That is, the revolution that, to paraphrase Hacking (1987: 45), led from a conception of the world at the end of the eighteenth century in which it was 'deemed to be governed by stern necessity and universal laws' to one established by around 1930 in which the world was 'run at best by laws of chance'.

At the beginning of the nineteenth century, probability theory had two main, though quite different, areas of application. On the one hand, within the 'moral sciences' of the Enlightenment, it served as the calculus through which rational individuals could—and should—form their beliefs and direct their actions wherever situations of risk or uncertainty arose. Thus, probability theory was urged (with varying degrees of success) as providing the proper basis for the settlement of interrupted games of chance; for deciding the terms of life insurance policies, annuities, and other aleatory contracts; and for fixing the ground rules for jury verdicts and electoral procedures. This tradition can be seen as reaching its culmination in the work of Condorcet, the 'last of the *philosophes*', but now recognised as one of the founders of the present-day theory of 'social choice' (Baker, 1975). On the other hand, in a number of nonexperimental natural sciences, especially astronomy and geodesy, probability theory was used as a means of handling observational error and arriving at 'best estimates' in the measurement of the properties of physical objects or systems. Mathematicians of the calibre of Gauss and Laplace provided the ultimate rationale and refinement of techniques that had, however, been applied by working scientists in a rule-of-thumb fashion for many decades previously (see further Stigler, 1986: part I).

It is then not a little surprising to find that when, from around 1830 to 1860, sociology and probability theory came together in a relatively brief but highly influential period of synergy, it was in fact from the theory's application in this *latter* field that inspiration derived. The 'social mathematics' of Condorcet were almost entirely ignored; it was the 'social physics' of Adolphe Quetelet, the Belgian astronomer-turned-sociologist, that were central (cf. Daston, 1987).

As an astronomer, Quetelet was familiar with what he and his colleagues knew as Laplace's 'error law' or 'error curve' or, in modern terminology, the normal distribution. Astronomers were well aware of the fallibility both of their instruments and of their own senses, and had for long sought to improve their measurements by making many equivalent observations of a phenomenon of interest (e.g., the position of a star) and then calculating the mean of the values recorded as the best approximation to the true value. The error curve of probability theory was of key importance in legitimating this procedure. If deviations from the mean value—that is, what were to be treated as errors—proved to be distributed around the mean in accordance with this curve, the validity of taking the mean as the best estimate was confirmed. It became possible to regard errors as resulting from many different 'accidental' causes which, in the mean, were in effect cancelled out. However, if deviations were not so distributed, a more problematic situation was indicated in which the observations made were for some reason or other not equivalent or in which they were influenced by systematic rather than merely random sources of error; and in these circumstances, their mean value could stand as no more than an arbitrary arithmetical result.[3]

Quetelet's scientific interests seem first to have moved beyond astronomy when he noted that much anthropometric data—measurements of individuals' physical features and capacities, such as height, weight, or strength—showed distributions very similar to the error curve. It was, he suggested, as if Nature were 'aiming' at a true value, represented by the mean, but, because of various accidental influences, was subject to inaccuracy, or error, in the same way as a marksman shooting at a target. But Quetelet made his crucial step, so far as social science was concerned, by then going on to discover, or at all events to propose, a similar phenomenon in the case of demographic and, further, of 'moral' statistics—the statistics of marriage, illegitimacy, suicide, crime, and so on. Like many others before him, Quetelet was impressed by the fact that such moral statistics, considered as, say, annual rates for some national or regional population, or in some other ratio form, showed a high degree of stability. But what distinguished his position was his suggestion that if one traced out the variation in such rates or ratios around a mean value for a large number of observations, what tended to be revealed was again the error curve.

Where this was the case, Quetelet then argued, the mean values could be taken as expressing distinctive features of the population to which they referred; or, alternatively, distinctive propensities (*penchants*) of its individual members: that is, their propensities to marry, have illegitimate children, kill themselves, or resort to crime. In other words, from these values one could be said to learn not just about the 'average man' (*l'homme moyen*) of a population in some purely arithmetical sense but also, because the means were ones derived from observations distributed according to the error curve, about the 'typical man' (*l'homme type*). In turn, then, Quetelet maintained, it was on such true mean values that scientific attention should focus. For these values would be purely influenced by, and would thus facilitate the identification of, those causal factors at work that were of a *constant* or, possibly, a *systematically varying* kind; whereas actually observed rates would, in addition, be influenced by a wide range of accidental causes of no particular interest. Thus, from astronomical observations, through anthropometric data to moral statistics, the same logic was pursued: where true means were to be found, as guaranteed by the error curve, true values were represented.[4]

The work of Quetelet has then to be seen as the first attempt at the study of regularities in social action that combined the use of extensive descriptive statistics with some elements of probability theory. However, in its own day it proved to have a wider significance still. The regularities to which Quetelet's efforts pointed were ones of a radically new kind—more so than he himself was able to appreciate. They were not the deterministic regularities of eighteenth-century science that could be directly explained in terms of laws of nature or of society, despite Quetelet's repeated references to the latter. Rather, they were probabilistic regularities, observable only at the level of the aggregate or 'mass', and relating to phenomena that, when viewed more locally, appeared as being inherently underdetermined.[5]

The significance of such regularities was in fact most rapidly grasped and effectively exploited by the physical scientists whom Quetelet had always sought to emulate. That is, in the development of the kinetic theory of gases and of 'statistical physics' more generally that set the probabilistic revolution on its triumphant way. Remarkably (cf. Porter, 1982, 1986: ch. 5; Gigerenzer et al., 1989: ch. 2) *both* of the leading figures in the field, Clerk Maxwell and Ludwig Boltzmann, were crucially, though independently, influenced by Quetelet. Both acknowledged his work on moral statistics as providing the basic model of how a higher-level order could emerge, and become open to study, from out of lower-level processes that, whether ultimately subject to deterministic laws or not, proved to be practically untreatable from this point of view. Thus, the rather ironic situation arose that while Quetelet aimed always to base his social science on the methods of physics in its classical era, those who in the mid-nineteenth century were creating a new physics felt free to take their lead from the insights of Quetelet's social science. As Krüger (1987: 80) has remarked, at this point 'the familiar hierarchy of the disciplines loses meaning'.

By 1860, Quetelet's own original work was virtually completed. He had, however, large numbers of devoted followers throughout Europe, and his ideas were to remain a major focus of commentary and critique within statistics for at least two decades more. Correspondingly, sociology continued to be one of the main subject-matter areas with reference to which key issues were pursued. Two such issues can, for present purposes at least, be taken as of main importance.

First, as moral statistics steadily increased in both quantity and quality, and were seized on by the disciples of Quetelet, doubts began to be voiced about the main postulate of his approach to the analysis and interpretation of such data: that is, that series of moral statistics revealed a long-term stability, in the sense that short-term deviations from their mean values conformed to the error curve. The enthusiasts of *Queteletismus,* still more than Quetelet himself, were, as Hacking has put it (1990: 113), ready to accept 'any empirical distribution that came up in a hump' as being that which they wished to find. But work in the 1870s by more critically minded statisticians, such as Emile Dormoy in France and Wilhelm Lexis in Germany, on evaluating dispersion in statistical series led to increased questioning in this regard. In the light of the tests that were developed, the indications were in fact that most series of moral statistics showed greater dispersion in their distributions than would be expected under the error curve (Porter, 1986: 240–55; Desrosières, 1993: 116–21). Thus, the idea that mean values captured general population characteristics that were causally specific was subverted. It seemed rather the case that rates of moral statistics calculated for, say, a national society were a composite of those specific to a number of different collectivities within that society, each of which was subject to its own particular set of causal processes.

In fact, Quetelet had always shown an awareness of this problem of 'heterogeneity'[6] and in many of his analyses had recognised, at least implicitly, that just a single 'average individual' would be quite inadequate to represent an entire society. A whole series of average men—and average women—further specified by age, ethnicity, occupation, social class, and so on, might need to be distinguished before true average rates could be isolated. Indeed, in pursuing this line of argument, Quetelet was led to produce, notably in his studies of crime rates (see esp. 1835/1842: part 3) some recognisable, though primitive, exercises in *multivariate* analysis.[7] And in this way he then himself anticipated what in the later nineteenth century was to mark the decisive break with *Queteletismus:* that is, the movement, as Desrosières has put it (1993: ch. 4), away from 'the statistics of the average' and towards 'the statistics of relationships'.

This movement was, however, yet more powerfully driven by debate on the second major issue that arose from Quetelet's work: that of the significance that should be attached in moral and other social statistics to deviations from mean values, regardless of whether these followed the error curve or not. As noted at the outset, the probabilistic ideas that informed Quetelet's social science were ones developed in order to deal with observational problems in the physical sciences. But the analogies that Quetelet was then forced to imply between true means and best estimates in, say, astronomy and in the study of regularities in social action were clearly open to question. Just what was the validity of regarding deviations from the mean in the case of moral statistics as being 'error' in the same sense as deviations from the mean in the case of observations of celestial bodies?

An incisive treatment of the matter was eventually provided by Edgeworth (1885) who insisted that 'observations' and 'statistics' should be clearly distinguished. Observations could be understood as more or less accurate representations of the attributes of some given object—'different copies of one original'; but statistics, at least of the kind analysed by social scientists, had their own autonomy—'different originals affording one "generic portrait"'. Thus, in the former case, true means as guaranteed by the error curve could indeed be regarded as the best approximation to true values, and deviation as being mere error. But in the latter case even true means could be no more than useful summaries, and deviations from them had to be seen not as error but as genuine variation that could in fact claim a greater reality, and interest, than the mean itself.

Indeed, for some time before Edgeworth's intervention, researchers in various fields had been using the error curve in ways that were inspired by Quetelet's work but that led them clearly beyond his preoccupation with population means. Most notably, Galton, in his pioneering studies of heredity (1869, 1889a), realised the potential of the error curve from Quetelet's sociological applications, but used it as more than simply a method of determining 'types' (cf. vol. I, ch. 4). For Galton, it became the basis for examining variation in, and the intergenerational transmission of, individual characteristics within populations. As a committed hereditarian, Galton stressed the degree of family likeness that was shared by parents and their offspring across a wide range of characteristics. But by studying the relations between error-curve distributions, he made the important finding that a class of parents with a similar value on a given characteristic—for example, height—would have offspring with a mean value in this regard that differed from their own, and that would in fact show 'regression' closer to the mean value for the population as a whole. Then in further work, also on Queteletian lines, in the field of anthropometry, Galton developed the concept of 'correlation' and recognised it as being, formally, an extension of that of regression.

Galton's analytic efforts in dealing with his substantive problems proved in fact to be of far greater consequence than these problems themselves. They marked the first breakthrough in what was to become a collective intellectual achievement of a quite outstanding kind (see esp. Stigler, 1986: chs. 8–10; also Porter, 1986: chs. 5, 9). Through the subsequent work of Edgeworth and then, crucially, of Karl Pearson and George Udny Yule, Galton's initial understanding of regression and correlation as specifically biological phenomena was transformed into the idea of regression and correlation as *general statistical methods* for treating the connection between two, and then, in principle, any number of variables, *of any kind whatever*. In this way, the foundations were established of multivariate statistical analysis as it is practised today, and indeed of what Stigler (1986: 361) has aptly described as 'a unified logic of empirical science', the significance of which went far beyond that of its component techniques.

However, paradoxically, at the same time as the 'new English statistics' were being thus created, the period of vital engagement of sociology in the probabilistic revolution was coming to its close. The application of probability theory to social data had played a central role in the recognition of a new kind of regularity—probabilistic regularity—and hence of a new kind of scientific *explanandum*, unknown to the classical determinists of the eighteenth century. And sociology had remained an important subject-matter area for the initial attempts at using probability theory in turn as the basis of establishing and analysing such regularities, and of making and testing inferences about the processes through which they were generated. But, by the end of the nineteenth century, even as the full potential of this project was becoming apparent, sociology and statistics began to draw apart. The subject-matter areas in which the new statistics became most effectively deployed were, first of all, evolutionary biology, then psychology, and then, with a curious but

short delay (Morgan, 1987), economics. In the early decades of the twentieth century, biometrics, psychometrics, and econometrics came into being
and were energetically developed, but without any sociological equivalent.[8]

It cannot be supposed that what is here revealed is simply a declining
interest in sociology on the part of statisticians, preoccupied, say, with demonstrating the value of their discipline to the 'harder' sciences. The makers
of the new statistics, Galton, Edgeworth, Pearson, and Yule alike, were ex-
traordinarily wide ranging in their intellectual interests, and on numerous
occasions showed themselves ready enough to try to apply their expertise to
social, and indeed sociological, issues.[9] However, as will later be shown, their
efforts in this regard found scant appreciation in the sociological circles of
the day. Often they were not well understood and, whether understood or
not, tended to meet with a response that was at best lukewarm. Furthermore,
the tendency of sociologists to distance themselves from the new statistics
meant that even where they sought to maintain the tradition of Quetelet in
using descriptive statistical data relating to patterns of social action as a basis for empirical argument, they were increasingly ill-equipped to exploit the
analytical opportunities that such data afforded. And neither then were they
well positioned to integrate their empirical work with the development of
a theory of action consistent with probabilistic thinking and offering some
explanatory purchase in regard to the substantive problems with which they
were concerned.

Why, then, did such a situation arise, and persist for more than half a
century?

FRANCE

France could be regarded as Quetelet's intellectual homeland, but the reception of his ideas there, and especially on the part of sociologists, was perhaps
less favourable than in any other European country. To begin with, Quetelet
greatly angered Auguste Comte, the founder of 'positivist philosophy', by
taking the term *physique sociale,* in which Comte had priority, to describe
the new science that he sought to base on the analysis of statistical data.
Comte then coined the word *sociologie* in an effort to ensure that no confusion between his work and that of Quetelet should arise. But far more was
involved here than personal rivalry. For not only did Comte lack all interest
in the kind of empirical enquiry in which Quetelet engaged, he repeatedly

and vehemently opposed any suggestion that probability theory could have a useful, or indeed a valid, application in the study of society. All attempts, whether in the style of Quetelet or of Condorcet, 'à rendre positives les études sociales d'après une subordination chimérique à l'illusoire théorie mathématique des chances' (1830–42/1908: vol. 4: 270–71; cf. vol. 2: 192) were to be rejected out of hand. Moreover, the main arguments that Comte levelled against a statistically grounded sociology were ones that remained influential in France for many decades after his death.

On the one hand, Comte upheld a theory of science (cf. Heilbron, 1995: chs. 11–13) of a strongly antireductionist character. Each of the sciences that had reached the 'positive' stage had, he insisted, created its own specific methodology. Mathematics, or more precisely geometry and mechanics, had become part of the proper methodology of astronomy, and could also play some role in physics. But in the more complex science of chemistry, mathematical reasoning had little place, and in biology and sociology, which were more complex still, had no place at all. The complexity to which Comte here referred was that deriving from the degree of interdependence of the phenomena that these latter sciences treated. This meant in effect that biology and sociology had to follow what would later be called a 'holistic' approach. Their concern must be with the study of organisms or societies as such, aimed at the discovery of the principles that govern their integration and their development. So far, then, as sociology was concerned, its evidential basis had to be found not in data on patterns of individual action occurring within societies but rather in the recorded history of societies, or of entire civilisations, considered as entities in themselves. Indeed, so thoroughgoing was Comte's holism that, as Aron (1965–67, vol. 1: 83) has aptly observed, its logical conclusion, from which Comte did not in fact resile, was that the ultimate goal of sociology should be the understanding of human history in its totality, 'regarded as the history of a single people'.

On the other hand, though, Comte opposed the introduction of probabilistic thinking into sociology through an argument that appealed to the unity of science rather than to its differentiation: namely, that 'le calcul de chances' offended against the idea of deterministic law that was fundamental to every science, no matter what its methodology (cf. Hacking, 1990: ch. 17). Comte adhered always to the eighteenth-century view, which the probabilistic revolution was destined to transform, that invoking chance simply testified to ignorance. It was, he contended, open to sociology to establish laws of human society and of the movement of human history—of 'social statics' and 'social dynamics'—that would be no less strict in their determinism than those of astronomy or physics. And indeed Comte believed that he had himself succeeded in formulating the most important of these laws, the 'law of the three stages', which showed how the development of human societies was necessarily governed by the progress, no less necessary, of the human mind. Moreover, Comte's determinism, allied with his holism, then led him in turn to an extreme anti-individualistic position—in effect, as Kolakowski (1972: 87) has noted, to a virtual refusal 'to ascribe a reality to the human individual'. Consequently, at the same time as Comte's sociology excluded any notion of the social world as probabilistic, it also excluded any serious consideration of human agency: the reality of chance and the reality of choice were together denied (cf. Daston, 1987).

Comte's attack on probabilistic thinking does not appear to have had any very widespread impact. In the larger scientific context, it became rather quickly outmoded. However, in the development of sociology, and in France in particular, a Comtean legacy can clearly be traced: most consequentially, in the work of Durkheim and then of the Durkheimian school, which remained preeminent up to the time of World War II (cf. Clark, 1973).[10]

In understanding the significance of this legacy, the key text is undoubtedly Durkheim's *Suicide* (1897/1952). This work has been widely regarded as a great pioneering study in quantitative sociology, pointing the way to twentieth-century achievements. However, such a view is not a little misleading. At least as regards the creation of a sociology in which the statistical analysis of regularities in social action is combined with the explanation and understanding of such action at the individual level, *Suicide* made no contribution, nor was it intended to. It can in fact be far better seen as exemplifying several of the more serious intellectual barriers that help explain why such a project was for so long delayed.

To begin with, *Suicide* does not display any major advances in the application of statistical technique in sociological work. Durkheim differed from Comte in that he recognised the need for detailed empirical research and saw official statistics as being in this respect a valuable resource. But in his treatment of such data, Durkheim did not go much beyond the moral statisticians who had preceded him and in some ways his analyses could be reckoned as less sophisticated than those of Quetelet.[11] This is all the more remarkable in that by the time of the writing of *Suicide* the early work of the English statisticians was available and, at least to some extent, actually known to Durkheim. Already in *The Division of Labour* (1893/1933: bk. II, ch. 4) he had discussed, approvingly if not with full understanding, Galton's analyses of regression towards the mean.[12] Nonetheless, in *Suicide* Durkheim made no use of the derived concept of correlation, which would have been well-suited to his purposes and would indeed have saved him from a number of serious errors.

One possible reason for this disregard is that Durkheim, in true Comtean fashion, believed that sociology should, like any other science, have its own distinctive methods, and did not therefore wish it to be seen as overly dependent on statistics, a field, moreover, in which he had no evident expertise. But of surely greater significance was the further Comtean insistence on determinism, which runs through *Suicide* and which makes it—received opinion notwithstanding—in most respects a profoundly *anti-statistical* work.

Thus, contrary to appearances, the method on which Durkheim chiefly relies in analysing the connection between rates of suicide in different populations and other of their characteristics is not statistical at all but rather a logical procedure designed to establish relations of a quite deterministic kind: that is, John Stuart Mill's method of 'concomitant variation' (Boudon, 1967: ch. 2; and see also vol. I, ch. 3, pp. 42–7). Before a link between suicide and another population characteristic can be claimed, Durkheim typically requires (and especially when attacking the theories of rival authors) what would in modern terms be called a perfect rank-order correlation. By this criterion, he is, for example, led to deny (1897/1952: bk. 1, chs. 1–2) that *any* connection exists between the suicide rate and the proportion of German speakers in data from the Austrian provinces, or again between the suicide rate and the consumption of alcohol in data for the French *départements*—although, in both cases, a fairly strong, if far from perfect, correlation is in fact present (Selvin, 1976; Skog, 1991; cf. Desrosières, 1985). For Durkheim, in other words, dependencies between social variables had to be either total or nonexistent; no intermediate position could be recognised.

Furthermore, Durkheim's commitment to deterministic rather than probabilistic thinking emerges strongly at a theoretical as well as a technical level: that is, in the way in which he seeks to explain those constancies and variations in suicide rates that he accepts as being well established. For the authors who first discovered regularity in moral statistics, this appeared as a clear manifestation of divine providence: the pioneering work of J. P. Süssmilch of 1741 bears the title *Die göttliche Ordnung* (see Westergaard, 1932: ch. 7). Quetelet remained to a large extent under the sway of this tradition of 'explanation from above', even though appealing not to divine power but rather to that of the 'social system'. He did, however, at the same time attempt, and at the cost of some ambivalence, to accommodate individual action. As well as recognising free will as one of the accidental causes that produced variation around stable average rates, he was, as earlier noted, also ready to interpret both constancy and systematic variation in rates as expressing individual 'propensities' to act.[13] In contrast, Durkheim, following the programme of *The Rules of Sociological Method* (1895/1938), reverted to a position of macro-to-micro determinism of a quite uncompromising kind.

In taking up suicide as a subject for study, Durkheim's very purpose was to show how this apparently most private act could not be understood, in the *rate*, as opposed to the *incidence*, of its occurrence, by reference to the attributes of individuals, such as, say, their material circumstances or mental states. Rates of suicide, and indeed of the different types of suicide that Durkheim distinguished, had to be seen as determined by 'realities' that were entirely external to and independent of the individual. These realities took the form of what Durkheim called suicidogenic 'currents' or 'impulses' that bore off their victims at a rate directly proportional to the strength with which they operated at particular times and in particular societies and their various milieux. In other words, what Durkheim had in mind here were not simply *conditions* of action that might influence individual decisions on whether or not to commit suicide but rather 'real, living, active forces' in which causal power inhered and to which individuals were subject (see 1897/1952: bk. 2, ch. 1; bk. 3 ch. 1 esp.).

As several commentators have observed, Durkheim could not himself always sustain the 'radical disjunction' (Lukes, 1975: 213) that he wished to set up between the explanation of suicide rates and of individual acts of suicide. Especially in his more detailed discussions of how rates of egoistic, altruistic, and anomic suicide are determined by the differing intensities of primary social relations and of moral regulation, Durkheim tends to move down from the level of suicidogenic currents and to treat statistical associations between suicide rates and specific social situations in terms of individuals' subjective responses. That is to say, he *does* refer, and despite his own prohibitions (e.g., 1897/1952: 43, 297), to the meanings that suicide carries for individuals and in turn to their motives and intentions in either killing themselves or being resistant to this course of action (see esp. Douglas, 1967: ch. 2; cf. also Aron, 1965–67, vol. 2: ch. 5; Lukes, 1975: ch. 9).

However, what, for present purposes, is important is that still at no stage does Durkheim come to contend seriously with the idea that statistically demonstrated regularities in suicide rates might be explained in a way quite different from that which his methodological programme would require. That is, not deterministically, by appeal to the operation of macrosocial forces external to and independent of individuals—and indeed of an altogether mysterious character (cf. Aron, 1965–67, vol. 2: 87–91)—but rather probabilistically, as the outcome of individual actions varying around some central tendency under a range of conditions that may themselves differ over time or from one population or subpopulation to another. At just one point in *Suicide* (1897/1952: 305–306) does Durkheim contemplate this possibility, with reference to the work of Moritz Drobisch (1867). Durkheim here clearly sees the import of the probabilistic argument—perhaps all too clearly. With this argument, he writes, 'One need not assume that they [potential suicides] yield to a superior influence; but merely that they reason generally in the same way when confronted by the same circumstances.' But he at once proceeds to a rejection that is based, first, on an entirely question-begging assertion—that we already *know* that the circumstances associated with suicides 'are not their real causes'—and, second, on the quite fallacious claim that if suicides did come about in this way, then suicide rates could not display the kinds of regularity that are apparent.

In sum, it was not for Durkheim conceivable that in accounting for these regularities no effect of a societal power existing over and above individuals need be invoked, but only the actions of individuals themselves, aggregated through the 'laws of chance' (cf. Oberschall, 1987: 117; Hacking, 1990: 177–78). Ironically, in his concern to make sociology a true Comtean science, dealing in holistic and deterministic causation rather than the uncertainties of human action and its interpretation, Durkheim failed to grasp one of the most potent ideas of the science of his day: that the operation of chance at one level could play a crucial role in the creation of order—of a kind—at a higher, emergent level.

After *Suicide*, Durkheim's interest in the use of statistical data waned. Work that he started on crime rates, intended, it seems, to form the basis of a sequel, was never completed (Lukes, 1975: 257). From the later 1890s Durkheim's main substantive concerns came in fact to centre on systems of *représentations collectives* as the ultimate source of the moral regulation of societies. The approach he pursued was primarily an evolutionary one, in the sense that he sought to identify the original, or at least the most 'elementary', expressions of the ideational and institutional phenomena that he wished to study, most famously, of course, in *The Elementary Forms of the Religious Life* (1912/1915). The empirical materials to which he chiefly resorted were then those of comparative history and, increasingly, ethnography, despite the strong reservations about the reliability of the latter that he had previously voiced.[14]

Moreover, this shift in the focus of Durkheim's work exerted a powerful influence on the Durkheimian school in the process of its formation around the journal, *L'Année sociologique,* the first volume of which appeared in 1898. Up to the time of Durkheim's death in 1917 and the disruption of the school in consequence of World War I, most of Durkheim's closer associates, such as Mauss, Hubert, and Hertz, also concentrated their attention on 'archaic' rather than modern societies and established strong ties with the emerging discipline of social anthropology (Karady, 1981, 1983; cf. also Clark, 1973: Appendix 2). In contrast, some others associated with the *Année* whose sociological interests directed them towards research in the society of their own day and of a more quantitative kind tended to be marginalised. For instance, the concerns of Paul Lapie with the role of education in social mobility (Lapie was the inventor of the mobility table) were apparently deemed 'not sociologisable', on the grounds that they were too much related to psychology (Besnard, 1983a; cf. also Cherkaoui, 1983)—or, one might say, to individual life events and courses of action that ideational and institutional structures conditioned but did not determine. For the true Durkheimians, any individualistic approach threatened to compromise the autonomy of their new discipline by implying psychological foundations.

This is not of course to say that the Durkheimian school was entirely monolithic. Both before and after the war, there were those who strove from within to free it from some of the rigidities that, in the name of Comtean science, it had imposed on itself. However, their efforts remained crucially lacking in the degree of confidence and coherence that would have been needed in order to give French sociology a radically new orientation. Thus, Bouglé (1896, 1899), under the influence of both French and German neo-Kantianism, was ready to question the dogma that required that the explanation of 'social facts' should be given always in terms of 'preceding social facts' (cf. Durkheim, 1895/1938: 110) rather than of the actions of individuals and their consequences. But although in the 1930s some of his students moved, in various directions, away from Durkheimian orthodoxy (Stoetzel, 1957), Bouglé himself had no apparent interest in, nor perhaps the ability to take up, the possibilities offered by new statistical thinking for translating his theoretical ideas into research and data analysis (cf. Vogt, 1983).

Conversely, Simiand and Halbwachs kept in close touch with 'official' statisticians in France (Desrosières, 1996) and also monitored the development of the new statistics in England and elsewhere, with advantage to their own empirical studies (e.g., Simiand, 1907, 1932; Halbwachs, 1930/1978, 1933). Both clearly favoured statistical over the ethnographic methods of the other Durkheimians—Simiand (1932) inveighing against the 'superstition de l'étude d'origine' and the 'tissu d'anecdotes' often involved in its pursuit (cf. Desrosières, 1985: 306), while Halbwachs upheld statistical analysis as the only means of reliably identifying social regularities (Craig, 1983: 283). Further, both Simiand and Halbwachs saw in emerging multivariate techniques a vital substitute for experimental methods in the testing of explanatory theory. However, their work did not bring into being any distinctively new style of sociological analysis. While their lack of more general influence may in some degree be attributable to personal characteristics and circumstances, neither in fact showed any tendency to waver in the defence of the essentials of Durkheim's meta-theoretical stance.[15] Indeed, they could together be ranked among their master's most faithful adherents in regarding the regularities that statistical or other research revealed as being expressions of a supra-individual reality sui generis, which were then to be accounted for at this same level and *not* by resorting to theories formulated in the perspective of actors themselves (cf. Desrosières, 1991, 1993: 267–71).[16] It was, moreover, chiefly on this account that they followed Durkheim into a polemical 'imperialism' that sought to represent other social sciences and various humanistic disciples as being ultimately subordinate to sociology (cf. Clark, 1973: ch. 6; Besnard, 1983b; Craig, 1983) and that blinded them, often, it must be said, in a rather embarrassing fashion, to the degree of success that an antideterministic and individualistic approach had elsewhere achieved, most notably, perhaps, in economics and historiography.

In sum, even though challenged in particular respects, and in some decline in the later 1920s and 1930s, the Durkheimian school still managed to maintain an intellectual influence too powerful to allow the emergence in France of any fundamentally different version of sociology, in which the concept of social action would provide the focus for statistical analysis and theoretical understanding alike.[17]

ENGLAND

Quetelet's work was viewed far more positively and exerted a far wider influence in England than in France. Quetelet was a frequent visitor to England and enjoyed the respect of leading figures in English science, such as Herschel and Whewell. Moreover, as earlier noted, it was in England in the later nineteenth century that, starting from Quetelet's exploitation of the error curve in his *physique sociale,* modern methods of multivariate statistics were created. It might therefore appear that England represented an unusually favourable context for the integration of sociology within the probabilistic revolution. And all the more so, perhaps, since the country had also a strong tradition of economics that, by the time in question, could offer a relatively well-developed model of 'micro-to-macro' analysis, in which regularities observable at an aggregate, societal level were theoretically explained by reference to individual action. However, from this standpoint, the actual progress of sociology turned out to be as disappointing in England as in France—in part for similar, but in part too for rather different reasons.

In England as well as France the influence of Comte stood for long as a barrier to statistical thinking in sociology. John Stuart Mill and Herbert Spencer, dominant figures of the Victorian era, tended alike to play down their intellectual debt to Comte on account, it would seem, of their strong disagreement with him on political issues (cf. Abrams, 1968: 53–58). Nonetheless, both were fully committed to the Comtean faith that the concept of deterministic law, the foundation of the natural sciences, was, in principle at least, equally applicable to the study of society. In his early years, Mill indeed followed Comte in attacking probability theory—'the real opprobrium of mathematics' (1843/1973: bk. vii, 583); and although he was ready, as was Spencer, to accept the regularities revealed by moral and other social statistics as data of some significance, this was always from a strictly deterministic position. Such regularities were to be understood as the outcome, albeit perhaps complex, of the operation of invariable laws that it was the task of sociology to discover.[18] Furthermore, Mill and Spencer were also at one with Comte in believing that the ultimate concern of sociology must be not with the laws of social statics but, rather, with those of social dynamics: the laws according to which one state or form of society succeeded another over the course of human history. In turn, then, for them, as for Comte, the empirical materials—and regularities—of crucial interest were those provided not by statistics but by historical, and also in Spencer's case, ethnographic enquiry.

The major scientific issue on which Mill and Spencer differed from Comte was that of the relation between sociology and psychology. Comte refused even to allow psychology a place in the structure of positivist science; there was no space between the claims of sociology and biology. Mill and Spencer, in contrast, were both sufficiently under the sway of the English individualistic tradition to wish to have sociological laws ultimately grounded in psychological ones, in the sense of 'laws of human nature'. However, what must still be recognised is that no relaxation of their determinism was here entailed of a kind that might have allowed a theory of social action, as distinct from social behaviour, to emerge.

The linkage between sociological and psychological laws envisaged by Mill (1843/1973: bk. vi, chs. 3–8) was highly complicated and, perhaps not surprisingly, remained no more than programmatic.[19] For Spencer, matters were simplified by his evolutionism and, more specifically, by his adherence to a theory of evolution of an unreservedly Lamarckian kind (cf. Peel, 1971: ch. 6). On this basis, he was able to integrate individualism and holism in an apparently seamless way. As societies struggled to survive and grow, evolutionary processes—ones of increasing social differentiation and integration—worked themselves out at an institutional level, but at the same time accommodative changes occurred, and were intergenerationally transmitted, in the behaviour patterns of individuals and indeed in human nature itself (Spencer, 1873/1961: ch. 3 esp.). Thus, without denying a role to psychology, Spencer's explanatory approach could still remain essentially 'macro-to-micro', being in effect, a pioneering version of structural-functionalism (cf. Burrow, 1966: ch.6; Abrams, 1968; Peel, 1971: ch. 7) reliant on a *highly* 'oversocialised conception of man' (Wrong, 1961; and cf. vol. 1, ch. 8). The individual was to be viewed 'as one whose will is a factor in social evolution and yet as one whose will is a product of all antecedent influences, social included'.[20]

An important methodological implication of this position was, then, that while the relevance of individual action was acknowledged in principle, *in the actual practice of empirical enquiry* institutions could be the almost exclusive focus of attention—as indeed they were throughout the volumes of Spencer's *Principles of Sociology* (1876–97). Because the process of social evolution was taken to guarantee what Spencer called (after Comte) a 'consensus' between the institutions of a society and the social character of its members (1873/1961: 47), all patterns of action, or rather behaviour, could be taken as, so to speak, instancing the presence of some institution or other. And, conversely, an adequate account of the institutional structure of a society could then stand as at very least an adequate synopsis of the behavioural regularities that its members displayed. In other words, the need for any direct statistical demonstration of these regularities was circumvented: an obvious convenience, one might add, so far as a wide-ranging treatment of historical and preliterate societies was concerned.

With Spencer there in fact originated a distinctive English tradition of sociology *defined as* the study of social institutions in comparative and evolutionary or developmental perspective. L. T. Hobhouse, who occupied the first chair in sociology in a British university—at the London School of Economics from 1907 to 1929—stood clearly in this tradition (e.g., 1906, 1924), even while striving to produce a version of social evolutionism more 'moralised' than that of Spencer and in turn more congenial to collectivist politics (cf. Collini, 1979). And his successor, Morris Ginsberg, upheld the tradition, if more through exposition than continuing research, until well after the World War II.

For present purposes, it need further be noted about this tradition only that its representatives' lack of enthusiasm for statistical methods was apparent even in the pursuit of their analyses at the level of institutions. In 1888 in a paper to the Anthropological Institute, Edward Tylor presented evidence of correlations (or what he called 'adhesions') among elements of economic and familial institutions across almost 400 societies (Tylor, 1889). Galton, at that time president of the Institute and himself an experienced ethnographer, questioned the validity of Tylor's analyses on the grounds of a probable lack of independence among his cases resulting from—to use a later term—'cultural diffusion', and thus initiated what remains well known in comparative sociology as the Galton problem (see vol. I, ch. 3). But what is less well known is that Galton (1889b) also offered various encouraging suggestions about how Tylor might deal with the problem and in other ways improve his statistical work as, for example, through what would now be called tests of significance.[21] Tylor did not, apparently, ever seek to follow this advice. However, what is far more remarkable is that when, a quarter of a century later, Hobhouse, Wheeler, and Ginsberg in their *Material Culture and Social Institutions of the Simpler Peoples* (1915) carried out analyses similar in form to Tylor's, they were content simply to follow his methods (cf. also Ginsberg, 1965). They made no **reference** whatever to Galton or to any of those who had followed him in **transforming** statistical thinking and technique—although they did regret that more had not been done to extend *Tylor's* methods to other issues! Perhaps the most plausible explanation that can be advanced for this almost studied disregard is that Hobhouse could not dissociate the new statistics from the eugenics movement that Galton had in effect initiated and Pearson promoted, and to which Hobhouse was strongly opposed (Collini, 1979: ch. 6).[22]

The other major tradition in the early history of English sociology, apart from that of comparative and evolutionary institutionalism, was represented by the study of social problems and policy—with particular reference to issues of poverty and 'the condition of the working class'. Such enquiry, though extending back to the 'political arithmeticians' of the seventeenth century (cf. Stone, 1997), revived strongly in the 1830s in association with a growing enthusiasm for the collection of statistical data and the organisation of local statistical societies, and also at this time had rather close links with political economy (Abrams, 1968; Cullen, 1975). But, despite these seemingly promising beginnings, the proponents of this tradition, too, proved more or less immune to the attractive opportunities for the empirical analysis of social data and their theoretical understanding that the probabilistic revolution afforded. In this case, the barrier was not determinism but rather a crude and unreflecting empiricism.

To begin with, the leaders of the 'statistical movement', anxious to avoid its disruption by political dissension, especially in regard to the principles of political economy, represented the role of statistics as being simply that of the production of *facts,* in numerical form, and not consideration of what these facts implied or how they might be explained. Thus, when in 1833 a statistical section was created within the British Association for the Advancement of Science, its president went out of his way to stress that should statistics once transgress its proper concern with matters of fact, 'that instant will the foul Daemon of discord find its way into our Eden of philosophy' (Cullen, 1975: 79). And when, the following year, the Statistical Society of London (the forerunner of the Royal Statistical Society) was established, it adopted the quite explicit motto of *Aliis Exterendum*—'It is for others to thresh out our results'. In this context, then, the study of social problems could rarely rise above unfocused, even if often profuse, description; insofar as investigators were bold enough to consider policy questions, they did so with little in the way of intervening analysis.

Furthermore, given the prevalence of this Gradgrind view of the role of statistics in social research, there was little incentive for its practitioners to keep abreast of technical advances. Indeed, there was resistance to what was called the 'mathematicisation' of statistics—that is, the grounding of statistical analysis in probability theory (cf. Lecuyer, 1987); and over the course of the nineteenth-century technical standards of social research using statistics would appear, if anything, to have declined rather than improved (cf. Cole, 1972; Oberschall, 1987).[23] Consequently, by the time the tradition of 'social problems and policy' research reached its culmination with the poverty surveys of Booth (1889–1903) and Rowntree (1901) a wide gulf had opened up between the conception of statistics that this work embodied and that which informed the new English statistics, concurrently emerging as one of the great achievements of the probabilistic revolution.

In this regard, the most revealing episode is the clash that occurred between Booth and Yule over whether a connection existed between pauperism and poor relief policy: specifically, the giving of relief outdoors rather than indoors (i.e., in workhouses). Booth had denied any such connection but Yule (1895), using the new technique of correlation, demonstrated that across English poor law unions the higher the proportion of out-relief—relief given without the requirement of entering workhouses—the higher, on average, was the rate of pauperism. From Booth's reply (1896), it was apparent that he suffered from exactly the same difficulty as Durkheim in understanding correlation. He conceded that Yule had shown what he called a 'general' relation between out-relief and pauperism but not, he insisted, a 'regular' one—by which he meant simply that the correlation was not perfect. To this Yule (1896: 613–14) made the obvious counter that a perfect correlation was scarcely to be expected wherever 'one quantity (e.g., pauperism) is a function of a great many others' and that the important point, both analytically and in respect of policy, was whether there was any correlation *at all*.

In a later paper (1899) Yule then took up another of Booth's objections (which he had in fact anticipated) that the correlation revealed might be spurious, with levels both of out-relief and of pauperism being determined by some other factor such as, say, the actual amount of poverty. This paper was of major technical importance in that it marked the final stage in the freeing of the ideas of correlation and regression from the particular biological contexts in which Galton had first developed them, and in turn illustrated their applicability to social data (Stigler, 1986: 345–58).[24] But the paper also represented, and still represents, a notable piece of quantitative sociology. Yule established that his correlation held up when several likely confounding factors were allowed for and also that it persisted when *changes* in levels of out-relief and pauperism were considered. Furthermore, while clearly concerned with the use of regression in treating causal questions regarding variation in pauperism, Yule was nonetheless aware that his analysis could in itself establish only association, not causation (see esp. 1899, n. 25; cf. Freedman, 1999 and vol. I, ch. 6), and indeed appeared to recognise that in the end the explanation of the regularities he displayed would need to be given in terms of the patterns of action of the different parties involved—the poor, paupers, poor law administrators, and so on. His paper, he emphasised, was, as it stood, incomplete and raised many issues to which he hoped to return.[25]

However, he received little encouragement to do so. Booth chose not to pursue the controversy, perhaps because he now felt out of his depth (despite being a former president of the Royal Statistical Society) and, as Selvin (1976) has suggested, preferred the intellectually less demanding world of 'newspaper editorials and Royal Commissions'. And when in 1905 such a Commission was appointed to consider reform of the Poor Laws, with Booth as a member and responsible for statistics, Yule's work was almost entirely ignored.[26] In fact, the tradition of research into poverty and working-class social conditions continued in the narrowly descriptive mode already established in the 1830s through to the mid-twentieth century. Although methods of data collection were significantly advanced, notably with Bowley's introduction of probability theory into sampling (Bowley, 1906, 1926; Bowley and Burnett-Hurst, 1915), the opportunities for improving analytical procedures, following on Yule's lead, were disregarded, and explanations of poverty and its consequences, if they were attempted at all, remained of a very limited kind (cf. Kent, 1985).[27]

Indeed, insofar as any significant development of the tradition did occur, it went in a clearly anti-statistical *and* anti-analytical direction. The studies of Beatrice and Sidney Webb (e.g., Webb, 1891; Webb and Webb, 1894, 1897) represented a shift of interest away from the social conditions of the working class to its social institutions—cooperatives, trade unions, and local governmental bodies. And with this work, institutionalism and the cult of 'the facts' were powerfully combined. Beatrice Webb numbered both Spencer and Booth among her mentors, and Spencer taught her, she recalled (1926: 38), 'to look on all social institutions exactly as if they were plants or animals' and to describe and classify them accordingly. In their textbook on methods of social research (1932), the Webbs gave only one rather hesitant chapter to statistics, which they still understood essentially as a means of univariate description. The creation of the 'statistics of relationships' over the preceding three decades was simply ignored. They did, however, echo the Spencerian lesson. 'The only right way to approach the subject-matter of sociology', they wrote (1932: 41), 'is not to focus the enquiry upon discovering the answer to some particular question' but to choose 'a particular social institution', treat it as if it were 'the type-specimen of a plant or some species of animal' and 'to acquire all possible information about it'. Their faith then was not only that 'the facts would speak for themselves' (cf. Kent, 1981: ch. 3) but further, following Spencer, that establishing the facts about social institutions was in effect the same thing as establishing the regularities present in social action.

In England the emergence of a version of sociology capable of exploiting the new technical and theoretical possibilities that the probabilistic revolution offered was not blocked, as it was in France, by an already well-entrenched school of sociology, inimical to developments in this direction. Sociology in the early decades of the twentieth century remained a quite ill-defined enterprise, and indeed one fragmented to a yet greater extent than the foregoing account has been able to bring out (see further Abrams, 1968; Halliday, 1968; Bulmer, ed., 1985). The disputatious history of the Sociological Society (founded in 1903) and the highly variegated contents of its journal, *The Sociological Review,* stand in marked contrast with the degree of intellectual coherence achieved by the Durkheimian school and *L'Année sociologique.* Nonetheless, the same negative outcome, from the standpoint of this essay, is to be observed in England as in France.

Perhaps the most notable comparative point here is that even though sociology was more loosely understood and organised in England than in France, it does not appear to have been any more open to new intellectual influences or better able to build positive relationships with neighbouring disciplines. As already indicated, English sociologists, or proto-sociologists, showed little appreciation of the transformation of statistics that was being achieved in their own country—far less in fact than did Simiand and Halbwachs. And at the same time they would appear to have been no more inclined than were the 'imperialistic' Durkheimians to respond to current work in other social sciences or the humanities that could have afforded them theoretical perspectives better suited to a probabilistic world than those they carried over in effect from the early nineteenth century.

Thus, for example, the efforts of Alfred Marshall (1890) to widen utility theory as a theory of action by elaborating the idea of 'wants' and relating it to that of 'activities' had a large, if undeveloped, sociological potential but one which aroused no interest at all within the English sociological community—although it was, of course, later seized on by Talcott Parsons (1937) as the starting point of his own theoretical odyssey. Similarly, Collingwood's attempts (1946/1993) to set the rational reconstruction of 'processes of action', rather than the 'external' narration of events, at the core of historiography were highly suggestive as regards alternative possibilities for explanation in sociology, but found no resonance among its English practitioners. And it is in turn then scarcely surprising that for most established scholars, including Marshall and Collingwood themselves, sociology should have remained a highly dubious undertaking, veering unpersuasively between grandiose but ill-supported claims of deterministic laws of society in the manner of Comte and Spencer and fact gathering and classifying of an essentially mindless kind.[28]

GERMANY

In Germany the main reception of Quetelet's ideas was of later date than in France or England, and followed their popularisation through the work of Buckle (1857), which first appeared in German translations in the 1860s. However, the debate that then ensued was in general of a more sophisticated and penetrating kind than occurred elsewhere, and formed an important strand within the complex *Methodenstreite* that were a feature of the social sciences and humanities in Germany (cf. Desrosières, 1996). The crucial issue was that of the significance, scientific and philosophical, that should be attached to the social regularities that Quetelet and his followers were able to display and, in particular, when these were viewed from the standpoint of the Kantian dualism of 'the realm of necessity' and 'the realm of freedom'. Did the demonstration of such regularities in the statistics of marriage, illegitimacy, suicide, or crime mean that the realm of necessity extended to human society? And, if so, did this then further mean that ideas of the freedom of human will and of the moral determination of individual conduct were illusory?

The answers offered to these questions were diverse (Porter, 1986: ch. 6 esp., 1987; Hacking, 1990: ch. 15 esp.). Most, and including those that were of major consequence for the development of sociology, entailed rejection of at least the larger claims of *Queteletismus,* but often on the basis of arguments that were of an appreciative as well as a critical kind. In fact, with benefit of hindsight, it could be said that in the period here under review it was in Germany that the implications of the probabilistic revolution for the nature of the social sciences were most seriously considered and, in turn, that the possibility of a sociology capable of assimilating these implications, both methodological and theoretical, came closest to realisation—even though, in the end, this was not achieved.

German philosophic and academic traditions, and notably those expressed in the distinction between *Geisteswissenschaften* and *Naturwissenschaften,* in themselves entailed a far greater resistance than in France or England to the idea that deterministic law could hold a similar place in the study of society to that which it held in the study of the natural world. For this reason, sociology as understood by Comte, or later Spencer, gained only a relatively limited following in nineteenth-century Germany and was the subject of many forceful attacks (Aron, 1936). In turn, the most typical reaction of German social scientists to the regularities demonstrated by the Queteletians was not to seize on these as manifesting the operation of underlying social laws but, rather, to emphasise their purely empirical character and to insist on the difference between such empirical regularities and true laws that carried causal force. Moreover, from this position it could further be argued that because no law had been established, there could be no question of the curtailment of the autonomy of the individual. It was 'statistical fatalism', not free will, that was illusory.

At the same time, though, such a position did not lead to acceptance of a radical individualism of the kind that was associated in Germany with the English utilitarian tradition—and thus again with supposedly deterministic laws, in this case those of political economy. The most significant group in the German reception of Quetelet was made up of adherents of the 'historical school' of economics, often also members of the Verein für Sozialpolitik, founded in 1872, who stood opposed to both the principles and practice of *laissez-faire* and who had in fact already established their own tradition of descriptive statistics in the course of their critique of abstract economic theory. For these thinkers, Queteletian statistics pointed a way to greater analytical rigour, but, given their dominant sociopolitical concerns with the growing differentiation and tensions of German society as rapid industrialisation took hold, a focus on population averages appeared to them inadequate. Although out of quite different interests, they followed Galton in insisting on the importance of *variation* as well as means, but with the emphasis on variation at the level of subpopulations, or social collectivities, rather than of individuals.

The key role in this regard was played by Wilhelm Lexis, one of the founders of the Verein. As earlier noted, Lexis's work on dispersion (1877, 1879/1903: ch.8) led to serious doubts over whether series of moral statistics could be regarded as showing merely random fluctuations around their mean values. This work was, however, more than just technical in ambition. The indication that such series were almost all 'supernormal'—that is, displayed greater dispersion than would be expected under the normal curve—led Lexis to argue, following in fact Quetelet's own logic, that the rates or ratios examined were actually a summation of ones that should have been regarded as specific to a number of component collectivities in which differing levels or trends over time were present. In other words, if the recorded statistics of marriage, illegitimacy, suicide, crime, and so on were to be properly understood, they must be treated in an appropriately disaggregated form—by age, sex, occupation, region, and also period. Statistics, in Lexis's view (1875, 1877), should aim to establish for each of the many social groupings that together made up a modern society their own 'probability schemes' (*Chancensysteme*) in regard to different kinds of act or life event, and then to trace out the nature of change in these differing probabilities. In this way, statistics could provide the 'natural-scientific foundation' for the social sciences (cf. Porter, 1986: 247–53) and free them from dependence on either spurious laws or analyses of an entirely abstract kind.

Moreover, Lexis also drew significance from a negative result: that none of the series that he examined proved to be 'subnormal'—that is, to show less dispersion than if it were indeed normal. Here the important point was that if in the various kinds of action represented by the statistics in question, all individuals within a society were alike subject to some constraining supra-individual force, then subnormality is what might have been expected, as it would be if a particular action was required of certain individuals by law in the sense of a statute—as, say, entering military service at a given age. Conversely, in the absence of subnormality, there would seem little reason why regularities in social statistics should not be seen as resulting simply from individuals acting, probabilistically, in similar ways insofar as they found themselves in similar circumstances—just as in fact Drobisch had suggested in the case of regularities in suicide rates, to Durkheim's uncomprehending disapproval (see further Porter, 1986: 248–49; Wise, 1987; Gigerenzer et al., 1989: 52–53).

Finally, though, Lexis acknowledged (1874/1903: ch. 10) that statistical analysis could not in itself provide causal accounts of patterns of human action. To arrive at such accounts, social scientists would need to complement the empirical results obtained through the natural science methodology of statistics with some form of understanding (*Verständnis*) of the subjective mental states of actors and of their motivations. In economics, Lexis argued, the causal explanation and the understanding of action alike derived from the postulate that individuals pursued their material interests to the best of their ability. On this basis, models of rational action could be constructed and their adequacy in relation to statistically established empirical regularities could in turn be assessed (cf. Oberschall, 1965: 48–49).[29] Some appropriate generalisation of this procedure, Lexis appeared to believe, would represent the best way ahead for the other social sciences.

With Lexis, then, one has at least an outline sketch of a kind of sociology in which the quantitative analysis of patterns of social action and the attempt at their explanation and interpretation would be combined. However, little in fact developed from Lexis's writings in this regard. His own substantive interests lay chiefly in economics and demography, and he would in any event seem to have become steadily less adventurous intellectually as his academic career progressed (Schumpeter, 1954: 852–53). Moreover, from the 1870s through to the 1890s other unfavourable conditions supervened.

On the one hand, this was the period in which in Germany positivist conceptions of sociology, and in particular different versions of Social Darwinism, achieved their greatest prominence, even though confined largely to the fringes of the academic community. Not only were their proponents themselves little interested in either statistics or the theory of social action but, further, their 'naturalistic' excesses had the effect of arousing the hostility of the mandarin defenders of the *Geisteswissenschaften* against sociology in general.[30] On the other hand, and, in the long view, yet more damagingly, German statistics fell into decline. Representatives of the older German tradition of statistics as a form of state bookkeeping (*Universitätsstatistik*) resisted the introduction of probability theory and the conception of statistics as a general methodology for empirical research (Lazarsfeld, 1961; Schad, 1972: 22–25), while the successors of Lexis reacted by concentrating more on mathematical problems of probability theory itself than on those of its application, at all events outside of the physical sciences (Porter, 1986: 253–55). Thus, statistics in Germany languished, in notable contrast with the situation in England where major theoretical advances were made largely in consequence of the pursuit of substantive concerns in the social and biological fields.

It was not in fact until the first decade of the twentieth century that the possibility returned that something on the lines of Lexis's programme, or indeed a yet more ambitious project, might be accomplished: that is, with the attempt, led by Max Weber, to create in Germany a sociology quite distinct in its conception from that of Comte or Spencer and that would impose both strong empirical *and* explanatory-cum-interpretative requirements.[31]

From an early stage in his career, and while still working primarily as an economic and legal historian, Weber took up a number of methodological positions (1903–1906/1975, 1904/1949, 1906/1949, 1907/1977, 1908/1975) that crucially shaped his understanding of what sociology could, and could not, hope to achieve and how it should proceed. To begin with, he rejected the idea that sociology should aim at the formulation of deterministic laws and in particular developmental or evolutionary laws claiming to provide some cognitive grasp on the general movement of human history. From this point of view, Weber thus came into opposition not only with Comte and Spencer and their intellectual heirs but likewise with Marx and the Marxist theoreticians of the German labour movement. Further, Weber was sceptical of what could be gained from 'organic' analogies in the study of societies that led to explanations of their institutional or other structural features in functional terms (cf. also 1922/1968: 14–15). He insisted, rather, that sociology must rely on causal explanations of a probabilistic kind that

were given 'micro-to-macro' in terms of individual action and its consequences, and he can indeed claim priority in the assertion of the principle of
methodological individualism (Ringer, 1997; Udéhn, 2001: ch. 4) and in the
more or less explicit counterposing of—to follow Boudon's (1987) distinction—the individualistic against the nomological paradigm in sociology (see
esp. 1913/1981: 158–59).

Thus, for Weber, social institutions could not be the ultimate units of
sociological analysis, nor their description an adequate substitute for the
study of social action itself. For institutions were no more than the products of action, and while they in turn obviously conditioned action, they
did not determine it: they implied only the probability that given forms of
action by individuals would occur. At the same time, though, Weber made
it abundantly clear that adopting such an individualistic approach did *not*
entail the grounding of sociology in a naturalistic psychology (1908/1975,
1913/1981). To the contrary, if sociological explanation had, as Weber believed, to entail the 'interpretative understanding' of action, this must derive from the sociologist's reconstruction of the meanings with which actors
themselves subjectively endowed their actions in the particular kinds of situation under study (Ringer, 1997: ch. 4 esp.).

For a basic model of such 'explanatory interpretation' (*erklärendes Verstehen*), which could make action intelligible at the same time as giving it
causal force, Weber in fact, in much the same way as Lexis, looked to economic analysis (Lachmann, 1970: ch. 1; Ringer, 1997; Swedberg, 1998: ch.
2). Here, a major advantage existed insofar as attention focused on action of
an instrumentally rational (*Zweckrational*) type, which was that most open
to intelligible reconstruction through the demonstration of logical links between actors' goals, their beliefs, and the courses of action they then in
fact followed (see esp. 1903–1906/1975: 186–91, 1913/1981: 151–56). But,
again like Lexis, Weber regarded the explanatory strategy involved—the
providing of causal narratives at the level of action—as being capable of
generalisation from instrumentally rational action to other types, such as
'value-rational' (*Wertrational*) action and even perhaps, at the limit, to action determined by tradition or habit or by actors' emotional states.[32]

However, while Weber can thus be seen as upholding the idea of sociology as a *Geisteswissenschaft,* he did at the same time insist that it must
also have a secure foundation in empirical research, and—like Halbwachs—

attached a particular importance to research findings in statistical form as the most reliable means by which social regularities could be displayed. As is by now well documented (Lazarsfeld and Oberschall, 1965; Oberschall, 1965; Käsler, 1988), over the first two decades of his academic life Weber was involved in a series of field studies of the German working classes, both agricultural and industrial, which were aimed at the collection and analysis of quantitative data (see esp. 1892, 1908). These studies are of great, but much neglected, interest in their own right.[33] They represent important contributions to the German debate on 'the social question', which was of a wider-ranging kind than the concurrent British debate on poverty, and have also to be seen (cf. Marianne Weber, 1926/1975: 367; Käsler, 1988) in the context of Weber's larger concerns with the changing nature of work and of employment relations and class formation under capitalism. They are thus closely allied with his major historical study of the same period, *The Protestant Ethic and the Spirit of Capitalism* (1904–1905/1930), which does indeed at various points draw on them.[34] Further, though, it is this body of research that would appear to provide the main basis for Weber's most explicit statements on the essential complementarity in sociological analysis of the demonstration of empirical, probabilistic regularities in social action and its consequences and the explanatory interpretation of such action. Passages such as the following are of particular note (1922/1968: 12; cf. also 18–19 and 1913/1981: 151, 157):

> If adequacy in respect to meaning is lacking, then no matter how high the degree of uniformity and how precisely [the] probability [of a course of action] can be numerically determined, it is still an incomprehensible statistical probability. On the other hand, even the most perfect adequacy on the level of meaning has causal significance from a sociological point of view only insofar as there is some proof for the existence of a probability that action in fact normally takes the course which has been held to be meaningful.[35]

Here, Weber's position on the articulation of research and theory does in fact come very close to that from which this essay started out. Social regularities that are empirically established need to be causally explained and also made intelligible by reference to the patterns of action through which they are created and sustained, with the idea of rationality playing a central role in the reconstruction of the subjective meaning of such action. At the same time, the whole point of elaborating theories and models of action is that they should be put to explanatory use in relation to empirical findings. It is, therefore, of evident interest to ask why in Germany at least *some* sociology did not develop that could be regarded as an expression of Weber's vision, and all the more so since it is clear that Weber himself engaged in a serious attempt to promote such a development.

In 1909, around the time when Weber first came to designate himself as a sociologist, he played a prominent role in the founding of the Deutsche Gesellschaft für Soziologie (DGfS) and became its treasurer (Käsler, 1988: 15). The main objective of Weber and his associates in this venture was to create an alternative context for large-scale social research to the Verein für Sozialpolitik (under the auspices of which much of Weber's empirical work had hitherto been carried out), and one within which the emphasis could be placed firmly on a 'value-neutral' linkage of research to *theory* rather than to social problems and policy (cf. Roth, 1968; Weyembergh, 1971; Hennis, 1996: ch. 3; Ringer, 2004: ch. 6). At the same time, Weber was anxious to promote greater cooperation between sociologists and statisticians, and encouraged the organisation of a new German statistical society, intended to have close relations with its sociological counterpart (Schad, 1972: 22–23). At the inaugural meeting of the DGfS in 1910, Weber outlined his ideas that it should serve as a collaborative 'workshop' and seek to raise funds for major empirical investigations. As an initial research programme, he suggested studies of three topics: voluntary associations, social mobility, and—his own current concern—the sociology of the press (Oberschall, 1965: 109; Schad, 1972: 42–43).

However, from these apparently promising beginnings, little of any substance emerged and after the second meeting of the DGfS in 1912 Weber withdrew in evident frustration (Marianne Weber, 1926/1975: 420–25). His subsequent efforts at developing a sociology aiming at 'the interpretive understanding of social action and thereby a causal explanation of its course and consequences' (1922/1968:4) were pursued entirely through his historically based studies—with, it seems, some relief on his part but also, it should be added, some clear methodological reservations.[36] Weber's personality appears not to have been well suited to organisational activity of the kind he attempted, and misunderstandings over the idea of value-neutral sociology persisted (Ringer, 2004: 175–76). But behind the failure of the DGfS initiative two further problems can be identified.

First, as Weber bitterly complained, other eminent figures in the association proved unwilling to abandon their individual scholarship in order to participate in empirical research of a kind that called for collaboration.[37] In this regard, the traditions of the German university system may perhaps be seen as an obstacle, although in other new disciplines, notably psychology, they would appear to have been far more successfully adapted.

Second, and more seriously, among the membership of the DGfS at large there was a lack of expertise in the conduct of social research and especially insofar as quantification was involved. Weber himself from the time of his earliest field studies had expressed worries about how to deal with issues of both data collection and data analysis—especially multivariate analysis—and about the difficulty of obtaining appropriate guidance (Lazarsfeld and Ober-schall, 1965).[38] Moreover, this problem was deepened in that the attempt to create an alliance with the statisticians did not succeed. As earlier noted, the more conservative of the latter still regarded their discipline as itself a kind of social science and thus tended to see sociology as a potential competitor (Schad, 1972: 17–35), while the more progressive, who understood statistics as a general methodology based on probability theory, appear for the most part to have adopted a rather unhelpful attitude towards the sociologists' efforts. Thus, in 1911, just when Weber's work with the DGfS was at a crucial stage, von Bortkiewicz, perhaps the most distinguished student of Lexis but a man noted for his negative temperament (Schumpeter, 1954: 851), sharply criticised reports from a study of industrial workers that Weber had led for the Verein, pointing out, among other failings, inadequacies in sample size and representativeness and also elementary computational errors. Weber made an uncomfortable reply in which he felt obliged to play down, to an undue degree, what the study had achieved (Verein für Sozialpolitik, 1912; Oberschall, 1965: 130–1; Käsler, 1988: 72–73).

Viewed in this way, the failure in the years before World War I to create a *verstehende Soziologie* that had also a secure quantitative basis then largely foreshadows the situation that developed in the Weimar period. German universities established chairs in sociology for the first time, but this institutional advance did little to further the intellectual coherence of the discipline. As Aron observed (1936: 167), in order to establish a claim to a chair, it seemed necessary for every aspirant to produce his own system of sociology—typically expressed in foundational terms, though with little reference to genuine theoretical issues, let alone to actual research. And as the political tensions of Weimar heightened, the ideological content of such discussions of basic methodology became increasingly apparent (cf. Ringer, 1969: 227–53).

Not surprisingly, then, the more serious attempts that were made to advance research were essentially divorced from theory, and vice versa. For example, Tönnies, one of the cofounders with Weber of the DGfS, enthusiastically pursued empirical—and quantitative—studies on a wide range of issues, but under the rubric of 'sociography' and without any relation to theoretical ideas, even his own. The earlier aspiration of seeking the greater integration of research and theory, Tönnies now believed, had been premature. He was also disinclined to renew Weber's plan of involving statisticians more constructively in sociological work. He showed no interest himself in acquiring knowledge of the new statistics, and relied in his sociography on techniques of correlation and multivariate analysis that were of a highly idiosyncratic, and in fact largely inadequate, kind (Oberschall, 1965: 52–62; Schad, 1972: 46–48, 66–73).

Conversely, the most sustained effort at elaborating the conception of a *verstehende Soziologie* was that made by Schütz (1932/1967). This was, however, aimed at giving such a sociology what Schütz believed to be a more secure philosophical—that is, phenomenological—basis, rather than at clarifying further how *erklärendes Verstehen* was to be applied in, and ultimately tested by, empirical research. Indeed, the 'phenomenological turn' in the reception of Weber's work served to make these matters appear considerably more rather than less problematic. As Campbell (1996; 31–37 esp.) has observed, Schütz extended Weber's understanding of what makes action 'social' so as to require that it involve not simply the actor 'taking account' in a general way of the action of others but indeed engaging continuously in the interpretation of the meaning of the action of all specific 'others' who were encountered. Thus, rather than the focus of sociological attention falling on the micro-to-macro link—on how social regularities are generated through central tendencies in action and interaction that can be understood as deriving from social situations of a particular type—it had in effect to be *confined to* the micro-level: that is, to the processes through which actors, as themselves microsociologists, 'make sense' together. Moreover, even at this level, it remained unclear just how Schütz and his followers envisaged that their supposed theoretical refinements of Weber's approach should be incorporated into substantive sociological enquiry.[39]

In sum, by the time of the Nazi accession to power in 1933, and the devastation of German sociology that followed, it could, from the standpoint of this essay, be said that the high promise of the period around 1910 had in fact already been dissipated.

The questions that have motivated this essay were posed at the outset as follows. Why was a version of sociology aiming to combine the quantitative analysis of probabilistic social regularities with their explanatory interpretation on the basis of a theory of social action so slow to appear? How far is this retardation to be understood as reflecting difficulties inherent in the project itself or, rather, historically specific barriers of an institutional or an intellectual kind or even perhaps still more contingent factors? In the light of the foregoing review of the early development of sociology in France, England, and Germany, I would now venture these answers.

To begin with, there is little indication that, insofar as a sociology of the kind in question was envisaged, its progress was impeded by serious internal contradictions. It is true that Quetelet and his followers had only an uncertain grasp of the significance of the probabilistic regularities in social life that they were able to demonstrate, and often regarded them as being but the (imperfect) manifestation of deterministic laws operating at a supra-individual level—the position that Mill and Spencer in England and the Durkheimians in France readily took up in direct opposition to probabilistic thinking.

However, within the German tradition of the *Geisteswissenschaften*, Lexis and then Weber saw such an explanation of social regularities as being neither necessary nor indeed appropriate, and outlined a quite different approach: that is, one of a 'micro-to-macro' rather than 'macro-to-micro' kind, which gave causal force to the typical or central courses of action pursued by collectivities of individuals within social situations of a given type. Thus, quite consistently, probabilistic regularities were addressed from the standpoint of probabilistic causation. And, in turn, the way was opened for sociological explanation to be grounded ultimately in the interpretation of individual action, through which it might at the same time be rendered intelligible.

The period in which this approach originated corresponded with that in which in England the new statistics were created—the ideal complement, it might be thought, so far as empirical enquiry was concerned, allowing, on the one hand, more reliable and revealing analyses of the character of social regularities and, on the other, more rigorous testing of hypotheses regarding their generation that might be formulated at the level of action. However, despite the eminent suitability of a marriage of research and theory on this basis, the historical fact remains that it did not take place. It is on external barriers, I would then maintain, that attention has chiefly to focus.

As regards the development of sociology at large, much of interest has been written on the problems of 'institutionalisation' that the emergent discipline faced as it struggled for acceptance by both academia and governments (e.g., Abrams, 1968; Oberschall, ed., 1972). Nonetheless, as regards the particular issues to which this essay is directed, such problems do not stand out as being ones of major significance. The failure to achieve a sociology that could in both research and theory exploit the potential of the probabilistic revolution was common to France, England, and Germany alike, despite very evident differences in the structuring of their academic and scientific communities and in the extent and manner in which sociology was accommodated. It could not, for example, be claimed that institutionalised rivalry between statisticians and sociologists was a generally adverse factor. As noted, such rivalry did indeed arise to some extent in the German case. But in France Simiand and Halbwachs were able to sustain a dialogue with statisticians even across quite sharply drawn organisational boundaries, while in England the loose institutionalisation of both disciplines clearly did not make for a high level of cooperation or even interaction. In accounting for the failure in question, I would then believe, far greater weight has to be given to intellectual rather than to institutional factors. Three intellectual barriers can be identified, as follows.

The first and most serious, at least in France and England and for at time in Germany also, was the Comtean legacy or, in other words, the positivist conception of science. In this conception, the goal of all sciences, whatever their specific methodologies, was the formulation of deterministic laws, and probabilistic thinking was thus viewed with hostility or at least great suspicion. Moreover, the sociology elaborated within positivist science was one that, largely on account of analogies drawn with biology, sought to take total societies or at all events their constituent institutions as its basic units of analysis, and to discover the laws that governed societal integration and long-term developmental, or evolutionary, trajectories. It followed, therefore, that sociological explanation proceeded always in a macro-to-micro fashion. If individual action and interaction were considered at all, they could be given little more than epiphenomenal status. Further, the essential empirical materials of such a sociology were ones that could serve to illustrate the functioning and change of institutions across the widest conceivable range of societies, and that had therefore to be largely derived from (what were taken to be) the preestablished findings of history or ethnography. No particular interest or privilege attached to the *direct* study of patterns of social action (as opposed to their inference from institutional descriptions), which would call for research in contemporary societies and of a kind likely to employ methods of data collection and analysis that the new statistics of the probabilistic revolution could inform. Thus, at virtually every point, the positivist version of sociology stood opposed to one in which the idea of social action would be central, as the focus of both research and theory, and in which, to revert to Boudon's distinction, the nomological would be replaced by the individualistic paradigm. The particular significance of the German case is that it reveals how the radical rejection of the Comtean legacy was a necessary condition for such an alternative sociology even to be programmatically envisaged—although not, of course, by any means a sufficient one for its realisation.[40]

Second, the barrier of positivism was in certain instances reinforced by that of an extreme empiricism. Where, on the one hand, such empiricism was associated with statistical work, as was most notably the case in mid-nineteenth century England but also and for a somewhat longer period in Germany, it restricted statistics, at best, to a form of numerical social description and, at worst, to a mindless 'cult of the facts'. It was, in other words, inimical to the development of statistics into a general scientific methodology, based on probability theory, which sociologists could then use in establishing and analysing social regularities and in testing the theoretically grounded explanations of these regularities that they might advance. Where, on the other hand, empiricism was associated with the idea of sociology as the study of social institutions, again as best exemplified in the English case and above all in the work of the Webbs, it resulted in such study being progressively divorced from the evolutionary theory that had initially inspired it and becoming another, qualitative form of descriptivism, lacking at least any explicit analytical or theoretical concerns.

Third, the creation of a sociology in which the concept of social action played a central role was also impeded by psychologism and in two different ways. It was above all a *fear* of psychologism—a fear that the autonomy of sociology might appear to be undermined by a dependence on laws of human nature—that led the Durkheimians, following Comte, to reject any kind of sociological explanation that referred ultimately to the action of individuals, and to insist that social facts be accounted for exclusively in terms of other social facts. But conversely, a recognition that sociological explanation could not in the end avoid reference to individual attributes and conduct led to the argument, as found in Mill and Spencer, that sociology did indeed need a specific psychology—in effect, a science of human behaviour—as its foundation. Only in the German tradition of the *Geisteswissenschaften,* and in particular through the work of Max Weber, was the crucial point eventually established that adopting the principle of methodological individualism in sociology did not in fact imply psychologism. Instead of the individualistic paradigm being associated with the idea of making individual behaviour explicable by subsuming it under general psychological laws, it could rather be associated with that of making individual action intelligible by placing it within its social context and, especially, by showing it to be rational within this context.

The intellectual barriers I have indicated were indeed formidable. Nonetheless, it would, I believe, be a mistake to suppose that the appearance of a sociology allying the quantitative analysis of social regularities with their explanation via a theory of social action was inevitably precluded in any one of the three cases reviewed. For this would be to discount factors of a yet more contingent kind than those I have so far considered but that are rather clearly in evidence. In their nature, such factors do not lend themselves to systematic treatment. They do, however, tend to prompt, and may in turn be highlighted by, counterfactual speculation.

For example, it is, as earlier remarked, a curious feature of the French case that Simiand and Halbwachs, the two sociologists of the early twentieth century who were perhaps best informed about the new statistics, should have remained throughout their academic careers committed, even militant, Durkheimians. It would be difficult to maintain that this could not have been otherwise. And it is not in turn absurd to contemplate the question of what might have happened in French sociology in the interwar years if the attachment of these two individuals to the Durkheimian school had been weaker or, alternatively, if others who were more ready to question its disregard for a theory of action had chosen to acquire a similar degree of statistical sophistication.

Similarly, to turn to the English case, the attempts made by the creators of the new statistics themselves to show its value to various kinds of sociological enterprise surely did not have to be spurned in quite the way that they were. Conflicts of ideology, especially over eugenics, very probably played a part here. But even if the rejection of Galton and Pearson by the evolutionary institutionalists is left aside, it cannot be regarded as unthinkable that poverty research, with stronger intellectual leadership than that provided by Booth, might have developed into a more serious form of applied sociology: that is, might have drawn more readily on advances in data analysis, especially following on Yule's intervention, and in this way have been better equipped to move beyond 'the cult of the facts' to pursue explanations of its empirical findings of a theoretically grounded kind.

Finally, in Germany above all a situation that was, in the years prior to World War I, in many respects highly favourable to a new sociology linking quantitative and interpretative concerns must be seen as being marred at least as much by a conjunction of particularities as by more systematic difficulties, whether institutional or intellectual. How might German sociology have developed, one is tempted to ask, if Weber had had the proclivity and capacity for academic mobilisation of a Durkheim, and if his quest for guidance and cooperation from statisticians could have met with the response of a Yule rather than a von Bortkiewicz?

All such 'what if' questions of historical possibility are of course in one sense vain: what happened, happened. Nonetheless, they do still serve to bring out that the issue to which this essay has been addressed—that of why a sociology more responsive to the probabilistic revolution in its conception of both research and theory did not earlier develop—has itself to be answered in probabilistic terms. There were indeed substantial barriers in the way of such a development, and it did not in fact occur. But from the vantage point of, say, the late nineteenth century, the situation was surely far more open than it might now appear in retrospect. Other things could have happened than actually did if individuals had acted and interacted in different ways. In other words, even in this relatively early period, the kind of sociology in the interests of which this essay is written was neither inconceivable nor unrealisable. However, it must of course by the same token be accepted that even if today there are encouraging signs that such a sociology is at last beginning to take recognisable shape, its eventual success is still by no means guaranteed.

CHAPTER NINE

Statistics and the Theory of Social Action

Failures in the Integration of American Sociology, 1900–1960*

This essay is a direct sequel to that of the previous chapter. It addresses the same central question: why, in historical perspective, has a version of sociology allying the quantitative analysis of social regularities with their explanation and understanding through a theory of social action been so slow to emerge? This question is, however, now pursued in a different context, that of early and mid-twentieth-century America. In the preceding chapter, I sought to show that in Europe over the period 1830 to 1930 the 'absent synthesis' cannot be accounted for simply in terms of its own inherent difficulties. At certain junctures, most notably perhaps in Germany in the years before World War I, there are good grounds for claiming the objective possibility of its realisation. That this did not in fact occur has then to be seen as the result largely of external factors. In some instances institutional barriers can be noted. But, I argued, intellectual barriers would in general appear to have been far more serious and, in particular, the persisting influence within European sociology of Comtean positivism and the resistance that it provided to the probabilistic revolution.[1] In what follows, my aim is to examine how far similar conclusions might be reached when attention moves to the United States and to the period from around 1900 to 1960, in the course of which American sociology moved clearly ahead of European sociology as regards both the security of its institutional bases and the material and human resources that it could command.

*I am indebted to Matthew Bond for an extended commentary on an earlier draft of this essay and also to Martin Bulmer, Jennifer Platt, and Stephen Stigler for helpful comments and advice.

228

In one respect, it is in fact evident from the outset that a different situation must here be recognised. As the twentieth century progressed, an acceptance of statistical methodology spread, albeit patchily, throughout sociology, but far more rapidly in America than elsewhere (cf. Platt, 1996). Thus, in the American context, the issue of the receptiveness of sociologists to the new opportunities in research and analysis afforded by the advance of statistics is in itself of less importance than a further issue that arose: namely, that of the actual part to be played by quantitative work in the larger sociological enterprise and, in particular, the nature of its linkage to theory.

This latter issue is, I believe, distinctively illuminated by three episodes in the history of American sociology. These relate to sociology at Columbia University from 1900 to 1929, at the University of Chicago from 1927 to around 1935, and then again at Columbia from 1940 to 1960. In each of these cases, quantitative work was pursued with vigour and with, on its own terms, some significant degree of success. But in each case, too, major difficulties are apparent in the integration of this work with prevailing theory, at all events in such a way that the statistically informed analysis of empirical social regularities could be joined with theoretically informed explanation and understanding at the level of social action. I proceed by examining these three episodes in turn.[2]

COLUMBIA, 1900–1929

Columbia is here of *prima facie* interest as the first university in the United States, or, probably, elsewhere, in which statistics was systematically incorporated into both teaching and research in the social sciences (Camic and Xie, 1994). Already in the 1880s Richmond Mayo-Smith—one of the first social scientists to be admitted to the National Academy of Sciences—was teaching statistics to students in economics and politics and was active in a variety of quantitative investigations in such fields as labour conditions and immigration. In 1891 Mayo-Smith helped promote the idea of a chair in sociology at Columbia, and in 1894 Franklin Giddings, who had for some time helped Mayo-Smith with his teaching, was appointed.

Giddings' early work, like that of most first-generation American sociologists, was in the tradition of 'evolutionary naturalism', under the influence of Comte and, especially, Spencer, and was based largely on secondary historical and ethnographic materials. However, chiefly, it seems, as a result of his association with Mayo-Smith and of his reading of the work of Karl Pearson, Giddings came to believe that statistics had a vital role to play in the future of sociology. It has also been suggested (Camic and Xie, 1994) that he saw an emphasis on statistical methods as an important means of strengthening both the disciplinary identity of sociology and its scientific credentials. By the turn of the century, Giddings had developed a new conception of sociology in which quantification played a central role (cf. Giddings, 1901, 1904) and, as Turner has written (1991: 277), 'this conception was impressed relentlessly on his students'. Giddings set up a well-equipped statistical laboratory in his department, published frequently in the *Journal of the American Statistical Association* as well as in sociological journals, and up to his retirement in 1929 supervised a steady stream of doctoral theses, the large majority of which involved quantitative work.

The statistics that Mayo-Smith taught at Columbia were essentially in the tradition of nineteenth-century German *Universitätsstatistik*, with an emphasis on the description and analysis of 'mass phenomena' as a source of intelligence for state policy. Giddings initially followed in this tradition, but then, via Pearson, became aware of the new English statistics. In his own work he did not in fact demonstrate any very impressive command of either the new techniques or the underlying probability theory. But he encouraged his students to venture further than he did himself, and there were others at Columbia who were able to provide statistical teaching at an advanced level, notably Henry Moore, a pioneer econometrician, who was a frequent visitor to Pearson and his colleagues in London. Thus, Columbia served as the 'portal' (Bernert, 1983: 238) through which the new English statistics entered American sociology—and indeed American social science more generally.[3] Over the years the statistical sophistication of the theses prepared by Giddings' students steadily advanced, with a reliance simply on descriptive counts, tabulations, and indexes giving way to correlational analyses and then, by the 1920s, to the use of multiple regression techniques (Turner, 1991).

The body of work produced at Columbia under the influence of Giddings, more so than that produced by Giddings himself, can then be seen as representing the realisation in the United States of the opportunity that was so obviously missed in Britain: that of restoring the close relationship that had initially existed between sociology and the probabilistic revolution, so that in their empirical research sociologists could take due advantage of the enormously enhanced analytical possibilities that had been created.

However, despite the undoubted historical significance of developments at Columbia—from which the tradition of American quantitative sociology can indeed be dated (cf. Bannister, 1987: ch. 5)—one negative consequence became increasingly evident: that is, a widening gap between research and theory, to the point in fact of a virtual divorce. Two main sources of this estrangement can be identified.

First, so far as Giddings himself was concerned, the immediate problem that arose was that of how the enthusiasm for statistics that he had conceived in mid-career should be related to his evolutionism. The solution he pursued was to move away from the study of social evolution in a broad historical and comparative perspective and to concentrate rather on its operation in contemporary America: in particular, on the way in which processes of 'social selection' could be seen as still working there to create a more advanced form of society, characterised by an appropriate balance of freedom and control. On the one hand, Giddings focused his attention on the Spencerian movement from 'homogeneity' to 'heterogeneity' that was evident in consequence of mass immigration and the widening of class differences, and, on the other hand, on what he took to be the offsetting tendencies of social selection through which 'harmful extremes' within the growing range of social variation were eliminated. A related concern that later emerged was that of the possibilities of change via purposive reform and of the likely costs of seeking to direct the course of social evolution in this way.

In this context, then, the key role to be played by statistics was that of measurement—for example, of the actual extent of heterogeneity in modern American society, racial, ethnic, and otherwise; of the social distance existing between different groups; of the 'state of political cooperation' in local communities; of the degree of 'social pressure' necessary to bring about effective change, and so on.[4] In all these respects, and many others too, Giddings laboured to produce numerical indices—of in fact a largely ad hoc kind—which, he believed, he and his students would be able to use so as to give some relatively precise empirical content to the concepts in terms of which his evolutionary theory was expressed.

However, no great advance was in this way achieved. From the start, while some students found Giddings' concepts and their accompanying indices of value in their research, others experienced them as tiresome and constraining. And in any event, they could serve as a basis only for the illustration of Giddings' theory rather than for its empirical testing and further development. Moreover, in the early decades of the twentieth century the intellectual attractiveness of social evolutionism was beginning to wane. Thus, at the same time as Giddings' students went beyond him in their statistical expertise, they tended also to lose interest in the problems that derived from his theoretical position, often making only passing reference to these before taking up their own concerns. These were in fact increasingly shaped by an explicitly reformist agenda, and one that was formulated with little, if any, theoretical underpinning (see further Turner, 1991: 277–84; also Bannister, 1987: 80–82; Ross, 1991: 228–29).

Second, and perhaps yet more important, Giddings' own methodological outlook changed significantly in his later life, and in such a way as to encourage a concentration on quantitative research of a largely atheoretical kind. Through his reading of Pearson, Giddings not only learnt about the new English statistics but was also introduced to a new philosophy of science, inspired primarily by the work of Ernst Mach (see esp. Pearson, 1892). This represented a reconstruction of the positivism of Comte and Spencer on yet more radically anti-metaphysical lines. The positivist insistence that knowledge should be derived only from phenomenal experience was now taken further so as to require the abandonment of all explanatory appeals to abstract general laws, whether of nature or of society (cf. Kolakowski, 1972: ch. 5). For the new 'critical', as opposed to 'systematic', positivism, science could in the end be no more than a form of factual description. Thus, theories were merely indirect descriptions, the function of which was to aid in the discovery of further, previously unknown facts. The idea that theory could be embodied in laws that allowed for causal explanation as something distinct from description was flatly rejected. Thus, for Pearson, the idea of causation was simply a 'fetish' (cf. vol. 1, ch. 9, p. 190); and also Porter, 2004: ch. 9). Apparent statements of causal relations were no more than statements of phenomenal sequence, the recurrence of which had, moreover, to be understood as only probable, not necessary. From this standpoint, then, a scientific sociology would consist essentially in the statistical study of characteristics of interest observed within social aggregates or collectivities and, more specifically, in the analysis of their variation and correlation under differing conditions.

In his early work (1896), Giddings had been attracted by the idea of explaining group formation, differentiation, and antagonism in terms of social processes that stemmed from individuals' 'consciousness of kind', in the sense of Adam Smith. But his exposure to critical positivism led him in his later writing to take up a far more behaviourist stance: 'consciousness of kind' became simply 'like response to the same given stimulus' (1904: 164). While not denying the reality of consciousness in principle, Giddings came to regard all mental states as being in themselves effectively beyond the reach of scientific enquiry or, that is to say, as being observable and measurable only through their expression in behaviour. His initial approach to the problems of social conflict and order via the rudiments of a theory of action was not therefore sustained. And, given the conception of sociology that followed from Pearson's philosophy, the aim was not in any event to understand how observed social phenomena were actually generated through individual action and interaction but simply to demonstrate how different aspects of the behaviour of individuals in society, and their consequences, were related to each other. As Bannister (1987: 76) summarises Giddings' ultimate position: 'why not focus on correlations alone, without attempting to explain social behaviour in any deeper sense?'

In the light of present concerns, Columbia sociology in the era of Giddings had thus a highly ambivalent outcome. It saw the successful reception of the new English statistics into sociological research, but in circumstances that proved to be highly detrimental to the integration of research with theory. The research programme through which Giddings sought to link statistical work to his evolutionary theory always appeared somewhat artificial, even perhaps in the end to Giddings himself (cf. Ross, 1991: 369), and it did not survive him. But as interest in evolutionary theory faded, no well-defined alternative emerged as a basis either for the definition of sociological problems—which in fact became increasingly derived from, if not equated with, social problems—or, yet more damagingly, for the construction of sociological explanations. Further, the philosophy of science that Giddings took over together with the new English statistics served to reinforce and legitimate the tendency towards a sociology of quantitative description that eschewed theory and that was leavened, if at all, simply by 'commonsense' interpretation.

It is, however, important here to emphasise that while the new English statistics could indeed be readily recruited in the service of critical positivism in the way that Pearson proposed, and that Giddings accepted as the basis for a scientific sociology, such a conjunction *was in no way necessary*. The other founders of the new English statistics do not appear to have displayed any obvious enthusiasm for Pearson's philosophy of science, and, as was earlier seen (ch. 8, p. 211, this volume), Yule at least clearly recognised both the reality and the importance of the distinction between correlation or more generally association, on the one hand, and causation, on the other.[5] In other words, the increasing use in sociological research of the powerful new methods of quantitative analysis that had become available, as occurred at Columbia, did not at all require the abandonment of attempts to develop theory. Indeed, it is not difficult to imagine how, in a different intellectual context, such attempts could have been directly stimulated: that is, in order to better explain and understand the social regularities that the new methods made it possible to display with greater refinement and reliability than before.

At Columbia, the crucial, though contingent, facts would appear to have been that Giddings was persuaded that the way ahead for sociology was that indicated by critical positivism *and* that, in the period in question, Giddings *was* Columbia sociology. In the foregoing, it may be noted, reference has repeatedly been made to Giddings and his students but not to Giddings and his colleagues. A domineering man who did not welcome criticism of his own views, Giddings filled the posts initially at his disposal with acolytes of only mediocre ability (Barnes, 1948: 763–74; Bannister, 1987: 77–78), and then over the years managed to alienate most other leading figures in the Columbia faculty. In this way, he effectively undermined his entire project. He lost the possibility of intellectual exchanges with a range of distinguished social scientists in other fields who were also much concerned with the implications of the new statistics and the results they produced (see esp. Camic and Xie, 1994);[6] and at the same time he destroyed the chances of expanding his department and thus of being able to recruit individuals more capable than he was himself of endowing the quantitative sociology that he had inspired with theoretical ambition (Oberschall, 1972: 236).

In consequence, Giddings' influence at Columbia ended rather abruptly with his retirement, when a virtually new department of sociology was formed. His students did, however, ensure that his ideas, and especially his commitment to quantitative sociology, lived on elsewhere. Often without prospects at Columbia, 'Giddings men' spread out widely across the other sociology departments that had become established in American universities, and in many cases rose to positions of academic eminence—six of their number being elected president of the American Sociological Society in the interwar period (Turner, 1991; cf. also Oberschall, 1972). The second episode I consider turns in fact on the arrival of perhaps the most able of all Giddings' students, William F. Ogburn, at the University of Chicago in 1927.

CHICAGO, 1927–1935

At Columbia, Giddings failed to establish a tradition of sociology that could maintain its vitality, or indeed its identity, after the end of his own career. In this regard, his counterpart at Chicago, Albion Small, achieved a far greater degree of success. Small became the first professor of sociology at Chicago in 1892 and remained there until his retirement in 1924. Although his intellectual influence on the development of American sociology was probably less than that of other leading figures of the founding generation, Small can claim the distinction of having created the first department in the United States in which a significant degree of continuity in teaching and research was maintained over several decades and in which in fact a generally recognised school of sociology emerged.

Three occurrences may be singled out as illustrative of different aspects of this achievement. First, in 1895, Small founded the *American Journal of Sociology*, published by the University of Chicago Press, which until the end of the period here considered was the leading journal in the field and served as the key medium through which, directly and indirectly, the Chicago school exerted its influence on American sociology at large (Abbott, 1999).[7] Second, over the years 1918 to 1920 W. I. Thomas, another founder-member of the Chicago department, published, together with Florian Znaniecki, the five volumes of *The Polish Peasant in America and Europe*. This study broke new ground in treating not just an issue of social importance, mass immigration, but also crucial disciplinary problems, those of the sources of social organisation and disorganisation, on the basis of extensive, firsthand empirical research. In 1937 it was voted the most significant research contribution to have been made to American sociology. Third, in 1921, Robert Park and E. W. Burgess brought out *Introduction to the Science of Sociology*, a text and collection of readings based on the introductory course they taught at Chicago, which skilfully interwove the work of members of the Chicago department with that of earlier American and European authors, and which could make a strong claim to be the first modern sociology textbook—and also one of the longest lasting.

A great deal has been written on the subject of the Chicago school (for a brief account of the historiography, see Abbott, 1999: ch. 1). But what is here of chief significance is the 'revisionist' history that has been provided by Bulmer (1981, 1984; cf. also 1991, 1997). Bulmer's work mounts a powerful challenge to the conventional understanding of Chicago sociology which would identify it almost exclusively with one particular type of research: that is, with case studies based on qualitative—ethnographic or 'personal document'—methods, and aimed primarily at revealing the intersubjective aspects of social life. While sociology in this style was indeed strongly represented at Chicago, it coexisted from an early stage, Bulmer shows (1981 esp.), with several different forms of quantitative sociology, which in previous accounts of the Chicago school were largely neglected or discounted.[8] For example, Burgess, and also several of his and Park's graduate students, engaged in studies of urban ecology that used increasingly sophisticated statistical mapping techniques, and Burgess was also a pioneer of census tract statistics and promoted quantitative criminological research. Park in turn was associated with research into race relations of a strongly quantitative character and also encouraged efforts at the measurement of social attitudes and 'social distance', including the development of the celebrated Bogardus scale.[9]

For present purposes, the importance of this more comprehensive understanding of the Chicago school is then the following. It enables the decision made, in 1926, to invite Ogburn to move from Columbia to a senior chair at Chicago to be seen in a very different light than was previously possible.[10] For so long as the Chicago department was taken to be committed to a version of 'soft', qualitative sociology in opposition to the 'hard', quantitative approach associated with Columbia, the recruitment of a noted 'Giddings man' and proponent of quantitative methods, could only appear as a strange aberration. Thus, Kuklick (1980: 207) speaks of Ogburn as a 'vehemently scientistic sociologist' who came to Chicago with 'a research program for sociology which in many ways violated Chicago ideals'. However, as Bulmer further shows (1984: 169–71), the invitation to Ogburn had the unanimous support of the members of the Chicago department; their express purpose was to strengthen the quantitative work currently being undertaken there by ensuring that it was given a sounder basis in statistical expertise, the need for which had in several instances become apparent.[11] Far from being problematic, the move to bring Ogburn to Chicago had then a clear rationale, and could indeed be viewed as, in Bannister's phrase (1987: 174), a 'bold stroke' in academic entrepreneurship.

What was in effect entailed was the introduction of the relatively advanced quantitative techniques deployed at Columbia into a research environment that could be thought far more favourable to the full realisation of their value for sociology than that which Giddings had been able to create. By the mid-1920s, Chicago sociology had largely freed itself from the spell of social evolutionary theory, to which Giddings had struggled to link his enthusiasm for statistics, and likewise from the tradition of atheoretical research into social problems into which many of Giddings' students had been drawn. Following the lead provided by *The Polish Peasant,* Chicago research, while often stimulated by issues of social concern, tended to be directed towards specifically sociological goals: most important, one might say, towards that of gaining a better understanding of the relationship between, on the one hand, the more overt aspects of 'social organisation' and, on the other, underlying processes of 'social interaction'—to use the key macro- and micro-level concepts of the school. In such research, a case-study approach relying chiefly on qualitative methods was that followed most readily and with greatest assurance, but quantitative methods were also used and their growing potential was clearly recognised. The recruitment of Ogburn represented an attempt to ensure that in this regard also the Chicago department should stand at the forefront of American sociology.

However, as against the great promise of the situation of 1927, when Ogburn arrived in Chicago, what in the end was achieved by the 'bold stroke' could only be regarded as a disappointment. It is true that in the following years Ogburn reached his own academic peak, producing impressive studies of voting patterns in the Hoover-Smith presidential election of 1928 (Ogburn and Talbot, 1929) and of changes in marriage and the family in America (1929, 1935), as well as his major work on social trends (to which I return below).[12] The quantitative tradition at Chicago was thus undoubtedly strengthened, and Ogburn began to attract high quality students.[13] But the transplantation of his statistical expertise into the Chicago environment did not in fact lead to the closer integration of quantitative analysis with theoretically directed substantive research in the way that, one may suppose, had been hoped for.

In explaining this outcome, strains in personal relationships, whether or not grounded in academic differences, were probably of some importance. From the start Ogburn had difficulties with Park and later, and more seriously, with Blumer. However, other colleagues, and notably Burgess, who attended Ogburn's statistics courses, were supportive (cf. Bulmer, 1984: ch. 10; Bannister, 1987: ch. 12).[14] Moreover, although by the 1930s disagreements and divisions between those favouring quantitative and qualitative approaches were readily apparent among both faculty and graduate students, they do not appear to have involved undue animosity,[15] and might in any event be seen as consequences as much as causes of the failure to achieve any degree of synergy between Ogburn's sociology and the preexisting Chicago style. The primary sources of this failure have, it would seem, to be recognised as intellectual, and can in fact be traced back to persisting problems that were to be found on both sides of the quantitative/qualitative divide.

To begin with Ogburn, it has to be noted that although he went far beyond Giddings in the sophistication of his quantitative work, he seems never to have escaped from the same quandary as that in which Giddings found himself over the relationship between such work and sociological theory. In his doctoral dissertation of 1912, on the development of child labour legislation, Ogburn made an explicit distinction between studies that, like his dissertation, were aimed solely at description and those that sought to go beyond description to causal explanation (cf. Bernert, 1983). Subsequently, though, and, one may suppose, following Giddings, he moved towards the position of the critical positivists in seeking to elide this distinction. Thus, in a paper on 'Sociology and Statistics', published in 1927, the year of his arrival in Chicago, Ogburn commended techniques of correlation and regression to sociologists as methods of studying 'the different causes of phenomena' on the grounds that 'causation is practically correlated variation' and that these methods could serve as the sociologist's substitute for controlled experiments (1927: 379–80).

However, given this standpoint, the problem then arose for Ogburn, as it had for Giddings, of what role theory was to play in sociological analysis or, more specifically, of what role was *left* for theory to play if statistics provided the means for description *and* explanation at one and the same time. This problem, it appears, Ogburn could not satisfactorily resolve. As several commentators have noted (Duncan, 1964; Bulmer, 1984: ch. 10; Ross, 1991: 430–33), he remained to the end of his career uneasy with the very idea of theory—in some instances treating it as mere speculation that would tend to disappear as sociology became more scientific, and in others, viewing it somewhat more favourably but even then only as a framework for the organisation of factual knowledge that might help in the further accumulation of such knowledge (see, e.g., Ogburn, 1930, 1955).

Moreover, this was more than simply a private intellectual difficulty. It was one that became fully exposed in the course of debates that arose over Ogburn's work and that led him into an embattled position. From the time of his first book, *Social Change* (1922), Ogburn had been interested in the relationship between different aspects of change, including the possibility of 'cultural lag': that is, the failure of certain elements of a culture to adapt effectively to other, more rapidly developing ones. He then sought to treat such questions statistically, concentrating at first on the social consequences of economic fluctuations—for rates of marriage and divorce, suicide, crime, strikes, and so on (e.g., Ogburn and Thomas, 1922; Ogburn, 1923). Later, though, his main concern came to be with longer-term changes, or 'social trends', and with building up data on these that would be equivalent to economic time series and that would permit systematic correlational analysis. Thus, for each year from 1927 to 1934 he edited a special issue of the *American Journal of Sociology* that served as a kind of annual abstract of social statistics. However, Ogburn's most ambitious, and controversial, efforts in this connection resulted from his appointment in 1929 as research director of a committee set up by President Hoover to investigate recent social trends in the United States. After a troubled period of gestation (Bannister, 1987: 181–85), the committee's multiauthored report (President's Research Committee on Social Trends, 1933) finally appeared—to a very mixed critical reception.

In the case both of disagreements within the committee and then, after the publication of the report, within the sociological community, the issue of theory was central. The report provided a mass of information on social trends but few authors made any attempt to apply theory in order to explain how the trends they described were actually produced or why it should be supposed—where this was supposed—that they could be projected into the future.[16] Critics could therefore ask just how much of scientific value had been achieved. Ogburn's conception of knowledge simply as organised facts, which clearly underlay the report, was directly called into question. A number of sociologists, notably Sorokin (1933), but also including Znaniecki (1934: chs. 5, 6) and later MacIver (1942: ch. 13) who disliked, feared, and, it must be said, were ill-equipped to understand the techniques of statistical analysis promoted by Ogburn, were given opportunity to attack quantitative sociology via the philosophy of science with which Ogburn linked it—and took full advantage. Facts, they insisted, could not 'speak for themselves'; causation could not be reduced to association or correlation; scientific knowledge was ultimately theoretical, not factual, in character.[17]

How far such criticism was fair could be debated, as also could the extent to which it was motivated merely by anti-Chicago sentiment (cf. Bannister, 1987: 185–86). But more to the point for present purposes is the fact that it was far stronger in its negative than in its positive aspects. Very little indication or illustration was provided by the critics of just what kind of theory Ogburn and his colleagues *might* have used and to what effect. It would therefore seem reasonable to suppose that the situation in which Ogburn found himself was one far more likely to reinforce his doubts or indeed hostility in regard to theory than to increase his appreciation of its claims. Moreover, the other side of the question has now to be raised. It has to be asked what—even supposing more favourable circumstances—Chicago itself had to offer Ogburn in the way of theory that might have proved attractive and of value to him in his work on social trends and more generally.

Bulmer (1997) has argued, as against several earlier commentators, that the Chicago school, especially through the work of Thomas and Park, did indeed make a significant contribution to sociological theory and, more specifically, in developing a social action perspective: that is, one in which the interpretation of subjectively meaningful individual action and interaction is seen as the ultimate basis of sociological explanation. However, Bulmer has himself to acknowledge that this contribution consisted primarily in the provision of a 'general orientation' and of related concepts that proved fruitful in empirical research in certain types of milieu. And in fact neither Thomas nor Park succeeded in or, one might say, were much concerned with, the more considered articulation of theory, even of a middle range kind. The more sceptical view has indeed been that the failure of the Chicago school to show 'a more explicit concern with theory' (Janowitz 1970: xi; cf. Shils, 1948; Turner and Turner, 1990) could be reckoned as its major weakness. Even if, then, Ogburn had actively looked to his new colleagues to suggest a theoretical approach with explanatory potential in relation to the macro-level empirical regularities revealed by his research, it is not at all apparent that they could have made a helpful response. There was at all events no clearly formulated body of theory already to hand to which Ogburn could have been directed.[18]

Furthermore, from the standpoint of the present essay at least, it is important to question how far even the 'general orientation' of Thomas and Park was towards social action theory. It is true that the position of these authors did imply a break with the Durkheimian insistence that the causal explanation of social phenomena had always to be sought in terms of other social phenomena rather than by resorting to the individual level, and likewise with the Spencerian assumption that the description of social institutions could in itself suffice to represent patterns of individual action and interaction (cf. ch. 8, this volume, pp. 202–204 and 207–208). But the concern of Thomas and Park with problems of—to use a modern phrase—the microfoundations of sociological analysis would appear to fall essentially within an established American tradition of social psychology, or of what might more specifically be called 'the psychology of social life', central figures in which were Cooley and Mead. And this tradition has then to be recognised as differing significantly from what might be taken as its European functional equivalent: that is, the attempt to explain higher-level social phenomena through interpretive accounts of social action and the tracing out of its, often unintended, consequences—as was envisaged by Lexis and pursued more systematically by Weber (cf. Faris, 1967: ch. 6; Ross, 1991: 348–67).[19]

In fact, the difference that here arises is one that could be thought crucial to understanding why, under *any* conditions, an effective melding of the kind of quantitative sociology that Ogburn brought to Chicago with the theoretical orientation of Thomas and Park would have been hard to achieve. Looking back in later life on the divisions in the department during the 1930s, Blumer aptly observed that while those favouring statistical methods concentrated on demonstrating regularities in 'the product of action, as it were', those who continued with the case-study approach wished to deal with 'the whole process whereby that action came into being'.[20] And Blumer was not here pointing to the recognition of at least a potential complementarity of interests but rather to the opposite: to a failure of interests to converge.

For Ogburn and his followers to be led beyond the idea that sociological analysis could stop with correlation, since this was 'practically' the only way of treating causation, they would have had to be shown a theory that could help explain how the 'products of action' that they studied—societal patterns and trends in marriage and divorce, voting, crime, or whatever—were actually generated: that is, by central tendencies discernible in individual action and interaction and their consequences across a range of differing milieux. But the Chicago concern with social action was not directed towards the construction of generalised narratives of such a kind. It was rather focused on the issue of how, at the interpersonal level, ordered social action became possible, and, further, with the way in which the particular patterns of action that 'came into being' were specifically shaped by their temporally and spatially defined contexts—by 'natural history' and 'natural area' (cf. Abbott, 1999: ch. 7). In this perspective, social action was not just the action of individuals that in some way involved others, whether face to face or more indirectly; it was action, the subjective meaning of which was socially shared and indeed socially constituted. And it was in turn on the psychological processes of this constitution—the interpersonal negotiation of social meanings and the common definition of situations—that attention centred.[21]

There was then no very evident way in which a social action orientation in *this* sense could play an explanatory role in relation to the results of research such as Ogburn's, the interest of which lay essentially in the demonstration of empirical regularities that were extensive in time and space. A parallel might be traced here (cf. Campbell 1996: ch. 2, and also ch. 8, p. 222, this volume), with the attempt made by Schütz to give Weber's *verstehende Soziologie* a more secure grounding—in this case in phenomenology rather than psychology—which had, however, the effect of making it difficult to see how the explanatory interpretation of action that was sought could in fact be achieved with any research that aimed to go beyond the small group or social milieu. The crucial point here is that made by Stinchcombe (1993: 27; cf. vol. I, ch. 6, pp. 124–5 and n. 9) when he argues that little can be gained in explanatory power if the processes that are invoked to account for regularities observed at a higher, more macro, level should then entail 'complex investigations' at a lower, more micro, level. Or, as he elaborates with a nice nod back to the Quetelet-Maxwell-Boltzmann link (see ch. 8, p. 194, this volume): 'There is no beauty in understanding pressure, temperature and volume of gases by the behavior of molecules if the molecules have to be a lot more complex than the behavior of the gases being explained, if all their quarks and colors have to enter into the statistical mechanics.'

In the light of the foregoing, it can then scarcely be regarded as surprising that, following Ogburn's entry into the Chicago department, no new synthesis arose. Rather, by the mid-1930s, a series of mutual accommodations had led to the 'new' and the 'old' Chicagoans reaching what Turner and Turner (1990: 49–50) refer to as 'a loose working consensus'. But as these authors further comment, this outcome could be taken as one of the first manifestations of American sociology as a 'culturally divided discipline': that is, one in which disputes on quite fundamental issues have to be set aside rather than resolved, in the interests of maintaining some viable degree of social cohesion, but in which then 'separate and virtually autonomous forms of intellectual life exist'.[22]

As for Ogburn himself, he remained a prominent figure in the Chicago department until his retirement in 1952. However, from around 1935 he changed the direction of his research and, subsequently, of his teaching. He moved on from his work in documenting and analysing social trends to a concern with what might now be called technological forecasting or 'futurology' and also developed interests in demography, in which field, too, he attracted some notable students. In these new ventures, he deployed largely descriptive statistics to good advantage, but his advocacy of statistical methods in mainstream sociology became less enthusiastic and he no longer kept up with the statistical literature—a decision over which he later had regrets.[23] When, in the 1940s, quantitative sociology in America gained a new impetus, it did not come from Chicago but, once more, from Columbia.

COLUMBIA, 1940–1960

As earlier noted, Giddings' retirement from his chair at Columbia in 1929 was followed by the creation of a more or less new department of sociology—under the leadership of Robert MacIver who was joined a few years later by Robert Lynd. For most of the 1930s Columbia remained in fact under the shadow of Chicago, but, from the end of the decade, the relative fortunes of the two departments began to change. Chicago faced a variety of problems—of internal organisation, of declining research grants, and most seriously, perhaps of 'succession'—while at Columbia two developments occurred that were destined to bring the department into a period of undoubted ascendancy.

First, in 1939, Paul Lazarsfeld accepted a courtesy appointment at Columbia and in the following year, with the support of Lynd, brought the Rockefeller-funded Office of Radio Research into association with the university. In 1941 Lazarsfeld was appointed associate professor of sociology, and then in 1943 the ORR, which had considerably widened the range of its enquiries, was transformed into the Bureau of Applied Social Research (BASR), under Lazarsfeld's directorship, and provided with financial support from the university as a supplement to its income from market research and other commercial work. Apart from the rather special case of an institute at the University of North Carolina, under Howard Odum, which was devoted to the study of the cultural history and social problems of the South, the BASR was the first academic research centre in sociology to be established in the United States.

Second, in 1941, at the same time as Lazarsfeld became an associate professor, Robert Merton was appointed to a similar position as a way of resolving a dispute between MacIver and Lynd over whether a full professorship should be occupied by a theorist or an empirical researcher. Despite this somewhat unpromising start, Merton and Lazarsfeld soon formed a friendship and in 1943 Merton became an associate director of the BASR. While continuing to pursue his theoretical interests, he worked closely with Lazarsfeld and other members of the bureau on a variety of research projects until the end of the 1950s (see further Lazarsfeld, 1975).

Thus, circumstances came into being at Columbia that were perhaps more propitious than any that had hitherto existed in America for the creation of a vital relationship between sociological research and theory. Furthermore, the general methodological positions taken up by Lazarsfeld and Merton at this time were such as to suggest that the basis of this relationship would indeed be found in the study of social action, in a way that had not proved possible at Chicago. That is, through the quantitative analysis of social regularities understood as the—intended and unintended—products of action, on the one hand, and the corresponding explanation of such regularities ultimately through intelligible narratives of individual action, on the other.

Lazarsfeld had first come to the United States from Austria in 1933 on a Rockefeller Fellowship and, following the banning of the Austrian Social Democratic Party, decided not to return. He had worked at the Psychological Institute of the University of Vienna, and had led a research team that produced a notable pioneering study of responses to unemployment (Jahoda, Lazarsfeld, and Zeisel, 1933). Some time later he remarked (1975: 45) that this and other enquiries in which he had been engaged in Vienna might best be described as the 'empirical study of aggregated actions'. That is to say, the research was concerned with relatively large numbers of individuals who had been involved in approximately the same social situations—for example, entering the labour market for the first time, moving from farm to industrial work, becoming unemployed, and so on—and who had then to decide how to act in these situations. Under the influence of Karl Bühler, the director of the Psychological Institute, and of his wife, Charlotte, also a distinguished psychologist, a rather distinctive methodology was developed. Samples of individuals in similar situations were interviewed and, through a technique labelled 'the art of asking why'—or, later, 'reason analysis'—the investigators sought to determine retrospectively both the inner experiences and the perceived external conditions that had shaped the courses of action, often widely varying, that different individuals had in fact pursued (cf. Fleck, 1998).

Since he retained his commitment to this approach (cf. Lazarsfeld and Rosenberg, eds., 1955: section V), Lazarsfeld found himself in opposition to what, by the 1940s, had become the behaviourist orthodoxy of American psychology, which sought to avoid all reference to unobservable mental states of the kind that the concept of action implied. However, Lazarsfeld aimed to show that the study of action could still claim scientific status through being grounded in systematic empirical research and, in particular, in well-designed survey research that was capable of producing generally reliable data indicative of individuals' goals, values, and preferences and their related beliefs and attitudes.

It is here important to recognise that while the quantitative work of Ogburn and his associates was almost entirely based on aggregate-level data—usually official statistics for various kinds of administrative unit— Lazarsfeld's 'empirical study of aggregated actions' was based on the extensive individual-level data that survey research could provide. Thus, not only could the technical pitfalls of 'ecological correlation' (Robinson, 1951) be avoided but, further, the collection of subjective data capable of quantitative treatment was for the first time made feasible. Indeed, with problems of the empirical study of action much in mind, Lazarsfeld took the lead in developing the survey methods of the BASR well beyond the routines of current market research or opinion polling. Panel designs were introduced, which enabled the formation, stability, and change of attitudes to be traced over time, and also 'contextual' designs, which made it possible to assess, at least in principle, the effects on individual action of interpersonal relations or group or organisational memberships (see, e.g., Lazarsfeld and Rosenberg, eds., 1955: sections III and IV; cf. Converse, 1987: 286–95).

Finally, it should be noted that although from his Viennese origins Lazarsfeld was entirely familiar with critical positivism, and indeed had known some of its leading proponents personally (Merton, 1998), he did not share in its rejection of the idea of causation. To the contrary, he regarded the question of how social phenomena were to be causally explained as quite fundamental, and addressed it in two different, though complementary, ways.

First, Lazarsfeld played a prominent part in restoring a concern with causal inference in the statistical analysis of social data. The actual statistical techniques that he utilised were for the most part no more advanced than those of Ogburn, and often in fact did not go beyond the percentage analysis of contingency tables of categorical data. This reflected Lazarsfeld's view (cf. 1961) that Yule's analysis of 'attribute variables' had at least as much to offer sociology as correlation and regression techniques.[24] However, far from accepting Ogburn's view that correlation or association were 'practically' the same as causation, Lazarsfeld sought to develop methods for what he called 'elaboration' in data analysis that would help to show which correlations or associations among a set of variables were of possible causal significance and which were not (Kendall and Lazarsfeld, 1950; Lazarsfeld and Rosenberg, eds., 1955: sect. II; and cf. vol. I, ch. 9, p. 193).

Second, though, Lazarsfeld also showed an awareness, even if never fully developed, that no matter how sophisticated a statistical analysis might be, it could lead to an adequate causal explanation of social phenomena only when linked with an account of how the statistical results that had been obtained were actually generated. In other words, some answer had to be given to the question 'What is going on here?'—and by means of what Lazarsfeld sometimes referred to as a 'story-line' that was given in terms of the action and interaction of the individuals involved (Jahoda, 1979: 7).

The further requirement that most obviously arose out of this programme was then for a well-articulated theory of action: that is, for a theory in the light of which story-lines or, that is, explanatory narratives, could be constructed in order to illuminate statistical results in a relatively consistent way, rather than being thought up on a merely ad hoc basis. And in this regard the work of Merton, as this had developed through to the early years of his association with Lazarsfeld, might well appear as holding out great promise.

In papers published during the 1940s Merton (1945, 1948, 1949: Part I) took up a distinctive position on theory in sociology. To begin with, he sought to differentiate theory not only from empirical generalisation but, further, from purely conceptual schemes. The regularities or (Merton's favourite word) 'patterns' that could be empirically demonstrated in different aspects of social life did not themselves constitute, nor necessarily point to, theory; rather, they formed the basic *explananda* of sociology (cf. Merton, 1987). The prime task of theory was then to provide explanations. Conceptual schemes played a part in the formulation of theory but they were not to be equated with theory itself. Theories had ultimately to take a propositional form so that they would, on the one hand, actually have explanatory potential and, on the other, be exposed to empirical test and possible refutation.

Furthermore, Merton questioned (see 1948 esp.), with direct reference to the work of Parsons, whether the aim in sociology should be to develop theory of a quite general kind or, rather, theories that sought to explain only particular types of phenomena: that is, what Merton called 'theories of the middle range'. In the various natural sciences, Merton argued, theories that were thus restricted were far more in evidence than general theory—although there was always a concern with their interrelation—whereas in sociology it had to be recognised 'how unimpressive' were the attempts that had been made to derive more specific theories from some 'master conceptual scheme' (1948: 166).

Finally, it is also of significance that, while Merton always held a fairly catholic view of the forms that sociological theory might take, at this early stage in his career, he did in fact chiefly deploy action theory on essentially Weberian lines. Most obviously, his essays on the sociology of science (e.g., 1936a, 1938, 1949: Part IV) were devoted to showing how in seventeenth-century England the Puritan ethos 'promoted a state of mind and a value-orientation' conducive to the pursuit of natural science, and were thus in direct and quite explicit continuation of Weber's work on capitalism. Their chief concern was to explain and make intelligible a salient feature of modern society by revealing its origins in individual action, even while emphasising that far more was involved than simply the *intended* results of such action.[25] And the more general methodological problems and possibilities arising from such micro-to-macro analysis of social action and its unanticipated consequences were the subject of a paper (1936b) that is now increasingly appreciated as a classic (cf. Elster, 1990).

At Columbia, then, Lazarsfeld and Merton, one might suppose, were brought together not only in friendship but also on the basis of a genuine convergence of interests. And there is indeed ample evidence that a close and highly fruitful collaboration occurred and extended well beyond their several joint publications. Merton readily acknowledged (e.g., 1949: ch. 3) the importance of Lazarsfeld's empirical work in compelling him to clarify concepts and to focus his theoretical concerns, while Lazarsfeld emphasised the major contribution that Merton made through the '"sociological radiation" of empirical action research' (1975: 53). However, for present purposes, the crucial questions that have to be raised are those of just what this collaboration led to and, in particular, of how far it actually succeeded in creating, around the concept of social action, an effective integration of quantitative data analysis and explanatory interpretation.

Attempts that have already been made at assessing Columbia, or more specifically BASR, sociology in the 1940s and 1950s show in fact a large measure of agreement as to its general character (see, e.g., Converse, 1987: ch. 9; Coleman, 1990). Empirically and theoretically, its central concern is seen to be with the social context of individual action: that is, with the diversity of social influences that bear on such action via the formation of goals, values, or preferences; the development of related beliefs and attitudes; and the eventual making of choices or arrival at decisions as expressed in action. The main objective was to trace out the detailed operation of these influences at a relatively micro-level: that is, at the level of relations within primary groups, social networks, local communities, workplaces, and so on. To this end, broadly the same approach in conceptualisation and in data collection and analysis was adapted so as to apply across a wide range of substantive topics: for example, responses to propaganda (Lazarsfeld and Merton, 1943/1949; Merton, 1946), party choice and ideological position (Lazarsfeld, Berelson, and Gaudet, 1948; Lazarsfeld and Thielens, 1958), consumption and community participation (Katz and Lazarsfeld, 1955), and occupational choice and socialisation (Merton, Reader, and Kendall, eds., 1957). Middle-range theory led to hypotheses concerning underlying processes such as the 'two-step flow of communication' from the mass media to mass publics via opinion leaders or 'influentials', the choice of 'reference groups' on individuals' aspirations, evaluations, and satisfactions,[26] and, most generally, the social pressures—including 'cross-pressures'—that are exerted on individuals through the structuring of their social networks and of their roles and role sets.

However, as regards the actual *value* of the Columbia achievement, as opposed to its character, opinion has remained rather sharply divided. Thus, Turner and Turner (1990: 105–107, 188–89) would concur with the early criticism of Mills (1959) that the BASR studies were shaped more by considerations of quantitative technique and also of clients' demands than by any coherent understanding of the nature of sociological problems. In contrast, Hedström and Swedberg (1998: 1) have argued that 'middle range sociology of the kind that Robert Merton and Paul Lazarsfeld tried to develop at Columbia University after World War II', was sociology at its 'most promising and productive'. I would myself certainly favour the latter over the former view. Turner and Turner seem seriously to neglect the extent to which, at least in the major BASR studies, theory was indeed used both in defining the problems to be addressed and in attempting to explain the results empirically produced. Nonetheless, from the standpoint of the present essay, the question remains of whether or in what sense this guiding theory was a theory of action. And the answer has to be that it was not in fact such a theory—or at least not in what might be called the Weberian or European sense. It was, rather, theory developed, even if with some European colouring, in the established American tradition previously noted in connection with the Chicago school of 'the psychology of social life'.

So far as Lazarsfeld is concerned, it is evident from his own writing that, although he made a detailed study of Weber's work, and especially of the methodological essays and empirical projects, he remained deeply dissatisfied and indeed perplexed over Weber's use of the concept of action (Lazarsfeld, 1972; Lazarsfeld and Oberschall, 1965). It appeared to Lazarsfeld that Weber, under the influence of the formal treatment of action in the German juridical tradition and also of the rationalist models of action of Austrian economics, was seeking to ground his sociology in an essentially a priori, nonempirical psychology and ultimately in fact in logic—when what was manifestly needed was an empirical analysis of action, informed by a nonbehaviourist but still scientific psychology, on the lines that he was himself pursuing (cf. Boudon, 1998–2000: vol. 1, ch. 7). Indeed, so strange did Lazarsfeld find Weber's approach that he was driven ultimately to an *ad hominem* explanation: Weber's own acute psychological problems, into which he seemed reluctant to gain much insight, were reflected in an 'unconscious resistance' to the claims of psychology (1972: 93–95).

What Lazarsfeld failed to appreciate, however, was that Weber, being committed to the idea of a *verstehende Soziologie,* had good reasons for not wishing to follow in the tradition of Mill and Spencer in linking his methodological individualism to psychologism: that is, to the view that sociology has to be given a systematic psychological grounding. Weber's position was that if social regularities were to be explained through the action that generated them being rendered *verständlich,* then it was in the end to the practical logic, or rationality, of this action rather than to its psychology that appeal would have to be made. It was through displaying the logical connections that modally prevailed between actors' goals or values, their beliefs and attitudes, and the courses of action that they then pursued under certain situational conditions that this action could best be made intelligible. And accounts of the psychological processes involved, no matter how elaborate they might be (or how illuminating in the individual case) could not in themselves lead to this end. The only psychological assumptions that were required were ones that would allow for individuals to be in fact *capable of* action, and including action that was in some sense rational, as distinct from mere behaviour (cf. ch. 8, pp. 217–8, this volume and also vol. I, ch. 8, pp. 179–81).

As Boudon implies (1998–2000: vol. 1, ch. 7; cf. also Oberschall, 1998), it is in fact Lazarsfeld's own position, rather than Weber's, that is the more difficult to account for. Why did Lazarsfeld so obviously fail to grasp the point of Weber's argument, even if he might still have wished to disagree with it—and especially when his own notion of the story-line that should accompany the empirical analysis of action would seem nothing other than an informal version of Weber's *erklärendes Verstehen?* A suggestion that Boudon makes, and that I find plausible, is that Lazarsfeld's lack of interest in, and indeed generally negative view of, the macrosociology of his day (see esp. Lazarsfeld, 1970) is at the heart of the matter.[27] Given the relatively small-scale studies in which the BASR specialised, and also the prevailing belief in the ability of new survey techniques to deliver reliable subjective data, it could appear feasible to Lazarsfeld and his collaborators to bring out the psychological processes that were involved in the contextual shaping of patterns of social action at a high level of detail—in all their 'quarks and colors', as it were. In contrast, they had little concern with micro-to-macro analyses that would entail the explanatory interpretation of macro-level regularities through narratives of social action of a necessarily quite generalised kind, nor even with macro-to-micro analyses that would aim in turn to show how processes of action were themselves facilitated or constrained by macrosocial factors. The key focus of Lazarsfeldian concerns was rather on what might be called the psychological-microsocial interplay; or, as Boudon remarks of Lazarsfeld (1971: 112): 'la sociologie lui apparut toujours refractée à travers la psychologie. De sorte que la réconciliation avec un Max Weber qui, lui, la percevait comme refractée à travers le droit, n'était guère possible.'

But what, then, of the contribution of Merton? Since, as earlier noted, one part at least of his research programme prior to his joining the BASR was of a manifestly Weberian character, did not his 'sociological radiation' of empirical action research serve in some way to offset Lazarsfeld's psychologism? In fact, it did not, or at least not in a way that might have brought Lazarsfeld closer to Weber, and again the attendant circumstances create something of a puzzle.

In the course of the 1940s Merton's theoretical thinking would appear to have undergone a significant change. When in 1949 his celebrated collection of essays, *Social Theory and Social Structure*, was first published, Merton made it clear in his introductory remarks that he now regarded 'functional analysis' as 'the most promising approach' to sociological explanation and that which would be most profitably followed in the construction of middle-range theory. His subsequently much-debated essay on 'Manifest and Latent Functions' opened the volume and was intended to inform all that followed. While some of his studies in the sociology of science that exemplified micro-to-macro analysis were nonetheless included, his earlier theoretical reflections on social action and its unanticipated consequences found no place.[28]

Merton's attempt at the elaboration and codification of functionalism could in fact be reckoned as his least successful intellectual venture (cf. Campbell, 1982; Elster, 1990). However, he showed no inclination to revert to a social action perspective. For reasons that remain unclear, he would appear to have largely abandoned his Weberian concerns and, insofar as he moved away from functionalism, it was in the direction of purely structural analysis, of the kind later developed in a more extreme form by his student, Peter Blau (e.g., 1994), in which interest centres on the alternative courses of action that are objectively available to individuals in different social situations. Thus, as Bierstedt (1981, 1990), among others, has pointed out, in Merton's mature work it is in fact a theory of action that is the most conspicuously missing element: that is, a theory by resort to which explanations might be developed of how individuals actually make the choices that they do, *given* the structurally determined opportunities and constraints that confront them.[29]

Against this background, therefore, it is scarcely surprising to find that Merton's contribution to empirical action research within the BASR was not to the theory of action itself but rather to the analysis of differing social contexts of action and their implications—which, as earlier remarked, was the prime distinguishing feature of the bureau's work. In other words, Merton's 'sociological radiation' of the research tradition that Lazarsfeld had imported from Vienna did not imply any shift from Lazarsfeld's understanding of action back to that of Weber. Rather, what was involved was a larger and more sophisticated awareness of how individual 'predispositions to act', which might initially appear to be of a quite random nature, could in fact be systematically conditioned by the positions that individuals held within different kinds of relational structure. What Merton added and emphasised, over and above Lazarsfeld's concern with primary, interpersonal relations, was the part played by larger and more institutionalised aspects of social structure, especially the structure of social roles. Nonetheless, in the middle-range theories inspired by Merton, the focus remained on the ways in which these structures shaped action, understood from this standpoint essentially as social behaviour. The subjective logic of differing patterns of action—through consideration of which it might be made intelligible just *why* individuals responded to structural constraints and pressures in the ways they did—was either ignored or was treated only via story-lines of an essentially ad hoc and underdeveloped kind.[30]

In sum, sociology at Columbia in the period under review did attain, largely through the BASR programme, a notable, and indeed arguably still unmatched, degree of integration of research and theory. But this integration, though an impressive accomplishment in itself, remained significantly restricted in both its range and character. The methodological advances made by Lazarsfeld in the collection and quantitative analysis of survey data and the successes of Merton in constructing middle-range theory were closely related and mutually supportive achievements. However, the style of sociology that Lazarsfeld and Merton together created had a twofold limitation.

On the one hand, its scope was confined to relatively microsocial situations. Although the detailed analyses of the various ways in which social processes shaped individual action were intended to have quite general application, rather than being specific to the particular localities within which research was undertaken, the problem was never solved of how such analyses might in fact be linked with results obtained from social surveys or other data sources that were extensive in time and space.[31] And on the other hand, no very serious attempt could therefore be made to start out from temporal and macro-level regularities, established and analysed via quantitative methods—in progressive continuity, say, with the work of Ogburn—and then to explain these regularities through story-lines, or narratives, of the central tendencies in action and interaction through which they were generated, sustained, or, possibly, changed.

At the start of this essay, I already remarked that it should not be expected that a sociology allying the quantitative analysis of social phenomena with their explanation and understanding through a theory of action should face the same difficulties in twentieth-century America as in Europe in the period considered in the preceding chapter. In particular, there was in America little principled resistance to probabilistic thinking, as was created in Europe by the legacy of Comte, nor then to the acceptance into sociology of the new statistical methodology that the probabilistic revolution engendered—although controversies certainly did arise over just what the role of this methodology should be.

Nonetheless, as should have by now become apparent, barriers to a sociology of the kind in question were indeed present. And, just as in the European case—indeed, if anything yet more clearly so—they have to be understood, I would argue, as being ones of an intellectual rather than an institutional character. Each of the episodes that has been considered does in fact serve to illustrate some aspect of the progressive institutional accommodation of sociology within the American university system that occurred in the course of the twentieth century. American sociologists, to a far greater degree than their European counterparts, were given the capacity, in terms of organisational and other resources, to shape their discipline in a relatively autonomous fashion.[32] What, then, was the nature of the intellectual barriers that stood in the way of this capacity being used in order to ally the quantitative analysis of 'the product of action', to resort to Blumer's phrase, with the development of a directly complementary theory of action?

In the European case, I identified three such barriers: those of positivism, empiricism, and psychologism. Interestingly, all three could be said to be present in the American case also, but, it must at once be added, in significantly differing forms.

For example, while positivism again appears as a serious intellectual barrier, it was not in America the systematic positivism of Comte that mattered but rather the critical positivism of Mach, Pearson, and their followers. For the latter, probabilistic thinking posed no problems. Indeed, it was heavily drawn on in order to replace the supposedly metaphysical idea of causation with that of correlation. But the dubious consequence of critical positivism then was that it could serve to legitimate quantitative analyses that had only a quite tenuous connection with theory of any kind—as, most notably, in the later work of Giddings and subsequently in that of Ogburn.

In turn, then, a supposedly self-sufficient empiricism also created difficulties in the American as in the European case, while, however, taking on for the most part a more sophisticated form. It was chiefly manifested not in atheoretical institutional descriptivism, such as that of the Webbs in England, nor in the mere accumulation of numerical social data, but rather as an expression of the probabilistic revolution and of the new English statistics *as infused by* critical positivism. Quantitative analysis was itself seen as the basis of sociological explanation, and theory as little more than a source of concepts or classificatory schemes in terms of which the conclusions emerging from correlation and regression analyses might be organised. It is true that in the hands of Lazarsfeld, quantitative analysis did become both more flexible and potentially more open to a serious alliance with theory than in the hands of Giddings or Ogburn. But still neither Lazarsfeld alone nor Lazarsfeld and Merton together were able to find a satisfactory way of fully realising this potential: that is, a way of accounting for statistical results through theoretically grounded explanatory interpretations of social action that could extend beyond particular relational contexts—groups, networks, communities, and so on. Lazarsfeld's sociological legacy has in fact been usually regarded as one of an undue empiricism—chiefly under the influence of Mills' attack (1959)—even if this is not the way in which Lazarsfeld himself would have wished his work to be understood, and is indeed far from fair.

Finally, the barrier of psychologism—the belief that sociological analysis has ultimately to be grounded in psychology—which could be reckoned as a source of still more serious problems in America than in the Europe, also had distinctively American features. In America it was not the case that a *fear* of psychologism created a damaging *reactive* effect, as with the Durkheim-ians in France, which then led to the rejection of any kind of individualistic explanatory paradigm in sociology. Rather, psychologism, in one version or another, seems often to have been taken more or less for granted, and it was then from this largely unconsidered acceptance that difficulties stemmed. On the one hand, behaviouristic psychologism, of the kind to which Giddings became increasingly attracted, ruled out the very concept of action as entail-ing impermissible reference to mental states. But, on the other hand, negative consequences also resulted from what I have referred to as the American tradition of the psychology of social life, with its evidently mentalistic char-acter, as this was represented both in Chicago in the 1920s and 1930s and then again, with a Lazarsfeldian gloss, in Columbia in the 1940s and 1950s. Although psychologism in this latter form allowed and indeed exploited the concept of action, it too was scarcely compatible with the development of a theory of action on Weberian lines. Its concern was with the origins and constitution of action in highly contextualised interpersonal relations, not with the development of generalised narratives of action and the analysis of the consequences of action as a means of explaining social regularities that might often be extensive in time and space. The incompatibility in question is well brought out in Lazarsfeld's inability to see the point of the Weberian programme. And it may also have been a factor—though this can be no more than speculation—behind Merton's mysterious abandonment of his previous, highly successful, Weberian investigations at around the time when his association with the BASR began.

In conclusion, then, it is natural to ask what are the implications of the foregoing for the state of American sociology today? Do problems of the in-tegration of research and theory of the kind illustrated in the three episodes that I have considered still continue, and for the same reasons as before? To provide any detailed answer to such questions, in the light of the large and complex evolution of American sociology from the 1960s to the present, would call for another lengthy essay or indeed an entire book, and is not therefore something that can here be attempted. However, in lieu of this, two fairly straightforward observations can be made and two illustrative instances offered that would together suggest that the early history reviewed above is, at all events, not irrelevant to the contemporary situation.

The first observation is that while American sociologists have remained in the forefront of quantitative analysis, such work as it appears today in, say, the leading American journals, is not evidently characterised by a concern to provide theoretically well-grounded explanations for the empirical results that are reported. The second observation is that within American sociology the theory of social action, at least as understood on broadly Weberian lines, would still seem to be at best a minority interest. In Europe efforts to build on the individualistic paradigm, and in particular to extend rational action theory beyond the rational choice theory of mainstream economics, have of late taken on new vigour (cf. vol. I, chs. 6–8 and ch. 1, this volume). But in American sociology—and in marked contrast, it may be added with American political science—such developments have met with resistance or, at best, indifference and would appear to have become to some large extent ghettoised.[33]

To illustrate my first observation, I can do no better than return to the particular field of research, that of social stratification and mobility, on which I have in fact concentrated in this volume. This is a field in which American sociologists can claim credit for pioneering major advances in quantitative analysis and for a large volume of highly sophisticated empirical work. At the same time, though, it would have to be regarded as a field in which, in the United States, the spirit of Machian critical positivism has a persistent afterlife, even if the underlying philosophy of science has been long since forgotten. While a distinction between causation and correlation is in principle recognised, the supposition would seem still to prevail, implicitly if not explicitly, that causal explanations can in some way or other be ground out of statistical analyses themselves, so that—essentially as in the work of Ogburn and his colleagues—the role of theory becomes uncertain if not quite marginal. The issues that are central here were clearly posed some time ago (cf. vol. I, ch. 6, p. 119 and n. 2) by Boudon (1976) in a celebrated exchange with Hauser (1976): that is, issues concerning the need, in explaining established empirical regularities in stratification processes, for generative mechanisms to be specified at the level of action, over and above the analysis of the variables involved. However, these issues appear never to have been taken as seriously among American students of social stratification as among their European counterparts, as citations in the earlier chapters in this volume will serve to indicate. Insofar as theory is invoked at all in the American literature, it tends to be functionalist theory, on the lines that I have indicated and criticised (see esp. ch. 7, this volume) or in effect social-psychological theory, and thus theory that one way or another short-circuits any consideration of action.[34]

I would illustrate my second observation by reference to a particular sociologist, James Coleman, who was a product of the Columbia of Lazarsfeld and Merton. A strong case could be made for Coleman as the outstanding American sociologist of his generation, and he must certainly rank among the most versatile. On the one hand, he undertook extensive research, notably in the sociology of education (e.g., Coleman et al., 1966; Coleman, Hoffer, and Kilgore, 1982; Coleman and Hoffer, 1987), that involved the quantitative analysis of large-scale data-sets and that established a series of important empirical regularities—concerning, for example, the relationship between children's educational performance and their social background, type of school attended, school resources, peer group influences, and so on. On the other hand, his *Foundations of Social Theory* (1990) represents the one major attempt made by a recent American author to develop a theory of social action for sociology—essentially through the development and adaptation of rational choice theory. However, the striking point then is that Coleman never succeeded in, and indeed appears to have made rather little attempt at, bringing these two aspects of his work together.

Thus, *Foundations of Social Theory* seems largely divorced from Coleman's research in educational sociology. He does not resort to this research in order to illustrate the explanatory potential of the kind of theory that he advocates or to test explanations derived from it. And this is all the more surprising in that some of the most cogent criticisms made of the research, notably by economists (e.g., Cain and Watts, 1970; Hanushek, 1972;), concern its lack of a clear theoretical basis and are, ironically, criticisms that Coleman himself, in different mode, might well have put forward (see esp. Coleman, 1986a). For example, it has been pointed out that, since the causal interpretations that Coleman offers of the results of his regression analyses are not grounded in any explicit narrative at the level of action, the possibility is not adequately treated that some regressors may, as a result of individual action, be at least partly determined by the very outcomes that they are supposed to account for. Thus, parents may choose schools for their children *because of* their good academic records or encourage their children to choose others as friends *because of* the latter's academic abilities and motivation. Not without reason, two—generally appreciative—commentators (Heckman and Neal, 1996: 82) have spoken of Coleman's 'multiple intellectual personalities' and have observed that 'Coleman the empiricist is clearly not the same person as Coleman the theorist'.

Rather clear indications do then exist, I would argue, that the difficulties in integrating quantitative analysis with an appropriate form of theory that I have documented for the earlier and mid-twentieth century are still far from resolution in American sociology at the present time—further in fact than in Europe. And perhaps the most serious question that now arises is that of whether, as American sociology appears to be moving into an increasingly unstructured and unreflective pluralism, these difficulties are any longer ones of central professional concern.

Notes to Chapter 1

1. It should be noted that in the course of the essays I do in fact use 'theory' in two rather different ways: sometimes to refer to the general basis of the explanatory accounts that are offered of particular phenomena—that is in effect to RAT, but sometimes, too, to refer to these accounts themselves as being 'theories of' something. While this double usage is not very tidy, it is, I think, innocuous.

2. It should be added that the danger here pointed to is far less likely to arise with statistical techniques such as, say, loglinear modelling, that, unlike regression, do not entail the specification of independent and dependent variables but are manifestly concerned only with description by means of revealing patterns of association among variables.

3. Lieberson's own illustration of his point is taken from physics. One may account for the varying velocities with which a feather, a coin, and a brick fall through the air by reference to differences in their density and shape. But more is involved in their falling in the first place. To explain this, one would need to invoke the further force of gravity—and not as a variable but as a constant.

4. This is not to say that the subject matter of sociology, or of other social sciences, is of no consequence whatever. I would agree with Cole that the greater mutability of social than of natural phenomena does carry implications for the nature of sociological theory, and in particular in limiting the degree of generality that it can hope to attain. But even so I would see the differences that thus arise between the social and natural sciences as being ones of degree rather than kind (cf. vol. I, ch. 1, pp. 5–7).

5. Research councils and other funding agencies in European nations would seem generally more ready than corresponding bodies in the United States to support comparative work in the social sciences. And in addition the EU is itself now heavily committed in this area. For example, as I write, the first activities are being planned of an EU 'network of centres of excellence' in the social sciences involving 14 centres (including my own institution), which will dispose of a budget of around 6 million euros over 5 years in order to develop and mobilise research

expertise in the general field of the comparative study of economic change, social differentiation and inequality, and social cohesion. Actual research funding is extra.

6. A negative consequence has, however, also to be noted: that is, the widening gap that is emerging in many European countries between what might be called the sociology of the research institutes and centres and the sociology of the university departments—or at least of those without a continuing tradition of systematic empirical research. I have discussed this problem in more detail elsewhere, with particular reference to the case of Ireland (Goldthorpe, 2002b).

7. There has so far been rather little time for the theory I outline to be subjected to any systematic empirical test. One study that purports to do so, at least in certain respects, is Devine (2004). However, despite what might be described as the author's qualified enthusiasm for the theory, I cannot regard the research she reports as having much relevance one way or another. Apart from problems of how to generalise from the rather strange 'samples' studied and from the qualitative material presented, Devine misunderstands the theory in two crucial respects: first, as regards the ways in which it does and does not invoke class differences in cultural resources (see further ch. 4, pp. 81–4, this volume); and second, in supposing that it is a theory concerned with absolute rates of mobility—like that of Bourdieu with which she recurrently compares it—when it is, very explicitly, concerned with explaining regularities in relative rates.

8. I am not just being wise after the event. My conditional prediction about decreasing fluidity was already made in the first edition of *On Sociology* before most of the research findings that would seem to lend support to it had appeared.

Notes to Chapter 2

1. Remarkably, this statement has led to the supposition (Pahl, 1993) that Marshall and I would conceive of class analysis as being entirely *a*theoretical!

2. As the above implies, the theory is functionalist in character and later, in Chapter 7, in regard to its specific application to social mobility, I do in fact refer to it as functionalist rather than liberal, since in this context it is its theoretical form rather than its ideological colouration that is chiefly relevant.

3. This and the next few paragraphs recapitulate arguments that are set out at greater length at various points in Volume I, Chapters 6–8.

4. In the first edition of this work, I used the terms 'service class' and 'salariat' interchangeably. However, in this edition I favour the latter. Although the idea of a service class (*Dienstklasse*) has an interesting and informative intellectual pedigree (Renner, 1953; Dahrendorf, 1959), it can, I have discovered, lead to some confusion: most notably, to the idea that the service class has some particular connection with the services sector of the economy, which is not of course the case.

5. The most influential advance in modelling in this respect was that made by Mare (1981; cf. also 1993). A further notable finding of research following the approach in question is that as young people progress through the educational sys-

tem, class differentials in attainment diminish (see esp. Shavit and Blossfeld, eds., 1993). Some debate has arisen over whether this is to be explained in terms of life-course effects (as children become older they are less dependent on and influenced by their families of origin) or by selection effects (children who in fact stay on in the educational system are more able and better motivated than those who drop out, independently of their class backgrounds).

6. It may be added that decreasing class differentials in particular transitions are most readily revealed when the analysis extends over a very lengthy period—say, half a century or so. This may be because the decrease is extremely slow. However, where repeated reforms of educational and qualificational systems have occurred, the problem arises of identifying the 'same' transition over time, and in turn the danger exists of taking as evidence of decreasing differentials what are in fact simply the effects of the restratification of different levels of education concomitantly with their expansion. In some further analyses a 'global' rather than a 'local' approach to class differentials is adopted (cf. Vallet, 2004b) in that attention focuses simply on the association between individuals' class origins and the highest level of qualification that they attain in the course of their educational careers. With this approach, and where long periods are also covered, evidence of decreasing differentials seems more often—though still by no means consistently—to be found (see, e.g., Breen et al., 2005), with the decrease often resulting from reduced differentials in early transitions 'feeding through' the educational system even where class differentials in later transitions do not decline in themselves. But this latter fact still of course remains to be accounted for, and simply to appeal to increasing heterogeneity among the growing number of students who continue in education after early transitions is more adequate statistically than sociologically, unless the particular respects in which heterogeneity increases, and the consequences thereof, are specified.

7. On the general difficulty in culturalist explanations of providing evidence of the independent variable that is sufficiently removed from that which constitutes the dependent one, see Barry (1970: ch. iv) and also the apt observations of Boudon (1990: 41) on the notion of *habitus* as introduced by Bourdieu and popularised by his followers. I would also include under culturalist explanations—and the foregoing critique—those advanced from anti-egalitarian positions that emphasise differences among classes simply in their 'taste' for education (see, e.g., Murphy, 1981, and esp. 1990: 49–50).

8. Thus, Bourdieu (1973) starts from the assumption that such mobility is 'controlled' and concerns only 'a limited category of individuals, carefully selected and modified by and for individual ascent'—but presents no supporting evidence. Similarly, Willis (1977: 126–28) believes that in Britain opportunities for upward mobility created by economic growth exist for the working class in 'only in relatively small numbers' (but compare the results reported in Goldthorpe, 1987: Tables 2.2 and 3.1 or in Goldthorpe and Mills, 2004), and then follows Bourdieu and Passeron (1970) in claiming that educational qualifications do not really help

working-class children to take up these opportunities, which is, again, demonstrably wrong (see, e.g., Goldthorpe and Jackson, 2006).

9. On the basis of the—very limited—evidence then available to him, Boudon was led to believe that inequalities of educational opportunity in advanced societies had in fact been in steady decline, and therefore took up the problem of why this had not apparently generated any increase in social mobility. See further Volume I, Chapter 6.

10. In fact evidence suggests that the educational and occupational aspirations actually expressed by children of different class backgrounds are now growing more similar (see, e.g., Furlong, 1992: ch. 7 and also the research reviewed in ch. 4, this volume). In other words, rather than the problem for the working class being one of a 'poverty of aspiration', it could, in the absence of change in differential attainment, be better seen as more one of aspirations frustrated.

11. With gender differentials, in contrast to class differentials, there is of course no reason to expect that, in the absence of secondary effects, they will still be sustained in some significant degree by primary effects. This does not, however, detract from the point that the virtual collapse of gender differentials indicates that purely normative influences on educational choice are likely to be rapidly modified as cost-benefit balances change.

12. It is also important to keep in mind here that working-class children— perhaps more than their parents—are well aware of the opportunity costs to themselves of staying on at school beyond the minimum leaving age (Micklewright, Pearson, and Smith, 1988; Bynner, 1991). If entry into higher education follows, the reduced material standard of living that they incur may of course extend up to their mid- or late twenties or longer still if, when in employment, they have to pay off high levels of debt. With children from more advantaged families, such disadvantages are likely to be offset by parental support in various forms (cf. Erikson and Jonsson, 1993, 1994).

13. In the spirit of David Lockwood's famous Steinian comment (1960) on the supposed normative significance of working-class families buying washing machines in the 1950s ('a washing machine is a washing machine is a washing machine'), one might observe that 'three years at university is three years at university is three years at university'. In other words, one could question whether, net of economic considerations, a taste for higher education should be any more class differentiated than that for standard consumer durables.

14. It is with considerations such as this that the approach here followed most obviously diverges from the 'human capital' approach taken by most economists of education. In their perspective, as Arum and Hout (1998: 471) have put it, education appears 'as a fungible linear accumulation, like a financial investment'; but in fact the actual institutional structures of modern educational systems 'offer an array of choices and constraints that defy the simple linear formulations' of the economists' models. For an interesting discussion from this point of view of the operation of the German apprenticeship system, see Jonsson, Mills, and Müller (1996).

15. A further question of potentially large importance here is that of whether returns to education, and especially at higher levels, as measured in terms of either income or class destinations, are lower for children of less advantaged than of more advantaged class backgrounds. Unfortunately, studies thus far undertaken show little consistency in either their methods or results. See, for example, Hauser (1973), Petit (1975), Papanicolaou and Psacharopoulos (1979), Björklund and Kjellström (1994), and Jonsson (1995). However, as regards returns in terms of class mobility chances, see further Chapter 7, this volume, pp. 176–7.

16. It has been argued, sometimes with apparently supporting evidence (e.g., Pissarides, 1981), that by reducing opportunity costs unemployment encourages children to stay on in full-time education. But for a well-documented case to the contrary, indicating that rising unemployment leads to more children taking jobs at the first opportunity rather than investing in further education, see Micklewright, Pearson, and Smith (1988).

17. On further Swedish distinctiveness, that is, as regards the relative equality of class mobility chances, see Erikson and Goldthorpe (1992: 164–65, 177–80) and also Chapter 7, this volume. Perhaps the main basis for challenging the interpretation of the decline in Swedish class differentials in education that is presented in the text, or at all events the significance that I would attach to it, is provided by the further case of France. For this country also evidence is emerging of a long-term decline in these differentials and also of an increase in social fluidity (Thélot and Vallet, 2000; Vallet, 2004a, 2004b), although in the absence of any social democratic hegemony. But, so far, both the processes through which educational attainment has become more equal across classes in France and the importance of this in accounting for the increase in fluidity remain unclear (again, see further ch. 7).

Notes to Chapter 3

1. We do in fact treat children and their parents as a single decision-making entity but there is nothing in the model that we shall go on to propose that need preclude the possibility of intrafamilial disagreements, bargaining, and compromises.

2. We need not, for present purposes, be committed to any particular theory of how different levels or kinds of resources derive from different class positions (but cf. chs. 14 and 15, this volume).

3. Arum and Shavit (1995) show that while opting for a vocational rather than an academic track in secondary education does reduce American students' chances of continuing into higher education, it also serves as an important safety net for those who do not in fact continue. In particular, for 'non-college-bound' students, vocational education improves labour market prospects relative to those associated with other tracks by raising the chances for males of entering skilled manual work and for females of entering routine nonmanual work as against less favourable outcomes, notably unemployment.

4. Empirical support for the idea of such a consensus on the general desir-

ability of different kinds of occupation (taken together with specific employment statuses) is provided in Goldthorpe and Hope (1974).

5. Strictly speaking, the mathematics of our model require a slightly weaker condition, namely that $(\alpha > \gamma_1 / (\gamma_1 + \gamma_2)$. This imposes a condition on the magnitude of the difference in the chances of access to the salariat as between remaining at school and passing the examination and leaving immediately. The conditional probability of access to the salariat for those who leave immediately should not be greater than $\gamma_1 + \gamma_2$ times the conditional probability of access to the salariat for those who remain at school and pass the examination. However, because of condition (3), condition (4) will always be met if $\gamma > 0.5$.

6. For further discussion of this assumption, see ch. 7, this volume, pp. 166–8.

7. Note that, whereas p_{iW} can take any value between 0 and 1, depending on the value of π, if $\beta_1 > \gamma_1$, then p_{iS} will exceed one-half for all values of π.

8. Of course, the risk of dropping into the underclass bears also on pupils of salariat origin. But, for these pupils, the more ambitious option of remaining at school entails no risk, relative to leaving, because their subjective probability of gaining access to the salariat is greater even if they remain at school and fail than it would be if they left. This follows from condition (1) of our model. Put another way, the inferior outcome for pupils of salariat origin is to end up in either the working class or the underclass, but, in contrast to the inferior outcome for working-class pupils, the risk of such an outcome is not reduced by taking the less ambitious educational option.

9. Though empirically this will be observed only if the proportion of salariat children who consider it in their best interests to remain in education does not change for other reasons. For example, given an increase over time in the importance of educational qualifications in obtaining jobs, we might see changes in the relative values of the α, β, and γ parameters causing the proportion for whom $p_i > 0.5$ to increase in both classes. Under these conditions a narrowing of the odds ratio will not necessarily follow.

10. In our model this will be the case for the salariat if (in addition to conditions [1] to [4]) $\beta_1 > \gamma_1$ but it need not be so if this inequality does not hold.

11. One respect in which gender differentials in education have proved relatively resistant to change is that of patterns of subject choice, with girls remaining underrepresented in mathematics and some of the applied sciences. An explanation of this in the spirit of our model would be that while women are nowadays much more likely to seek their own careers, they nevertheless anticipate quite lengthy breaks from the labour force or periods of part-time work arising for domestic reasons. They are therefore likely to choose those subjects that give access to careers that afford some flexibility in working arrangements or allow for career interruptions. So, secretarial work, which provides a great deal of flexibility, is likely to be more attractive to girls than is, say, skilled manual work, although there is little difference in the level of educational attainment required by, or in the general

desirability of, the two kinds of employment. Similar arguments might be made in respect of the choice between teaching or law, on the one hand, and engineering or management, on the other. If women were better enabled as, say, through adequate childcare provision, to maintain their availability for full-time employment over the life course, the expectation would then be that gender differences in subject choice would diminish far more rapidly than hitherto. Note that this explanation can again be set in contrast with one couched in terms of—in this case gender-specific— values and norms. For attempts to apply rational action theory more systematically to the explanation of gender-based and other regularities in choice of field of education, see Jonsson (1999) and Van de Werfhorst, Sullivan, and Cheung (2003).

12. As regards the tendency for children from more advantaged class backgrounds to make more ambitious educational choices than those from less advantaged backgrounds even when level of previous academic performance is held constant, see Chapter 2, this volume, p. 39; and as regards generally declining class effects on educational attainment at successive transitions within educational systems, see Chapter 2, note 5.

13. Elster (1991) criticises several different versions of the argument that action taken in conformity with social norms is reducible to rational action. However, his efforts to show that no version entails that such a reduction is *always* possible are of greater philosophical than sociological interest. One could entirely agree with Elster, yet still wish to maintain that, in a particular instance of sociological explanation, a reductionist view could in fact be upheld.

Notes to Chapter 4

1. Various commentators have also referred, for reasons that will become apparent, to the 'relative risk aversion' (or RRA) theory of educational choice. In Breen and Yaish (2006) it is shown how the formal model of the previous chapter can be presented in a somewhat more generalised way. It is also shown, first, that certain of the more restrictive or disputable assumptions initially made can be relaxed, most notably assumption (2) (p. 52) that staying on in education and failing may be more risky than leaving; and, second, that the model amounts in fact to a special case of 'prospect theory' as advanced by Kahneman and Tversky (1979)— with, thus, some degree of support from experimental psychology. However, this development of the model has no major consequences for the discussion of this chapter.

2. An illuminating contrast between economists' approaches to educational attainment and perhaps the best-known and empirically best-implemented sociological approach, that embodied in the 'Wisconsin model' of educational (and status) attainment, is provided in Morgan (1998). See further, pp. 96–7.

3. Other problems apart from that of realism that arise from economists' assumptions about how young people form expectations about returns from education are analysed in a trenchant way by Manski (1993). Somewhat heretically for

an economist, Manski advocates the use of subjective data on expectations. See further, pp. 98–100.

4. For example, with the multilevel modelling techniques usually applied, apparent contextual effects may simply reflect model misspecification through the omission of relevant individual characteristics, or again contextual effects may indeed be present but stem from various other processes than social interaction.

5. It may be noted that the ethnography to which Akerlof chiefly refers in discussing educational choice—Whyte's (1943) *Street Corner Society*—is a prime example of a 'disputed' ethnography that raises the problem I earlier discussed (vol. I, ch. 4), of how any rational evaluation of rival claims might be made. See, as the starting point of the dispute, Boelen (1992). Moreover, as I also argued, a recourse to ethnography does not in itself automatically overcome the difficulties of establishing contextual effects in the way that Akerlof would seem to suppose. In fairness to Akerlof, it should be said that he does at one point (1997: 1020) accept that 'snippets of ethnography, autobiography, and biography, of course do not statistically prove that people try to conform to the social norms of their friends and relatives.' Rather, they serve as 'token reminders of what most of us already appreciate instinctively . . . we know that the education sought by most people will be the education that meets the approval of friends and relatives.' But I would then have to respond by saying that my biography, at least, leads me, for what it is worth, to 'appreciate instinctively' and 'know' something significantly different from this.

6. In addition, as indicated in the two preceding chapters, the theory does also aim to provide a basis for explaining changes in class differentials in cases where these can in fact be observed—such as the decline in differentials found in Sweden, and now, it appears, also in France and possibly elsewhere over the last decades of the twentieth century.

7. It may further be noted that both these authors seem greatly to underestimate the difficulty of actually determining the relative contributions made by primary and secondary effects to any particular level of class differentials in educational attainment. Only recently has it been possible to propose a method for so doing (Erikson et al., 2005; cf. also Jackson et al., 2005)

8. Nash does at one point (2003: 442) remark that 'There is, perhaps, a subtle difference between seeking to explain how class differences in educational attainment are caused and how the *persistence* or *stability* of such differences is caused, but the distinction is a point of such academic fineness that it should not be admitted.' I can of course only apologise for the fact that, as an academic, I do have a preference for fineness over qualities with which it might be contrasted.

9. For example, Savage (2000: 86) describes this move as 'a piece of intellectual chutzpah'. It ought of course to be evident that what is primarily at issue here is not how classes should be conceptualised but what aspects of class should be taken as being of relevance and importance for the explanatory purposes in hand. As already indicated, the BG theory in no way seeks to deny the part played by

class differences in levels of cultural (as of other) *resources* in creating differentials in educational attainment via primary effects—that is, those relating to differences in students' academic ability and performance. But it does not then follow that differences in subcultural *values* and related norms are similarly important in regard to students' educational goals and choices—their readiness to take up opportunities that their demonstrated ability would make available to them. Thus, parents and children may have quite similar views on the purposes and importance of education across classes but with class differences still being marked in the capacity of parents to help the their children achieve their educational goals. See further, ch. 7.

10. I would refer back here to the arguments of Abell (1992), Coleman and Fararo (1992), and Stinchcombe (1993), previously cited (vol. I, ch. 6, pp. 124–7). I suspect that the critics under consideration are more favourably disposed towards 'grounded theory', which, one might say, 'does a little with a lot': that is, involves the ever more elaborate conceptualisation and reconceptualisation of empirical data with negligible explanatory gain.

11. Class differentials in this regard, as measured by odds ratios, did, however, change little over the period in question—widening, if anything, as between children of working-class and salariat background, while narrowing slightly as between children of working-class and intermediate-class background.

12. It may, though, be again pointed out that while the BG theory is not dependent on the operation of class-specific norms relating to educational choice, it does not need to claim that such norms do not exist; only that, insofar as they do exist, they do not represent a satisfactory 'bottom line' for explanatory purposes. Such norms can in fact be viewed—and themselves explained—as 'serving as guides to rational action that have evolved over time out of distinctive class experience and that may substitute for detailed calculation where educational choices arise' (p. 69, this volume, and cf. also vol. I., ch. 8). However, two implications follow. First, the influence that norms exert on individuals' actions will not take the form of a blanket effect but will vary widely with individuals' particular circumstances and attributes (e.g., in the case in point, with their ability). Second, norms should be understood as being quite mutable—as likely to change once they no longer appear to be useful guides to rational action, even if with some amount of lag. Thus, as earlier suggested (pp. 65–7), the undermining of norms associated with former gender differentials in educational attainment (to the disadvantage of females), the disappearance of which contrasts so sharply with the persistence of class differentials, can be understood as following from changing conditions in labour and marriage markets that significantly increased the returns that young women can expect from education.

13. The reference here is to the title of a powerful attack by Kerr and Fisher (1957) on the industrial sociology of Elton Mayo and his followers. In such 'plant sociology', Kerr and Fisher observe, a pervasive dualism is to be found. Workers are seen as essentially nonrational actors, driven by a desire for security and so-

cial approval, who blindly follow the norms of their group (e.g., output norms), whereas managers are rational actors aiming, under unreformed capitalism, at maximising profits but, once appropriately trained in 'human relations', capable of leading workers, through the reshaping of their loyalties, to a new kind of industrial society. Compare at a macro-level, the dualism criticised in Volume I, Chapter 8 that divides cultures taken to be characterised by a predominance of rational action from those still in the grip of traditionalism, and, in turn, logical from prelogical mentalities.

14. It may also be noted that such a view leaves the way open for politicians and others to account for class differentials simply by invoking a 'poverty of aspirations' among working-class children and their parents, which, as well as being eminently question begging, provides a nice illustration of blaming the victim. I suspect that what often lies behind the suggestion that middle-class but not working-class educational decision making is rational is some confusion between the processes through which decisions are reached and the effectiveness with which they can then be implemented—the latter being more a matter of resources rather than of rationality.

15. See, for example, the studies referred to in the articles by Devine, Hatcher, and Nash previously cited. More recent examples of qualitative work, focusing in fact on 'middle-class' educational decision making, are Ball (2003) and Devine (2004). What is meant by 'intensive' or 'in-depth' is often far from clear. While in some cases repeated interviews with respondents are carried out over an extended period, in others just one interview is undertaken and sometimes of apparently no longer duration than might occur in the context of a large-scale survey. Typically, such studies do not produce data that can be—or at least is—placed in the public domain in the way that now routinely occurs with survey data (cf. Vol. 1, ch. 1, p. 15) and it is thus not possible to carry out any check on authors' interpretations of their findings or on the representativeness of the snippets from interviews that constitute the main supporting evidence that is made available to the reader.

16. See, for example, the studies reviewed by Payne (2003: 13–14) in discussing 'pragmatic rationality' in educational decision making.

17. I earlier argued (vol. I, ch. 4) that properly designed ethnographical research might also play an important part in the testing of theories of the generative processes underlying macro-level regularities: that is, by investigating whether evidence was to be found of these processes actually at work 'on the ground' in particular locales. However, in the particular case in point, some major difficulties arise. Educational choices are likely to be made—or, one might better say, to 'emerge'—over periods of weeks or months and, moreover, in a number of different contexts of interaction, involving parents, teachers, and peer groups in and out of school. Consequently, relevant ethnography following classic techniques of participant or nonparticipant observation is not easily undertaken. This explains, I would suggest, why, with the exception of a number of school ethnographies, that tend to

neglect family and other out-of-school relations, qualitative work has been largely interview based.

18. I am in fact aware of several other research projects in train that are concerned in part at least with evaluating the BG theory but that are not at this time complete. For example, Van de Werfhorst and Anderson (2005; also Van de Werfhorst, 2005), using American and Dutch data, seek to provide indirect tests of the theory, as against human capital theory, by deriving implications that would follow under conditions of credentials 'inflation' or 'deflation' in relation to class attainment; and Holm and Jaeger (2005), using Danish data, aim at more direct and comprehensive tests of the theory, in this case as against cultural reproduction theory, via the econometric technique of dynamic decision process modelling. So far, results from these projects, in much the same way as those reviewed in the text below, give broad support to the BG theory or are at all events more supportive of this theory than of its rivals.

19. Need and de Jong (2000) recognise that the theory was in fact developed to explain persistence in class differentials over time but argue that, as they are concerned only with the question of whether relative risk aversion can be shown to be at work, they do not need over-time data. They also suggest their own extension of the BG theory to apply to gender differentials but since, as they acknowledge, this involves claims not made or implied by the theory itself, I do not consider the, mainly negative, results that they report in this regard.

20. As Sullivan (2006) observes, this is a notable result given that a strong, positive association does exist between parental level of qualification and examination performance.

21. Sullivan does in fact also find an association with parental educational level, though this is weaker than that with class. And it may be added that both Sullivan and Need and de Jong find that boys tend to have higher estimations of their own abilities than do girls.

22. The possibility should also be noted of limits on information leading to mistaken beliefs being in fact formed in a rational way. This possibility is discussed by Boudon (see vol. I, ch. 7, p. 144) and also by Breen (1999). The latter's work is especially relevant here in that it draws on Bayesian learning theory to suggest how students, by being caught in a 'confounded learning equilibrium', may come to hold quite mistaken beliefs about the importance of effort to educational success. A parallel argument could perhaps be developed in regard to students coming quite rationally to mistaken conclusions in the process of learning what level of ability they possess.

23. This model differs from the formal BG model chiefly in that Esser specifically provides for an effect on educational choice of parental concern to minimise the risk of children's downward mobility.

24. I have to admit that I did not myself see this implication of the theory.

Perhaps one of the main advantages of the representation of a theory in a formal model is that it helps others to make 'discoveries within an invention'.

25. It is not in fact clear, to me at least, exactly how this expectation is derived from Akerlof's theory and in any event I would doubt if as strong test of this theory is involved as is in the case of the BG theory where a fairly distinctive implication is identified.

26. What would have been of greater interest, if appropriate data had existed, would have been to derive proxies for the beliefs of members of the 1958 birth cohort from the labour market experience of members of a birth cohort just a few years younger.

27. As Payne observes (and cf. Becker's findings for Germany referred to in the text above), important class differences do exist in the extent to which, through deploying such resources, parents can intervene effectively so as to influence, in one way or another, the course of their children's academic careers.

28. While not primarily concerned with the BG theory, Beattie does however recognise that her results could be regarded consistent with it (2002: 36). The relative unresponsiveness of young men from more advantaged backgrounds to prevailing earnings returns when opting for courses leading to high-level educational qualifications could be taken to reflect the overriding priority that they give to avoiding downward mobility in class (or status) terms and their belief that such qualifications give the best long-term protection. And it is of course also possible that they are motivated by other class-related economic considerations than level of earnings alone, such as employment security, stability of earnings, and career prospects.

29. One could also note in this connection the models of educational choice developed in Erikson and Jonsson (1996), Jonsson and Erikson (2000), and in Hillmert and Jacob (2003), which have evident similarities with the BG model.

30. From the work referred to in note 7 above, it would appear (Erikson et al., 2005; Jackson et al., 2005) that in a crucial transition within the British educational system—that to A-level work in secondary school, which is the normal route to securing university entry—secondary effects regularly account for somewhere between a quarter and a half of the class differentials in this transition as represented by odds ratios.

Notes to Chapter 5

1. The schema is known, in consequence of its rather complex genesis, by several different names. In a British context it is usually referred to as the Goldthorpe schema; in an international context, as the EGP (Erikson-Goldthorpe-Portocarero) schema, the Erikson-Goldthorpe schema or the CASMIN schema, after its use in the Comparative Analysis of Social Mobility in Industrial Societies project.

2. NS-SEC can in effect be regarded as a new instantiation of the class schema in which the allocation of occupations to the categories of the classification was

undertaken in the light of more extensive information on aspects of the employment relations with which occupations are typically associated than was previously
available (Rose and Pevalin, 2003). However, a quite close correspondence can be
established between the original classes and NS-SEC in its 'analytical' version (see
Goldthorpe and McKnight, 2006: Table 1). The labelling of the new classification
as one of 'socioeconomic status' is somewhat unfortunate, though not very consequential, and has perhaps to be attributed to the concern of a New Labour government to avoid the language of class at all costs.

3. In this last respect, a particularly sharp debate has of late developed among
social epidemiologists concerning the relative importance of 'subjective' and 'objective' aspects of social stratification—or, that is, of what sociologists would regard
as status and class—with the latter being in some instances operationalised via the
class schema. See, for example, on the one side, Marmot (2004) and, on the other,
Macleod et al. (2005).

4. Although the distinction here made between construct and criterion validity is widely recognised, the terminology by which it is identified can differ and
sometimes in quite confusing ways. For a useful discussion, see Rose and O'Reilly
(1998: Appendix 10).

5. Evans and Mills (1999) have in fact extended their work to newly capitalist eastern European nations, with again generally encouraging results. Further
comparative findings will emerge from current research led by David Rose at the
University of Essex and directed towards the development of a common European
Union social classification, for which NS-SEC is being taken as the prototype (see
www.iser.essex/ac/uk/esec).

6. Why this very skewed distribution of individuals among the three categories should be found *does* of course constitute a significant problem: as Simon
(1991) has put it, that of why, to go to extremes, there are employing organisations
and employees at all, rather than simply independent contractors, or, alternatively,
of why there is not just a single, encompassing organisation by which everyone is
employed. This problem is in fact centrally addressed by the organisational and
transaction cost economics on which I later draw and is one of obvious relevance
to understanding how class structures of different 'shape' have evolved. However, it
is not that with which I am here concerned.

7. Most important in this regard are the latent class analyses undertaken by
Evans and Mills (1998, 2000; and cf. also Birkelund, Goodman, and Rose, 1996).
The indicators used in these analyses were constructed from responses to questions on their employment relations that were put directly to members of samples
of the employed population. Substantially better results than those reported could
not, I believe, be expected in view of difficulties encountered in eliciting the precise
information required and resulting high levels of 'noise' in the data. For example,
respondents reporting that they were paid weekly might in fact mean not that they
had a fixed weekly wage but rather that, while being paid, say, by the hour or shift,

they actually *received* their earnings weekly; respondents might confuse being on an incremental salary scale with receiving annual cost-of-living increases; or they might report on their own *personal* promotion chances rather than on those generally associated with the jobs they held. Better quality data could almost certainly be obtained directly from employers, provided that sampling problems could then be overcome.

8. This statement may appear less surprising if certain common sources are recognised, most notably Barnard (1938) and the first edition (1946) of Simon (1961), and also a similar starting point in the critique of the conceptualisation of work, the firm, and employment relations within orthodox neoclassical economics.

9. In particular, I seek to avoid, on the one hand, the self-indulgence of those Marxists who assume that in some future world the abolition of capitalist institutions will make possible the production of 'new' men and women with preferences, orientations to work, and so on, such that present-world problems of efficiency will be entirely transcended; and, on the other hand, the Panglossian tendencies of those economists who assume that 'whatever is, is efficient' and fail to give due recognition to the conflictual or contested aspects of employment relations.

10. I do not assume, I should stress, that employers' rationality implies that they subject their contractual relations with employees to some continuous process of review and revision; only that they are ready to reexamine and modify these relations from the point of view of organisational effectiveness when prompted to do so by changing circumstances (cf. Osterman, 1987; also vol. I, chs. 7 and 8). I also recognise that although employers have the initiative in the design and implementation of employment contracts, the constraints under which they act are likely to include those created by employee responses to their initiatives, whether individually or collectively expressed, and also those that follow from the legislative and regulatory framework that is imposed on employment relations by the state. The nature of such constraints can, however, be expected to show great variation by time and place; and thus, a focus on the actions of employers in dealing with highly generalised contractual problems would seem appropriate, given that my concern is with explaining broad probabilistic regularities in the association between forms of contract and types of work rather than with the deviations from these regularities that will certainly be found.

11. In what follows, 'employer' should be understood as also covering what is in fact the more likely case of 'employing organisation'. It should also be noted that throughout I use 'agent' only in (explicit or implicit) contradistinction to 'principal', and not as a synonym for 'actor'.

12. The idea of implicit contracts or of implicit provisions in contracts has taken on particular importance in the economics literature. Ehrenberg and Smith (1991: 409) refer in this connection to 'a set of shared, informal understandings about how firms and workers will respond to contingencies' and Gibbons (1997: 11) refers to 'an understanding backed by the parties' reputations instead of law'.

13. If only workers have such knowledge, employers are exposed to oppor-

tunism. Workers may shirk in order to conceal this knowledge from their employer and in this way seek to get a higher rate of pay than they would if the employer were better informed (cf. Gibbons, 1987, 1997). One has here a prime illustration of the similarity of concern but divergence of approach of the contemporary economics on which I draw and the industrial sociology of the 1940s and 1950s. In the latter, the restriction of output was indeed recognised as a likely problem of piece-rate payment but was represented as the outcome of a failure in human relations—specifically, management had failed to build up workgroup norms supportive of organisational goals—with the result that workers then behaved irrationally in not responding to financial incentives. Interestingly, a yet earlier account of the phenomenon, that of Max Weber (1908), himself trained as an institutional economist, comes much closer in spirit to that of his present-day counterparts in treating the restriction of output under piece rates as in many circumstances an entirely rational strategy for workers to pursue—since increasing output might lead simply to a cut in rates.

14. Various authors have pointed out that general qualifications are valued by employers not only on account of the skills, expertise, and knowledge to which they directly attest but further, and perhaps primarily, as indicators or 'signals' of the individual's *capacity to learn*. Correspondingly, employees often report that in the course of their work they draw on their prior qualifications only to a surprisingly limited extent (see, e.g., Thurow, 1972; Wilensky and Lawrence, 1980; Cohen and Pfeffer, 1986; Bills, 1988).

15. It is in this connection of interest to note that in the paper that in effect inaugurated transaction-cost economics, Coase (1937) draws attention to the legal distinction made in (then) current British law between an agent and a 'servant', which turns not on the absence or presence of a fixed wage or the payment of commission but rather 'on the freedom with which an agent may carry out his employment'.

16. Milgrom and Roberts (1992: 413) point out that while in the late 1980s it was known that around 30 percent of all U.S. firms operated profit-sharing schemes, the proportion of total employee income received through such schemes was very small, perhaps no more than 1 percent. Goldthorpe and McKnight (2006) note that while in 1998 around 12 percent of professional and managerial employees in Britain (Classes I and II) received some performance related pay, this averaged out at only around 4 percent of their total earnings and exceeded 10 percent only for a few specific groups of business professionals and marketing and sales managers. Where close employee monitoring is not possible, profit-sharing and group-based bonus schemes are of course always likely to give rise to free-rider problems.

17. Empirical support for Lazear's theory can be found in Medoff and Abraham (1981) and Hutchens (1987). As Lazear notes (1995: 71), the upward-sloping experience-earnings profile would appear in many ways similar to an 'efficiency wage' or, as Marxists such as Wright (1997) would have it, a 'loyalty wage'. But, as

Lazear also notes, a major difference is that deferred payment contracts need imply no breach of the principle of payment in accordance with marginal productivity—nor therefore involuntary unemployment; at the start of the earnings profile wages can be sufficiently low to clear markets.

18. The above differs from my earlier discussion of the service relationship (Goldthorpe, 1982) chiefly in that it dispenses with the idea of 'trust' as being central to this relationship. I found my own increasing doubts in this regard expressed in a more cogent way than I was able to formulate myself in Williamson's critique (1996: ch. 10) of the concept of trust as applied in recent sociological work (e.g., Gambetta, ed., 1988; Coleman, 1990). The gist of Williamson's argument (1996: 256) is that 'it is redundant at best and can be misleading to use the term "trust" to describe commercial exchange for which cost-effective safeguards have been devised in support of more efficient exchange. Calculative trust is a contradiction in terms.'

19. In this connection, it is of some interest to note that Savage and his associates (Savage et al., 1992; Savage and Butler, 1995) have argued, in critique of the idea of a salariat or service class, that a line of class demarcation should be seen as falling between professionals, on the one hand, and managers, on the other. This is on account of the different kinds of asset that they typically possess—in the case of the former, *cultural* assets, and of the latter, *organisational* assets. Professionals are then taken to be advantaged over managers in that cultural assets are less specific than organisational assets and therefore more 'storable': that is, more readily accumulated in transferable form. This analysis can be related to, and may perhaps enhance, that which I have made in suggesting that agency problems may be more acute than asset specificity problems among some kinds of professionals—such as, say, those employed in less senior positions in health, education, and other state welfare services; while the converse situation may apply with some lower-level administrators and managers whose decision-making role is more local than strategic. But what, from the position I adopt, must tell against the claim that different class positions are thus created is the fact that the service relationship would appear an appropriate response to the contractual hazards that arise in *either* eventuality, even if certain features of this relationship are more fully expressed in some instances than in others. Moreover, Savage and his colleagues seem to miss the key insight of transaction-cost economics that asset specificity gives rise to *bilateral* dependency. Thus, insofar as the assets that managers acquire are of an organisationally specific kind, they may indeed be lost or much diminished if these employees lose their jobs; but, at the same time, there will be costs to employers who fail to retain employees with such assets. I have developed elsewhere (Goldthorpe, 1995) a more general critique of the 'assets theory' of the differentiation of the service class. See also Li (1997, 2002). In some contrast to Savage and his associates, Tåhlin (2005) bases a critique of the theory of class that I advance on the—mistaken—supposition that I see bilateral dependence as a necessary feature of the service relationship itself, when in fact it will be associated

with this relationship only insofar as this form of contract represents a response to problems of human asset specificity as distinct from those of work monitoring.

20. Findings of the validation exercises referred to in the text above and note 6 point to such a conclusion, as also do results from work in progress by Colin Mills (personal communication). On the specific issue of variable elements in pay, see Goldthorpe and McKnight (2006: Table 2).

21. From this same point of view (as has been pointed out to me by Jerker Denrell), it is then not surprising that secretarial and similar workers should often be engaged on a temporary basis via employment agencies. A further occupational group that is in this connection of interest is that of sales personnel. With these employees, payment on the basis of a fixed salary *plus* commission is often found. The rationale here would appear to be that while quantity of output, that is, sales made, can rather easily be measured, thus allowing piece-rate payment, problems of monitoring quality do also arise, notably as regards maintaining the firm's reputation with its customers. I would therefore hypothesise that it is with the employees of firms having least to lose in this respect, for example, firms selling double-glazing or door and window frames, that the largest commission element will occur.

22. It should, however, be noted that the job ladders in question are typically much shorter than those available to professional and managerial staff. Compare the distinction made by Osterman (1987) between the 'industrial' and 'salaried' forms of internal labour markets.

23. Delayering could perhaps make the service relationship more difficult to implement in that promotion opportunities would be reduced; but it would still be possible to maintain the upward-sloping earnings-experience profile by allowing incremental salary scales or appraisal-related pay increases to operate *within* given hierarchical levels (cf. Lazear, 1995: 79–80).

24. As Holmström and Milgrom (1991) stress, the ultimate source of difficulty here lies in the diversity of tasks performed and in finding a way of appropriately relating pay to all of them, rather than in work monitoring and measurement per se. On further problems of performance-related pay see Prendergast (1999) and Marsden, French, and Kubo (2001).

25. It might be added here that satisfactory evidence of the kind in question could not be derived merely from ad hoc case studies. Research based on representative samples both of employing organisations and of their employees would seem essential (see further Kalleberg, 1990).

26. For example, while employees in manual supervisory and technical positions (Class V) may have comparable or even higher average earnings than employees in routine nonmanual work (Class III), their earnings are more likely to show short-term variation (cf. Goldthorpe and McKnight, 2006); or again while small employers and self-employed workers (Class IV) are generally exposed to more insecurity than intermediate-class employees, they have better chances of accumulating capital—and so on. It has sometimes been seen as a disadvantage of the class schema that its categories cannot be fully ordered in any unambiguous way.

However, studies of its construct validity have shown its capacity, on the one hand, to reveal marked class differences in regard to political partisanship, educational choice, health, and so on, especially as between the salariat (Classes I and II) and the working class (Classes VI and VII) and, on the other hand, more subtle but still intelligible differences in these respects involving the intermediate classes (Classes III, IV, and V), of a kind that would have been obscured by the use of instruments that are one-dimensional by construction, such as classifications or scales of socio-economic status.

27. Morris and Western (1999) have chided sociologists working in field of social stratification for their failure to produce explanations for rising income inequality over recent decades. However, in seeking such explanations it would seem essential to take a comparative approach, rather than focusing, as Morris and Western do, on just one country (the United States), and thus to recognise from the start that wide cross-national variation is apparent in the extent of the increase in inequality and that factors operative only in particular nations or groups of nations may well be of major importance (cf. Atkinson, 1999).

28. From this point of view, interesting British-Italian and British-German comparisons are those provided by Bernadi et al. (2000) and McGinnity and Hill-mert (2004), respectively.

Notes to Chapter 6

1. Tragically, Aage Sørensen became ill shortly after publishing two papers (Sørensen, 2000a, 2000b; and see also his posthumous 2005) that represented a summation of his theoretical work to date, and died without being able either to reply to the critical commentaries that I (Goldthorpe, 2000) and various others made on these papers or to undertake related empirical projects that he envisaged. I take this opportunity of saluting one of the outstanding sociologists of his generation and of recording my personal sorrow at the loss of a good friend. Much of David Grusky's work has been carried out with colleagues, as will be apparent from the citations given, although in the main body of the text I refer, simply for convenience, to Grusky alone.

2. See, for example, Clark and Lipset (1991), Clark, Lipset, and Rempel (1993), and Pakulski and Waters (1996). As I have elsewhere argued (Goldthorpe, 2001), this is a case of 'flogging a very dead horse'.

3. Given the general 'action frame of reference' that I apply throughout this work, I prefer here to speak of 'life choices' (with of course the understanding that choices are always choices under constraints) rather than, say, of 'attitudes and behaviour', although I will resort to this locution, as appropriate, in presenting and discussing the views of other authors.

4. What I refer to here as the non-Marxist tradition of class analysis may be thought to correspond, to some extent, to what, in textbooks, is now routinely called the Weberian tradition. However, the tradition, as I would understand it,

is one formed from the later nineteenth to the mid-twentieth century by a series of European authors, including, as well as Weber, Schumpeter (1927), Geiger (1951), Halbwachs (1933, 1955), Marshall (1938, 1947), Renner (1953), Croner (1954), Lockwood (1958), and early Dahrendorf (1959). I would in fact agree with Sørensen's observation (2000b: 1527, n. 3) that the overwhelming importance usually attached to Weber in the literature on class analysis is 'a bit curious', given his only rather fragmentary, even if highly suggestive, writing on this topic. Sørensen, Danish by origin, shows a detailed knowledge of the European tradition to which I refer, even though he does not follow in it. But in American sociology in general it would appear to be largely neglected—a reflection, perhaps, of the polarisation that exists between, on the one hand, the tendency to think of social stratification in terms merely of 'socioeconomic' status and, on the other hand, the Marxist tradition of class analysis as revived especially by Erik Olin Wright.

5. Somewhat surprisingly, neither Sørensen nor Grusky give much attention to the problem of collective action as classically formulated, from a rational action standpoint, by Olson (1965)—in effect, the problem of free riding. However, insofar as they do, the theoretical differences between them clearly emerge. Sørensen (2000b: 1545) recognises the problem as posed by Olson, and comments that this is 'what the class formation literature is about, or rather what it should be about', but that work on resource mobilisation and social movements prompted by Olson is often in fact 'curiously separated' from discussion of class formation. Grusky would appear to assume that insofar as classes can be treated as sociocultural entities, then the Olson problem will not arise: free riding will, presumably, be prevented by the existence of shared values and social norms.

6. Sørensen allows an exception in this regard for rents that accrue to outstanding natural abilities, such as those, say, of leading professional athletes or opera singers. It should also be noted that he makes an important, and somewhat problematic (see Goldthorpe, 2000), extension of his concept of rent to take in what he calls 'welfare rents' and regards (see further below) as being of growing importance in modern societies. In this case, rent derives not from the possession of assets in limited or controlled supply but rather from the possession of a legal right to benefit (see further Sørensen, 1998b).

7. Sørensen here draws, though with a change of idiom, on his earlier work (e.g., 1983) on 'open' and 'closed' social positions.

8. In a presentation to a conference organised by the European Consortium for Sociological Research on 'Rational Action Theory in Social Analysis', held in Stockholm in 1997.

9. Wright (2005) makes it clear that, for Marxists, the fundamental pay-off of the concept of exploitation is the way in which it infuses class analysis with moral critique. Given that Sørensen clearly does *not* wish to use the word with such rhetorical intent, I find it odd, and potentially misleading, that he should retain it simply in order to flag the existence of structurally opposed class interests that lead to zero-sum conflict.

10. In order to avoid the confusion into which at least one commentator appears already to have fallen, it is important to distinguish between (Jesper) Sørensen *fils,* the collaborator of Grusky here referred to, and (Aage) Sørensen *père,* the author discussed in the previous section.

11. Grusky, it should be said, does not usually refer to the degree of formation of classes but rather adopts Giddens' (1973) concept of 'structuration'. Since this seems to me to add nothing to the older concept (and in addition means using an ugly word), I stick with 'formation'.

12. Grusky is indeed generally appreciative of Sørensen's emphasis on rent-seeking collective action and especially of the latter's critique of Wright's 'aggregate model' of the class structure on the grounds that it conceals the rent-seeking, and thus exploitative, strategies of craft workers and of more strongly organised professionals as against other employees. However, Grusky is doubtful if any reaggregation is possible that would allow 'big classes' to be identified in terms of their members' shared position in conflicts over rents—on account of 'the highly disaggregate level at which rent is extracted and interests are thus formed.' (Grusky and Sørensen, 1998: 1211). This is an argument that I would also make from my own position (see pp. 141–2).

13. It may, however, be noted that, elsewhere, Grusky appears a good deal more cautious on this matter, recognising, for example (Grusky and Weeden, 2001: 207), that 'disaggegation may reveal only small pockets of realist occupations interspersed in far larger regions of purely nominal categories'. It is in this regard, I would suggest, that a crucial empirical issue for Grusky's programme arises—and is not, as yet, resolved.

14. It may be noted that evidence *has* been forthcoming, at least for the United States, of *selective* rent destruction that has impacted primarily on the earnings of manual wage workers and has thus been a factor in widening both class and racial inequalities in earnings. See Morgan and McKerrow (2004) and Morgan and Tang (2005). To repeat, from the position I would adopt, employers can indeed always be expected to try to eliminate employment rents where these are *not* integral to efficient employment contracts.

15. As already noted, the most demanding tests of the criterion validity of the class schema described in the previous chapter (see pp. 102–104) are ones based on latent class analyses of various features of individuals' employment relations indicative of the kind of employment contract in which they are involved. The latent classes found to underlie these features prove to map in a broadly satisfactory way onto the allocation of individuals to the classes of the schema on the basis of their occupation (and, where relevant, employment status). The implication thus is that occupations can be meaningfully aggregated in terms of shared features of the employment relations that are typically associated with them.

16. See, for example, the British data on the relationship of 'objective' and 'subjective' class reported in Heath et al. (1991: Table 5.9 esp.).

17. Much has in fact already been written by economists on insider-outsider conflict in labour markets (cf. Lindbeck and Snower, 2002).

18. In this regard, as I have already implied, there is a close affinity between Sørensen's position and my own. Indeed Sørensen argues (e.g., 2000b: 1538–539), in standard fashion for a rational action theorist, that even if value differences can be demonstrated among classes, this 'only moves the question one level back': that is, to that of 'What is it about the living conditions of different classes that accounts for these differences?' He then goes on to suggest explanations for class differences in time horizons, risk aversion, and so on in terms of individuals' rational responses to quite objective differences in their economic security, stability, and prospects—that is, explanations on lines that I would entirely endorse (cf. chs. 2–4, this volume). It should be added here that Grusky does not seek to deny the validity of explanations of this kind and has indeed written appreciatively of the rational action approach in regard to my own work (Grusky and Di Carlo, 2001). His critical point is that insofar as classes can be treated as 'real' social groupings, a wider range of causal processes is in principle available for explanatory purposes (cf. Grusky and Weeden, 2004). However, the crucial issue then is whether class analysis has to be dependent on this availability.

19. As I have earlier noted (ch. 2: pp. 30–31, this volume), it is a gross empirical flaw in the claims of 'social reproduction' pushed by Bourdieu and his followers that they disregard the high absolute rates of class mobility in modern societies and suppose that such mobility is 'controlled' and concerns only a 'limited category' of individuals. It is especially remarkable that Bourdieu should have neglected, and have persisted in neglecting, the excellent data and analyses available for his own country, France, from the 1950s onwards (see, e.g., Vallet, 1999) that show that his views are in this regard without any serious foundation.

20. It is likely that, at the level of relative rates, some quite marked propensities for intergenerational occupational 'inheritance' could be shown up. But of course such inheritance is only one aspect of the total pattern of association between social origins and destinations that forms endogenous mobility regimes. And how other aspects are to be treated on the basis of occupational groupings must be regarded as unclear, at least until the issue is resolved of whether—and, if so, how—such groupings are to be seen as hierarchically ordered (cf. p. 146). In some work in progress, Grusky and his associates appear inclined to resort to an ordering in terms of socioeconomic status. But, as appears at other points to be recognised (e.g., Weeden and Grusky, 2005: 189–90), to draw thus on a scaling that derives from quite *generic* features of occupations, such as average earnings and educational levels, would scarcely be consistent with a theoretical emphasis on the importance of the institutional boundaries of occupations and their distinctive subcultures. It may be noted that Grusky and Weeden (2006) outline a quite new approach to questions of social mobility.

21. In other words, Grusky does not, at this stage of his empirical work, at-

tempt to demonstrate the operation of the wider range of actual causal processes that he believes it will be possible to show as underlying class effects if class analysis is based on 'real', occupational groupings.

22. For example, in the life-chances domain there are no outcome variables relating to respondents' experience of job loss and unemployment or to instability in their earnings or to differences in their earnings prospects (cf. Goldthorpe and McKnight, 2006). Thus, it is somewhat misleading for Weeden and Grusky to claim that 'the disaggregated class model outperforms big class model even when modeling life chances that are conventionally regarded as the home ground of big class analysis' (2005: 143). It would also be of interest to consider in this regard such other life-chance variables as individuals' risks of serious ill health and premature death or their children's risks of dying in infancy or dropping out of full-time education.

23. This point is often overlooked (see, e.g., Grusky and Weeden, 2006:88–91). In seeking to emphasise it in a seminar at the University of Mannheim, my colleague, Robert Erikson, was led to remark—breaking into German so that his meaning could not be lost on the audience—'Der Klassenbegriff ist nicht ein Mädchen für alles' ('The class concept is not a maid-of-all-work.').

24. It is, I would suggest, essentially to this substantive point that the *bic* statistic (Raftery, 1986) should be seen as drawing attention when, in contrast to conventional tests of statistical significance, it often prefers 'big class' models to the detailed occupational classification (Weeden and Grusky, 2005: 170–71). Since I would regard *bic*'s penalising of additional parameters as being fairly arbitrary (Weakliem, 1999; Firth and Kuha, 1999), I do not wish to question that models using this classification will generally give the better fit to data on 'outcomes'. But *bic*'s preference for the far more parsimonious approach of conventional class analysis might be taken as a warning that seeking simply to maximise association, or variance explained, need not be, sociologically, the most illuminating route to follow.

25. For reasons already indicated in note 20 above, socioeconomic scaling would be theoretically quite inappropriate—as Weeden and Grusky (2006) recognise.

26. Thus, Grusky more than once takes sociologists themselves as a notable example of an occupational grouping where processes of self-selection, formal and informal socialisation, and institutional arrangements all serve to create a relatively distinctive subculture. However, none of this speaks to the question of whether or not, or in what ways, sociologists are socially advantaged or disadvantaged in comparison with, say, economists or physicists, or academics in general in comparison with, say, accountants or civil servants. I might add here that while I would also favour a shift down to the occupational level as a means of complementing (not replacing) conventional class analysis and of thus treating social stratification multidimensionally, my approach would be a quite different one to that favoured by Grusky: that is, one involving a return to the Weberian distinction between class

and *status*—in contrast both to the casual obliteration of this distinction through the use of socioeconomic status scales and to Bourdieu's (1984) elaborate, and, I would say, quite unconvincing, conceptual manoeuvres aimed at overcoming it. In modern societies, occupation may be regarded as the most salient single marker of status; and a status order, expressing, especially through intimate relationships, generalised social superiority, equality, and inferiority—and thus taking an inherently hierarchical form—is still, I believe, identifiable. For work that pursues this approach, see Chan and Goldthorpe (2004, 2006, 2007a, 2007b).

27. For example, in the context of labour markets, insiders (i.e., workers with relative security of employment in firm-internal labour markets) would be seen by Sørensen as exploiting outsiders. But insofar as outsiders become unemployed, then, in the context of a welfare state, it is they, in holding a right to receive unemployment benefit, who are to be seen as exploiting insiders as taxpayers.

28. It is of interest that Sørensen (1998b) should question how far the development of the Danish welfare state can in fact be understood as the outcome of the power of organised labour exercised through societal bargaining with employers and governments. Sørensen seeks rather to emphasise the influence on state social policy, from the eighteenth century onwards, of a combination of royalist absolutism and Lutheran pietism. There are, moreover, indications that he would wish to extend this argument to other Scandinavian nations, although in the paper cited he does not attempt to do so. It would, I believe, be a difficult task. For a detailed comparison of the historical development of Scandinavian welfare states, see Esping-Andersen (1985); and for a forceful demonstration of the continuing relevance of class-based political action to the cross-national evolution of welfare states in the late twentieth century, see Korpi and Palme (2003).

29. In this connection, Elster's (1985: 347) definition of class consciousness, with the Olson problem (see n. 5 above) in mind, has a particular aptness: that is, 'the ability [of a class] to overcome the free rider problem in realizing class interests'—essential to which, at the occupational or other lower levels, may thus be class oriented *in*action.

30. The literature cited in the above paragraph, which is representative of the 'varieties of capitalism' approach in contemporary political economy, does of course stand in sharp contrast and opposition to arguments of globalisation theorists who would believe that, in consequence of globalisation, 'Every type of currently existing capitalism is thrown into the melting pot' (Gray, 1998: 78). For further analyses of emerging new versions of political exchange and societal bargaining, see the special number of the *British Journal of Industrial Relations,* vol. 41, 4, 2003, devoted to the theme of 'Politics and Employment Relations'.

31. To concentrate, in the first place, on work of this kind (cf. Weeden, 2002) would, in my view, be a more logical way of developing the general research programme envisaged by Grusky than the analyses referred to in the text—the results of which would themselves be more readily interpretable if more were known

about how far the occupational groupings distinguished could in fact be regarded as 'real' in Grusky's sense.

Notes to Chapter 7

1. Although this is the most obvious case to take in order to make my point, it is by no means the only one available. For example, the application of techniques of event history analysis has greatly advanced the study of intragenerational or worklife mobility and has raised many new theoretical issues, especially regarding the causation of such mobility (see esp. Blossfeld and Rohwer, 1995a).

2. Of late, there has been some tendency for models of this kind to be rather over-enthusiastically applied, and for parameters estimated under them to be taken as demonstrating trends in fluidity—usually in fact trends towards greater fluidity—when the model does not in fact give a good fit to the data. In this case, as Firth (2005) has shown, the parameters of the logmultiplicative model will in fact be influenced by the marginal distributions of the mobility table and could therefore be misleading. Fitting linear trends to such parameters, a further recent development, would seem likely to accentuate any problems that might arise.

3. This approach might thus be seen as providing an equivalent to path analysis as classically exploited within the field of mobility research by Blau and Duncan (1967). However, it should be noted that within the context of logistic regression the separation of 'direct' and 'indirect' effects can only be achieved in some approximate way (cf. Winship and Mare, 1983; Breen and Luijkx, 2004b: Appendix B), and it is not clear that the most satisfactory approximation has yet been found.

4. These two different conceptual approaches can be traced back virtually to the beginning of social mobility research. Since the 1980s a revival of the class structural perspective has occurred, and versions of the class schema referred to in Chapter 5 have become widely used as a basis for the construction of mobility tables. However, even though the findings of mobility research subsequently discussed in the text tend to be shown up more clearly and in greater detail in a class structural perspective, they are still usually apparent in a prestige or status perspective also, and thus little here turns on which of the two approaches is favoured.

5. Breen and Luijkx (2004a) show that among European societies in the last decades of the twentieth century some convergence in the shapes of their class structures, and thus in their rates and patterns of absolute mobility, has in fact occurred. This comes about chiefly as a result, first, of the rapid decline in size of agricultural classes in those countries where this had not occurred earlier in the century and, second, of the general growth of the professional and managerial salariat. But, as Breen and Luijkx recognise, there is little theoretical basis for predicting whether or not such convergent trends of change will continue.

6. In Chapter 2 (and cf. Erikson and Goldthorpe, 1992: ch. 1) this theory is in fact described as the 'liberal' theory of industrialism. However, I here refer to it as the functionalist theory since it is now its theoretical form rather than its ideological colouration that is of main relevance.

7. Although the theory antedates the distinction between absolute and relative mobility rates, more sophisticated versions of it, such as that of Treiman (1970), do in effect imply such a distinction, and no difficulty has therefore arisen in making this explicit in later formulations.

8. The two major comparative studies that have been undertaken are Erikson and Goldthorpe (1992) and Breen, ed. (2004), on which the following text chiefly draws. However, these works provide references to many other studies of importance, both national and comparative, that are also taken into account.

9. These adjectives are taken from one study in which such a tendency, albeit very slow and so far slight, is in fact claimed (Ganzeboom, Luijkx, and Treiman, 1989). However, this claim has subsequently been called into question on various grounds and has failed to find support from alternative analyses carried out on the same data-set (Erikson and Goldthorpe, 1992: 100–101; Jones, 1992; Wong, 1994). In regard to recent work on European societies, Breen and Luijkx refer at one point to a 'widespread tendency' for social fluidity to increase during the later twentieth century (2004a: 73) but elsewhere emphasise the difficulties involved in establishing trends and the need for caution in the interpretation of results (and cf. n. 2 above in regard to possibly misleading parameters from nonfitting logmultiplicative models). In fact (see Breen and Luijkx, 2004a, Tables 3.8 and 3.18 and Figures 3.2 and 3.4; Breen and Luijkx, 2004b, Table 15.1) in only two of the eight countries chiefly considered—that is, France and the Netherlands—do the results for men point unambiguously to a sustained trend towards greater fluidity. In two cases, Hungary and Ireland, fluidity was somewhat higher in the 1990s than the 1970s but in Ireland decreased in the 1980s and in Hungary in the 1990s. In three further cases, Germany, Poland, and Sweden, whether trends towards greater fluidity exist or not is very much a matter of interpretation. And finally for Britain there is clearly no trend. In the case of women, consistent increases in fluidity show up in five cases (i.e., France, Hungary, the Netherlands, Poland, and Sweden) but the theoretical significance of these increases is uncertain because of the possibility of 'perverse fluidity' deriving from increasing downward worklife mobility among married women (Goldthorpe and Mills, 2004). As regards the general degree of temporal stability that exists in relative rates, it may be noted that in mobility research generally a model postulating *no* change in such rates—the 'constant social fluidity' model—is usually found to account for around 95 percent of the total association existing between class origins and destinations, and to misclassify under 3 percent of all individual cases. While this figure obviously reflects the overall extent to which cell values in mobility tables are determined by their marginal distributions, it is still relevant to contrast it with, on the one hand, the 15–20 percent of all cases misclassified under the assumption of independence of origins and destinations—that is, when marginal distributions totally determine cell values—and, on the other hand, the further reduction in cases misclassified of usually less than 1 percent that is achieved where a model allowing for directional change in odds ratios is preferred to the constant social fluidity model.

10. On the supposed exceptionalism of American society—that is, as showing clearly greater openness than that found elsewhere—see Erikson and Goldthorpe (1985; 1992: ch. 9) and Ferrie (2005). Taking together analyses in Erikson and Goldthorpe (1992, ch. 11) and Breen and Luijkx (2004b), between which there is little disagreement insofar as their coverage overlaps, the societies that over the middle and the later twentieth century would appear to lie towards the more fluid end of the range of variation are Australia, the former Czechoslovakia, Israel, Norway, Poland, and Sweden, and towards the less fluid end, France, Germany, Ireland, and Italy. The attempt made in Erikson and Goldthorpe (1992, chs. 4 and 5) to capture the commonality in the endogenous mobility regimes of modern societies through a 'core model' of social fluidity is sometimes misunderstood. The aim was to hold on to the important insight of the FJH hypothesis (Featherman, Jones, and Hauser, 1975), claiming a 'basic similarity' in such regimes, while recognising that if this hypothesis is taken strictly and represented by a 'common social fluidity' model, it is clearly rejected by the available comparative data. Where applied in later studies (e.g., in Breen, ed., 2004; and see also Torche, 2005), the core model continues to prove illuminating.

11. The Swedish case is discussed further below, pp. 181–2. In France, there are indications that declining sectoral barriers to mobility between agricultural and nonagricultural classes are important (Vallet, 2005). The weakening of such barriers is widely found as conditions of life in rural and urban areas become more similar, but may be of greater consequence in France than elsewhere since France maintained a relatively large agricultural sector until well into the twentieth century.

12. There is no purely statistical way of deciding between the two interpretations but it would seem natural to condition on the variable, that is, class origins, that is earliest in the supposed time sequence. In addition, in a regression context, to condition on origins would seem most consistent with the argument made by Cox (1984), in a general discussion of the treatment of interaction effects, in favour of conditioning on 'intrinsic' variables—that is, ones on which individuals' levels have to be regarded as given—and to then focus on the effects on the dependent variable, at each 'intrinsic' level, of those explanatory variables on which individuals *could* conceivably have been at a different level. In the case in point, the relevant consideration is that while individuals cannot choose their class origins, they do have some degree of choice, subject of course to various constraints, on the level of their educational attainment.

13. The essential functionalist argument is that any persisting feature of a social system is to be explained by its function for that system—that is, by what it contributes to the system's self-maintenance and survival in an environment that is in some degree selective. In turn, it is *because* the system survives that the feature persists and thus can be observed as an *explanandum*. In all of this, social action can be regarded as of little importance, since patterns of action that do not 'follow the script' laid down by functional exigencies will simply be eliminated. Thus, to take an example from economics, one can explain the fact that entrepreneurs maxi-

mise profits because, if they did not, competitive pressures would ensure that they would not be there to be observed in the first place. To analyse profit maximisation as a form of action is thus in the end redundant. Whether such an explanatory approach is a compelling one is disputed even in economics (see vol. I, ch. 7), where an appeal to the selectivity of competitive markets might in some contexts at least be plausible. So far as sociology is concerned, the potential of the approach seems to me even more limited. It should be noted that the functionalist theory of mobility processes says nothing about what will happen to societies where achievement does *not* progressively prevail over ascription. It does not specify any mechanism through which these societies will disappear so that lasting counterexamples to the theory are unlikely to be observed (cf. Breen, 1997b).

14. The use of the concept of 'strategy' has been the subject of some debate, in British sociology at least, though not, in my view, of a very illuminating or helpful kind. I understand by a strategy a course of action, involving the use of resources, that is chosen in the pursuit of a given goal on the basis of some kind of cost-benefit evaluation. This implies a situation in which action is constrained but in which there are still at least two possible courses of action within the feasible set. For my present purposes, it is of no consequence whether a strategy is chosen through some explicit decision-making procedure or only emerges over time in a more or less implicit and piecemeal fashion. Nor indeed is it necessary, in order to explain the kind of probabilistic regularities with which I am concerned, that all relevant actors should actually have mobility strategies of the kind that I would attribute to them: only that such strategies represent central tendencies in action considered in aggregate and that deviations from these central tendencies are not systematic (see further vol. I, chs. 6 and 8).

15. The foregoing argument does of course imply that the objective mobility opportunities provided by class structures are determined exogenously relative to the mobility strategies that individuals pursue. I would accept that this may not be entirely correct: that is, it is possible that the nature of the supply of individuals with differing attributes may influence demand for them and in turn the structure of class positions. However, the empirical indications are that, even if such effects do occur, they are slight, and I therefore believe that making the assumption of exogeneity will not undermine the theory I suggest.

16. Small employers are theoretically best understood as employers whose businesses are not incorporated. In modern societies, most larger enterprises, in terms of numbers employed and so on, are incorporated, so that even if ownership remains with particular individuals or families, those owners who also work for the enterprise will have the status of employees.

17. Data in the form of individuals' own expressions of their ambitions, and aspirations are notoriously difficult to interpret. One basic problem is that of knowing the degree to which such expressions are already conditioned by a recognition of likely constraints—that is, represent 'adaptive preferences'.

18. This position is derived in part from what has become known as the

structural theory of aspirations (see further Keller and Zavalloni, 1964, and ch. 2, this volume) and it can also be expressed in terms of identical *relative* risk aversion across classes (see further ch. 3). From a psychological standpoint, it is highly consistent with—indeed could be regarded as an application of—'prospect theory', as developed by Kahneman and Tversky (1979), according to which the slope of individuals' utility curves is steeper in the 'domain of losses' than in the 'domain of gains'. However, I would see no need to accept the view of these authors that simply because their theory is incompatible with standard expected utility theory, it must *ipso facto* imply action of an irrational or at least nonrational kind (see further vol. I, ch. 8: 180–1).

19. As is here implied, I suppose the possibility of downward mobility, that is, into the ranks of the long-term or recurrently unemployed, even for members of the class of nonskilled wage workers. Whether or not this should be regarded as itself class mobility, that is, into a yet more disadvantaged class—for example, an 'underclass' of some kind—or rather as mobility out of the class structure altogether, as implied by the loss of any kind of stable employment relationship, is an interesting conceptual issue but not one that much affects the argument regarding mobility strategies.

20. Just as I would suppose the possibility of downward mobility even for members of the class of nonskilled wage workers, so I would suppose the possibility of upward mobility for members of the salariat—that is, from the lower to the higher echelons of this class or into 'elite' positions. Again, the conceptual issue might be debated of the nature of this mobility but, for present purposes, the important point is that maximising educational attainment would be no less relevant to strategies aimed at such advancement as to those aimed simply at maintaining class stability.

21. In the latter respect, Sørensen (2000a) aptly observes that insofar as an investment is threatened by uncertainty, as, say, over the adequacy of the resources available to back it, then to apply in effect a high discount rate to future returns may be considered as entirely rational. Culturalist explanations have often emphasised the difference between the short time horizons of the working class and the often much more extended ones of the 'lower middle class' of routine nonmanual employees, despite the average income levels of these classes being fairly similar. But this is again to neglect the importance of differences in employment relations and their implications for both the security and stability of incomes and their life-course trajectories (see Goldthorpe and McKnight, 2006).

22. In the case of the daughters of the petty bourgeoisie, in contrast, education would seem, at least up to the very recent past, to have played an important part in mobility strategies conducted within the marriage market. In fact, the main way in which the pattern of women's relative class mobility chances via marriage deviates overall from men's chances via employment is that while the sons of the petty bourgeoisie are significantly more likely to be themselves found in this class through their employment than are their 'sisters' to marry into it, the daughters

of the petty bourgeoisie are more likely to marry into the salariat than are their 'brothers' to gain access to professional or managerial positions (see further Erikson and Goldthorpe, 1992: ch. 7). I do not, however, seek here to treat class mobility via marriage markets in any systematic way.

23. As Hayek (1960, 1976) has argued, the idea of meritocracy as based on an understanding of merit that is in some way externally imposed on employers is not compatible with the operation of a market economy. In this context, merit in employees or potential employees can only be what employers define it to be, and their definitions are likely to be various.

24. The original proponents of the functionalist theory (see esp. Bell, 1973, 1980) were greatly impressed by the growth of professional occupations in the mid-twentieth century, and thus saw universities as the powerhouses of modern economies. Indeed, there is still much talk of 'knowledge-based' economies, for the success of which an ever more highly qualified workforce is essential. But for a far more sceptical view of the role of education in economic advance see Wolf (2002). It is, moreover, of note that economists, more so in fact than sociologists, have of late become interested in various noncognitive attributes of individuals as possible determinants of their economic success. See, for example, Bowles, Gintis, and Groves, eds. (2005).

25. Other causes could of course also operate. For example, the increasing number of people having a greater variety of qualifications could mean that the 'signalling' function of qualifications is impaired, and especially where—as, for example, in Britain—there have been repeated changes to qualification systems and their nomenclature. That is to say, employers find it increasingly difficult to make inferences from qualifications to desirable but not immediately observable attributes of potential employees (see further Jackson, Goldthorpe, and Mills, 2005).

26. Moreover, in this way another possible cause of a weakening ED association is suggested: that is, as a compositional effect of the general expansion of the salariat in modern societies over the second half of the twentieth century. Proportionately more children now come from backgrounds where family resources are available that can help them preserve their relatively advantaged positions even if their educational performance is substandard.

27. An issue that could seriously be raised here, as it was previously in regard to class differentials in educational choice, is that of how far individuals' responses to the conditions under which they must act are *over*adaptive and, further, of whether such overadaptation, insofar as it occurs, can be brought within the scope of rational action theory. In the work of both Boudon (1996, 1998) and Breen (1999) attempts are made to show how belief formation—and including the formation of mistaken beliefs—might be endogenised to rational action theory, so that socially structured differences in beliefs can then be explained rather than merely redescribed as aspects of subculture. As these authors recognise (and cf. the conclusions to ch. 4, this volume) the main challenge ahead is that of developing better

methods through which beliefs and related goals and expectations can be empirically established.

28. A clear contrast here arises, it may be noted, with the case of class differentials in educational attainment, in that the expansion of higher-level educational provision has to a large extent been demand-led, so that the tendency of children of more advantaged class origins to maintain or increase their take-up of opportunities has not itself seriously limited the possibilities for children of less advantaged origins to do likewise.

29. An arithmetic illustration of the point here being made might be helpful, and one can in fact be provided using actual British data (see further Goldthorpe, 1987: ch. 9). As of the early 1970s, the chances of men of salariat, intermediate-class, and working-class origins respectively being themselves found in the salariat showed disparity ratios of approximately 4:2:1, while their chances, or risks, of being found in working-class positions were more or less in the reverse ratios of 1:2:4. By the late 1980s, the former disparities had moved to something closer to 3:1.5:1: that is, men of working-class origins did improve their relative chances of access to what could be regarded as the most desirable class positions. However, at the same time, the latter disparities also changed, to around 1:3:5—that is, men of salariat origins improved *their* relative chances of avoiding the least desirable class positions. And disparity ratios changing on the pattern in question would then imply odds ratios remaining little altered, or moving in marginally different directions, rather than showing any general shift towards unity and thus indicating increased social fluidity.

30. For example, the widely differing agrarian histories of modern societies and their institutional and cultural legacies have exerted clearly traceable effects on the detail of their mobility regimes, though not ones necessarily implying greater or less fluidity overall. Similar effects also derive from the differing historical formation of educational and vocational training systems.

31. Apart from the questionable adequacy of income inequality as a proxy for all forms of class-linked inequalities in resources, the small N problem (cf. vol. I, ch. 3) also arises, and further the problem of what lag should be allowed between the periods to which measures of inequality and of social fluidity relate. Other complexities arise and are discussed in Torche (2005).

32. It should be noted that of the authors cited Szelényi is the one most sceptical about the effectiveness of policies of destratification and comments on the 'almost eerie constancy' (1998: viii) in relative rates of class mobility in Hungary over half a century. But even she recognises evidence of some decline in the intergenerational stability of managers, if not professionals, during the earlier years of communist rule.

33. The decreasing fluidity that was noted above for post-communist Hungary during the 1990s may well have some parallel with the Russian case, although in Hungary, so far at least, the decrease seems less marked and is only clearly evident with men.

34. This last statement is based on my own current work with Michelle Jackson. One methodological point that should be made in this connection is the following. It will be of growing importance in mobility research in all contemporary societies to give due attention to data quality and, in particular, to problems that may arise from the fairly general decline in survey response rates *becoming increasingly class biased.* Analyses of response in British cohort studies (Despotidu and Shepherd, 1998; Nathan, 1999) indicate that attrition rates are especially high among individuals who are from disadvantaged class backgrounds *and* who have low levels of educational attainment—that is, who are likely themselves to be found in disadvantaged class positions. Neglect of this potential problem could lead to a real decline in social fluidity not being recognised. Breen and Luijkx (2004b: Appendix A) carry out simulations based on increasing the proportion of nonskilled workers (Classes VIIa and VIIb of the schema in Table 5.1 above) in both the origin and destination distributions of mobility tables. However, while these exercises give generally reassuring results, they do not address the possibility of increasing nonresponse from individuals who, had they responded, would have been found in the VII-VII cell.

Notes to Chapter 8

1. Although marred by the limitations of available data and techniques (see ch. 2, this volume), Boudon's *Education, Opportunity and Social Inequality* (1974) could be taken as a key pioneering work in sociology in the style in question.

2. One exception is S. P. Turner (1985). This work does, however, suffer from having been written before the publication of most of the remarkable series of studies on the history of the probabilistic revolution (including those cited in the text) that emerged from the 1982–83 programme of the *Zentrum für interdisziplinäre Forschung* of the University of Bielefeld.

3. It is also of interest to note that the extension of this use of the error curve to situations where two quantities were being measured simultaneously led to the method of estimation through 'least squares' long before it was applied to the choice of the best-fitting regression line (see Stigler, 1986: ch. 1).

4. I draw here mainly on Quetelet (1835/1842, 1846, 1869). However, tracing exactly the development of Quetelet's thought is hindered by the extensive but fragmented nature and often complex publication history of his work. A new critical edition is badly needed.

5. As Stigler has observed (1999: 55–57), Quetelet's 'social physics' in fact owed little to Newton and would in fact have been better labeled as 'social meteorology'.

6. This awareness went back in fact to an early episode in Quetelet's career—the forceful critique by de Keverberg of Laplace's 'ratio' method for estimating the size of national populations that Quetelet had endorsed (Stigler, 1986: 163–99).

7. Quetelet in effect treated as causally relevant those attributes that, if ignored in the categorisation of data, revealed a lack of homogeneity in that average

rates were produced that were clearly not true ones. For critical commentary, see Stigler (1987).

8. When the terms 'sociometry' and 'sociometrics' eventually made their appearance, it was not with reference to a statistical methodology adapted to the needs of sociology but rather to an approach to the study of primary social relations. Sociology's failure to respond positively to the new English statistics in the same way as the other disciplines referred to meant that when in the course of the twentieth-century interest in quantitative analysis revived, there was for some time a far from satisfactory dependence on previously established '-ometrics'. It is in fact only quite recently that sociologists have managed to free themselves from this dependence by developing techniques more suited to the kinds of data and problems with which they typically deal (cf. Clogg, 1992).

9. This point is unfortunately obscured in the work of MacKenzie (1981) who, apparently in his concern to validate the 'strong programme' in the sociology of science (see vol. I, ch. 1, n. 4), puts too great an emphasis on the eugenicist preoccupations of the English statisticians—as, perhaps, contemporaries were also inclined to do (see text below and n. 27). As MacKenzie in fact acknowledges, while Galton and Pearson were leaders of the eugenicist movement, Edgeworth was never seriously involved and Yule tended to be hostile. It should in any event be noted that in the years before World War I the Galton Laboratory at University College London, under Pearson's leadership, did produce much work of real sociological interest—and high technical standards—despite its eugenicist preoccupations (cf. Stigler, 1999: ch. 1).

10. An implication of moving thus directly from Comte to Durkheim is neglect of Tocqueville, who is in fact regarded by Aron (1965–67), Boudon (1998–2000), and others as one of the great representatives of the individualistic tradition in sociology and thus set in contrast with Durkheim. However, Tocqueville's influence on the development of sociology, in France or elsewhere, would appear, at least until recently, to have been very slight.

11. For example, Durkheim did not show Quetelet's concern with the question of whether deviations from average suicide rates were normally distributed; nor did he give as much attention as had Quetelet to problems of the reliability and validity of official statistics. It is in fact these latter problems that most immediately undermine Durkheim's analyses (see, e.g., Day, 1987; van Poppel and Day, 1996). Durkheim's own criticisms (1897/1955: 300–4) of Quetelet's work are not easy to follow but could be taken to imply some misunderstanding of the ideas of *l'homme moyen* and *l'homme type*, as distinguished in the text above.

12. Selvin (1976) gives other reasons for supposing that Durkheim was probably aware of English statistical work but neglects the actual reference to Galton. On Durkheim's failure to grasp the point of Galton's argument, see Desrosières (1985) and Hacking (1990: 178).

13. Quetelet saw such propensities as explaining why individuals might act differently in similar circumstances. However, he seems never to have reached any

settled view about whether propensities were to be understood as biological, psychological, or social.

14. Parsons (1937) has argued that also at this stage Durkheim began to move towards a voluntaristic theory of action and even a Weberian notion of *Verstehen*. This view would, however, seem difficult to sustain. Even if, by the time of *The Elementary Forms of Religious Life,* Durkheim had come to adhere to some kind of idealist position, there is little indication that he was led to accord any greater autonomy to individuals in relation to *représentations collectives* than in relation to the normative constraints of the institutional order that he had stressed in his earlier work.

15. This is apparent even in their reception of the new statistics. Thus, Halbwachs, from his early study of Quetelet (1912), through a primer on probability theory written with the mathematician Maurice Fréchet (1924), to some of his last essays, returned always to the argument that the application of statistical models in sociology must be limited by the fact that individual actions are not independent of each other but are, rather, influenced by shared beliefs and norms. However, as Lazarsfeld has pointed out (1961), this is no serious objection; for insofar as such interdependence is known to exist, it too can be statistically modelled if appropriate changes in underlying assumptions are made—as, for example, in well-known 'contagion' models (cf. also Oberschall, 1987).

16. It is, incidentally, for this reason that criticism of Durkheim's and likewise of Halbwachs' own work on suicide (1930/1978) for relying largely on 'ecological' rather than individual-level correlations is scarcely to the point (cf. Isambert, 1973; S. P. Turner, 1985: 135–38), and notwithstanding Halbwachs' concerns to go somewhat beyond Durkheim in reconciling sociological and psychiatric explanations of suicide.

17. As Clark has observed (1973: 200) the 'non-Durkheimian alternatives', such as the highly eclectic 'international sociology' promoted by René Worms or the remnants of Le Playism, were in fact 'most dismal'.

18. Both Mill, in his later work, and Spencer tended to refer in this regard to the work of Buckle (1857), which was important in disseminating Quetelet's ideas, rather than to Quetelet's own writings. Mill's difficulties with probability theory are indicated by the number of changes he made in passages dealing with this topic over the successive editions of *A System of Logic*. His initial hostility to it was, however, perhaps more related to its use in the manner of Condorcet than of Quetelet.

19. Various intermediary 'special sciences' were involved, the most important being, apparently, 'ethology'—the science of human character and its modification by circumstance—on which, however, Mill has little of substance to say. Economics was another special science: that concerned with the behaviour of individuals, *given* that they seek to increase their wealth and are able to compare the efficacy of different means to that end. Mill supposed that the conclusions of economics would need ultimately to be qualified in the light of sociology, but appears never

to have contemplated the possibility that sociology might proceed on the basis of a generalisation of the methodology of economics. For further relevant commentary on the limitations of Mill's conception of human action, see Ryan (1970: 162–66).

20. Several authors (see esp. J. H. Turner, 1985) have noted the extent to which Spencer's work prefigures that of the later Parsons—despite Parsons having begun his first major treatise (1937: 3) with the rhetorical question: 'Who now reads Spencer?' and also that differences between Spencer and Durkheim on the nature of social order are in fact fewer than Durkheim sought to make out. It is of further interest to note that at one point where Spencer does address the problem specifically of social action and its interpretation (1873/1961: ch. 6), he is chiefly concerned to show that this is more or less insuperable, at all events where actors from remote 'races' or 'civilisations' are concerned: 'we must represent their thoughts and feelings in terms of our own' but 'in so representing them we can never be more than partially right, and are frequently very wrong'. Thus, such 'automorphic' interpretation can never be of great scientific value. The idea of rationality as the *passe partout* is absent.

21. Tylor's foray into comparative institutionalism was something of a departure from his main concern with cultural issues. It is possible that Galton's response to Tylor's work was intended as an implicit reproach to Spencer in regard to his *Descriptive Sociology* (1873–1934), a multivolume compilation of ethnographic extracts, largely undertaken by research assistants and continued after Spencer's death, which is often regarded as the prototype for the Yale Human Relations Area Files. Spencer made no attempt at all at the statistical analysis of his data, despite being ready to advance claims that would appear to entail such analysis.

22. However, another serious possibility is that neither Hobhouse nor his collaborators were equipped to understand the new statistics. One of the few other pieces of empirical research in which Ginsberg was involved was a study of social mobility (1929) that is also technically very limited and that again entirely ignores valuable leads in earlier statistical work, in this case by Pearson (e.g., 1904), of a kind that were quite readily detachable from the latter's eugenicist preoccupations.

23. One possible exception here is the use of statistics in the sociomedical field, chiefly due to the work of William Farr and his associates. Another version of 'social science' in the mid-Victorian period was that represented by the Social Science Association (see Goldman, 2002): that is, social science as the basis for the rational reform of social policy and its administration—but social science itself based more on (supposedly) expert knowledge and testimony than on systematic research and data analysis or theoretical argument. Goldman may well be right in questioning the claims of Abrams (1968) and Anderson (1968) that the activities of the SSA actually frustrated the development of a more serious sociology in nineteenth-century Britain; but it is at the same time difficult to see what positive contribution it made.

24. More specifically, in this and a more technical paper (1897), Yule showed that the coefficient of correlation was not as closely dependent as had been previ-

ously supposed on the bivariate normal distribution, and also described and applied the technique of what later became known as multiple regression.

25. It is thus evident that Yule wished to think in terms of causation, even while recognising that this was not necessarily implied by association, in marked contrast to Pearson (1892) who, under the influence of the new critical positivism of Mach, dismissed the idea of causation as a mere 'fetish' for which that of association, or more specifically correlation, should be substituted (cf. vol. I, ch. 9).

26. The main reference to it came in the form of a critical submission from the economist, A. C. Pigou, on which, and on the general hostility of Cambridge economists to the new statistics, see the revealing commentary of Stigler (1986: 356, and 1999: ch. 1). After his work on pauperism Yule largely abandoned the social sciences and worked in a variety of other subject-matter areas, making pioneering contributions to the 'statistics of attributes', which led eventually to loglinear modelling techniques.

27. It might seem especially strange that Bowley, a leading expert in economic statistics, should not have applied his abilities to data analysis as well as data collection. Indeed, as Kent (1985: 66) has observed, in his statistics textbook (1910), Bowley made no mention at all of the work of Galton, Pearson, or Yule—although he did, very briefly, in an earlier work. In *his* textbook (1911) Yule reciprocated by failing to refer to Bowley. It could be, as Kent suggests, that the issue of eugenics was again the divisive one, but, if so, Yule suffered guilt by association. Conflict over eugenics would again seem the most likely explanation for the fact that the group around Lancelot Hogben at the LSE in the 1930s who sought to revive the 'political arithmetic' tradition (Hogben, ed., 1938) also used the new statistics to only a very limited extent, even though by no means lacking in mathematical sophistication.

28. On Marshall's views, see Soffer (1978: 106–108). Dismissive references to Comte and Spencer are scattered throughout Collingwood (1946/1993). Also relevant in this regard (see further vol. I, ch. 2) is the scathing attack launched on Spencer by Maitland (1911).

29. Although Lexis rejected, along with other members of the German historical school, the idea of general and deterministic laws in economics, he nonetheless differed from its more extreme representatives in seeing theoretical models as being necessary if economists were to go beyond mere description, statistical or institutional.

30. Of particular significance and influence in this respect was Dilthey's *Einleitung in die Geisteswissenschaften* (1883/1959). It has, however, subsequently become apparent, largely from Dilthey's *Nachlass,* that he had a long-standing interest in the work of Quetelet and in fact took up a position on the possible linking of statistical and interpretative accounts of social action broadly similar to that formulated by Lexis and, later, Max Weber (see Ermarth, 1978: 297–303).

31. There is little evidence of any close intellectual ties between Weber and Lexis, although in 1896 they sat alongside each other as the two academic partici-

pants in a governmental committee concerned with the reform of the German stock exchange (Marianne Weber, 1926/1975: 197–98); and it is evident from Weber's correspondence that he had a high regard for Lexis.

32. Thus, an example that Weber several times took up (e.g., 1922/1968: 10–11, 18–19) is that of Gresham's Law—actually, an empirical generalisation to the effect that when a coinage becomes debased, 'the bad money drives out the good' from circulation. Weber notes that in seeking to account for this regularity modern economists do not in fact aim to subsume it under some higher-level covering law but rather to explain it *and* to render it intelligible as the outcome of rational action on the part of individuals. The causal narrative is a very simple one: it makes sense, under conditions of debasement, to trade with bad coin and hold on to good. However, another empirical regularity Weber considers (e.g., 1904–1905/1930: 59–60) is that revealed when workers, under certain conditions, work *less* as their rates of pay increase (the 'backward sloping supply curve for labour'). In this case, the regularity could be seen as deriving from traditionally determined action. But such action might also be rendered rationally intelligible if a traditional standard of living, strictly delimiting workers' economic wants, is accepted as a situational factor.

33. Their neglect, notably by interpreters of Weber entirely reliant on such of his work as is available in English translation, has indeed often led to very partial, if not distorted, accounts.

34. Weber in fact begins this study by referring to a regularity in German official statistics, which, he claims, is confirmed in a more detailed study of Baden by one of his students, Martin Offenbacher: namely, 'that business leaders and owners of capital, as well as the higher grades of skilled labour, and even more the higher technically and commercially trained personnel of modern enterprises, are overwhelmingly Protestant' (cf. Hernes, 1989 and for a more sceptical view, Hamilton, 1996: ch. 3). Moreover, the general *explanandum* of the study—the 'spirit of capitalism'—can itself be understood as referring to recurrent patterns of action: that is, those in which individuals engage in relation to work and money (cf. Marshall, 1980, 1982: ch.2)

35. It should be noted that Weber began writing the work here cited as early as 1909 or 1910 (Marianne Weber, 1926/1975: 418–19) and that an early version of the opening section was published a few years later (Weber, 1913/1981).

36. These chiefly concerned the difficulties inherent in using secondary historical materials as the major empirical resource for sociological analysis and especially where this went beyond institutional description to the level of individual action. Weber was acutely aware, and to an extent that commentators have usually failed to bring out—exceptions are Roth (1968) and Marshall (1982)—of the fallibility of such sources, of the problem of conflicting accounts, and, above all, of the ever-present possibility that on theoretically crucial issues secondary works might have nothing to say simply because 'primary' evidence did not exist (cf. also Marianne Weber, 1926/1975: 331–32 and the discussion in vol. I, ch. 2). In 1909 Weber

in fact declined an invitation to join the Baden Academy of Science on account of its neglect of the more systematic social sciences and of its 'stifling overemphasis on the historical approach' (Ringer, 2004: 175).

37. When Weber felt disqualified from continuing as director of the research into the press because of his involvement in a lawsuit with a newspaper, he was unable to find anyone ready to take over from him even though he had already secured financial support for the project (Marianne Weber, 1926/1975: 423–24, 429–39).

38. It would seem fairly clear that Weber himself had no serious knowledge of statistics. Some commentators have been led to speculate otherwise on account of the frequent references in his work to 'probability', 'likelihood', or 'chances'. However, these should rather be seen as reflecting Weber's *legal* training. In Weber's day, the concept of probability played a key role in German jurisprudential theory: that is, in the determination of individual responsibility, or liability, for particular outcomes under given sets of conditions (cf. Turner and Factor, 1981, 1994; Ringer, 2004: 80–82). Thus, while Weber readily invoked the concept of probabilistic regularity and viewed causality in probabilistic rather than deterministic terms, there is no reason to suppose that he was technically equipped to translate these ideas into research design or the analysis of quantitative data.

39. Whether there is any serious warrant for a phenomenological reading of Weber I would in fact regard as highly debatable. Weber's neglect of the way in which the subjective meanings of actions are actually formed—from which Schütz begins—may well have been quite deliberate. That is, because Weber simply did not believe that direct access to 'other minds' was possible and, as Hollis (1987: 7–8) has suggested, saw the rational reconstruction of action as providing the essential interpretative bridge. For an illuminating commentary on the directly opposing developments (or distortions?) of Weber's ideas by Schütz and by Parsons, see Wagner (1983: 74–79).

40. In this perspective it is of course rather remarkable that from the 1960s onwards sociological analysis using quantitative methods and conducted on the basis of methodological individualism has itself been routinely condemned as 'positivistic'. Responsibility for this philosophically unhelpful, and historically highly misleading, use of the term must, I believe, rest largely with members of the Frankfurt school who initiated the *Postivismusstreit*.

Notes to Chapter 9

1. I also suggested that the part played by various adverse contingencies in individual lives and relationships should not be underestimated.

2. It may be that other episodes could be identified that would be similarly revealing or that indeed might point to somewhat different, perhaps more positive, conclusions. Colleagues have made various suggestions to me. However, lack of source materials is a common problem. It would, for example, be of great interest to know more about the collaboration, in teaching and research, between Samuel

Stouffer, as a pioneering quantitative sociologist, and Talcott Parsons, as a leading theorist, in the Department (and Laboratory) of Social Relations at Harvard after 1946. Some fascinating glimpses are provided by Toby (1980; see also Abbott, 1999: 78, 215–26). However, as Toby notes, little emerged in published form from the main collaborative work in which the two men engaged, namely, the Harvard Social Mobility Project, apparently started in 1948. Merton (1998: 181–83) suggests that the attempted partnership in fact failed, despite good intentions, because Stouffer and Parsons, unlike himself and Lazarsfeld (see further below), lacked 'elective affinities' and 'simply could not understand each other'.

3. Also at Columbia at this same time new statistical methods were introduced into psychology by James McKeen Cattell and into anthropology by Franz Boas, the latter in particular emphasising the English approach. Indeed, Camic and Xie (1994) point out that in the United States it was essentially through the social sciences that statistical methodology made academic headway in general, rather than, as in Britain and elsewhere in Europe, through the biological sciences.

4. From his reading of Pearson's work in the philosophy of science as well as statistics (see further below), Giddings took over Pearson's reformulation of Comte's 'law of the three stages', through which any body of thought must pass, as being not those of the 'theological', 'metaphysical', and positivist' but rather those of the 'ideological', the 'observational', and the 'metrical'.

5. Porter (2004: 244–45) has also drawn attention to criticisms of Pearson made by Edgeworth to the effect that a preoccupation with 'curve fitting', to the neglect of underlying causal processes that might give a rationale for the curve chosen, must raise questions about what can thus be learnt about the actual phenomena under study.

6. Especially serious would appear to have been Giddings' little concealed anti-Semitism and his consequent poor relations with his Jewish colleagues at Columbia, notably Boas (Oberschall, 1972: 226).

7. Stephen Stigler has pointed out to me (personal communication) that the founding president of the University of Chicago, William Rainey Harper, in fact required that each department should publish a journal. So Small was in effect following orders, but did so with energy and flair.

8. An exception is the 'insider' account of Faris (1967: ch. 7 esp.) which in certain respects anticipates Bulmer.

9. Jennifer Platt has added the comment (personal communication) that even in work usually taken to exemplify the Chicago qualitative case-study style, quantitative data were often also used, even if only rather crudely analysed.

10. Ogburn had been appointed to a chair at Columbia in 1919, with support from the Columbia economists, after working for some time as a statistician with the National War Labor Board and the Bureau of Statistics. See further Bannister (1987: 173–74).

11. For example, a major study, with which Park had been closely associated, subsequently published by the Chicago Commission on Race Relations as *The Ne-*

gro in Chicago (1922), collected a large amount of numerical data that was never satisfactorily analysed. See further Bulmer (1984: ch. 5); also Oberschall (1972: 232–40).

12. This body of work is all the more impressive when one remembers the very primitive data-processing technology that was available at this time. Calculating a simple correlation could be a very lengthy and tiresome operation.

13. Perhaps most notable among these was Samuel Stouffer who, after taking his doctorate, spent the academic year 1931–32 in London working with Pearson, Yule, Bowley, and Fisher, and who could perhaps be regarded as the most sophisticated sociological exponent of the new statistics in the United States during the 1930s. He became full professor at Chicago in 1935 and then after his work during World War II, which led to *The American Soldier* (Stouffer et al., 1949) took a chair at Harvard. As remarked in note 2 above, it is unfortunate that more is not known about his efforts together with Parsons to achieve a closer integration of research and theory within the Department of Social Relations, even though they had little tangible outcome.

14. Ogburn also had close and rewarding interdisciplinary relationships, notably with Harold F. Gosnell in political science and L. L. Thurstone in psychology (Bulmer, 1984: ch. 10).

15. Philip Hauser, another of Ogburn's highly talented students, recalls (Bulmer, 1984: 184) that at departmental picnics softball teams would be formed on the basis of quantifiers versus case-study proponents.

16. In this latter respect, matters were not helped by the fact that between the completion of the report and its publication America had been plunged into the Great Depression.

17. Ironically, the report itself in the end made little use of advanced statistics. The reasons for this are not entirely clear. It may be that technical difficulties prevented systematic correlational analyses from being carried out on the data that were assembled or simply that the work involved (cf. n. 11 above) was too onerous.

18. 'Symbolic interactionism' has often taken by later commentators to be the theory chiefly associated with the Chicago school. However, this term was introduced by Blumer only in 1937 and was never systematically explicated either by Blumer himself or anyone else at Chicago. It is noteworthy that in his monograph on symbolic interactionism, Rock (1979) sees its lack of explicitness as an essential—and, apparently, a not unattractive—feature.

19. In particular, in the American tradition, a strong emphasis persisted on the formation of the individual self through social influences rather than on individual action as the 'animating principle' of the social (Popper, 1994); and there is then some validity in speaking in the American case of 'social behaviourism', even though individuals' mental states were readily referred to. Ross has acutely observed (1991: 356) that in *The Polish Peasant*, Thomas and Znaniecki appear to treat the individuals they study as 'objects rather than agents'. In this connection,

I would agree with Abbott's judgment (1999: 70) that, for Blumer—and, I would add, most other Chicagoans—'social psychology was the master science', and that symbolic interactionism was simply a label under it was sought to represent the entire Chicago tradition as being one grounded in social psychology. On the other hand, it should be noted that during the 1920s and 1930s Weber's work seems to have aroused little interest in, and in turn to have had little influence on, American sociology, Chicago included (see Platt, 1985).

20. Interview with James T. Carey in May, 1972, cited in Bulmer (1984: 188).

21. Blumer's position in this regard would appear to be in direct continuation of that of Thomas (cf. Ross, 1991: 355).

22. This seems an excellent way of characterising the spurious pluralism that, I have suggested, is today widely found in sociology at large (see vol. I, ch.1, pp. 2–3).

23. See the extracts from Ogburn's diaries cited by Laslett (1991: 529) and Bannister (1987: 224). These report *inter alia* a particularly sad episode when, after Ogburn's retirement, the distinguished British statistician, R. A. Fisher, was awarded an honorary degree at Chicago, followed by a lunch of which Ogburn was not informed. Apparently seeing this as somehow symbolic of his failure to 'stay by' statistics, Ogburn poignantly wrote 'There was a vacant place at R. A. Fisher's table'.

24. Lazarsfeld once remarked to David Sills that 'his whole career had been a footnote to Yule' (Sills, 1998: 153).

25. A further parallel may be noted in that Merton's *explanandum* (like Weber's) was ultimately grounded in a quantitative claim: that is, that at a certain critical period in the development of the institutions of science (capitalism) a disproportionate number of scientists (capitalists) were of Puritan background.

26. The 'reference group concept' was taken from Stouffer et al., *The American Soldier* (1949), a work that appears to have been a major source of inspiration for Lazarsfeld's and Merton's attempts at achieving a closer integration of research and theory.

27. Fleck (1998) notes that in his youth Lazarsfeld was an adherent of Austro-Marxism but that, even before leaving Vienna, he had come to doubt its validity as social science while still adhering to its sociopolitical values. In his early days in America Lazarsfeld described himself as 'a Marxist on leave of absence' and was criticised by exiled members of the Frankfurt school for having abandoned his earlier views (Sills, 1998).

28. Merton's essay on 'The Unanticipated Consequences of Purposive Social Action' (1936b) was included in a later collection of essays, *Sociological Ambivalence* (1976), but without any explanation of its previous exclusion from the canon or of its restoration.

29. Coleman (1986a) arrives at much the same conclusion regarding Merton's strange eschewal of the theory of action but through a rather different route. He observes that the modifications that Merton made to the basic functionalist para-

digm were such as to strip away most of its distinctive explanatory potential—that is, its potential to explain social phenomena by their effects via an appeal to some 'homeostatic principle'. In fact, Coleman argues, Merton's recognition of 'functional alternatives' and of 'eufunctions' and 'dysfunctions' means that all of his uses of 'function' could be systematically replaced with 'consequence of action (intended or unintended)' without any theoretical loss. But while Merton may thus be seen as bringing action back into sociological analysis, he does so in an almost entirely implicit way, or, as Coleman aptly puts it (1986a: 1323), 'without letting the second shoe drop'.

30. The most obvious, and most discussed, illustration of this point arises in the case of Merton's famous essay on 'Social Structure and Anomie' (Merton, 1949). In this paradigmatic attempt at demonstrating how 'social structures generate the circumstances in which infringement of social codes constitutes a "normal" (that is to say, an expectable) response', Merton develops a well-known fivefold typology of possible responses or 'individual adaptations' to the tensions existing in American society between culturally prescribed goals and institutionally limited opportunities for attaining these goals. However, he has little to say on why individuals who would appear similarly exposed to such tensions should opt for one response rather than another and would seem to regard this question as being one entirely of individual psychology. For illustrations of what I would regard as highly suggestive but largely implicit and unsystematic action story-lines in Lazarsfeld's work, see Boudon (1998: 373–77).

31. It could indeed be said that this problem remains largely unsolved, although of late some promising suggestions have been made about how it could perhaps be overcome: for example, by obtaining data on the social networks of members of national samples and by then moving beyond these ego-centred networks through, say, snowball sampling. Note further in this connection the comments of Coleman (1990: ch. 23) on both the Columbia and the earlier Chicago schools in the context of an intriguing 'sociology of American sociology' that emphasises the declining importance of local communities and of locally bounded social networks and the impact of this decline on research strategies.

32. From this point of view, the attempt of Turner and Turner (1990) to account for the intellectual incoherence of American sociology in largely institutional terms must seem not a little parochial.

33. As, for example, in the journal *Rationality and Society* or in 'special interest' sections within the American Sociological Association.

34. In the case of the two new approaches to class analysis that I consider at length in Chapter 6, it may be noted that while Sørensen's neo-Ricardian approach is rather naturally grounded in rational action theory, Grusky's neo-Durkheimian approach does not in fact entail a determined macro-to-macro explanatory strategy. It represents, rather, Durkheimianism *à la americaine*: that is, the emphasis is on the essentially social psychological processes—(self-) selection, socialisation, interpersonal influence, and so on—through which individual behaviour is shaped

by the specificities of its micro-level (in this case, occupational) contexts. The continuity with the Columbia BASR tradition is evident, even though Grusky does not much stress this. If some new theoretical input to American stratification research is to ensue, then my analysis in the text above must lead me to predict that this will come predominantly from Grusky's work rather than from Sørensen's.

Abbott, A. (1999), *Department and Discipline: Chicago Sociology at One Hundred* (Chicago: Chicago University Press).

Abell, P. (1992), 'Is Rational Choice Theory a Rational Choice of Theory?' in J. S. Coleman and T. J. Fararo (eds.) *Rational Choice Theory: Advocacy and Critique* (Newbury Park: Sage).

Åberg, R., Selén, J., and Tham, H. (1987), 'Economic Resources' in R. Erikson and R. Åberg (eds.) *Welfare in Transition* (Oxford: Clarendon).

Abrams, P. (1968), *The Origins of British Sociology* (Chicago: University of Chicago Press).

Akerlof, G. A. (1997), 'Social Distance and Social Decisions', *Econometrica*, 65: 1005–27.

Andersen, R. and Heath, A. F. (2002), 'Class Matters: The Persisting Effects of Contextual Social Class on Individual Voting in Britain, 1964–97', *European Sociological Review*, 18: 125–38.

Anderson, P. (1968), 'Components of the National Culture', *New Left Review*, 50: 3–57.

Andorka, R. (1990), 'Half a Century of Trends in Social Mobility in Hungary' in J. L. Peschar (ed.) *Social Reproduction in Eastern and Western Europe* (Nijmegen: Institute for Applied Social Sciences).

Aron, R. (1936), *La sociologie allemande contemporaine* (Paris: Presses Universitaires de France).

Aron, R. (1965–67), *Main Currents in Sociological Thought*, 2 vols. (London: Weidenfeld and Nicolson).

Arum, R. and Hout, M. (1998), 'The Early Returns: The Transition from School to Work in the United States' in Y. Shavit and W. Müller (eds.) *From School to Work* (Oxford: Clarendon).

Arum, R. and Shavit, Y. (1995), 'Secondary Vocational Education and the Transition from School to Work', *Sociology of Education*, 68: 187–204.

Atkinson, A. B. (1999), 'Is Rising Inequality Inevitable? A Critique of the Transatlantic Consensus,' WIDER Annual Lecture, Nov.3, 1999, United Nations University, Helsinki.

301

Atkinson, J. (1985), 'The Changing Corporation' in D. Clutterbuck (ed.) *New Patterns of Work* (Aldershot: Gower).

Baker, K. M. (1975), *Condorcet: from Natural Philosophy to Social Mathematics* (Chicago: University of Chicago Press).

Baldamus, W. (1961), *Efficiency and Effort* (London: Tavistock).

Ball, S. (2003), *Class Strategies and the Education Market* (London: Routledge-Falmer).

Banks, O. (1971), *The Sociology of Education*, 2nd ed. (London: Batsford).

Bannister, R. C. (1987), *Sociology and Scientism: The American Quest for Objectivity, 1880–1940* (Chapel Hill: University of North Carolina Press).

Barnard, C. (1938), *The Functions of the Executive* (Cambridge, Mass.: Harvard University Press).

Barnes, H. E. (1948), *An Introduction to the History of Sociology* (Chicago: Chicago University Press).

Barry, B. (1970), *Sociologists, Economists and Democracy* (London: Collier-Macmillan).

Bartley, M., Carpenter, L., Dunnell, K., and Fitzpatrick, R. (1996), 'Measuring Inequalities in Health: An Analysis of Mortality Patterns Using Two Social Classifications', *Sociology of Health and Illness*, 18: 455–74.

Beattie, I. R. (2002), 'Are All "Adolescent Econometricians" Created Equal? Racial, Class and Gender Differences in College Enrollment', *Sociology of Education*, 75: 19–43.

Becker, R. (2003), 'Educational Expansion and Persistent Inequalities of Education in Germany', *European Sociological Review*, 19: 1–24

Bell, D. (1973), *The Coming of Post-Industrial Society* (New York: Basic Books).

Bell, D. (1980), 'Liberalism in the Post-Industrial Society' in *Sociological Journeys* (London: Heinemann).

Beller, E. and Hout, M. (2005), 'Inequality and Intergenerational Mobility: Change across Cohorts'. Department of Sociology, University of California, Berkeley.

Bernadi, F., Layte, R., Schizzerotto, A., and Jacobs, S. (2000), 'Who Exits Unemployment? Institutional Features, Individual Characteristics and Chances of Getting a Job: A Comparison of Britain and Italy' in D. Gallie and S. Paugam (eds.) *Welfare Regimes and the Experience of Unemployment in Europe* (Oxford: Oxford University Press).

Bernert, C. (1983), 'The Career of Causal Analysis in American Sociology', *British Journal of Sociology*, 24: 230–54.

Besnard, P. (1983a), 'The *"Année Sociologique"* Team' in *idem* (ed.) *The Sociological Domain* (Cambridge: Cambridge University Press).

Besnard, P. (1983b), 'The Epistemological Polemic: François Simiand' in *idem* (ed.) *The Sociological Domain* (Cambridge: Cambridge University Press).

Bierstedt, R. (1981), *American Sociological Theory: A Critical History* (New York: Academic Press).

Bierstedt, R. (1990) 'Merton's Systematic Theory' in J. Clark, C. Modgil, and

S. Modgil (eds.) *Robert K. Merton: Consensus and Controversy* (London: Falmer).

Bills, D. B. (1988), 'Credentials and Capacities: Employers' Perceptions of the Acquisition of Skills', *Sociological Quarterly*, 29: 439–49.

Birkelund, G. E. (2002), 'A Class Analysis for the Future? Comment on Grusky and Weeden', *Acta Sociologica*, 45: 217–21.

Birkelund, G. E., Goodman, L. A., and Rose, D. (1996), 'The Latent Structure of Job Characteristics of Men and Women', *American Journal of Sociology*, 102: 80–113.

Björklund, A. and Kjellström, C. (1994), 'Avkastningen på Utbildning i Sverige 1968 till 1991' in R. Erikson and J. O. Jonsson (eds.) *Sorteringen i Sverige* (Stockholm: Carlsson).

Blanden, J., Goodman, A., Gregg, P., and Machin, S. (2004), 'Changes in Intergenerational Mobility in Britain' in M. Corak (ed.), *Generational Income Mobility in North America and Europe* (Cambridge: Cambridge University Press).

Blau, P. M. and Duncan, O. D. (1967), *The American Occupational Structure* (New York: Wiley).

Blau, P. M. (1994), *Structural Contexts of Opportunities* (Chicago: Chicago University Press).

Blossfeld, H.-P. and Rohwer, G. (1995), *Techniques of Event History Modeling: New Approaches to Causal Analysis* (Hillsdale, N.J.: Erlbaum).

Boelen, W. F. (1992), 'Street Corner Society: Cornerville Revisited', *Journal of Contemporary Ethnography*, 21: 11–51.

Booth, C. (1889–1903), *Life and Labour of the People of London* (London: Macmillan).

Booth, C. (1896), 'Poor Law Statistics', *Economic Journal*, 6: 70–74.

Boudon, R. (1967), *L'analyse mathématique des faits sociaux* (Paris: Plon).

Boudon, R. (1971), 'La metasociologie de Lazarsfeld' in *La crise de sociologie* (Geneva: Droz).

Boudon, R. (1974), *Education, Opportunity and Social Inequality* (New York: Wiley).

Boudon, R. (1976), 'Comment on Hauser's Review of *Education, Opportunity and Social Inequality*', *American Journal of Sociology*, 81: 1175–187.

Boudon, R. (1987), 'The Individualistic Tradition in Sociology' in J. C. Alexander, B. Giesen, R. Münch, and N. J. Smelser (eds.) *The Micro-Macro Link* (Berkeley: University of California Press).

Boudon, R. (1990), 'Individualism or Holism in the Social Sciences' in P. Birnbaum and J. Leca (eds.) *Individualism* (Oxford: Clarendon).

Boudon, R. (1996), 'The "Cognitivist Model": A Generalized "Rational-Choice" Model', *Rationality and Society*, 8: 123–50.

Boudon, R. (1998), 'Social Mechanisms Without Black Boxes' in P. Hedström and R. Swedberg (eds.) *Social Mechanisms* (Cambridge: Cambridge University Press).

Boudon, R. (1998–2000), *Études sur les sociologues classiques*, 2 vols. (Paris: Presses Universitaires de France).

Boudon, R. (2003a), 'Beyond Rational Choice Theory', *Annual Review of Sociology*, 29: 1–21.

Boudon, R. (2003b), *Raison, bonnes raisons* (Paris: Presses Universitaires de France).

Bouglé, C. (1896), *Les Sciences sociales en Allemagne* (Paris: Alcan).

Bouglé, C. (1899), *Les Idées égalitaires* (Paris: Alcan).

Bourdieu, P. (1973), 'Cultural Reproduction and Social Reproduction' in R. K. Brown (ed.) *Knowledge, Education and Cultural Change* (London: Tavistock).

Bourdieu, P. (1984), *Distinction: A Social Critique of the Judgment of Taste* (London: Routledge).

Bourdieu, P. and Passeron. J.-C. (1970), *La Reproduction* (Paris: Editions de Minuit).

Bowles, S. and Gintis, H. (1976), *Schooling in Capitalist America* (London: Routledge).

Bowles, S., Gintis, H., and Osborne Groves, M. (eds.) (2005), *Unequal Chances* (Princeton: Russell Sage Foundation and Princeton University Press).

Bowley, A. L. (1906), 'Address to the Economic Science and Statistics Section of the British Association for the Advancement of Science', *Journal of the Royal Statistical Society*, 47: 607–25.

Bowley, A. L. (1910), *An Elementary Manual of Statistics* (London: Macdonald and Evans).

Bowley, A. L. (1926), 'Measurement of the Precision Obtained in Sampling', *Bulletin of the International Statistical Institute*, 22, Supplement: 6–62.

Bowley, A. L. and Burnett-Hurst, A. R. (1915), *Livelihood and Poverty* (London: Bell).

Breen, R. (1994), 'Individual Level Models for Mobility Tables and Other Cross-Classifications', *Sociological Methods and Research*, 23: 147–73.

Breen, R. (1997a), 'Risk, Recommodification and Stratification', *Sociology*, 31: 473–89.

Breen, R. (1997b), 'Inequality, Economic Growth and Social Mobility', *British Journal of Sociology*, 48: 429–49.

Breen, R. (1999), 'Beliefs, Rational Choice and Bayesian Learning', *Rationality and Society*, 11: 463–79.

Breen, R. (ed.) (2004), *Social Mobility in Europe* (Oxford: Oxford University Press).

Breen, R. and Goldthorpe, J. H. (1999), 'Class Inequality and Meritocracy: A Critique of Saunders and an Alternative Analysis', *British Journal of Sociology*, 50: 1–27.

Breen, R. and Goldthorpe, J. H. (2001), 'Class, Mobility and Merit: the Experience of Two British Birth Cohorts', *European Sociological Review*, 17: 81–101.

Breen, R. and Luijkx, R. (2004a), 'Social Mobility in Europe between 1970 and 2000' in R. Breen (ed.) *Social Mobility in Europe* (Oxford: Oxford University Press).

Breen, R. and Luijkx, R. (2004b), 'Conclusions' in R. Breen (ed.) *Social Mobility in Europe* (Oxford: Oxford University Press).

Breen, R., Luijkx, R., Müller, W., and Pollak, R. (2005), 'Non-Persistent Inequality in Educational Attainment: Evidence from Eight European Countries'. ISA Research Committee on Social Stratification and Mobility, Los Angeles.

Breen, R. and Yaish, M. (2006), 'Testing the Breen-Goldthorpe Model of Educational Decision-Making' in S. Morgan, D. B. Grusky, and G. S. Fields (eds.) *Mobility and Inequality: Frontiers of Research from Sociology and Economics* (Stanford: Stanford University Press).

Brooks, C., Nieuwbeerta, P., and Manza, J. (2006), 'Cleavage-Based Votings Behaviour in Cross-National Perspective: Evidence from Six Post-War Democracies', *Social Science Research*, 35: 88–128.

Brown, P. (1995), 'Cultural Capital and Social Exclusion: Some Observations on Recent Trends in Education, Employment and the Labour Market', *Work, Employment and Society*, 9: 29–51.

Buckle, T. H. (1857), *History of Civilisation in England* (London: J. W. Parker).

Bulmer, M. (1981), 'Quantification and Chicago Social Science in the 1920s: A Neglected Tradition', *Journal of the History of the Behavioral Sciences*, 17: 312–31.

Bulmer, M. (1984), *The Chicago School of Sociology* (Chicago: University of Chicago Press).

Bulmer, M. (ed.) (1985), *Essays on the History of British Sociological Research* (Cambridge: Cambridge University Press).

Bulmer, M. (1991), The Decline of the Social Survey Movement and the Rise of American Empirical Sociology' in M. Bulmer, K. Bales, and K. K. Sklar (eds.) *The Social Survey in Historical Perspective* (Cambridge: Cambridge University Press).

Bulmer, M. (1997), 'W. I. Thomas and Robert E. Park: Conceptualising, Theorising and Investigating Social Processes' in C. Camic (ed.) *Reclaiming the Sociological Classics: The State of Scholarship* (Oxford: Blackwell).

Burrow, J. W. (1966), *Evolution and Society: A Study in Victorian Social Theory* (Cambridge: Cambridge University Press).

Bynner, J. (1991), 'Transitions to Work' in D. Ashton and G. Lowe (eds.) *Making Their Way* (Milton Keynes: Open University Press).

Cain, G. and Watts, H. (1970), 'Problems in Making Inferences from the Coleman Report', *American Sociological Review*, 35: 228–42.

Camic, C. and Xie, Y. (1994), 'The Statistical Turn in American Social Science: Columbia University, 1890 to 1915', *American Sociological Review*, 59: 773–805.

Campbell, C. (1982), 'A Dubious Distinction? An Inquiry into the Value and Use of Merton's Concepts of Manifest and Latent Function', *American Sociological Review*, 47: 29–44.

Campbell, C. (1996), *The Myth of Social Action* (Cambridge: Cambridge University Press).

Capelli, P. (1995), 'Rethinking Employment', *British Journal of Industrial Relations*, 33: 563–602.

Castles, F. G. (1978), *The Social Democratic Image of Society* (London: Routledge).

Chan, T. W. and Goldthorpe, J. H. (2004), 'Is There a Status Order in Contemporary British Society?', *European Sociological Review*, 20: 383–401.

Chan, T. W. and Goldthorpe, J. H. (2006), 'Class and Status: The Conceptual Distinction and Its Empirical Relevance', Department of Sociology, University of Oxford, Working Paper 2006–3.

Chan, T. W. and Goldthorpe, J. H. (2007a), 'Social Status and Newspaper Readership', *American Journal of Sociology*, forthcoming.

Chan, T. W. and Goldthorpe, J. H. (2007b), 'Social Stratification and Cultural Consumption: Music in England', *European Sociological Review*, forthcoming.

Cherkaoui, M. (1983), 'Education and Social Mobility: Paul Lapie's Pathbreaking Work' in P. Besnard (ed.) *The Sociological Domain* (Cambridge: Cambridge University Press).

Chicago Commission on Race Relations (1922), *The Negro in Chicago* (Chicago: University of Chicago Press).

Clark, T. N. (1973), *Prophets and Patrons: The French University and the Emergence of the Social Sciences* (Cambridge, Mass.: Harvard University Press).

Clark, T. N. and Lipset, S. M. (1991), 'Are Social Classes Dying?', *International Sociology*, 6: 397–410.

Clark, T. N. and Lipset, S. M. (eds.) (2001), *The Breakdown of Class Politics* (Washington, D.C.: Woodrow Wilson Centre).

Clark, T. N., Lipset, S. M., and Rempel, M. (1993), 'The Declining Political Significance of Social Class', *International Sociology*, 8: 293–316.

Clogg, C. C. (1992), 'The Impact of Sociological Methodology on Statistical Methodology', *Statistical Science*, 7: 183–207.

Coase, R. H. (1937), 'The Nature of the Firm', *Economica*, 4: 386–405.

Cohen, Y. and Pfeffer, J. (1986), 'Organizational Hiring Standards', *Administrative Science Quarterly*, 31: 1–24.

Cole, S. (1972), 'Continuity and Institutionalisation in Science: A Case Study of Failure' in A. Oberschall (ed.) *The Establishment of Empirical Sociology* (New York: Harper and Row).

Cole, S. (1994), 'Why Sociology Doesn't Make Progress Like the Natural Sciences', *Sociological Forum*, 9: 133–54.

Coleman, J. S. (1986a), 'Social Theory, Social Research and a Theory of Action', *American Journal of Sociology*, 91: 1309–335.

Coleman, J. S. (1986b), *Individual Interests and Collective Action* (Cambridge: Cambridge University Press).

Coleman, J. S. (1990), *Foundations of Social Theory* (Cambridge, Mass.: Belknap).

Coleman, J. S., Campbell, E. Q., Hobson, C. J., McPartland, J., Mood, A. M., Weinfeld, F. D., and York, R. L. (1966), *Equality of Educational Opportunity* (Washington, D.C.: U.S. Government Printing Office).

Coleman, J. S. and Fararo, T. J. (1992), 'Introduction' in *idem* (eds.) *Rational Choice Theory: Advocacy and Critique* (Newbury Park: Sage).

Coleman, J. S. and Hoffer, T. (1987), *Public and Private High Schools: The Impact of Community* (New York: Basic Books).

Coleman, J. S., Hoffer, T., and Kilgore, S. (1982), *High School Achievement: Public, Catholic and Private Schools Compared* (New York: Basic Books).

Collingwood, R. G. (1946/1993), *The Idea of History*, 2nd ed. (Oxford: Oxford University Press).

Collini, S. (1979), *Liberalism and Sociology* (Cambridge: Cambridge University Press).

Commons, J. R. (1924), *Institutional Economics* (Madison: University of Wisconsin Press).

Comte, A. (1830–42/1908), *Cours de philosophie positive* (Paris: Schleicher Frères).

Converse, J. (1987), *Survey Research in the United States: Roots and Emergence, 1890–1960* (Berkeley: University of California Press).

Cox, D. R. (1984), 'Interaction', *International Statistical Review*, 52: 1–31.

Craig, J. E. (1983), 'Sociology and Related Disciplines between the Wars: Maurice Halbwachs and the Imperialism of the Durkheimians' in P. Besnard (ed.) *The Sociological Domain* (Cambridge: Cambridge University Press).

Crompton, R. (1998), *Class and Stratification* (Cambridge: Polity).

Croner, F. (1954), *Die Angestellten in der modernen Gesellschaft* (Vienna: Humboldt).

Cullen, M. (1975), *The Statistical Movement in Early Victorian Britain* (New York: Harvester).

Dahrendorf, R. (1959), *Class and Class Conflict in Industrial Society* (London: Routledge).

Daston, L. J. (1987), 'Rational Individuals versus Laws of Society: From Probability to Statistics' in L. Krüger, L. J. Daston, and M. Heidelberger (eds.) *The Probabilistic Revolution*, vol.1, *Ideas in History* (Cambridge, Mass.: MIT Press).

Davies, R., Heinesen, E., and Holm, A. (2002), 'The Relative Risk Aversion Hypothesis of Educational Choice', *Journal of Population Economics*, 15: 683–713.

Day, L. H. (1987), 'Durkheim on Religion and Suicide—a Demographic Critique', *Sociology*, 21: 449–61.

De Graaf, P. M. and Ganzeboom, H. G. B. (1993), 'Family Background and Educational Attainment in the Netherlands for the 1891–1960 Birth Cohorts' in

Y. Shavit and H.-P. Blossfeld (eds.) *Persistent Inequality: Changing Educational Attainment in Thirteen Countries* (Boulder: Westview).

Despotidu, S. and Shepherd, P. (1998), *1970 British Cohort Study: Twenty-Six Year Follow-Up, 1996* (London: City University, Social Statistics Research Unit).

Desrosières, A. (1985), 'Histoire de formes: statistiques et sciences sociales avant 1940', *Revue française de sociologie*, 26: 277–310.

Desrosières, A. (1991), 'The Part in Relation to the Whole: How to Generalise? The Prehistory of Representative Sampling' in M. Bulmer, K. Bales, and K. K. Sklar (eds.) *The Social Survey in Historical Perspective, 1880–1940* (Cambridge: Cambridge University Press).

Desrosières, A. (1993), *La politique des grands nombres* (Paris: La Découverte).

Desrosières, A. (1996), 'Quetelet et la sociologie quantitative: du piédestal à l'oubli'. Paper presented at the Quetelet Bicentenary Colloquium, Brussels.

Devine, F. (1998), 'Class Analysis and the Stability of Class Relations', *Sociology*, 32: 23–42.

Devine, F. (2004), *Class Practices* (Cambridge: Cambridge University Press).

Devine, F. and Savage, M. (2000), 'Conclusion: Renewing Class Analysis' in R. Crompton, F. Devine, M. Savage, and J. Scott (eds.), *Renewing Class Analysis* (Oxford: Blackwell).

Dilthey, W. (1883/1959), *Einleitung in die Geisteswissenschaften* in *Gesammelte Schriften*, vol. 1 (Stuttgart: Teubner).

Doeringer, P. and Piore, M. (1971), *Internal Labor Markets and Manpower Analysis* (Lexington: Heath).

Dominitz, J. and Manski, C. (1999), 'The Several Cultures of Research on Subjective Expectations' in R. Willis and J. Smith (eds.) *Wealth, Work and Health* (Ann Arbor: University of Michigan Press).

Douglas, J. (1967), *The Social Meanings of Suicide* (Princeton: Princeton University Press).

Drobisch, M. (1867), *Die moralische Statistik und die menschliche Willensfreiheit* (Leipzig: Voss).

Duncan, O. D. (1964), 'Introduction' to *William F. Ogburn: On Culture and Social Change* (Chicago: Chicago University Press).

Duncan, O. D. (1968), 'Inheritance of Poverty or Inheritance of Race?' in D. P. Moynihan (ed.) *On Understanding Poverty* (New York: Basic Books).

Durkheim, E. (1893/1933), *The Division of Labour in Society* (Glencoe, Ill.: Free Press).

Durkheim, E. (1895/1938), *The Rules of Sociological Method* (Glencoe, Ill.: Free Press).

Durkheim, E. (1897/1952), *Suicide* (London: Routledge and Kegan Paul).

Durkheim, E. (1912/1915), *The Elementary Forms of the Religious Life* (London: Allen and Unwin).

Duru-Bellat, M., Jarousse, J.-P., and Mingat, A. (1992), *De l'orientation en fin de cinquième au fonctionnement du collège*, vol. 3 (Dijon: Presses de l'Université de Bourgogne).

Duru-Bellat, M. and Mingat, A. (1989), 'How do French Junior Secondary Schools Operate? Academic Achievement, Grading and Streaming of Students', *European Sociological Review*, 5: 47–64.

Ebbinghaus, B. and Visser, J. (2000), 'A Comparative Profile' in *idem* (eds.), *Trade Unions in Western Europe since 1945* (London: Macmillan).

Edgeworth, F. Y. (1885), 'Observations and Statistics: An Essay on the Theory of Errors and the First Principles of Statistics', *Transactions of the Cambridge Philosophical Society*, 14: 138–69.

Edwards, R. (1979), *Contested Terrain: The Transformation of the Workplace in the Twentieth Century* (London: Heinemann).

Eggertsson, T. (1990), *Economic Behavior and Institutions* (Cambridge: Cambridge University Press).

Ehrenberg, R. G. and Smith, R. S. (1991), *Modern Labor Economics: Theory and Public Policy* (New York: Harper Collins).

Elias, P. and McKnight, A. (2003), 'Earnings, Unemployment and the NS-SEC' in D. Rose and D. J. Pevalin (eds.), *A Researcher's Guide to the National Statistics Socio-economic Classification* (London: Sage).

Elster, J. (1985), *Making Sense of Marx* (Cambridge: Cambridge University Press).

Elster, J. (1990), 'Merton's Functionalism and the Unintended Consequences of Action' in J. Clark, C. Modgil, and S. Modgil (eds.) *Robert K. Merton: Consensus and Controversy* (London: Falmer).

Elster, J. (1991), 'Rationality and Social Norms', *Archives européennes de sociologie*, 32: 109–29.

Erikson, R. (1983), 'Changes in Social Mobility in Industrial Nations: The Case of Sweden', *Research in Social Stratification and Mobility*, 2: 165–95.

Erikson, R. (1996), 'Can We Account for the Change in Inequality of Educational Opportunity?' in R. Erikson and J. O. Jonsson (eds.) *Can Education be Equalized? The Swedish Case in Comparative Perspective* (Boulder: Westview).

Erikson, R. and Goldthorpe, J. H. (1985), 'Are American Rates of Social Mobility Exceptionally High? New Evidence on an Old Issue', *European Sociological Review*, 1: 1–22.

Erikson, R. and Goldthorpe, J. H. (1992), *The Constant Flux: A Study of Class Mobility in Industrial Societies* (Oxford: Clarendon).

Erikson, R., Goldthorpe, J. H., Jackson, M., Yaish, M., and Cox, D. R. (2005), 'On Class Differentials in Educational Attainment', *Proceedings of the National Academy of Sciences*, 102: 9730–733.

Erikson, R., Goldthorpe, J. H., and Portocarero, L. (1979), 'Intergenerational Class Mobility in Three Western European Societies', *British Journal of Sociology*, 30: 415–41.

Erikson, R. and Jonsson, J. O. (1993), *Ursprung och Utbildning* (Stockholm: Statens Offentliga Utredningar).

Erikson, R. and Jonsson, J. O. (1994), 'Ökade Löneskillnader—Ett Sätt att ta till vara Begåvningsreserven', *Ekonomisk Debatt*, 22: 581–94.

Erikson, R. and Jonsson, J. O. (eds.) (1994), *Sorteringen i Sverige* (Stockholm: Carlsson).

Erikson, R. and Jonsson, J. O. (1996), 'Explaining Class Inequality in Education: the Swedish Test Case' in *idem* (eds.) *Can Education be Equalized? The Swedish Case in Comparative Perspective* (Boulder: Westview).

Erikson, R. and Jonsson, J. O. (eds.) (1996), *Can Education Be Equalized? The Swedish Case in Comparative Perspective* (Boulder: Westview).

Ermarth, M. (1978), *Wilhelm Dilthey: The Critique of Historical Reason* (Chicago: University of Chicago Press).

Esping-Andersen, G. (1985), *Politics Against Markets* (Princeton: Princeton University Press).

Esping-Andersen, G. (1990), *The Three Worlds of Welfare Capitalism* (Princeton: Princeton University Press).

Esping-Andersen, G. (1993), 'Post-Industrial Class Structures' in *idem* (ed.) *Changing Classes: Stratification and Mobility in Post-Industrial Societies* (London: Sage).

Esser, H. (1999), *Soziologie: Spezielle Grundlagen*, Band 1, *Situationslogik und Handeln* (Frankfurt: Campus).

Evans, G. (1992), 'Testing the Validity of the Goldthorpe Class Schema', *European Sociological Review*, 8: 211–32.

Evans, G. (1993), 'Class, Prospects and the Life-Cycle: Explaining the Association between Class Position and Political Preferences', *Acta Sociologica*, 36: 263–76.

Evans, G. (1996), 'Putting Men and Women into Classes: An Assessment of the Cross-Sex Validity of the Goldthorpe Class Schema', *Sociology*, 30: 209–234.

Evans, G. (1999), 'Class Voting: from Premature Obituary to Reasoned Appraisal' in G. Evans (ed.), *The End of Class Politics? Class Voting in Comparative Context* (Oxford: Clarendon).

Evans, G. (ed.) (1999), *The End of Class Politics? Class Voting in Comparative Context* (Oxford: Clarendon).

Evans, G. (2000), 'The Continued Significance of Class Voting', *Annual Review of Political Science*, 3: 401–17.

Evans, G., Heath, A. F., and Payne, C. (1991), 'Modelling the Class/Party Relationship 1964–87', *Electoral Studies*, 10: 99–117.

Evans, G., Heath, A. F., and Payne, C. (1996), 'Class and Party Revisited: A New Method for Estimating Changes in Levels of Class Voting', *British Elections and Parties Yearbook, 1995* (London: Frank Case).

Evans, G. and Mills, C. (1998), 'Identifying Class Structures: A Latent Class Analysis of the Criterion-Related and Construct Validity of the Goldthorpe Class Schema', *European Sociological Review*, 14: 87–106.

Evans G. and Mills, C. (1999), 'Are There Classes in Post-Communist Societies? A New Approach to Identifying Class Structure', *Sociology*, 33: 23–46.

Evans, G. and Mills, C. (2000), 'In Search of the Wage-Labour/Service Contract: New Evidence on the Validity of the Goldthorpe Class Schema', *British Journal of Sociology*, 51: 641–62.

Fama, E. F. (1991), 'Time, Salary, and Incentive Payoffs in Labor Contracts', *Journal of Labor Economics*, 9: 25–44.

Faris, R. E. L. (1967), *Chicago Sociology: 1920–1932* (Chicago: Chicago University Press).

Featherman, D. L., Jones, F. L., and Hauser, R. M. (1975), 'Assumptions of Social Mobility Research in the U.S.: The Case of Occupational Status', *Social Science Research*, 4: 329–60.

Featherman, D. L. and Spenner, K. I. (1990), 'Class and the Socialization of Children: Constancy, Chance or Irrelevance?' in E. M. Hetherington, R. M. Lerner, and M. Perlmutter (eds.) *Child Development in Life-Span Perspective* (Hillsdale, N.J.: Erlbaum).

Ferrie, J. P. (2005), 'The End of American Exceptionalism? Mobility in the U.S. since 1850'. NBER Washington, Working Paper 11324.

Firth, D. (2005), 'Some Topics in Social Statistics' in A. C. Davison, Y. Dodge, and N. Wermuth (eds.) *Celebrating Statistics: Papers in Honour of Sir David Cox on his 80th Birthday* (Oxford: Oxford University Press).

Firth, D. and Kuha, J. (1999), 'Comments on "A Critique of the Bayesian Information Criterion for Model Selection"', *Sociological Methods and Research*, 27: 398–402.

Fleck, C. (1998), 'The Choice between Market Research and Sociography, or What Happened to Lazarsfeld in the United States? in J. Lautman and B.-P. Lécuyer (eds.) *Paul Lazarsfeld (1901–1976) La Sociologie de Vienne à New York* (Paris: L'Harmattan).

Fox, T. G. and Miller, S. M. (1965), 'Economic, Political and Social Determinants of Mobility', *Acta Sociologica*, 9: 76–93.

Fox, T. G. and Miller, S. M. (1966), 'Occupational Stratification and Mobility: Inter-Country Variations' in R. Merritt and S. Rokkan (eds.) *Comparing Nations* (New Haven: Yale University Press).

Fréchet, M. and Halbwachs, M. (1924), *Le Calcul des probabilités à la portée de tous* (Paris: Dunod).

Freedman, D. A. (1999), 'From Association to Causation: Some Remarks on the History of Statistics', *Statistical Science*, 14: 243–58.

Fritzell, J. (1993), 'Income Inequality Trends in the 1980s: A Five Country Comparison', *Acta Sociologica*, 36: 47–62.

Furlong, A. (1992), *Growing Up in a Classless Society?* (Edinburgh: Edinburgh University Press).

Gallie, D. White, M., Cheng, Y., and Tomlinson, M. (1998), *Restructuring the Employment Relationship* (Oxford: Clarendon).

Galton, F. (1869), *Hereditary Genius* (London: Macmillan).

Galton, F. (1889a), *Natural Inheritance* (London: Macmillan).

Galton, F. (1889b), 'Comments' on E. B. Tylor 'On a Method of Investigating the Development of Institutions; Applied to Laws of Marriage and Descent', *Journal of the Royal Anthropological Institute*, 18: 245–56, 261–69.

Gambetta, D. (1987), *Were They Pushed or Did They Jump? Individual Decision Mechanisms in Education* (Cambridge: Cambridge University Press).

Gambetta, D. (ed.) (1988), *Trust: Making and Breaking Co-operative Relations* (Cambridge: Cambridge University Press).

Ganzeboom, H. G. B., Luijkx, R., and Treiman, D. J. (1989), 'Intergenerational Class Mobility in Comparative Perspective', *Research in Social Stratification and Mobility*, 8: 3–55.

Garrett, G. (1998), *Partisan Politics in the Global Economy* (Cambridge: Cambridge University Press).

Geiger, T. (1951), *Soziale Umschichtungen in einer dänischen Mittelstadt* (Aarhus: Aarhus University Press).

Gerber, T. P. (2002), 'Structural Change and Post-Socialist Stratification: Labor Market Transitions in Contemporary Russia', *American Sociological Review*, 67: 629–59.

Gerber, T. P. and Hout, M. (2004), 'Intergenerational Class Mobility in Russia, 1998–2000: Stronger Origin Effects During Market Transition', *American Sociological Review*, 69: 677–703.

Gibbons, R. (1987), 'Piece-Rate Incentive Schemes', *Journal of Labor Economics*, 5: 413–29.

Gibbons, R. (1997), 'Incentives and Careers in Organizations' in D. M. Kreps and K. F. Wallis (eds.) *Advances in Economics and Econometrics: Theory and Applications* (Cambridge: Cambridge University Press).

Giddens, A. (1973), *The Class Structure of the Advanced Societies* (London: Hutchinson).

Giddings, F. H. (1896), *Principles of Sociology* (New York: Macmillan).

Giddings, F. H. (1901), *Inductive Sociology* (New York: Macmillan).

Giddings, F. H. (1904) 'The Concepts and Methods of Sociology', *American Journal of Sociology*, 10: 161–76.

Gigerenzer, G., Swijtink, Z., Porter, T., Daston, L., Beatty, J., and Krüger, L. (1989), *The Empire of Chance* (Cambridge: Cambridge University Press).

Ginsberg, M. (1929), 'Interchange between Social Classes', *Economic Journal*, 39: 554–65.

Ginsberg, M. (1965), 'Introduction to the 1965 Reprint' of L. T. Hobhouse, G. C. Wheeler, and M. Ginsberg, *The Material Culture and Social Institutions of the Simpler Peoples* (London: London School of Economics).

Goldman, L. (2002), *Science, Reform and Politics in Victorian Britain: The Social Science Association, 1857–1886* (Cambridge: Cambridge University Press).

Goldthorpe, J. H. (1982), 'On the Service Class: Its Formation and Future' in A. Giddens and G. Mackenzie (eds.) *Social Class and the Division of Labour* (Cambridge: Cambridge University Press).

Goldthorpe, J. H. (ed.) (1984) *Order and Conflict in Contemporary Capitalism* (Oxford: Clarendon).

Goldthorpe, J. H. (with Llewellyn, C. and Payne, C.) (1987), *Social Mobility and Class Structure in Modern Britain* (Oxford: Clarendon).

Goldthorpe, J. H. (1995), 'The Service Class Revisited' in T. Butler and M. Savage (eds.) *Social Change and the Middle Classes* (London: UCL Press).

Goldthorpe, J. H. (2000), 'Rent, Class Conflict, and Class Structure: A Commentary on Sørensen', *American Journal of Sociology*, 105: 1572–582.

Goldthorpe, J. H. (2001), 'Class and Politics in Advanced Industrial Societies' in T. Clark and S. M. Lipset (eds.), *The Breakdown of Class Politics* (Washington, D.C.: Woodrow Wilson Centre).

Goldthorpe, J. H. (2002a), 'Occupational Sociology, Yes: Class Analysis, No. Comment on Grusky and Weeden's Research Agenda', *Acta Sociologica*, 45: 211–25.

Goldthorpe, J. H. (2002b), 'A Sociology of Ireland', *Irish Journal of Sociology*, 11: 97–109.

Goldthorpe, J. H. (2005), 'Progress in Sociology: The Case of Social Mobility Research' in S. Svallfors (ed.) *Analyzing Inequality: Life Chances and Social Mobility in Comparative Perspective* (Stanford: Stanford University Press)

Goldthorpe, J. H. and Heath, A. F. (1992), 'Revised Class Schema, 1992'. JUSST Working Paper 13, Nuffield College, Oxford.

Goldthorpe, J. H. and Hope, K. (1974), *The Social Grading of Occupations* (Oxford: Clarendon).

Goldthorpe, J. H. and Jackson, M. (2006), 'Education-Based Meritocracy: The Barriers to Its Realisation'. Russell Sage Foundation Conference on Social Class, New York.

Goldthorpe, J. H. and Llewellyn, C. (1977), 'Class Mobility in Modern Britain: Three Theses Examined', *Sociology*, 11: 257–87.

Goldthorpe, J. H., Lockwood, D., Platt, J., and Bechhofer, F. (1969), *The Affluent Worker in the Class Structure* (Cambridge: Cambridge University Press).

Goldthorpe, J. H. and Marshall, G. (1992), 'The Promising Future of Class Analysis: A Response to Recent Critiques', *Sociology*, 26: 381–400.

Goldthorpe, J. H. and McKnight, A. (2006), 'The Economic Basis of Social Class' in S. Morgan, D. B. Grusky, and G. S. Fields (eds.) *Mobility and Inequality: Frontiers of Research from Sociology and Economics* (Stanford: Stanford University Press).

Goldthorpe, J. H. and Mills, C. (2004), 'Trends in Intergenerational Class Mobility in Britain in the Late Twentieth Century' in R. Breen (ed.) *Social Mobility in Europe* (Oxford: Oxford University Press).

Goldthorpe, J. H., Payne, C., and Llewellyn, C. (1978), 'Trends in Class Mobility', *Sociology*, 12: 441–68.

Goodin, R. and Le Grand, J. (1987), *Not Only the Poor: The Middle Classes and the Welfare State* (London: Allen and Unwin).

Gottschalk, P. and Smeeding, T. M. (1997), 'Cross-National Comparisons of Earnings and Income Inequality', *Journal of Economic Literature*, 35: 633–87.

Goux, D. and Maurin, E. (1997), 'Meritocracy and Social Heredity in France', *European Sociological Review*, 13: 159–77.

Gray, J. (1998), *False Dawn: The Delusions of Global Capitalism* (London: Granta).

Grusky, D. B. (ed.) (2001), *Social Stratification: Class, Race and Gender in Sociological Perspective* (Boulder: Westview).

Grusky, D. B. (with Galescu, G.) (2005a), 'Is Durkheim a Class Analyst?' in J. Alexander and P. Smith (eds.) *The Cambridge Companion to Durkheim* (Cambridge: Cambridge University Press).

Grusky, D. B. (with Galescu, G.) (2005b), 'Foundations of a Neo-Durkheimian Class Analysis' in E. O. Wright (ed.), *Approaches to Class Analysis* (Cambridge: Cambridge University Press).

Grusky, D. B. and Di Carlo, M. (2001), 'Should Sociologists Plod Along and Establish Empirical Regularities or Seek a Grand Explanation for Them?', *European Sociological Review*, 17: 457–64.

Grusky, D. B. and Sørensen, J. B. (1998), 'Can Class Analysis be Salvaged?', *American Journal of Sociology*, 103: 1187–234.

Grusky, D. B. and Weeden, K. A. (2001), 'Decomposition Without Death: A Research Agenda for a New Class Analysis', *Acta Sociologica*, 44: 203–18.

Grusky, D. B. and Weeden, K. A. (2002), 'Class Analysis and the Heavy Weight of Convention', *Acta Sociologica*, 45: 229–36.

Grusky, D. B. and Weeden, K. A. (2006), 'Does the Sociological Approach to Studying Social Mobility Have a Future?' in S. L. Morgan, D. B. Grusky, and G. S. Fields (eds.), *Mobility and Inequality: Frontiers of Research in Economics and Sociology* (Stanford: Stanford University Press).

Grusky, D. B., Weeden, K. A., and Sørensen, J. B. (2000), 'The Case for Realism in Class Analysis', *Political Power and Social Theory*, 14: 291–305.

Guzzo, S. (2002), 'Getting in Through the Back Door: Equal Educational Qualifications, Unequal Occupational Returns'. ISA Research Committee on Social Stratification and Mobility, Oxford.

Hacking, I. (1987), 'Was There a Probabilistic Revolution 1800–1930?' in L. Krüger, L. J. Daston, and M. Heidelberger, (eds.) *The Probabilistic Revolution*, vol. 1, *Ideas in History* (Cambridge, Mass.: MIT Press).

Hacking, I. (1990), *The Taming of Chance* (Cambridge: Cambridge University Press).

Halbwachs, M. (1912), *La théorie de l'homme moyen* (Paris: Alcan).

Halbwachs, M. (1930/1978), *The Causes of Suicide* (London: Routledge).

Halbwachs, M. (1933), *L'Evolution des besoins dans les classes ouvrières* (Paris: Alcan).

Halbwachs, M. (1955), *Esquisse d'une psychologie des classes sociales* (Paris: Rivière).

Halford, S. and Savage, M. (1995), 'The Bureaucratic Career: Demise or Adaptation?' in T. Butler and M. Savage (eds.) *Social Change and the Middle Classes* (London: UCL Press).

Hall, P. A. and Soskice, D. (2001), 'An Introduction to Varieties of Capitalism' in *idem* (eds.) *Varieties of Capitalism: The Institutional Foundations of Comparative Advantage* (New York: Oxford University Press).

Halliday, R. (1968), 'The Sociological Movement, the Sociological Society and the Genesis of Academic Sociology in Britain', *Sociological Review*, 16: 377–98.

Halsey, A. H. (1977), 'Towards Meritocracy? The Case of Britain' in J. Karabel and A. H. Halsey (eds.) *Power and Ideology in Education* (New York: Oxford University Press).

Halsey, A. H., Floud, J., and Anderson, C. A. (eds.) (1961), *Education, Economy and Society* (New York: Free Press).

Halsey, A. H., Heath, A. F., and Ridge, J. M. (1980), *Origins and Destinations* (Oxford: Clarendon).

Hamilton, R. F. (1996), *The Social Misconstruction of Reality* (New Haven: Yale University Press).

Hanushek, E. A. (1972), *Education and Race* (Cambridge, Mass.: Ballinger).

Hatcher, R. M. (1998), 'Class Differentiation in Education: Rational Choice', *British Journal of Sociology of Education*, 19: 5–24.

Hauser, R. M. (1973), 'Socioeconomic Background and Differential Returns to Education' in L. C. Solmon and P. J. Taubman (eds.) *Does College Matter?* (New York: Academic Press).

Hauser, R. M. (1976), 'On Boudon's Model of Social Mobility', *American Journal of Sociology*, 81: 911–28.

Hauser, R. M., Koffel, J. N., Travis, H. P., and Dickinson, P. J. (1975), 'Temporal Change in Occupational Mobility: Evidence for Men in the United States', *American Sociological Review*, 40: 279–97.

Hayek, F. (1960), *The Constitution of Liberty* (London: Routledge).

Hayek, F. (1976), *Law, Legislation and Liberty* (London: Routledge).

Heath, A. F., Curtice, J., Jowell, R., Evans, G., and Field, J. (1991), *Understanding Political Change* (Oxford: Pergamon).

Heckman, J. J. and Neal, D. (1996), 'Coleman's Contribution to Education: Theory, Research Styles and Empirical Research' in J. Clark (ed.) *James Coleman* (London: Falmer).

Hedström, P. and Swedberg, R. (1998), 'Social Mechanisms: An Introductory Essay' in *idem* (eds.) *Social Mechanisms* (Cambridge: Cambridge University Press).

Heilbron, J. (1995), *The Rise of Social Theory* (Cambridge: Polity Press).

Hendrickx, J. and Ganzeboom, H. G. B. (1998), 'Occupational Status Attainment in the Netherlands, 1920–1990: A Multinomial Logistic Analysis', *European Sociological Review*, 14: 387–403.

Hennis, W. (1996), *Max Webers Wissenschaft vom Menschen* (Tübingen: J. C. B. Mohr).

Hernes, G. (1989), 'The Logic of *The Protestant Ethic*', *Rationality and Society*, 1: 123–62.

Hibbs, D. A. (1991), 'Market Forces, Trade Union Ideology and Trends in Swedish Wage Dispersion', *Acta Sociologica*, 34: 89–102.

Hillmert, S. and Jacob, M. (2003), 'Social Inequality in Higher Education: Is Vocational Training a Pathway Leading to or Away from University?', *European Sociological Review*, 19: 319–34.

Hirsch, F. (1976), *Social Limits to Growth* (Cambridge, Mass.: Harvard University Press).

Hobhouse, L. T. (1906), *Morals in Evolution* (London: Allen and Unwin).

Hobhouse, L. T. (1924), *Social Development* (London: Allen and Unwin).

Hobhouse, L. T., Wheeler, G. C., and Ginsberg, M. (1915), *The Material Culture and Social Institutions of the Simpler Peoples* (London: Chapman and Hall).

Hogben, L. T. (ed.) (1938), *Political Arithmetic* (London: Allen and Unwin).

Hollis, M. (1977), *Models of Man* (Cambridge: Cambridge University Press).

Hollis, M. (1987), *The Cunning of Reason* (Cambridge: Cambridge University Press).

Holm, A. and Jaeger, M. M. (2005), 'Relative Risk Aversion and Social Reproduction in Intergenerational Educational Attainment: Application of a Dynamic Discrete Choice Model'. Department of Sociology and Centre of Applied Microeconometrics, University of Copenhagen.

Holmström, B. and Milgrom, P. (1991), 'Multitask Principal–Agent Analyses: Incentive Contracts, Asset Ownership, and Job Design', *Journal of Law, Economics and Organization*, 7: 25–51.

Holton, G. (1996), 'Has Class Analysis a Future?' in D. J. Lee and B. S. Turner (eds.) *Conflicts About Class* (London: Longman).

Hout, M. (1988), 'More Universalism, Less Structural Mobility: the American Occupational Structure in the 1980s', *American Journal of Sociology*, 93: 1358–400.

Hout, M. and DiPrete, T. (forthcoming), 'What Have We Learned? RC-28's Contributions to Knowledge about Social Stratification', *Research in Social Stratification and Mobility*.

Hout, M., Raftery, A. E., and Bell, E. O. (1993), 'Making the Grade: Educational Stratification in the United States, 1925–1989' in Y. Shavit and H.-P. Blossfeld (eds.) *Persistent Inequality: Changing Educational Attainment in Thirteen Countries* (Boulder: Westview).

Hutchens, R. M. (1987), 'A Test of Lazear's Theory of Delayed Payment Contracts', *Journal of Labor Economics*, 5: S153–70.

Hyman, H. (1954), 'The Value Systems of Different Classes' in R. Bendix and S. M. Lipset (eds.) *Class, Status and Power* (Glencoe, Ill.: Free Press).

Isambert, F.-A. (1973), 'Durkheim et la statistique écologique' in *Une nouvelle civilisation? Hommage à Georges Friedmann* (Paris: Gallimard).

Ishida, H. (1995), 'Intergenerational Class Mobility and Reproduction' in *idem* (ed.) *Social Stratification and Mobility: Basic Analysis and Cross-National Comparison* (Tokyo: SSM Research Series).

Ishida, H. and Miwa, S. (2005), 'Social Mobility and Education in Post-War Japan'. Institute of Social Sciences, University of Tokyo.

Ishida, H., Müller, W., and Ridge, J. M. (1995), 'Class Origin, Class Destination, and Education: A Cross-National Study of Ten Industrial Nations', *American Journal of Sociology*, 60: 145–93.

Iversen, T. and Pontusson, J. (2000), 'Comparative Political Economy: A Northern European Perspective' in T. Iversen, J. Pontusson, and D. Soskice (eds.) *Unions, Employers and Central Banks* (Cambridge: Cambridge University Press).

Jackson, M. (2001), 'Meritocracy, Education and Occupational Attainment: What Do Employers Really See as Merit?' Department of Sociology, University of Oxford, Working Paper 2001–003.

Jackson, M. (2004), 'Resource Rich, Ability Poor: Why Even at Low Levels of Education Middle-Class Kids Get Middle-Class Jobs'. ISA Research Committee on Social Stratification and Mobility, Neuchcirâtel.

Jackson, M., Erikson, R., Goldthorpe, J. H., and Yaish, M. (2005), 'Primary and Secondary Effects in Class Differentials in Educational Attainment: The Transition to A-Level Courses in England and Wales'. Paper presented to the Royal Statistical Society, Oxford.

Jackson, M., Goldthorpe, J. H., and Mills, C. (2005), 'Education, Employers and Class Mobility', *Research in Social Stratification and Mobility*, 23: 3–34.

Jahoda, M. (1979), 'PFL: Hedgehog or Fox?' in R. K. Merton, J. S. Coleman, and P. Rossi (eds.), *Qualitative and Quantitative Research: Papers in Honor of Paul F. Lazarsfeld* (New York: Free Press).

Jahoda, M., Lazarsfeld, P. M., and Zeisel, H. (1933), *Die Arbeitslosen von Marienthal* (Leipzig: Hirzel).

Janowitz, M. (1970), 'Foreword' to R. E. L. Faris, *Chicago Sociology, 1920–1932* (Chicago: Chicago University Press).

Jones, F. L. (1992), 'Common Social Fluidity: A Comment on Recent Criticisms', *European Sociological Review*, 8: 255–59.

Jonsson, J. O. (1988), *Utbildning, Social Reproduktion och Social Skiktning* (Stockholm: Institutet för Social Forskning).

Jonsson, J. O. (1991), 'Education, Social Mobility and Social Reproduction in Sweden: Patterns and Changes' in E. J. Hansen et al. (eds.) *Scandinavian Trends in Welfare and Living Conditions* (Armonck, NY: Sharpe).

Jonsson, J. O. (1993), 'Persisting Inequalities in Sweden?' in Y. Shavit and H.-P. Blossfeld (eds.) *Persisting Inequality: Changing Educational Attainment in Thirteen Countries* (Boulder: Westview).

Jonsson, J. O. (1995), 'A Note on the Differential Incentive to Continue in Higher Education', Swedish Institute for Social Research, Stockholm.

Jonsson, J. O. (1996), 'Stratification in Post-Industrial Society: Are Educational Qualifications of Growing Importance?' in R. Erikson and J. O. Jonsson (eds.)

Can Education Be Equalized?: The Swedish Case in Comparative Perspective (Boulder: Westview).

Jonsson, J. O. (1999), 'Explaining Sex Differences in Educational Choice: An Empirical Assessment of a Rational Choice Model', *European Sociological Review*, 15: 391–404.

Jonsson, J. O. (2004), 'Equality at a Halt? Social Mobility in Sweden, 1976–99' in R. Breen (ed.) *Social Mobility in Europe* (Oxford: Oxford University Press).

Jonsson, J. O and Erikson, R. (2000), 'Understanding Educational Inequality: The Swedish Experience', *L'année sociologique*, 50: 345–82.

Jonsson, J. O. and Mills, C. (1993), 'Social Class and Educational Attainment in Historical Perspective', *British Journal of Sociology*, 44: 213–47, 403–428.

Jonsson, J. O., Mills, C., and Müller, W. (1996), 'A Half Century of Increasing Educational Openness? Social Class, Gender and Educational Attainment in Sweden, Germany and Britain' in R. Erikson and J. O. Jonsson (eds.) *Can Education be Equalized? The Swedish Case in Comparative Perspective* (Boulder: Westview).

Kahnemann, D. and Tversky, A. (1979), 'Prospect Theory: An Analysis of Decision under Risk', *Econometrica*, 47: 263–91.

Kalleberg, A. J. (1990), 'The Comparative Study of Business Organizations and their Employees: Conceptual and Methodological Issues', *Comparative Social Research*, 12: 153–75.

Karady, V. (1981), 'French Ethnology and the Durkheimian Breakthrough', *Journal of the Anthropological Society of Oxford*, 12: 165–76.

Karady, V. (1983), 'The Durkheimians in Academe: A Reconsideration' in P. Besnard (ed.) *The Sociological Domain* (Cambridge: Cambridge University Press).

Käsler, D. (1988), *Max Weber* (Cambridge: Polity Press).

Katz, E. and Lazarsfeld, P. F. (1955), *Personal Influence* (New York: Free Press).

Kay, J. (1993), *The Foundations of Corporate Success* (Oxford: Oxford University Press).

Keller, S. and Zavalloni, M. (1964), 'Ambition and Social Class: A Respecification', *Social Forces*, 43: 58–70.

Kelley, J., Robinson, R. V., and Klein, H. S. (1981), 'A Theory of Social Mobility, with Data on Status Attainment in a Peasant Society', *Research in Social Stratification and Mobility*, 1: 27–66.

Kendall, P. L. and Lazarsfeld, P. F. (1950), 'Problems of Survey Analysis' in R. K. Merton and P. F. Lazarsfeld (eds.) *Continuities in Social Research: Studies in the Scope and Method of 'The American Soldier'* (Glencoe, Ill.: Free Press).

Kent, R. (1981), *A History of British Empirical Sociology* (Aldershot: Gower).

Kent, R. (1985), 'The Emergence of the Sociological Survey' in M. Bulmer (ed.) *Essays on the History of British Sociological Research* (Cambridge: Cambridge University Press).

Kerr, C. (1983), *The Future of Industrial Societies* (Cambridge, Mass.: Harvard University Press).

Kerr, C., Dunlop, J. T., Harbison, F. H., and Myers, C. A. (1973), *Industrialism and Industrial Man* (Cambridge, Mass.: Harvard University Press).

Kerr, C. and Fisher, L. H. (1957), 'Plant Sociology: The Elite and the Aborigines' in M. Komarowsky (ed.) *Common Frontiers of the Social Sciences* (Glencoe, Ill.: Free Press).

King, G., Keohane, R. O., and Verba, S. (1994), *Designing Social Inquiry* (Princeton: Princeton University Press).

Kolakowski, L. (1972), *Positivist Philosophy* (Harmondsworth: Penguin).

Korpi, W. (1983), *The Democratic Class Struggle* (London: Routledge).

Korpi, W. and Palme, J. (2003), 'New Politics and Class Politics in the Context of Austerity and Globalization: Welfare State Regress in 18 Countries, 1975–95', *American Political Science Review*, 97: 425–46.

Krüger, L. (1987), 'The Slow Rise of Probabilism: Philosophical Arguments in the Nineteenth Century' in L. Krüger, L. J. Daston, and M. Heidelberger (eds.) *The Probabilistic Revolution*, vol. 1, *Ideas in History* (Cambridge, Mass.: MIT Press).

Krüger, L., Daston, L. J., and Heidelberger, M. (eds.) (1987), *The Probabilistic Revolution*, vol. 1, *Ideas in History* (Cambridge, Mass.: MIT Press).

Krüger, L., Gigerenzer, G., and Morgan, M. S. (eds.) (1987), *The Probabilistic Revolution*, vol. 2, *Ideas in the Sciences* (Cambridge, Mass.: MIT Press).

Kuklick, H. (1980), 'Boundary Maintenance in American Sociology: Limits to Academic "Professionalisation"', *Journal of the History of the Behavioural Sciences*, 16: 201–219.

Kunst, A. E. (1996), *Socioeconomic Inequalities in Morbidity and Mortality in Europe: A Comparative Study* (Rotterdam: Department of Public Health, Erasmus University).

Lachmann, L. M. (1970), *The Legacy of Max Weber* (London: Heinemann).

Lane, M. (1972), 'Explaining Educational Choice', *Sociology*, 6: 255–66.

Laslett, B. (1991), 'Biography as Historical Sociology: The Case of William Fielding Ogburn', *Theory and Society*, 20: 511–38.

Lazarsfeld, P. F. (1961), 'Notes on the History of Quantification in Sociology—Trends, Sources and Problems', *Isis*, 52: 277–333.

Lazarsfeld, P. F. (1970), *Qu'est-ce que la sociologie?* (Paris: Gallimard).

Lazarsfeld, P. F. (1972), *Qualitative Analysis: Historical and Other Essays* (Boston: Allyn and Bacon).

Lazarsfeld, P. F. (1975), 'Working with Merton' in L. Coser (ed.), *The Idea of Social Structure* (New York: Harcourt Brace Jovanovich).

Lazarsfeld, P. F., Berelson, B., and Gaudet, H. (1948), *The People's Choice*, 2nd ed. (New York: Columbia University Press).

Lazarsfeld, P. F. and Merton, R. K. (1943/1949), 'Studies in Radio and Film Propaganda', *Transactions of the New York Academy of Sciences*, 6, reprinted in R. K. Merton (1949) *Social Theory and Social Structure* (New York: Free Press).

Lazarsfeld, P. F. and Oberschall, A. (1965), 'Max Weber and Empirical Social Research', *American Sociological Review*, 30: 185–99.

Lazarsfeld, P. F. and Rosenberg, M. (eds.) (1955), *The Language of Social Research* (New York: Free Press).

Lazarsfeld, P. F. and Thielens, W. (1958), *The Academic Mind* (Glencoe, Ill.: Free Press).

Lazear, A. P. (1981), 'Agency, Earnings Profiles, Productivity and Hours Restrictions', *American Economic Review*, 71: 606–620.

Lazear, A. P. (1995), *Personnel Economics* (Cambridge, Mass.: MIT Press).

Lecuyer, B.-P. (1987), 'Probability in Vital and Social Statistics: Quetelet, Farr, and the Bertillons' in L. Krüger, L. J. Daston, and M. Heidelberger (eds.) *The Probabilistic Revolution*, vol. 1, *Ideas in History* (Cambridge, Mass.: MIT Press).

Lee, D. J. and Turner, B. S. (eds.) (1996), *Conflicts about Class* (London: Longman).

Lehmbruch, G. and Schmitter, P. (eds.) (1982), *Patterns of Corporatist Policy-Making* (London: Sage).

Lexis, W. (1875), *Einleitung in die Theorie der Bevölkerungsstatistik* (Strassburg: Trübner).

Lexis, W. (1877), *Zur Theorie der Massenerscheinungen in der menschlichen Gesellschaft* (Freiburg: Wagner).

Lexis, W. (1874/1903), 'Naturwissenschaft und Sozialwissenschaft' in *Abhandlungen zur Theorie der Bevölkerungs- und Moralstatistik* (Jena: Fischer).

Lexis, W. (1879/1903), 'Über die Theorie der Stabilität statistischer Reihen' in *Abhandlungen zur Theorie der Bevölkerungs- und Moralstatistik* (Jena: Fischer).

Li, Y. (1997), *The Service Class: Theoretical Debate and Empirical Value*, University of Oxford, D. Phil. thesis.

Li, Y. (2002), 'Falling Off the Ladder? Professional and Managerial Career Trajectories and Unemployment Experiences', *European Sociological Review*, 18: 253–70.

Lieberson, S. (1987), *Making It Count* (Berkeley: University of California Press).

Lindbeck, A. and Snower, D. (2002), 'The Insider-Outsider Theory: A Survey'. IZA Bonn, Discussion Paper, 534.

Lipset, S. M. (1960), *Political Man* (London: Heinemann).

Lipset, S. M. and Zetterberg, H. L. (1956), 'A Theory of Social Mobility', *Transactions of the Third World Congress of Sociology*, vol. 3 (London: International Sociological Association).

Lockwood, D. (1958), *The Blackcoated Worker* (London: Allen and Unwin).

Lockwood, D. (1960), 'The "New Working Class"', *Archives européennes de sociologie*, 1: 248–69.

Lockwood, D. (1981), 'The Weakest Link in the Chain? Some Comments on the Marxist Theory of Action', *Research in the Sociology of Work*, 1: 435–81.

Lockwood, D. (1992), *Solidarity and Schism* (Oxford: Clarendon).

Logan, J. A. (1983), 'A Multivariate Model for Mobility Tables', *American Journal of Sociology*, 89: 324–49.

Lukes, S. (1975), *Émile Durkheim: His Life and Work* (London: Peregrine).

MacIver, R. (1942), *Social Causation* (Boston: Ginn).

MacKenzie, D. A. (1981), *Statistics in Britain, 1865–1930* (Edinburgh: Edinburgh University Press).

Macleod, J., Davey Smith, G., Metcalfe, C., and Hart, C. (2005), 'Is Subjective Social Status a More Important Determinant of Health than Objective Social Status? Evidence from a Prospective Observational Study of Scottish Men', *Social Science and Medicine*, 61: 1916–929.

Maitland, F. M. (1911), 'The Body Politic' in H. A. L. Fisher (ed.) *F. M. Maitland, Collected Papers* (Cambridge: Cambridge University Press).

Manski, C. F. (1993), 'Adolescent Econometricians: How Do Youth Infer the Returns to Schooling?' in C. T. Clotfelter and M. Rothschild (eds.) *Studies of Supply and Demand in Higher Education* (Chicago: Chicago University Press).

Manski, C. M. (2004), 'Measuring Expectations'. Department of Economics and Institute for Policy Research, Northwestern University.

Mare, R. D. (1981), 'Change and Stability in Educational Stratification', *American Sociological Review*, 46: 72–87.

Mare, R. D. (1993), 'Educational Stratification on Observed and Unobserved Components of Family Background' in Y. Shavit and H.-P. Blossfeld (eds.) *Persistent Inequality: Changing Educational Attainment in Thirteen Countries* (Boulder: Westview).

Marglin, S. (1974), 'What Do Bosses Do?', *Review of Radical Political Economics*, 6: 60–112.

Marmot, M. (2004), *Status Syndrome* (London: Bloomsbury).

Marsden, D., French, S., and Kubo, K. (2001), *Does Performance Pay De-Motivate, and Does it Matter?* (London: Centre for Economic Performance).

Marshall, A. (1890), *Principles of Economics* (London: Macmillan).

Marshall, G. (1980), *Presbyteries and Profits: Calvinism and the Development of Capitalism in Scotland* (Oxford: Clarendon).

Marshall, G. (1982), *In Search of the Spirit of Capitalism* (London: Hutchinson).

Marshall, G. (1997), *Repositioning Class* (London: Sage).

Marshall, T. H. (1938), 'The Nature of Class Conflict' in *idem* (ed.), *Class Conflict and Social Stratification* (London: Le Play House).

Marshall, T. H. (1947), *Citizenship and Social Class* (Cambridge: Cambridge University Press).

McGinnity, F. and Hillmert, S. (2004), 'Persisting Class Inequality', *European Societies*, 6: 383–408.

McKnight, A. (2004), 'The Dynamics of Low Pay over Different Time Horizons'. University of London, PhD thesis.

Medoff, J. L. and Abraham, K. G. (1981), 'Are Those Paid More Really More Productive? The Case of Experience', *Journal of Human Resources*, 16: 186–216.

Merton, R. K. (1936a), 'Puritanism, Pietism and Science', *Sociological Review*, 28: 165–71.

Merton, R. K. (1936b), 'The Unanticipated Consequences of Purposive Social Action', *American Sociological Review*, 1: 894–904.

Merton, R. K. (1938), 'Science, Technology and Society in Seventeenth Century England', *Osiris* 4: 360–632.

Merton, R. K. (1945), 'Sociological Theory', *American Journal of Sociology*, 50: 462–73.

Merton, R. K. (1946), *Mass Persuasion* (New York: Harper and Brothers).

Merton, R. K. (1948), 'The Position of Sociological Theory', *American Sociological Review*, 13: 164–68.

Merton, R. K. (1949), *Social Theory and Social Structure* (New York: Free Press).

Merton, R. K. (1976), *Sociological Ambivalence and Other Essays* (New York: Free Press).

Merton, R. K. (1987), 'Three Fragments from a Sociologist's Notebook: Establishing the Phenomenon, Specified Ignorance and Strategic Research Materials', *Annual Review of Sociology*, 13: 1–28.

Merton, R. K. (1998), 'Working with Lazarsfeld: Notes and Contexts' in J. Lautman and B.-P. Lécuyer (eds.) *Paul Lazarsfeld (1901–1976): La sociologie de Vienne à New York* (Paris: L'Harmattan).

Merton, R. K., Reader, G., and Kendall, P. (eds.) (1957), *The Student Physician* (Cambridge, Mass.: Harvard University Press).

Micklewright, J. (1989), 'Choice at Sixteen', *Economica*, 56: 25–39.

Micklewright, J., Pearson, M., and Smith, S. (1988), 'Unemployment and Early School Leaving'. Institute for Fiscal Studies, London.

Miles, A. and Vincent, D. (eds.) (1993), *Building European Society* (Manchester: Manchester University Press).

Milgrom, P. and Roberts, J. (1992), *Economics, Organization and Management* (London: Prentice Hall).

Mill, J. S. (1843/1973–4), *A System of Logic Ratiocinative and Inductive* in M. Robson (ed.) *Collected Works of John Stuart Mill* (Toronto: University of Toronto Press).

Miller, D. C. and Form, W. H. (1951), *Industrial Sociology* (New York: Harper).

Miller, R. (1998), 'The Limited Concerns of Social Mobility Research', *Current Sociology*, 46: 145–63.

Mills, C. W. (1959), *The Sociological Imagination* (New York: Oxford University Press).

Morgan, M. S. (1987), 'The Probabilistic Revolution in Economics' in L. Krüger, G. Gigerenzer, and M S. Morgan (eds.) *The Probabilistic Revolution*, vol. 2, *Ideas in the Sciences* (Cambridge, Mass.: MIT Press).

Morgan, S. L. (1998), 'Adolescent Educational Expectations: Rationalized, Fantasized or Both?' *Rationality and Society*, 10: 131–62.

Morgan, S. L. (2002), 'Modeling Preparatory Commitment and Non-Repeatable Decisions: Information-Processing, Preference Formation and Educational Attainment', *Rationality and Society*, 14: 387–429.

Morgan, S. L. (2005), *On the Edge of Commitment: Educational Attainment and Race in the United States* (Stanford: Stanford University Press).

Morgan, S. L. and McKerrow, M. W. (2004), 'Social Class, Rent Destruction, and the Earnings of Black and White Men, 1982–2000', *Research in Social Stratification and Mobility*, 21: 215–51.

Morgan, S. L. and Tang, Z. (2005), 'Social Class and Workers' Rent, 1983–2001'. Department of Sociology, Cornell University.

Morris, M. and Western, B. (1999), 'Inequality in Earnings at the Close of the Twentieth Century', *Annual Review of Sociology*, 25: 623–57.

Müller, W. and Haun, D. (1994), 'Bildungsungleichheit im Sozialen Wandel', *Kölner Zeitschrift für Soziologie und Sozialpsychologie*, 46: 1–42.

Müller, W. and Shavit, Y. (1998), 'The Institutional Embeddedness of the Stratification Process: A Comparative Study of Qualifications and Occupations in Thirteen Countries' in Y. Shavit and W. Müller (eds.) *From School to Work* (Oxford: Clarendon).

Murphy, J. (1981), 'Class Inequality in Education: Two Justifications, One Evaluation but No Hard Evidence', *British Journal of Sociology*, 32: 182–201.

Murphy, J. (1990), 'A Most Respectable Prejudice: Inequality in Educational Research and Policy', *British Journal of Sociology*, 32: 182–201.

Nash, R. (2003), 'Inequality/Difference in Education: Is a Real Explanation of Primary and Secondary Effects Possible?' *British Journal of Sociology*, 54: 433–51.

Nathan, G. (1999), *A Review of Sample Attrition and Representativeness in Three Longitudinal Surveys* (London: Governmental Statistical Service Methodology Series, 13).

Need, A. and de Jong, U. (2000), 'Educational Differentials in the Netherlands: Testing Rational Action Theory', *Rationality and Society*, 13: 71–98.

Oberschall, A. (1965), *Empirical Social Research in Germany, 1848–1914* (The Hague: Mouton).

Oberschall, A. (1972), 'The Institutionalisation of American Sociology' in *idem* (ed.), *The Establishment of Empirical Sociology* (New York: Harper and Row).

Oberschall, A. (ed.), (1972), *The Establishment of Empirical Sociology* (New York: Harper and Row).

Oberschall, A. (1987), 'The Two Empirical Roots of Social Theory and the Probability Revolution' in L. Krüger, G. Gigerenzer, and M. S. Morgan (eds.) *The Probabilistic Revolution*, vol. 2, *Ideas in the Sciences* (Cambridge, Mass.: MIT Press).

Oberschall, A. (1998), 'Rational Choice and the Empirical Analysis of Action' in J. Lautman and B.-P. Lécuyer (eds.), *Paul Lazarsfeld (1901–1976): La sociologie de Vienne à New York* (Paris: L'Harmattan).

Ogburn, W. F. (1912), *Progress and Uniformity in Child-Labor Legislation: A Study in Statistical Measurement* (New York: Columbia University Press).

Ogburn, W. F. (1922), *Social Change with Respect to Culture and Original Nature* (New York: Huebsch).

Ogburn, W. F. (1923), 'The Fluctuations of Business as Social Forces', *Journal of Social Forces*, 1: 73–78.

Ogburn, W. F. (1927), 'Sociology and Statistics' in W. F. Ogburn and A. Goldenweiser (eds.) *The Social Sciences and their Interrelations* (London: Allen and Unwin).

Ogburn, W. F. (1929), 'The Changing Family', *Publications of the American Sociological Society*, 23: 124–33.

Ogburn, W. F. (1930), 'Three Obstacles to the Development of a Scientific Sociology', *Social Forces*, 8: 347–50.

Ogburn, W. F. (1935), 'Recent Changes in Marriage', *American Journal of Sociology*, 41: 285–98.

Ogburn, W. F. (1955), 'Some Observations on Sociological Research', *Social Forces*, 34: 10–18.

Ogburn, W. F. and Talbot, N. S. (1929), 'A Measurement of the Factors in the Presidential Election of 1928', *Social Forces*, 8: 175–83.

Ogburn, W. F. and Thomas, D. S. (1922), 'The Influence of the Business Cycle on Certain Social Conditions', *Quarterly Publication of the American Statistical Association*, 18: 324–40.

Olson, M. (1965), *The Logic of Collective Action* (Cambridge, Mass.: Harvard University Press).

Osterman, P. (1987), 'Choice of Employment Systems', *Industrial Relations*, 26: 46–67.

Pahl, R. (1993), 'Does Class Analysis without Class Theory Have a Promising Future? A Reply to Goldthorpe and Marshall', *Sociology*, 27: 253–58.

Pakulski, J. and Waters, M. (1996), *The Death of Class* (London: Sage).

Papanicolaou, J. and Psacharopoulos, G. (1979), 'Socioeconomic Background, Schooling and Monetary Rewards in the United Kingdom', *Economica*, 46: 435–39.

Park, R. and Burgess, E. W. (1921), *Introduction to the Science of Sociology* (Chicago: University of Chicago Press).

Parsons, T. (1937), *The Structure of Social Action* (Glencoe, Ill.: Free Press).

Parsons, T. (1967), *Sociological Theory and Modern Society* (New York: Free Press).

Parsons, T (1971), *The System of Modern Societies* (Englewood Cliffs, N.J.: Prentice Hall).

Payne, J. (2003), *Choice at the End of Compulsory Schooling: A Research Review* (London: Department of Education and Skills).

Pearson, K. (1892), *The Grammar of Science* (London: Black).

Pearson, K. (1904), *On the Theory of Contingency and Its Relation to Association and Normal Correlation* (London: Drapers' Company Research Memoirs).

Peel, J. D. Y. (1971), *Herbert Spencer: The Evolution of a Sociologist* (London: Heinemann).

Persson, I. (ed.) (1990), *Generating Equality in the Welfare State: The Swedish Experience* (Oslo: Norwegian University Press).

Petit, P. (1975), 'Rendement de l'enseignement supérieur et origine sociale', *Revue Economique*, 26: 587–64.

Pfeffer, J. (1997), *New Directions for Organization Theory* (Oxford: Oxford University Press).

Piore, M. and Sabel, C. F. (1984), *The Second Industrial Divide: Possibilities for Prosperity* (New York: Basic Books).

Pissarides, C. A. (1981), 'Staying on at School in England and Wales', *Economica*, 48: 345–63.

Pizzorno, A. (1978), 'Political Exchange and Collective Identity in Industrial Conflict' in C. Crouch and A. Pizzorno (eds.) *The Resurgence of Class Conflict in Western Europe since 1968*, vol. 2 (London: Macmillan).

Platt, J. (1985), 'Weber's Verstehen and the History of Qualitative Research: the Missing Link', *British Journal of Sociology*, 36: 448–66.

Platt, J. (1996), *A History of Sociological Research Methods in America* (Cambridge: Cambridge University Press).

Popper, K. R. (1972), *Objective Knowledge* (Oxford: Clarendon).

Popper, K. R. (1994), *The Myth of the Framework* (London: Routledge).

Porter, T. M. (1982), 'A Statistical Survey of Gases: Maxwell's Social Physics', *Historical Studies in the Physical Sciences*, 8: 77–116.

Porter, T. M. (1986), *The Rise of Statistical Thinking, 1820–1900* (Princeton: Princeton University Press).

Porter, T. M. (1987), 'Lawless Society: Social Science and the Reinterpretation of Statistics in Germany, 1850–1880' in L. Krüger, L. J. Daston, and M. Heidelberger (eds.) *The Probabilistic Revolution*, vol. 1, *Ideas in History* (Cambridge, Mass.: MIT Press).

Porter, T. M. (2004), *Karl Pearson: The Scientific Life in a Statistical Age* (Princeton: Princeton University Press).

Pratt, J. W. and Zeckhauser, R. J. (1984), 'Principals and Agents' in *idem* (eds.) *Principals and Agents: The Structure of Business* (Boston: Harvard Business School Press).

Prendergast, C. (1999), 'The Provision of Incentives within Firms', *Journal of Economic Literature* 37: 7–63.

President's Research Committee on Social Trends (1933), *Recent Social Trends in the United States* (New York: McGraw-Hill).

Quetelet, A. (1835/1842), *A Treatise on Man and the Development of his Faculties* (Edinburgh: Chambers).

Quetelet, A. (1846): *Lettres à S.A.R. le Duc Régnant de Saxe-Coburg-Gotha, sur la théorie des probabilités, appliquée aux sciences morales et politiques* (Brussels: Hayez).

Quetelet, A. (1869), *Physique sociale* (Brussels: Muquardt).

Raftery, A. E. (1986), 'Choosing Models for Cross-Classifications', *American Sociological Review* 51: 145–56.

Raftery, A. E. and Hout, M. (1990), 'Maximally Maintained Inequality: Expansion, Reform and Opportunity in Irish Education, 1921–1975'. ISA Research Committee on Social Stratification and Mobility, Madrid.

Renner, K. (1953), *Wandlungen der Modernen Gesellschaft: Zwei Abhandlungen über die Probleme der Nachkriegszeit* (Vienna: Wiener Volksbuchhandlung).

Richardson, C. J. (1977), *Contemporary Social Mobility* (London: Francis Pinter).

Ringer, F. (1969), *The Decline of the German Mandarins* (Cambridge, Mass.: Harvard University Press).

Ringer, F. (1997), *Max Weber's Methodology: The Unification of the Cultural and Social Sciences* (Cambridge, Mass.: Harvard University Press).

Ringer, F. (2004), *Max Weber: An Intellectual Biography* (Chicago: Chicago University Press).

Robinson, R. V. (1984), 'Reproducing Class Relations in Industrial Capitalism', *American Sociological Review*, 49: 182–96.

Robinson, W. S. (1951), 'The Logical Structure of Analytic Induction', *American Sociological Review*, 16: 812–18.

Róbert, P. and Bukodi, E. (2004), 'Changes in Intergenerational Class Mobility in Hungary, 1973–2000' in R. Breen (ed.) *Social Mobility in Europe* (Oxford: Oxford University Press).

Rock, P. (1979), *The Making of Symbolic Interactionism* (Totowa, N.J.: Rowman and Littlefield).

Rose, D. and O'Reilly, K. (1998), *The ESRC Review of Government Social Classifications* (London: Office for National Statistics and Economic and Social Research Council).

Rose, D. and O'Reilly, K. (eds.) (1997), *Constructing Classes: Towards a New Social Classification for the UK* (London: Economic and Social Research Council and Office for National Statistics).

Rose, D. and Pevalin, D. (2003), 'The NS-SEC Explained' in D. Rose and D. Pevalin (eds.) (2003), *A Researchers Guide to the National Statistics Socio-Economic Classification* (London: National Statistics and Sage).

Rose, D. and Pevalin, D. (eds.) (2003), *A Researchers Guide to the National Statistics Socio-Economic Classification* (London: National Statistics and Sage).

Rose, D., Pevalin, D. and O'Reilly, K. (2005), *The National Statistics Socio-Economic Classification: Origins, Development and Use* (London: National Statistics and Palgrave Macmillan).

Rosen, B. (1956), 'The Achievement Syndrome: A Psychocultural Dimension of Social Stratification', *American Sociological Review*, 21: 203–11.

Ross, D. (1991), *The Origins of American Social Science* (Cambridge: Cambridge University Press).

Roth, G. (1968), 'Introduction' to G. Roth and C. Wittich (eds.) Max Weber, *Economy and Society* (Berkeley: University of California Press).

Rowntree, S. (1901), *Poverty: A Study of Town Life* (London: Macmillan).

Ryan, A. (1970), *The Philosophy of John Stuart Mill* (London: Macmillan).

Sacker, A., Firth, D., Fitzpatrick, R., Lynch, K., and Bartley, M. (2000), 'Comparing Health Inequality in Men and Women: Prospective Study of Mortality, 1986–96', *British Medical Journal*, 320: 1303–07.

Savage, M. (2000), *Class Analysis and Social Transformation* (Buckingham: Open University Press).

Savage, M., Barlow, J., Dickens, P., and Fielding, T. (1992), *Property, Bureaucracy and Culture: Middle-Class Formation in Contemporary Britain* (London: Routledge).

Savage, M. and Butler, T. (1995), 'Assets and the Middle Classes in Contemporary Britain' in T. Butler and M. Savage (eds.) *Social Change and the Middle Classes* (London: UCL Press).

Schad, S. P. (1972), *Empirical Social Research in Weimar-Germany* (Paris: Mouton).

Schizzerotto, A. (1997), 'Perché in Italia ci sono pochi diplomati e pochi laureate? Vincoli strutturali e decisione razionali degli attori come cause della contenuta espansione della scolarità superiore', *Polis*, 11: 345–65,

Schneider, L. and Lysgaard, S. (1953), 'The Deferred Gratification Pattern', *American Sociological Review*, 18: 142–49.

Schumpeter, J. A. (1927), 'Die sozialen Klassen in ethnische homogenen Milieu' in *Aufsätze zur Soziologie* (Tübingen: Mohr).

Schumpeter, J. A. (1954), *History of Economic Analysis* (London: Routledge).

Schütz, A. (1932/1967), *The Phenomenology of the Social World* (New York: Northwestern University Press).

Selvin, H. C. (1976), 'Durkheim, Booth and Yule: The Non-Diffusion of an Intellectual Innovation', *Archives européennes de sociologie*, 17: 39–51.

Sewell, W. H. and Hauser, R. M. (1976), 'Causes and Consequences of Higher Education: Models of the Status Attainment Process' in W. H. Sewell, R. M. Hauser, and D. L. Featherman (eds.) *Schooling and Achievement in American Society* (New York: Academic Press).

Shavit, Y. and Blossfeld, H.-P. (eds.) (1993), *Persistent Inequality: Changing Educational Attainment in Thirteen Countries* (Boulder: Westview).

Shils, E. A. (1948), *The Present State of American Sociology* (Glencoe, Ill.: Free Press).

Sills, D. L. (1998), 'The Lazarsfeld Story as Genre' in J. Lautman and B.-P. Lécuyer (eds.), *Paul Lazarsfeld (1901–1976): La sociologie de Vienne à New York* (Paris: L'Harmattan).

Simiand, F. (1907), *Le Salaire des ouvriers des mines de charbon en France* (Paris: Société Nouvelle).

Simiand, F. (1932), *Le Salaire: l'évolution sociale et la monnaie* (Paris: Alcan).

Simkus, A., Jackson, J., Yip, K., and Treiman, D. J. (1990), 'Changes in Social Mobility in Two Societies in the Crux of Transition: A Hungarian-Irish Comparison, 1943–73', *Research in Social Stratification and Mobility*, 8: 33–78.

Simon, H. A. (1951), 'A Formal Theory of the Firm', *Econometrica*, 19: 293–305.

Simon, H. A. (1946, 2nd ed. 1961), *Administrative Behavior* (New York: Macmillan).

Simon, H. A. (1991), 'Organizations and Markets', *Journal of Economic Perspectives*, 5: 25–44.

Skog, O.-J. (1991), 'Alcohol and Suicide—Durkheim Revisited', *Acta Sociologica*, 34: 193–206.

Smeeding, T. M., O'Higgins, M., and Rainwater, L. (1990), *Poverty, Inequality and the Distribution of Income in Comparative Perspective* (London: Wheatsheaf).

Soffer, R. N. (1978), *Ethics and Society in England: The Revolution in the Social Sciences, 1870–1914* (Berkeley: University of California Press).

Sørensen, A. B. (1983), 'Processes of Allocation to Open and Closed Positions in Social Structure', *Zeitschrift für Soziologie*, 12: 203–24.

Sørensen, A. B. (1998a), 'Theoretical Mechanisms and the Empirical Study of Social Processes' in P. Hedström and R. Swedberg (eds.) *Social Mechanisms* (Cambridge: Cambridge University Press).

Sørensen, A. B. (1998b), 'On Kings, Pietism and Rent-Seeking in Scandinavian Welfare States', *Acta Sociologica* 41: 364–75.

Sørensen, A. B. (2000a), 'Employment Relations and Class Structure' in R. Crompton, F. Devine, M. Savage, and J. Scott (eds.) *Renewing Class Analysis* (Oxford: Blackwell).

Sørensen, A. B. (2000b), 'Toward a Sounder Basis for Class Analysis', *American Journal of Sociology*, 105: 1523–558.

Sørensen, A. B. (2005), 'Foundations of a Neo-Ricardian Class Analysis' in E. O. Wright (ed.) *Approaches to Class Analysis* (Cambridge: Cambridge University Press).

Sørensen, J. B. and Grusky, D. B. (1996), 'The Structure of Career Mobility in Microscopic Perspective' in J. N. Baron, D. B. Grusky, and D. J. Treiman (eds.) *Social Differentiation and Social Inequality* (Boulder: Westview).

Sorokin, P. A. (1933), 'Recent Social Trends: A Criticism', *Journal of Political Economy*, 41: 194–210.

Spånt, R. (1979), *The Distribution of Income in Sweden, 1920–1976* (Stockholm: Swedish Institute for Social Research).

Spencer, H. (1873/1961), *The Study of Sociology* (Ann Arbor: University of Michigan Press).

Spencer, H. (1876–97), *The Principles of Sociology*, 3 vols. (London: Williams and Norgate).

Spencer, H. and associates (1873–1934), *Descriptive Sociology* (London: various publishers).

Steuer, M. (2002), *The Scientific Study of Society* (Boston: Kluwer).

Stigler, S. M. (1986), *The History of Statistics: the Measurement of Uncertainty before 1900* (Cambridge, Mass.: Harvard University Press).

Stigler, S. M. (1987), 'The Measurement of Uncertainty in Nineteenth-Century Social Science' in L. Krüger, L. J. Daston, and M. Heidelberger (eds.) *The Probabilistic Revolution*, vol. 1, *Ideas in History* (Cambridge, Mass.: MIT Press).

Stigler, S. M. (1999), *Statistics on the Table* (Cambridge, Mass.: Harvard University Press).

Stinchcombe, A. L. (1993), 'The Conditions of Fruitfulness of Theorizing about Mechanisms in Social Science' in A. B. Sørensen and S. Spilerman (eds.) *Social Theory and Social Policy: Essays in Honor of James S. Coleman* (Westport: Praeger).

Stoetzel, J. (1957), 'Sociology in France: An Empiricist View' in H. Becker and B. Boskoff (eds.) *Modern Sociological Theory* (New York: Holt, Rinehart and Winston).

Stone, K. (1974), 'The Origins of Job Structures in the Steel Industry', *Review of Radical Political Economics*, 6: 61–97.

Stone, R. (1997), *Some British Empiricists in the Social Sciences, 1650–1900* (Cambridge: Cambridge University Press).

Stouffer, S. A., Suchman, E. A., DeVinney, L. C., Star, S. A., and Williams, R. M. (1949), *The American Soldier* (Princeton: Princeton University Press).

Sullivan, A. (2006), 'Students as Rational Decision Makers: The Question of Beliefs and Desires', *London Review of Education*, 46, forthcoming.

Swedberg, R. (1998), *Max Weber and the Idea of Economic Sociology* (Princeton: Princeton University Press).

Szelényi, S. (1998), *Equality by Design: The Grand Experiment in Destratification in Socialist Hungary* (Stanford: Stanford University Press).

Tåhlin, M. (2005), 'Class Clues'. Swedish Institute for Social Research, Stockholm.

Taylor, R. (2002), *Britain's World of Work—Myths and Realities* (London: Economic and Social Research Council).

Thelen, K. (2001), 'Varieties of Labor Politics in the Developed Democracies' in P. A. Hall and D. Soskice (eds.) *Varieties of Capitalism: The Institutional Foundations of Comparative Advantage* (New York: Oxford University Press).

Thélot, C. and Vallet, L.-A. (2000), 'La reduction des inégalités sociales devant l'école depuis le début du siècle', *Economie et statistique* 334: 3–32.

Thomas, W. I. and Znaniecki, F. (1918–20), *The Polish Peasant in Europe and America*, 5 vols. (Chicago: University of Chicago Press).

Thurow, L. C. (1972), 'Education and Economic Inequality', *The Public Interest*, no. 28, Summer.

Tilton, T. (1990), *The Political Theory of Swedish Social Democracy* (Oxford: Clarendon).

Toby, J. (1980), 'Samuel Stouffer: Social Research as a Calling' in R. K. Merton and M. W. Riley (eds.) *Sociological Traditions from Generation to Generation* (Norwood, N.J.: Ablex).

Torche, F. (2005), 'Unequal but Fluid: Social Mobility in Chile in Comparative Perspective', *American Sociological Review*, 70: 422–50.

Treiman, D. J. (1970), 'Industrialization and Social Stratification' in E. O. Laumann (ed.) *Social Stratification: Research and Theory for the 1970s* (Indianapolis: Bobbs Merrill).

Turner, J. H. (1985), *Herbert Spencer* (Beverly Hills: Sage).

Turner, S. P. (1985), *The Search for a Methodology of Social Science* (Dordrecht: Reidel).

Turner, S. P. (1991), 'The World of the Academic Quantifiers: The Columbia University Family and Its Connections' in M. Bulmer, K. Bales, and K. K. Sklar (eds.) *The Social Survey in Historical Perspective, 1880–1940* (Cambridge: Cambridge University Press).

Turner, S. P. and Factor, R. A. (1981), 'Objective Possibility and Adequate Causation in Weber's Methodological Writings', *Sociological Review*, 29: 5–28.

Turner, S. P. and Factor, R. A. (1994), *Max Weber: The Lawyer as Social Thinker* (London: Routledge).

Turner, S. P. and Turner, J. H. (1990), *The Impossible Science: An Institutional Analysis of American Sociology* (Newbury Park: Sage).

Tylor, E. B. (1889), 'On a Method of Investigating the Development of Institutions: Applied to Laws of Marriage and Descent', *Journal of the Royal Anthropological Institute*, 18: 245–56, 261–69.

Tyree, A., Semyonov, M., and Hodge, R. W. (1979), 'Gaps and Glissandos: Inequality, Economic Development, and Social Mobility in 24 Countries', *American Sociological Review*, 44: 410–24.

Udéhn, L. (2001), *Methodological Individualism* (London: Routledge).

Vallet, L.-A. (1999), 'Quarante années de mobilité sociale en France', *Revue française de sociologie*, 40: 3–64.

Vallet, L.-A. (2004a), 'Change in Intergenerational Class Mobility in France: From the 1970s to the 1990s and Its Explanation: An Analysis Following the CASMIN Approach' in R. Breen (ed.) *Social Mobility in Europe* (Oxford: Oxford University Press).

Vallet, L.-A. (2004b), 'The Dynamics of Educational Opportunity in France: Change in the Association between Social Background and Education in Thirteen Five-Year Birth Cohorts (1908–1972)'. CREST-INSEE, Paris.

Vallet, L.-A. (2005), 'Expliquer l'augmentation de la fluidité social entre generations: la France entre 1970 et 1993 et une perspective comparative'. CREST-INSEE, Paris.

Van de Werfhorst, H. (2005), 'Credential Inflation and Educational Inequality'. Department of Sociology and Anthropology, University of Amsterdam.

Van de Werfhorst, H. and Andersen, R. (2005), 'Social Background, Credential Inflation and Educational Strategies', *Acta Sociologica*, 48: 321–40.

Van de Werfhorst, H., Sullivan, A., and Cheung, S.-Y. (2003), 'Social Class, Ability and Choice of Subject in Secondary and Tertiary Education in Britain', *British Educational Research Journal*, 29: 41–62.

Van Poppel, F. and Day, L. H. (1996), 'A Test of Durkheim's Theory of Suicide—without Committing the "Ecological Fallacy"', *American Sociological Review*, 61: 500–507.

Vogel, J. (1987), *Det Svenska Klassamhället* (Stockholm: Statistika Centralbyrån).

Vogt, W. P. (1983), 'Durkheimian Sociology versus Philosophical Rationalism: The Case of Célestin Bouglé' in P. Besnard (ed.) *The Sociological Domain* (Cambridge: Cambridge University Press).

Verein für Sozialpolitik (1912), *Verhandlungen der Generalversammlung in Nürnberg, 1911* (Leipzig: Dunker and Humblot).

Wadsworth, M. E. J. (1991), *The Impact of Time: Childhood, History and Adult Life* (Oxford: Clarendon).

Wagner, H. R. (1983), *Alfred Schutz: An Intellectual Biography* (Chicago: University of Chicago Press).

Warhurst, C. and Nickson, D. (2001), *Looking Good, Sounding Right: Style Counselling in the New Economy* (London: The Industrial Society).

Weakliem, D. L. (1989), 'The Employment Contract: A Test of the Transaction Cost Theory', *Sociological Forum*, 4: 203–26.

Weakliem, D. L. (1999), 'A Critique of the Bayesian Information Criterion for Model Selection', *Sociological Methods and Research*, 27: 359–97.

Weakliem, D. L. and Heath, A. F. (1994), 'Rational Choice and Class Voting', *Rationality and Society*, 6: 243–70.

Webb, B. (1891), *The Cooperative Movement in Great Britain* (London: Sonnenschein).

Webb, B. (1926), *My Apprenticeship* (London: Longmans).

Webb, S. and Webb, B. (1894), *The History of Trade Unionism* (London: Longmans).

Webb, S. and Webb, B. (1897), *Industrial Democracy* (London: Longmans).

Webb, S. and Webb, B. (1932), *Methods of Social Study* (London: Longmans).

Weber, Marianne (1926/1975), *Max Weber: A Biography* (New Brunswick: Transaction).

Weber, Max (1892), *Die Verhältnisse der Landarbeiter im ostelbischen Deutschland* (Leipzig: Schriften des Vereins für Sozialpolitik).

Weber, Max (1903–06/1975), *Roscher and Knies: The Logical Problems of Historical Economics* (New York: Free Press).

Weber, Max (1904/1949), '"Objectivity" in Social Science and Social Policy' in *The Methodology of the Social Sciences* (Glencoe, Ill.: Free Press).

Weber, Max (1904–1905/1930), *The Protestant Ethic and the Spirit of Capitalism* (London: Allen and Unwin).

Weber, Max (1906/1949), 'A Critique of Eduard Meyer's Methodological Views' in *The Methodology of the Social Sciences* (Glencoe, Ill.: Free Press).

Weber, Max (1907/1977), *Critique of Stammler* (New York: Free Press).

Weber, Max (1908), 'Zur Psychophysik der industriellen Arbeit', *Archiv für Sozial-wissenschaft und Sozialpolitik*, 27: 730–70.

Weber, Max (1908/1975), 'Marginal Utility Theory and "The Fundamental Law of Psychophysics"', *Social Science Quarterly*, 56: 21–36.

Weber, Max (1913/1981), 'Some Categories of Interpretative Sociology', *Sociological Quarterly*, 22: 145–80.

Weber, Max (1922/1968), *Economy and Society* (Berkeley: University of California Press).

Weeden, K. A. (2002), 'Why Do Some Occupations Pay More than Others? Social Closure and Earnings Inequality in the United States', *American Journal of Sociology*, 108: 55–101.

Weeden, K. A. and Grusky, D. B. (2005), 'The Case for a New Class Map', *American Journal of Sociology*, 111: 141–212.

Westergaard, H. (1932), *Contributions to the History of Statistics* (London: King).

Weyembergh, M. (1971), *Le volontarisme rationnel de Max Weber* (Brussels: Académie Royale de Belgique).

Whyte, W. F. (1943), *Street Corner Society* (Chicago: Chicago University Press).

Wilensky, H. L. and Lawrence, A. T. (1980), 'Job Assignment in Modern Societies: A Re-examination of the Ascription-Achievement Hypothesis' in A. H. Hawley (ed.) *Societal Growth: Processes and Implications* (New York: Free Press).

Williamson, O. E. (1985), *The Economic Institutions of Capitalism* (New York: Free Press).

Williamson, O. E. (1994), 'The Economics and Sociology of Organizations: Promoting a Dialogue' in G. Farkas and P. England (eds.) *Industries, Firms and Jobs* (New York: Aldine De Gruyter).

Williamson, O. E. (1996), *The Mechanisms of Governance* (New York: Oxford University Press).

Willis, P. (1977), *Learning to Labour* (Farnborough: Saxon House).

Winship, C. and Mare, R. D. (1983), 'Structural Equations and Path Analysis for Discrete Data', *American Journal of Sociology*, 89: 54–110.

Wise, M. N. (1987), 'Do Sums Count? On the Cultural Origins of Statistical Causality' in L. Krüger, L. J. Daston, and M. Heidelberger (eds.) *The Probabilistic Revolution*, vol.1, *Ideas in History* (Cambridge, Mass.: MIT Press).

Wolf, A. (2002), *Does Education Matter?* (London: Penguin).

Wong, R. S.-K. (1994), 'Postwar Mobility Trends in Advanced Industrial Societies', *Research in Social Stratification and Mobility*, 13: 121–44.

Wong, R. S.-K. and Hauser, R. M. (1992), 'Trends in Occupational Mobility in Hungary under Socialism', *Social Science Research*, 21: 419–44.

Wright, E. O. (1985), *Classes* (London: Verso).

Wright, E. O. (1989), 'Rethinking, Once Again, the Concept of Class Structure' in E. O. Wright et al. (eds.) *The Debate on Classes* (London: Verso).

Wright, E. O. (1997), *Class Counts* (Cambridge: Cambridge University Press).

Wright, E. O. (2000), 'Class, Exploitation, and Economic Rents: Reflections on Sørensen's "Sounder Basis"', *American Journal of Sociology*, 105: 1559–571.

Wright, E. O. (2005), 'Foundations of a Neo-Marxist Class Analysis' in *idem* (ed.) *Approaches to Class Analysis* (Cambridge: Cambridge University Press).

Wrong, D. (1961), 'The Oversocialized Conception of Man in Modern Sociology', *American Sociological Review*, 26: 183–93.

Xie, Y. (1992), 'The Log-Multiplicative Layer Effect Model for Comparing Mobility Tables', *American Sociological Review*, 57: 380–95.

Yaish, M. (2000), 'Old Debate, New Evidence: Class Mobility in Israeli Society, 1974–91', *European Sociological Review*, 16: 159–83.

Yaish, M (2004a), *Class Mobility Trends in Israeli Society, 1974–1991* (Lewiston: Mellen).

Yaish, M. (2004b), 'Opportunities, Little Change: Class Mobility in Israeli Society, 1974–91' in R. Breen (ed.) *Social Mobility in Europe* (Oxford: Oxford University Press).

Yule, G. U. (1895), 'On the Correlation of Total Pauperism with Proportion of Out-relief, I: All Ages', *Economic Journal*, 5: 603–11.

Yule, G. U. (1896), 'On the Correlation of Total Pauperism with Proportion of Out-Relief, II: Males over 65', *Economic Journal*, 6: 613–23.

Yule, G. U. (1897), 'On the Theory of Correlation', *Journal of the Royal Statistical Society*, 60: 812–54.

Yule, G. U. (1899), 'An Investigation into the Causes of Changes in Pauperism in England, Chiefly During the Last Two Intercensal Decades', *Journal of the Royal Statistical Society*, 62: 249–95.

Yule, G. U. (1911), *An Introduction to the Theory of Statistics* (London: Griffin).

Znaniecki, F. (1934), *The Method of Sociology* (New York: Farrar and Rinehart).

STUDIES IN SOCIAL INEQUALITY

*After the Fall of the Wall: Life Courses in the Transformation
of East Germany*
EDITED BY MARTIN DIEWALD, ANNE GOEDICKE, AND KARL ULRICH MAYER
2006

*The Moral Economy of Class: Class and Attitudes
in Comparative Perspective*
BY STEFAN SVALLFORS
2006

The Global Dynamics of Racial and Ethnic Mobilization
BY SUSAN OLZAK
2006

Poverty and Inequality
EDITED BY DAVID B. GRUSKY AND RAVI KANBUR
2006

*Mobility and Inequality: Frontiers of Research in Sociology
and Economics*
EDITED BY STEPHEN L. MORGAN, DAVID B. GRUSKY, AND GARY S. FIELDS
2006

*Analyzing Inequality: Life Chances and Social Mobility in Comparative
Perspective*
EDITED BY STEFAN SVALLFORS
2005

*On the Edge of Commitment: Educational Attainment and Race
in the United States*
BY STEPHEN L. MORGAN
2005